The Definitive Guide to symfony

François Zaninotto and
Fabien Potencier

The Definitive Guide to symfony

Copyright © 2007 by Sensio SA

ISBN-13 (pbk): 978-1-59059-786-6

ISBN-10 (pbk): 1-59059-786-9

Printed and bound in the United States of America 9 8 7 6 5 4 3 2 1

Lead Editor: Jason Gilmore
Editorial Board: Steve Anglin, Ewan Buckingham, Gary Cornell, Jason Gilmore, Jonathan Gennick, Jonathan Hassell, James Huddleston, Chris Mills, Matthew Moodie, Dominic Shakeshaft, Jim Sumser, Matt Wade
Project Manager: Kylie Johnston
Copy Edit Manager: Nicole Flores
Copy Editors: Marilyn Smith and Ami Knox
Assistant Production Director: Kari Brooks-Copony
Production Editor: Katie Stence
Compositor: Susan Glinert
Proofreaders: Linda Marousek and April Eddy
Indexer: Toma Mulligan
Artist: April Milne
Cover Designer: Kurt Krames
Manufacturing Director: Tom Debolski

Distributed to the book trade worldwide by Springer-Verlag New York, Inc., 233 Spring Street, 6th Floor, New York, NY 10013. Phone 1-800-SPRINGER, fax 201-348-4505, e-mail orders-ny@springer-sbm.com, or visit http://www.springeronline.com.

For information on translations, please contact Apress directly at 2560 Ninth Street, Suite 219, Berkeley, CA 94710. Phone 510-549-5930, fax 510-549-5939, e-mail info@apress.com, or visit http://www.apress.com.

The source code for this book is available to readers at http://www.apress.com in the Source Code/ Download section.

To Anne-Marie.
—François Zaninotto

For Thomas and Hélène, with love.
—Fabien Potencier

Contents at a Glance

PART 1 ■■■ The Basics

PART 2 ■■■ The Core Architecture

PART 3 ■■■ Special Features

PART 4 ■■■ Development Tools

PART 5 ■■■ Becoming a Symfony Expert

Contents

PART 1 ■■■ The Basics

PART 2 ■■■ The Core Architecture

PART 3 ■■■ Special Features

PART 4   ■■■ Development Tools

PART 5 ■■■ Becoming a Symfony Expert

About the Authors

FRANÇOIS ZANINOTTO is a consultant and project manager for Internet application projects. He graduated from the French business school Ecole des Mines in 1997 with a specialization in computer science. He tried quite a few jobs before settling on the Internet business: social worker in a children's facility, manager of a bike rental shop, web project manager for a tire manufacturer, writer of a travel guide on Germany for the same tire manufacturer, logistician for Médecins Sans Frontières, and IT architect for a consumer credit company. He joined the Sensio web agency in 2003, and since then has managed many Internet and intranet web application projects, dealing with complex usability issues, agile development methodologies, and cutting-edge web techniques. When the symfony project started, he took responsibility for the documentation, and wrote the symfony online book and tutorials.

FABIEN POTENCIER is a serial entrepreneur. Since he was ten, he always dreamed of creating and running companies. He started his career with an engineering degree from the French business school Ecole des Mines and an MBA in entrepreneurship from HEC Paris. In 1998, right after graduation, Fabien founded his very first company with a fellow student. The company was a web agency focused on simplicity and open source technologies, and was called Sensio. His acute technical knowledge and his endless curiosity won him the confidence of many French big corporate companies. While Sensio kept growing (at the time of writing, it has more than 30 employees), Fabien started other businesses: an indoor go-kart circuit in Lille (France), an auto spare parts e-commerce shop, and an autopilot training business riding on the most famous French racetracks. Fabien is the main developer of the symfony framework and is responsible for 95% of its code. Today, Fabien spends most of his time as Sensio's CEO and as the symfony project leader.

About Sensio Labs

Sensio is a French web agency well known for its innovative ideas on web development. Founded in 1998 by Fabien Potencier, Gregory Pascal, and Samuel Potencier, Sensio benefited from the Internet growth of the late 1990s and situated itself as a major player for building complex web applications. It survived the Internet bubble burst by applying professional and industrial methods to a business where most players seemed to reinvent the wheel for each project. Most of Sensio's clients are large French corporations, who hire its teams to deal with small- to middle-scale projects with strong time-to-market and innovation constraints.

Today, Sensio's activity is divided in two business lines:

- **Extreme Sensio** deals with the interactive marketing projects and provides consulting on Internet communication strategies. It builds online communication campaigns from early conception to final product (websites, mailings, videos, viral marketing, and so on).

- **Sensio Labs** develops interactive web applications, both for dot-com and traditional companies. This division also provides auditing, consulting, and training on Internet technologies and complex application deployment. It helps define the global Internet strategy of large-scale industrial players. Sensio Labs has projects in France and abroad.

For its own needs, Sensio Labs develops the symfony framework and sponsors its deployment as an open source project. This means that symfony is built from experience and is really employed in many web applications, including those of large corporations.

Since its beginnings nine years ago, Sensio has always based its strategy on strong technical expertise. The company focuses on open source technologies, and as for dynamic scripting languages, Sensio offers developments in all LAMP platforms (Perl, Python, PHP, and Ruby, even if the latter doesn't start with a *P*). Sensio acquired strong experience on the best frameworks using these languages, and often develops web applications in Django, Rails, and, of course, symfony.

Sensio is always open to new business opportunities, so if you ever need help developing a web application, learning symfony, or evaluating a symfony development, feel free to contact us at info@sensio.com. The consultants, project managers, web designers, and developers of Sensio can handle projects from A to Z.

Acknowledgments

The authors would like to thank the Apress team, including Jason, Kylie, Marilyn, Katie, Ami, and all the people who collaborated on the writing of this book.

Acknowledgments also go to the Sensio team, particularly to those who were willing to take their personal time to develop and write this book.

The symfony community, who asked thousands of questions about the framework, is also to be thanked, for they made us understand that this book should contain many practical tips.

And lastly, the authors would like to thank the reader of this book, who contributes to the development of the symfony project by this purchase, and would like to welcome every reader into the community.

Introduction

When symfony first appeared in October 2005, many people heard about it mainly because of its extensive documentation. Unlike with other open source projects, you don't have to dig into the symfony code to understand how a method works or what a feature does. Documentation has always been a major concern among the symfony core team, and that's why we wrote this book: to leverage the adoption of the framework we initiated, to serve as a reference for the 1.0 release, and to allow enterprise use of a framework written primarily for professionals.

Who This Book Is For

For this book, you need a basic understanding of PHP 5 and object-oriented programming. Of course, having already developed web applications in PHP before reading this book is a plus, for you will see this book as a collection of answers to the questions you regularly ask yourself.

How This Book Is Structured

In this book, you will learn how to use symfony to build web applications. The chapters are grouped into five parts:

- *The Basics* covers all the general concepts and prerequisites for starting symfony.

- *The Core Architecture* describes how the three layers of the Model-View-Controller (MVC) architecture are implemented in symfony, and how to build pages and applications according to this separation.

- *Special Features* explains how to use symfony's mechanisms for shortening the development of smart URLs, forms and validation, Ajax interactions, caching, and internationalized applications.

- *Development Tools* covers the resources provided by symfony to make day-to-day development tasks easier: code generators, unit testing framework, command-line tasks, and plug-ins.

- *Becoming a Symfony Expert* reveals a few secret corners of the symfony code and shows you how to tweak the framework's behavior.

Conventions Used in This Book

In the code examples, the names starting with my are just examples of actual names. For instance, you will see myproject, myapp, and mymodule. In your own code, replace these with the real names of your project, application, and module. Not surprisingly, the words Foo and Bar (and sometimes FooBar) will be used as sample content for strings. Also, in syntax explanations, three Xs represent a sample name. For instance, validateXXX() is the syntax of a method that can be named validateUpdate(), validateEdit(), and so on.

Code lines longer than the book page width are indicated with a ➥ character. When you see this symbol at the end of a line, it means that you should read this line and the following as a single line. Here's an example:

```
<?php echo link_to('I never say my name', 'mymodule/myaction?name=anonymous', ➥
'class=foobar') ?>
```

Each command that should be typed in a *nix shell or a Windows command line starts with a greater-than sign:

```
> symfony clear-cache
```

In some code examples, the output of a script when viewed by a browser is written directly after the script code, preceded by an arrow, as follows:

```
<?php echo "Hello, World!" ?>
 => Hello, World!
```

On the other hand, the output of a command appears between two horizontal separators, as follows:

```
> php symfony -V
```

```
symfony version 1.0.0
```

Contacting the Authors

You can chat with François and Fabien on the #symfony IRC channel on freenode (irc://irc. freenode.net/symfony) or send them an e-mail at the following addresses:

```
francois.zaninotto@symfony-project.com
fabien.potencier@symfony-project.com
```

Be aware that they both live in France, so depending where you're writing from, there might be a delay in the response due to the difference in time zone.

License

The symfony framework is available under the MIT license, reproduced hereafter.
Copyright © 2004-2007 Fabien Potencier

Symfony integrates and/or uses code from third-party projects: **Mojavi3** (MVC framework), **Propel** (object-relational mapping), **Creole** (database abstraction), **Phing** (CLI utility), **Unicode** (i18n), **Dynarch** (JavaScript calendar), **Prototype** (JavaScript library), **script.aculo.us** (JavaScript library), **famfamfam** (icons), **Prado** (i18n classes), **PHPMailer** (mail functions), **Spyc** (YAML parser), **pake** (CLI utility), and **lime** (testing framework). Refer to the online copyright file at `http://www.symfony-project.com/trac/browser/trunk/COPYRIGHT`.

PART 1

The Basics

CHAPTER 1

■ ■ ■

Introducing Symfony

What can symfony do for you? What's required to use it? This chapter answers these questions.

Symfony in Brief

A *framework* streamlines application development by automating many of the patterns employed for a given purpose. A framework also adds structure to the code, prompting the developer to write better, more readable, and more maintainable code. Ultimately, a framework makes programming easier, since it packages complex operations into simple statements.

Symfony is a complete framework designed to optimize the development of web applications by way of several key features. For starters, it separates a web application's business rules, server logic, and presentation views. It contains numerous tools and classes aimed at shortening the development time of a complex web application. Additionally, it automates common tasks so that the developer can focus entirely on the specifics of an application. The end result of these advantages means there is no need to reinvent the wheel every time a new web application is built!

Symfony was written entirely in PHP 5. It has been thoroughly tested in various real-world projects, and is actually in use for high-demand e-business websites. It is compatible with most of the available databases engines, including MySQL, PostgreSQL, Oracle, and Microsoft SQL Server. It runs on *nix and Windows platforms. Let's begin with a closer look at its features.

Symfony Features

Symfony was built in order to fulfill the following requirements:

- Easy to install and configure on most platforms (and guaranteed to work on standard *nix and Windows platforms)

- Database engine-independent

- Simple to use, in most cases, but still flexible enough to adapt to complex cases

- Based on the premise of convention over configuration—the developer needs to configure only the unconventional

- Compliant with most web best practices and design patterns

- Enterprise-ready—adaptable to existing information technology (IT) policies and architectures, and stable enough for long-term projects

- Very readable code, with phpDocumentor comments, for easy maintenance

- Easy to extend, allowing for integration with other vendor libraries

Automated Web Project Features

Most of the common features of web projects are automated within symfony, as follows:

- The built-in internationalization layer allows for both data and interface translation, as well as content localization.

- The presentation uses templates and layouts that can be built by HTML designers without any knowledge of the framework. Helpers reduce the amount of presentation code to write by encapsulating large portions of code in simple function calls.

- Forms support automated validation and repopulation, and this ensures a good quality of data in the database and a better user experience.

- Output escaping protects applications from attacks via corrupted data.

- The cache management features reduce bandwidth usage and server load.

- Authentication and credential features facilitate the creation of restricted sections and user security management.

- Routing and smart URLs make the page address part of the interface and search-engine friendly.

- Built-in e-mail and API management features allow web applications to go beyond the classic browser interactions.

- Lists are more user-friendly thanks to automated pagination, sorting, and filtering.

- Factories, plug-ins, and mixins provide a high level of extensibility.

- Ajax interactions are easy to implement thanks to one-line helpers that encapsulate cross-browser-compatible JavaScript effects.

Development Environment and Tools

To fulfill the requirements of enterprises having their own coding guidelines and project management rules, symfony can be entirely customized. It provides, by default, several development environments and is bundled with multiple tools that automate common software-engineering tasks:

- The code-generation tools are great for prototyping and one-click back-end administration.

- The built-in unit and functional testing framework provides the perfect tools to allow test-driven development.

- The debug panel accelerates debugging by displaying all the information the developer needs on the page he's working on.

- The command-line interface automates application deployment between two servers.

- Live configuration changes are possible and effective.

- The logging features give administrators full details about an application's activities.

Who Made Symfony and Why?

The first version of symfony was released in October 2005 by project founder Fabien Potencier, coauthor of this book. Fabien is the CEO of Sensio (http://www.sensio.com/), a French web agency well known for its innovative views on web development.

Back in 2003, Fabien spent some time inquiring about the existing open source development tools for web applications in PHP. He found that none fulfilled the previously described requirements. When PHP 5 was released, he decided that the available tools had reached a mature enough stage to be integrated into a full-featured framework. He subsequently spent a year developing the symfony core, basing his work on the Mojavi Model-View-Controller (MVC) framework, the Propel object-relational mapping (ORM), and the Ruby on Rails templating helpers.

Fabien originally built symfony for Sensio's projects, because having an effective framework at your disposal presents an ideal way to develop applications faster and more efficiently. It also makes web development more intuitive, and the resulting applications are more robust and easier to maintain. The framework entered the proving grounds when it was employed to build an e-commerce website for a lingerie retailer, and subsequently was applied to other projects.

After successfully using symfony for a few projects, Fabien decided to release it under an open source license. He did so to donate this work to the community, to benefit from user feedback, to showcase Sensio's experience, and because it's fun.

■**Note** Why "symfony" and not "FooBarFramework"? Because Fabien wanted a short name containing an *s*, as in Sensio, and an *f*, as in framework—easy to remember and not associated with another development tool. Also, he doesn't like capital letters. *symfony* was close enough, even if not completely English, and it was also available as a project name. The other alternative was "baguette."

For symfony to be a successful open source project, it needed to have extensive documentation, in English, to increase the adoption rate. Fabien asked fellow Sensio employee François Zaninotto, the other author of this book, to dig into the code and write an online book about it. It took quite a while, but when the project was made public, it was documented well enough to appeal to numerous developers. The rest is history.

The Symfony Community

As soon as the symfony website (http://www.symfony-project.com/) was launched, numerous developers from around the world downloaded and installed the framework, read the online documentation, and built their first application with symfony, and the buzz began to mount.

Web application frameworks were getting popular at that time, and the need for a full-featured framework in PHP was high. Symfony offered a compelling solution due to its impressive code quality and significant amount of documentation—two major advantages over the other players in the framework category. Contributors soon began to surface, proposing patches and enhancements, proofreading the documentation, and performing other much-needed roles.

The public source repository and ticketing system offer a variety of ways to contribute, and all volunteers are welcome. Fabien is still the main committer in the trunk of the source code repository, and guarantees the quality of the code.

Today, the symfony forum, mailing lists, and Internet Relay Chat (IRC) channel offer ideal support outlets, with seemingly each question getting an average of four answers. Newcomers install symfony every day, and the wiki and code snippets sections host a lot of user-contributed documentation. The number of known symfony applications increases by an average of five per week, and counting.

The symfony community is the third strength of the framework, and we hope that you will join it after reading this book.

Is Symfony for Me?

Whether you are a PHP 5 expert or a newcomer to web application programming, you will be able to use symfony. The main factor in deciding whether or not to do so is the size of your project.

If you want to develop a simple website with five to ten pages, limited access to a database, and no obligations to ensuring its performance or providing documentation, then you should stick with PHP alone. You wouldn't gain much from a web application framework, and using object orientation or an MVC model would likely only slow down your development process. As a side note, symfony is not optimized to run efficiently on a shared server where PHP scripts can run only in Common Gateway Interface (CGI) mode.

On the other hand, if you develop more complex web applications, with heavy business logic, PHP alone is not enough. If you plan on maintaining or extending your application in the future, you will need your code to be lightweight, readable, and effective. If you want to use the latest advances in user interaction (like Ajax) in an intuitive way, you can't just write hundreds of lines of JavaScript. If you want to have fun and develop fast, then PHP alone will probably be disappointing. In all these cases, symfony is for you.

And, of course, if you are a professional web developer, you already know all the benefits of web application frameworks, and you need one that is mature, well documented, and has a large community. Search no more, for symfony is your solution.

■**Tip** If you would like a visual demonstration, take a look at the screencasts available from the symfony website. You will see how fast and fun it is to develop applications with symfony.

Fundamental Concepts

Before you get started with symfony, you should understand a few basic concepts. Feel free to skip ahead if you already know the meaning of OOP, ORM, RAD, DRY, KISS, TDD, YAML, and PEAR.

PHP 5

Symfony is developed in PHP 5 (http://www.php.net/) and dedicated to building web applications with the same language. Therefore, a solid understanding of PHP 5 is required to get the most out of the framework.

Developers who already know PHP 4 but not PHP 5 should mainly focus on the language's new object-oriented model.

Object-Oriented Programming (OOP)

Object-oriented programming (OOP) will not be explained in this chapter. It needs a whole book itself! Because symfony makes extensive use of the object-oriented mechanisms available as of PHP 5, OOP is a prerequisite to learning symfony.

Wikipedia explains OOP as follows:

> *The idea behind object-oriented programming is that a computer program may be seen as comprising a collection of individual units, or objects, that act on each other, as opposed to a traditional view in which a program may be seen as a collection of functions, or simply as a list of instructions to the computer.*

PHP 5 implements the object-oriented paradigms of class, object, method, inheritance, and much more. Those who are not familiar with these concepts are advised to read the related PHP documentation, available at http://www.php.net/manual/en/language.oop5.basic.php.

Magic Methods

One of the strengths of PHP's object capabilities is the use of *magic methods*. These are methods that can be used to override the default behavior of classes without modifying the outside code. They make the PHP syntax less verbose and more extensible. They are easy to recognize, because the names of the magic methods start with two underscores (__).

For instance, when displaying an object, PHP implicitly looks for a __toString() method for this object to see if a custom display format was defined by the developer:

```
$myObject = new myClass();
echo $myObject;
// Will look for a magic method
echo $myObject->__toString();
```

Symfony uses magic methods, so you should have a thorough understanding of them. They are described in the PHP documentation (http://www.php.net/manual/en/language.oop5.magic.php).

PHP Extension and Application Repository (PEAR)

PEAR is "a framework and distribution system for reusable PHP components." PEAR allows you to download, install, upgrade, and uninstall PHP scripts. When using a PEAR package, you don't need to worry about where to put scripts, how to make them available, or how to extend the command-line interface (CLI).

PEAR is a community-driven project written in PHP and shipped with standard PHP distributions.

■**Tip** The PEAR website, `http://pear.php.net/`, provides documentation and packages grouped by categories.

PEAR is the most professional way to install vendor libraries in PHP. Symfony advises the use of PEAR to keep a central installation point for use across multiple projects. The symfony plug-ins are PEAR packages with a special configuration. The symfony framework itself is available as a PEAR package.

You don't need to know all about the PEAR syntax to use symfony. You just need to understand what it does and have it installed. You can check that PEAR is installed in your computer by typing the following in a CLI:

```
> pear info pear
```

This command will return the version number of your PEAR installation.

The symfony project has its own PEAR repository, or channel. Note that channels are available only since version 1.4.0 of PEAR, so you should upgrade if your version is older. To upgrade your version of PEAR, issue the following command:

```
> pear upgrade PEAR
```

Object-Relational Mapping (ORM)

Databases are *relational*. PHP 5 and symfony are *object-oriented*. In order to access the database in an object-oriented way, an interface translating the object logic to the relational logic is required. This interface is called an object-relational mapping, or ORM.

An ORM is made up of objects that give access to data and keep business rules within themselves.

One benefit of an object/relational abstraction layer is that it prevents you from using a syntax that is specific to a given database. It automatically translates calls to the model objects to SQL queries optimized for the current database.

This means that switching to another database system in the middle of a project is easy. Imagine that you have to write a quick prototype for an application, but the client has not decided yet which database system would best suit his needs. You can start building your application with SQLite, for instance, and switch to MySQL, PostgreSQL, or Oracle when the client is ready to decide. Just change one line in a configuration file, and it works.

An abstraction layer encapsulates the data logic. The rest of the application does not need to know about the SQL queries, and the SQL that accesses the database is easy to find. Developers who specialize in database programming also know clearly where to go.

Using objects instead of records, and classes instead of tables, has another benefit: you can add new accessors to your tables. For instance, if you have a table called `Client` with two fields, `FirstName` and `LastName`, you might like to be able to require just a `Name`. In an object-oriented world, this is as easy as adding a new accessor method to the `Client` class, like this:

```
public function getName()
{
  return $this->getFirstName.' '.$this->getLastName();
}
```

All the repeated data-access functions and the business logic of the data can be maintained within such objects. For instance, consider a class ShoppingCart in which you keep items (which are objects). To retrieve the full amount of the shopping cart for the checkout, you can add a getTotal() method, like this:

```
public function getTotal()
{
  $total = 0;
  foreach ($this->getItems() as $item)
  {
    $total += $item->getPrice() * $item->getQuantity();
  }
  return $total;
}
```

And that's it. Imagine how long it would have required to write a SQL query doing the same thing!

Propel, another open source project, is currently one of the best object/relational abstraction layers for PHP 5. Symfony integrates Propel seamlessly into the framework, so most of the data manipulation described in this book follows the Propel syntax. This book will describe how to use the Propel objects, but for a more complete reference, a visit to the Propel website (http://propel.phpdb.org/trac/) is recommended.

Rapid Application Development (RAD)

Programming web applications has long been a tedious and slow job. Following the usual software engineering life cycles (like the one proposed by the Rational Unified Process, for instance), the development of web applications could not start before a complete set of requirements was written, a lot of Unified Modeling Language (UML) diagrams were drawn, and tons of preliminary documentation were produced. This was due to the general speed of development, to the lack of versatility of programming languages (you had to build, compile, restart, and who knows what else before actually seeing your program run), and most of all, to the fact that clients were quite reasonable and didn't change their minds constantly.

Today, business moves faster, and clients tend to constantly change their minds in the course of the project development. Of course, they expect the development team to adapt to their needs and modify the structure of an application quickly. Fortunately, the use of scripting languages like Perl and PHP makes it easy to apply other programming strategies, such as rapid application development (RAD) or agile software development.

One of the ideas of these methodologies is to start developing as soon as possible so that the client can review a working prototype and offer additional direction. Then the application gets built in an iterative process, releasing increasingly feature-rich versions in short development cycles.

The consequences for the developer are numerous. A developer doesn't need to think about the future when implementing a feature. The method used should be as simple and straightforward as possible. This is well illustrated by the maxim of the KISS principle: Keep It Simple, Stupid.

When the requirements evolve or when a feature is added, existing code usually has to be partly rewritten. This process is called *refactoring*, and happens a lot in the course of a web application development. Code is moved to other places according to its nature. Duplicated portions of code are refactored to a single place, thus applying the Don't Repeat Yourself (DRY) principle.

And to make sure that the application still runs when it changes constantly, it needs a full set of unit tests that can be automated. If well written, unit tests are a solid way to ensure that nothing is broken by adding or refactoring code. Some development methodologies even stipulate writing tests before coding—that's called test-driven development (TDD).

■**Note** There are many other principles and good habits related to agile development. One of the most effective agile development methodologies is called *Extreme Programming* (abbreviated as XP), and the XP literature will teach you a lot about how to develop an application in a fast and effective way. A good starting place is the XP series books by Kent Beck (Addison-Wesley).

Symfony is the perfect tool for RAD. As a matter of fact, the framework was built by a web agency applying the RAD principle for its own projects. This means that learning to use symfony is not about learning a new language, but more about applying the right reflexes and the best judgment in order to build applications in a more effective way.

The symfony project website proposes a step-by-step tutorial illustrating the development of an application in an agile way. It is called *askeet* (http://www.symfony-project.com/askeet), and is recommended reading for those who want to learn more about agile development.

YAML

According to the official YAML website (http://www.yaml.org/), YAML is "a straightforward machine parsable data serialization format designed for human readability and interaction with scripting languages." Put another way, YAML is a very simple language used to describe data in an XML-like way but with a much simpler syntax. It is especially useful to describe data that can be translated into arrays and hashes, like this:

```
$house = array(
  'family' => array(
    'name'     => 'Doe',
    'parents'  => array('John', 'Jane'),
    'children' => array('Paul', 'Mark', 'Simone')
  ),
  'address' => array(
    'number'   => 34,
    'street'   => 'Main Street',
    'city'     => 'Nowheretown',
    'zipcode'  => '12345'
  )
);
```

This PHP array can be automatically created by parsing the YAML string:

```
house:
  family:
    name:        Doe
    parents:
      - John
      - Jane
    children:
      - Paul
      - Mark
      - Simone
  address:
    number: 34
    street: Main Street
    city: Nowheretown
    zipcode: 12345
```

In YAML, structure is shown through indentation, sequence items are denoted by a dash, and key/value pairs within a map are separated by a colon. YAML also has a shorthand syntax to describe the same structure with fewer lines, where arrays are explicitly shown with [ ] and hashes with { }. Therefore, the previous YAML data can be written in a shorter way, as follows:

```
house:
  family: { name: Doe, parents: [John, Jane], children: [Paul, Mark, Simone] }
  address: { number: 34, street: Main Street, city: Nowheretown, zipcode: 12345 }
```

YAML is an acronym for Yet Another Markup Language and pronounced "yamel." The format has been around since 2001, and YAML parsers exist for a large variety of languages.

■**Tip** The specifications of the YAML format are available at `http://www.yaml.org/`.

As you can see, YAML is much faster to write than XML (no more closing tags or explicit quotes), and it is more powerful than .ini files (which don't support hierarchy). That is why symfony uses YAML as the preferred language to store configuration. You will see a lot of YAML files in this book, but it is so straightforward that you probably don't need to learn more about it.

Summary

Symfony is a PHP 5 web application framework. It adds a new layer on top of the PHP language, providing tools that speed up the development of complex web applications. This book will tell you all about it, and you just need to be familiar with the basic concepts of modern programming to understand it—namely object-oriented programming (OOP), object-relational mapping (ORM), and rapid application development (RAD). The only required technical background is knowledge of PHP 5.

■■■

## CHAPTER 2

Exploring Symfony's Code

At first glance, the code behind a symfony-driven application can seem quite daunting. It consists of many directories and scripts, and the files are a mix of PHP classes, HTML, and even an intermingling of the two. You'll also see references to classes that are otherwise nowhere to be found within the application folder, and the directory depth stretches to six levels. But once you understand the reason behind all of this seeming complexity, you'll suddenly feel like it's so natural that you wouldn't trade the symfony application structure for any other. This chapter explains away that intimidated feeling.

The MVC Pattern

Symfony is based on the classic web design pattern known as the MVC architecture, which consists of three levels:

- The *model* represents the information on which the application operates—its business logic.

- The *view* renders the model into a web page suitable for interaction with the user.

- The *controller* responds to user actions and invokes changes on the model or view as appropriate.

Figure 2-1 illustrates the MVC pattern.

The MVC architecture separates the business logic (model) and the presentation (view), resulting in greater maintainability. For instance, if your application should run on both standard web browsers and handheld devices, you just need a new view; you can keep the original controller and model. The controller helps to hide the detail of the protocol used for the request (HTTP, console mode, mail, and so on) from the model and the view. And the model abstracts the logic of the data, which makes the view and the action independent of, for instance, the type of database used by the application.

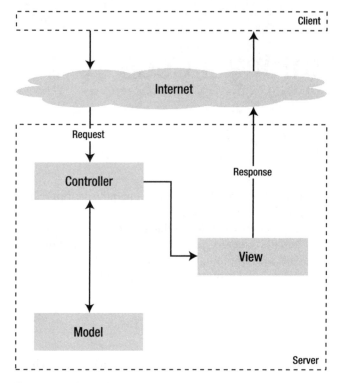

Figure 2-1. *The MVC pattern*

MVC Layering

To help you understand MVC's advantages, let's see how to convert a basic PHP application to an MVC-architectured application. A list of posts for a weblog application will be a perfect example.

Flat Programming

In a flat PHP file, displaying a list of database entries might look like the script presented in Listing 2-1.

Listing 2-1. *A Flat Script*

```php
<?php

// Connecting, selecting database
$link = mysql_connect('localhost', 'myuser', 'mypassword');
mysql_select_db('blog_db', $link);

// Performing SQL query
$result = mysql_query('SELECT date, title FROM post', $link);
```

```
?>

<html>
  <head>
    <title>List of Posts</title>
  </head>
  <body>
    <h1>List of Posts</h1>
    <table>
      <tr><th>Date</th><th>Title</th></tr>
<?php
// Printing results in HTML
while ($row = mysql_fetch_array($result, MYSQL_ASSOC))
{
echo "\t<tr>\n";
printf("\t\t<td> %s </td>\n", $row['date']);
printf("\t\t<td> %s </td>\n", $row['title']);
echo "\t</tr>\n";
}
?>
    </table>
  </body>
</html>

<?php

// Closing connection
mysql_close($link);

?>
```

That's quick to write, fast to execute, and impossible to maintain. The following are the major problems with this code:

- There is no error-checking (what if the connection to the database fails?).

- HTML and PHP code are mixed, even interwoven together.

- The code is tied to a MySQL database.

Isolating the Presentation

The echo and printf calls in Listing 2-1 make the code difficult to read. Modifying the HTML code to enhance the presentation is a hassle with the current syntax. So the code can be split into two parts. First, the pure PHP code with all the business logic goes in a *controller* script, as shown in Listing 2-2.

Listing 2-2. *The Controller Part, in* index.php

```php
<?php

// Connecting, selecting database
$link = mysql_connect('localhost', 'myuser', 'mypassword');
mysql_select_db('blog_db', $link);

// Performing SQL query
$result = mysql_query('SELECT date, title FROM post', $link);

// Filling up the array for the view
$posts = array();
while ($row = mysql_fetch_array($result, MYSQL_ASSOC))
{
    $posts[] = $row;
}

// Closing connection
mysql_close($link);

// Requiring the view
require('view.php');

?>
```

The HTML code, containing template-like PHP syntax, is stored in a *view* script, as shown in Listing 2-3.

Listing 2-3. *The View Part, in* view.php

```html
<html>
  <head>
    <title>List of Posts</title>
  </head>
  <body>
    <h1>List of Posts</h1>
    <table>
      <tr><th>Date</th><th>Title</th></tr>
```

```php
  <?php foreach ($posts as $post): ?>
    <tr>
      <td><?php echo $post['date'] ?></td>
      <td><?php echo $post['title'] ?></td>
    </tr>
  <?php endforeach; ?>
  </table>
 </body>
</html>
```

A good rule of thumb to determine whether the view is clean enough is that it should contain only a minimum amount of PHP code, in order to be understood by an HTML designer without PHP knowledge. The most common statements in views are echo, if/endif, foreach/endforeach, and that's about all. Also, there should not be PHP code echoing HTML tags.

All the logic is moved to the controller script, and contains only pure PHP code, with no HTML inside. As a matter of fact, you should imagine that the same controller could be reused for a totally different presentation, perhaps in a PDF file or an XML structure.

Isolating the Data Manipulation

Most of the controller script code is dedicated to data manipulation. But what if you need the list of posts for another controller, say one that would output an RSS feed of the weblog posts? What if you want to keep all the database queries in one place, to avoid code duplication? What if you decide to change the data model so that the post table gets renamed weblog_post? What if you want to switch to PostgreSQL instead of MySQL? In order to make all that possible, you need to remove the data-manipulation code from the controller and put it in another script, called the *model*, as shown in Listing 2-4.

Listing 2-4. *The Model Part, in* model.php

```php
<?php

function getAllPosts()
{
  // Connecting, selecting database
  $link = mysql_connect('localhost', 'myuser', 'mypassword');
  mysql_select_db('blog_db', $link);

  // Performing SQL query
  $result = mysql_query('SELECT date, title FROM post', $link);
```

```
// Filling up the array
$posts = array();
while ($row = mysql_fetch_array($result, MYSQL_ASSOC))
{
    $posts[] = $row;
}

// Closing connection
mysql_close($link);

return $posts;
}

?>
```

The revised controller is presented in Listing 2-5.

Listing 2-5. *The Controller Part, Revised, in* `index.php`

```php
<?php

// Requiring the model
require_once('model.php');

// Retrieving the list of posts
$posts = getAllPosts();

// Requiring the view
require('view.php');

?>
```

The controller becomes easier to read. Its sole task is to get the data from the model and pass it to the view. In more complex applications, the controller also deals with the request, the user session, the authentication, and so on. The use of explicit names for the functions of the model even makes code comments unnecessary in the controller.

The model script is dedicated to data access and can be organized accordingly. All parameters that don't depend on the data layer (like request parameters) must be given by the controller and not accessed directly by the model. The model functions can be easily reused in another controller.

Layer Separation Beyond MVC

So the principle of the MVC architecture is to separate the code into three layers, according to its nature. Data logic code is placed within the *model*, presentation code within the *view*, and application logic within the *controller*.

Other additional design patterns can make the coding experience even easier. The model, view, and controller layers can be further subdivided.

Database Abstraction

The model layer can be split into a *data access layer* and a *database abstraction layer*. That way, data access functions will not use database-dependent query statements, but call some other functions that will do the queries themselves. If you change your database system later, only the database abstraction layer will need updating.

An example of a MySQL-specific data access layer is presented in Listing 2-6, followed by a sample database abstraction layer in Listing 2-7.

Listing 2-6. *The Database Abstraction Part of the Model*

```php
<?php

function open_connection($host, $user, $password)
{
  return mysql_connect($host, $user, $password);
}

function close_connection($link)
{
  mysql_close($link);
}

function query_database($query, $database, $link)
{
  mysql_select_db($database, $link);

  return mysql_query($query, $link);
}

function fetch_results($result)
{
  return mysql_fetch_array($result, MYSQL_ASSOC);
}
```

Listing 2-7. *The Data Access Part of the Model*

```php
function getAllPosts()
{
  // Connecting to database
  $link = open_connection('localhost', 'myuser', 'mypassword');

  // Performing SQL query
  $result = query_database('SELECT date, title FROM post', 'blog_db', $link);
```

```
// Filling up the array
$posts = array();
while ($row = fetch_results($result))
{
   $posts[] = $row;
}

// Closing connection
close_connection($link);

return $posts;
}

?>
```

You can check that no database-engine dependent functions can be found in the data access layer, making it database-independent. Additionally, the functions created in the database abstraction layer can be reused for many other model functions that need access to the database.

■**Note** The examples in Listings 2-6 and 2-7 are still not very satisfactory, and there is some work left to do to have a full database abstraction (abstracting the SQL code through a database-independent query builder, moving all functions into a class, and so on). But the purpose of this book is not to show you how to write all that code by hand, and you will see in Chapter 8 that symfony natively does all the abstraction very well.

View Elements

The view layer can also benefit from some code separation. A web page often contains consistent elements throughout an application: the page headers, the graphical layout, the footer, and the global navigation. Only the inner part of the page changes. That's why the view is separated into a *layout* and a *template*. The layout is usually global to the application, or to a group of pages. The template only puts in shape the variables made available by the controller. Some logic is needed to make these components work together, and this view logic layer will keep the name *view*. According to these principles, the view part of Listing 2-3 can be separated into three parts, as shown in Listings 2-8, 2-9, and 2-10.

Listing 2-8. *The Template Part of the View, in* mytemplate.php

```
<h1>List of Posts</h1>
<table>
<tr><th>Date</th><th>Title</th></tr>
<?php foreach ($posts as $post): ?>
  <tr>
    <td><?php echo $post['date'] ?></td>
    <td><?php echo $post['title'] ?></td>
  </tr>
<?php endforeach; ?>
</table>
```

Listing 2-9. *The View Logic Part of the View*

```php
<?php

$title = 'List of Posts';
$content = include('mytemplate.php');

?>
```

Listing 2-10. *The Layout Part of the View*

```html
<html>
  <head>
    <title><?php echo $title ?></title>
  </head>
  <body>
    <?php echo $content ?>
  </body>
</html>
```

Action and Front Controller

The controller doesn't do much in the previous example, but in real web applications, the controller has a lot of work. An important part of this work is common to all the controllers of the application. The common tasks include request handling, security handling, loading the application configuration, and similar chores. This is why the controller is often divided into a *front controller*, which is unique for the whole application, and *actions*, which contain only the controller code specific to one page.

One of the great advantages of a front controller is that it offers a unique entry point to the whole application. If you ever decide to close the access to the application, you will just need to edit the front controller script. In an application without a front controller, each individual controller would need to be turned off.

Object Orientation

All the previous examples use procedural programming. The OOP capabilities of modern languages make the programming even easier, since objects can encapsulate logic, inherit from one another, and provide clean naming conventions.

Implementing an MVC architecture in a language that is not object-oriented raises namespace and code-duplication issues, and the overall code is difficult to read.

Object orientation allows developers to deal with such things as the *view object*, the *controller object*, and the *model classes*, and to transform all the functions in the previous examples into methods. It is a must for MVC architectures.

■**Tip** If you want to learn more about design patterns for web applications in an object-oriented context, read *Patterns of Enterprise Application Architecture* by Martin Fowler (Addison-Wesley, ISBN: 0-32112-742-0). Code examples in Fowler's book are in Java or C#, but are still quite readable for a PHP developer.

Symfony's MVC Implementation

Hold on a minute. For a single page listing the posts in a weblog, how many components are required? As illustrated in Figure 2-2, we have the following parts:

- Model layer
  - Database abstraction
  - Data access
- View layer
  - View
  - Template
  - Layout
- Controller layer
  - Front controller
  - Action

Seven scripts—a whole lot of files to open and to modify each time you create a new page! However, symfony makes things easy. While taking the best of the MVC architecture, symfony implements it in a way that makes application development fast and painless.

First of all, the front controller and the layout are common to all actions in an application. You *can* have multiple controllers and layouts, but you *need* only one of each. The front controller is pure MVC logic component, and you will never need to write a single one, because symfony will generate it for you.

The other good news is that the classes of the model layer are also generated automatically, based on your data structure. This is the job of the Propel library, which provides class skeletons and code generation. If Propel finds foreign key constraints or date fields, it will provide special accessor and mutator methods that will make data manipulation a piece of cake. And the database abstraction is totally invisible to you, because it is dealt with by another component, called Creole. So if you decide to change your database engine at one moment, you have zero code to rewrite. You just need to change one configuration parameter.

And the last thing is that the view logic can be easily translated as a simple configuration file, with no programming needed.

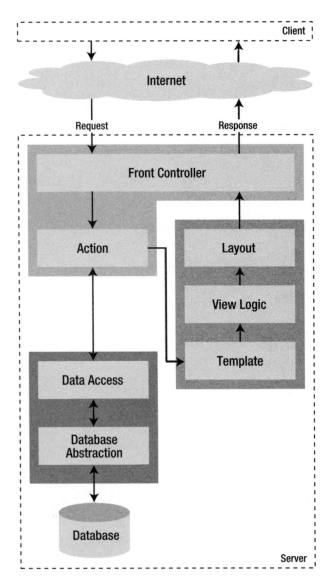

Figure 2-2. *Symfony workflow*

That means that the list of posts described in our example would require only three files to work in symfony, as shown in Listings 2-11, 2-12, and 2-13.

Listing 2-11. *list Action, in myproject/apps/myapp/modules/weblog/actions/actions.class.php*

```php
<?php
class weblogActions extends sfActions
{
  public function executeList()
  {
    $this->posts = PostPeer::doSelect(new Criteria());
  }
}

?>
```

Listing 2-12. *list Template, in myproject/apps/myapp/modules/weblog/templates/ listSuccess.php*

```php
<h1>List of Posts</h1>
<table>
<tr><th>Date</th><th>Title</th></tr>
<?php foreach ($posts as $post): ?>
  <tr>
    <td><?php echo $post->getDate() ?></td>
    <td><?php echo $post->getTitle() ?></td>
  </tr>
<?php endforeach; ?>
</table>
```

Listing 2-13. *list View, in myproject/apps/myapp/modules/weblog/config/view.yml*

```yaml
listSuccess:
  metas: { title: List of Posts }
```

In addition, you will still need to define a layout, as shown in Listing 2-14, but it will be reused many times.

Listing 2-14. *Layout, in myproject/apps/myapp/templates/layout.php*

```php
<html>
  <head>
    <?php echo include_title() ?>
  </head>
  <body>
    <?php echo $sf_data->getRaw('sf_content') ?>
  </body>
</html>
```

And that is really all you need. This is the exact code required to display the very same page as the flat script shown earlier in Listing 2-1. The rest (making all the components work together) is handled by symfony. If you count the lines, you will see that creating the list of posts in an MVC architecture with symfony doesn't require more time or coding than writing a flat file. Nevertheless, it gives you huge advantages, notably clear code organization, reusability, flexibility, and much more fun. And as a bonus, you have XHTML conformance, debug capabilities, easy configuration, database abstraction, smart URL routing, multiple environments, and many more development tools.

Symfony Core Classes

The MVC implementation in symfony uses several classes that you will meet quite often in this book:

- `sfController` is the controller class. It decodes the request and hands it to the action.

- `sfRequest` stores all the request elements (parameters, cookies, headers, and so on).

- `sfResponse` contains the response headers and contents. This is the object that will eventually be converted to an HTML response and be sent to the user.

- The context singleton (retrieved by `sfContext::getInstance()`) stores a reference to all the core objects and the current configuration; it is accessible from everywhere.

You will learn more about these objects in Chapter 6.

As you can see, all the symfony classes use the `sf` prefix, as do the symfony core variables in the templates. This should avoid name collisions with your own classes and variables, and make the core framework classes sociable and easy to recognize.

■**Note** Among the coding standards used in symfony, UpperCamelCase is the standard for class and variable naming. Two exceptions exist: core symfony classes start with `sf`, which is lowercase, and variables found in templates use the underscore-separated syntax.

Code Organization

Now that you know the different components of a symfony application, you're probably wondering how they are organized. Symfony organizes code in a project structure and puts the project files into a standard tree structure.

Project Structure: Applications, Modules, and Actions

In symfony, a *project* is a set of services and operations available under a given domain name, sharing the same object model.

Inside a project, the operations are grouped logically into *applications*. An application can normally run independently of the other applications of the same project. In most cases, a project will contain two applications: one for the front-office and one for the back-office, sharing the same database. But you can also have one project containing many mini-sites, with each site as a different application. Note that hyperlinks between applications must be in the absolute form.

Each application is a set of one or more *modules*. A module usually represents a page or a group of pages with a similar purpose. For example, you might have the modules home, articles, help, shoppingCart, account, and so on.

Modules hold *actions*, which represent the various actions that can be done in a module. For example, a shoppingCart module can have add, show, and update actions. Generally, actions can be described by a verb. Dealing with actions is almost like dealing with pages in a classic web application, although two actions can result in the same page (for instance, adding a comment to a post in a weblog will redisplay the post with the new comment).

■Tip If this represents too many levels for a beginning project, it is very easy to group all actions into one single module, so that the file structure can be kept simple. When the application gets more complex, it will be time to organize actions into separate modules. As mentioned in Chapter 1, rewriting code to improve its structure or readability (but preserving its behavior) is called *refactoring*, and you will do this a lot when applying RAD principles.

Figure 2-3 shows a sample code organization for a weblog project, in a project/ application/module/action structure. But be aware that the actual file tree structure of the project will differ from the setup shown in the figure.

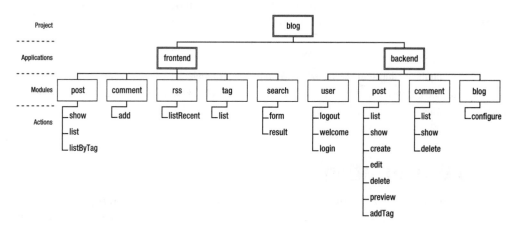

Figure 2-3. *Example of code organization*

File Tree Structure

All web projects generally share the same types of contents, such as the following:

- A database, such as MySQL or PostgreSQL

- Static files (HTML, images, JavaScript files, style sheets, and so on)

- Files uploaded by the site users and administrators

- PHP classes and libraries

- Foreign libraries (third-party scripts)

- Batch files (scripts to be launched by a command line or via a cron table)

- Log files (traces written by the application and/or the server)

- Configuration files

Symfony provides a standard file tree structure to organize all these contents in a logical way, consistent with the architecture choices (MVC pattern and project/application/module grouping). This is the tree structure that is automatically created when initializing every project, application, or module. Of course, you can customize it completely, to reorganize the files and directories at your convenience or to match your client's requirements.

Root Tree Structure

These are the directories found at the root of a symfony project:

```
apps/
  frontend/
  backend/
batch/
cache/
config/
data/
  sql/
doc/
lib/
  model/
log/
plugins/
test/
  unit/
  functional/
web/
  css/
  images/
  js/
  uploads/
```

Table 2-1 describes the contents of these directories.

Table 2-1. *Root Directories*

Directory	Description
apps/	Contains one directory for each application of the project (typically, frontend and backend for the front and back office).
batch/	Contains PHP scripts called from a command line or a scheduler, to run batch processes.
cache/	Contains the cached version of the configuration, and (if you activate it) the cache version of the actions and templates of the project. The cache mechanism (detailed in Chapter 12) uses these files to speed up the answer to web requests. Each application will have a subdirectory here, containing preprocessed PHP and HTML files.
config/	Holds the general configuration of the project.
data/	Here, you can store the data files of the project, like a database schema, a SQL file that creates tables, or even a SQLite database file.
doc/	Stores the project documentation, including your own documents and the documentation generated by PHPdoc.
lib/	Dedicated to foreign classes or libraries. Here, you can add the code that needs to be shared among your applications. The model/ subdirectory stores the object model of the project (described in Chapter 8).
log/	Stores the applicable log files generated directly by symfony. It can also contain web server log files, database log files, or log files from any part of the project. Symfony creates one log file per application and per environment (log files are discussed in Chapter 16).
plugins/	Stores the plug-ins installed in the application (plug-ins are discussed in Chapter 17).
test/	Contains unit and functional tests written in PHP and compatible with the symfony testing framework (discussed in Chapter 15). During the project setup, symfony automatically adds some stubs with a few basic tests.
web/	The root for the web server. The only files accessible from the Internet are the ones located in this directory.

Application Tree Structure

The tree structure of all application directories is the same:

```
apps/
  [application name]/
    config/
    i18n/
    lib/
    modules/
    templates/
      layout.php
      error.php
      error.txtdelete
```

Table 2-2 describes the application subdirectories.

Table 2-2. *Application Subdirectories*

Directory	Description
config/	Holds a hefty set of YAML configuration files. This is where most of the application configuration is, apart from the default parameters that can be found in the framework itself. Note that the default parameters can still be overridden here if needed. You'll learn more about application configuration in the Chapter 5.
i18n/	Contains files used for the internationalization of the application—mostly interface translation files (Chapter 13 deals with internationalization). You can bypass this directory if you choose to use a database for internationalization.
lib/	Contains classes and libraries that are specific to the application.
modules/	Stores all the modules that contain the features of the application.
templates/	Lists the global templates of the application—the ones that are shared by all modules. By default, it contains a layout.php file, which is the main layout in which the module templates are inserted.

■**Note** The i18n/, lib/, and modules/ directories are empty for a new application.

The classes of an application are not able to access methods or attributes in other applications of the same project. Also note that hyperlinks between two applications of the same project must be in absolute form. You need to keep this last constraint in mind during initialization, when you choose how to divide your project into applications.

Module Tree Structure

Each application contains one or more modules. Each module has its own subdirectory in the modules directory, and the name of this directory is chosen during the setup.

This is the typical tree structure of a module:

```
apps/
  [application name]/
    modules/
      [module name]/
          actions/
            actions.class.php
          config/
          lib/
          templates/
            indexSuccess.php
          validate/
```

Table 2-3 describes the module subdirectories.

Table 2-3. *Module Subdirectories*

Directory	Description
actions/	Generally contains a single class file named actions.class.php, in which you can store all the actions of the module. You can also write different actions of a module in separate files.
config/	Can contain custom configuration files with local parameters for the module.
lib/	Stores classes and libraries specific to the module.
templates/	Contains the templates corresponding to the actions of the module. A default template, called indexSuccess.php, is created during module setup.
validate/	Dedicated to configuration files used for form validation (discussed in Chapter 10).

■**Note** The config/, lib/, and validate/ directories are empty for a new module.

Web Tree Structure

There are very few constraints for the web directory, which is the directory of publicly accessible files. Following a few basic naming conventions will provide default behaviors and useful shortcuts in the templates. Here is an example of a web directory structure:

```
web/
  css/
  images/
  js/
  uploads/
```

Conventionally, the static files are distributed in the directories listed in Table 2-4.

Table 2-4. *Typical Web Subdirectories*

Directory	Description
css/	Contains style sheets with a .css extension.
images/	Contains images with a .jpg, .png, or .gif format.
js/	Holds JavaScript files with a .js extension.
uploads/	Must contain the files uploaded by the users. Even though the directory usually contains images, it is distinct from the images directory so that the synchronization of the development and production servers does not affect the uploaded images.

■**Note** Even though it is highly recommended that you maintain the default tree structure, it is possible to modify it for specific needs, such as to allow a project to run in a server with different tree structure rules and coding conventions. Refer to Chapter 19 for more information about modifying the file tree structure.

Common Instruments

A few techniques are used repeatedly in symfony, and you will meet them quite often in this book and in your own projects. These include parameter holders, constants, and class autoloading.

Parameter Holders

Many of the symfony classes contain a parameter holder. It is a convenient way to encapsulate attributes with clean getter and setter methods. For instance, the sfResponse class holds a parameter holder that you can retrieve by calling the getParameterHolder() method. Each parameter holder stores data the same way, as illustrated in Listing 2-15.

Listing 2-15. *Using the sfResponse Parameter Holder*

```
$response->getParameterHolder()->set('foo', 'bar');
echo $response->getParameterHolder()->get('foo');
 => 'bar'
```

Most of the classes using a parameter holder provide proxy methods to shorten the code needed for get/set operations. This is the case for the sfResponse object, so you can do the same as in Listing 2-15 with the code of Listing 2-16.

Listing 2-16. *Using the sfResponse Parameter Holder Proxy Methods*

```
$response->setParameter('foo', 'bar');
echo $response->getParameter('foo');
 => 'bar'
```

The parameter holder getter accepts a default value as a second argument. This provides a useful fallback mechanism that is much more concise than possible with a conditional statement. See Listing 2-17 for an example.

Listing 2-17. *Using the Attribute Holder Getter's Default Value*

```
// The 'foobar' parameter is not defined, so the getter returns an empty value
echo $response->getParameter('foobar');
 => null
```

```
// A default value can be used by putting the getter in a condition
if ($response->hasParameter('foobar'))
{
  echo $response->getParameter('foobar');
}
else
{
  echo 'default';
}
 => default

// But it is much faster to use the second getter argument for that
echo $response->getParameter('foobar', 'default');
 => default
```

The parameter holders even support namespaces. If you specify a third argument to a setter or a getter, it is used as a namespace, and the parameter will be defined only within that namespace. Listing 2-18 shows an example.

Listing 2-18. *Using the sfResponse Parameter Holder Namespace*

```
$response->setParameter('foo', 'bar1');
$response->setParameter('foo', 'bar2', 'my/name/space');
echo $response->getParameter('foo');
 => 'bar1'
echo $response->getParameter('foo', null, 'my/name/space');
 => 'bar2'
```

Of course, you can add a parameter holder to your own classes to take advantage of its syntax facilities. Listing 2-19 shows how to define a class with a parameter holder.

Listing 2-19. *Adding a Parameter Holder to a Class*

```
class MyClass
{
  protected $parameter_holder = null;

  public function initialize ($parameters = array())
  {
    $this->parameter_holder = new sfParameterHolder();
    $this->parameter_holder->add($parameters);
  }

  public function getParameterHolder()
  {
    return $this->parameter_holder;
  }
}
```

Constants

Surprisingly, you will find very few constants in symfony. This is because constants have a major drawback in PHP: you can't change their value once they are defined. So symfony uses its own configuration object, called sfConfig, which replaces constants. It provides static methods to access parameters from everywhere. Listing 2-20 demonstrates the use of sfConfig class methods.

Listing 2-20. *Using the sfConfig Class Methods Instead of Constants*

```
// Instead of PHP constants,
define('SF_FOO', 'bar');
echo SF_FOO;
// Symfony uses the sfConfig object
sfConfig::set('sf_foo', 'bar');
echo sfConfig::get('sf_foo');
```

The sfConfig methods support default values, and you can call the sfConfig::set() method more than once on the same parameter to change its value. Chapter 5 discusses sfConfig methods in more detail.

Class Autoloading

Classically, when you use a class method or create an object in PHP, you need to include the class definition first.

```
include 'classes/MyClass.php';
$myObject = new MyClass();
```

But on large projects with many classes and a deep directory structure, keeping track of all the class files to include and their paths takes a lot of time. By providing an __autoload() function (or a spl_autoload_register() function), symfony makes include statements unnecessary, and you can write directly:

```
$myObject = new MyClass();
```

Symfony will then look for a MyClass definition in all files ending with php in one of the project's lib/ directories. If the class definition is found, it will be included automatically.

So if you store all your classes in lib/ directories, you don't need to include classes anymore. That's why the symfony projects usually do not contain any include or require statements.

■**Note** For better performance, the symfony autoloading scans a list of directories (defined in an internal configuration file) during the first request. It then registers all the classes these directories contain and stores the class/file correspondence in a PHP file as an associative array. That way, future requests don't need to do the directory scan anymore. This is why you need to clear the cache every time you add or move a class file in your project by calling the symfony clear-cache command. You will learn more about the cache in Chapter 12, and about the autoloading configuration in Chapter 19.

Summary

Using an MVC framework forces you to divide and organize your code according to the framework conventions. Presentation code goes to the view, data manipulation code goes to the model, and the request manipulation logic goes to the controller. It makes the application of the MVC pattern both very helpful and quite restricting.

Symfony is an MVC framework written in PHP 5. Its structure is designed to get the best of the MVC pattern, but with great ease of use. Thanks to its versatility and configurability, symfony is suitable for all web application projects.

Now that you understand the underlying theory behind symfony, you are almost ready to develop your first application. But before that, you need a symfony installation up and running on your development server.

CHAPTER 3

■■■

Running Symfony

As you've learned in previous chapters, the symfony framework is a set of files written in PHP. A symfony project uses these files, so installing symfony means getting these files and making them available for the project.

Being a PHP 5 framework, symfony requires PHP 5. Make sure you have it installed by opening a command line and typing this command:

```
> php -v
```

```
PHP 5.2.0 (cli) (built: Nov 2 2006 11:57:36)
Copyright (c) 1997-2006 The PHP Group
Zend Engine v2.2.0, Copyright (c) 1998-2006 Zend Technologies
```

If the version number is 5.0 or higher, then you're ready for the installation, as described in this chapter.

Installing the Sandbox

If you just want to see what symfony is capable of, you'll probably go for the fast installation. In that case, you need the sandbox.

The sandbox is a simple archive of files. It contains an empty symfony project including all the required libraries (symfony, pake, lime, Creole, Propel, and Phing), a default application, and basic configuration. It will work out of the box, without specific server configuration or any additional packages.

To install it, download the sandbox archive from `http://www.symfony-project.com/get/ sf_sandbox.tgz`. Unpack it under the root web directory configured for your server (usually web/ or www/). For the purposes of uniformity, this chapter will assume you unpacked it to the directory sf_sandbox/.

■**Caution** Having all the files under the root web directory is fine for your own tests in a local host, but is a bad practice in a production server. It makes all the internals of your application visible to end users.

Test your installation by executing the symfony CLI. Go to the new sf_sandbox/ directory and type the following on a *nix system:

```
> ./symfony -V
```

On Windows, issue this command:

```
> symfony -V
```

You should see the sandbox version number:

```
symfony version 1.0.0
```

Now make sure that your web server can browse the sandbox by requesting this URL:

```
http://localhost/sf_sandbox/web/frontend_dev.php/
```

You should see a congratulations page that looks like Figure 3-1, and it means that your installation is finished. If not, then an error message will guide you through the configuration changes needed. You can also refer to the "Troubleshooting" section later in this chapter.

Figure 3-1. *Sandbox congratulations page*

The sandbox is intended for you to practice with symfony on a local computer, not to develop complex applications that may end up on the Web. However, the version of symfony shipped with the sandbox is fully functional and equivalent to the one you can install via PEAR.

To uninstall a sandbox, just remove the sf_sandbox/ directory from your web/ folder.

Installing the Symfony Libraries

When developing an application, you will probably need to install symfony twice: once for your development environment and once for the host server (unless your host already has symfony installed). For each server, you will probably want to avoid duplication by keeping all the symfony files in a single place, whether you develop only one application or several applications.

Since the symfony framework evolves quickly, a new stable version could very well be released only a few days after your first installation. You need to think of the framework upgrade as a major concern, and that's another reason why you should share one instance of the symfony libraries across all your symfony projects.

When it comes to installing the libraries for a real application development, you have two alternatives:

- The *PEAR installation* is recommended for most people. It can be easily shared and upgraded, and the installation process is straightforward.

- The *Subversion (SVN) installation* is meant to be used only by advanced PHP developers, who want to take advantage of the latest patches, add features of their own, and/or contribute to the symfony project.

Symfony integrates a few other packages:

- *pake* is a CLI utility.

- *lime* is a unit testing utility.

- *Creole* is a database abstraction engine. Just like PHP Data Objects (PDO), it provides an interface between your code and the database SQL code, and makes it possible to switch to another engine.

- *Propel* is for ORM. It provides object persistence and query service.

- *Phing* is a CLI for Propel.

Pake and lime are developed by the symfony team. Creole, Propel, and Phing come from another team and are released under the GNU Lesser Public General License (LGPL). All these packages are bundled with symfony.

Installing the Symfony PEAR Package

The symfony PEAR package contains the symfony libraries and all its dependencies. It also contains a script that will extend your CLI to include the symfony command.

The first step to install it is to add the symfony channel to PEAR, by issuing this command:

```
> pear channel-discover pear.symfony-project.com
```

To see the libraries available in this channel, type the following:

```
> pear remote-list -c symfony
```

Now you are ready to install the latest stable version of symfony. Issue this command:

```
> pear install symfony/symfony
```

```
downloading symfony-1.0.0.tgz ...
Starting to download symfony-1.0.0.tgz (1,283,270 bytes)
.............................................................
.............................................................
............done: 1,283,270 bytes
install ok: channel://pear.symfony-project.com/symfony-1.0.0
```

That's it. The symfony files and CLI are installed. Check that the installation succeeded by calling the new symfony command line, asking for the version number:

```
> symfony -V
```

```
symfony version 1.0.0
```

■**Tip** If you prefer to install the most recent beta, which has the latest bug fixes and enhancements, type pear install symfony/symfony-beta instead. Beta releases are not completely stable and are generally not recommended for production environments.

The symfony libraries are now installed in directories as follows:

- $php_dir/symfony/ contains the main libraries.

- $data_dir/symfony/ contains the skeleton of symfony applications; default modules; and configuration, i18n data, and so on.

- $doc_dir/symfony/ contains the documentation.

- $test_dir/symfony/ contains unit tests.

The _dir variables are part of your PEAR configuration. To see their values, type the following:

```
>pear config-show
```

Checking Out Symfony from the SVN Repository

For production servers, or when PEAR is not an option, you can download the latest version of the symfony libraries directly from the symfony Subversion repository by requesting a checkout:

```
> mkdir /path/to/symfony
> cd /path/to/symfony
> svn checkout http://svn.symfony-project.com/tags/RELEASE_1_0_0/ .
```

The `symfony` command, available only for PEAR installations, is a call to the `/path/to/symfony/data/bin/symfony` script. So the following would be the equivalent to the `symfony -V` command for an SVN installation:

```
> php /path/to/symfony/data/bin/symfony -V
```

```
symfony version 1.0.0
```

If you chose an SVN installation, you probably already have an existing symfony project. For this project to make use of the symfony files, you need to change the two variables defined in your project's `config/config.php` file, as follows:

```
<?php

$sf_symfony_lib_dir  = '/path/to/symfony/lib/';
$sf_symfony_data_dir = '/path/to/symfony/data/';
```

Chapter 19 proposes other ways to link a project with a symfony installation (including symbolic links and relative paths).

■**Tip** Alternatively, you can also download the PEAR package (`http://pear.symfony-project.com/get/symfony-1.0.0.tgz`) and unpack it somewhere. You will have the same result as with a checkout.

Setting Up an Application

As you learned in Chapter 2, symfony gathers related applications in projects. All the applications of a project share the same databases. In order to set up an application, you must first set up a project.

Creating the Project

Each symfony project follows a predefined directory structure. The symfony command line automates the creation of new projects by initiating the skeleton of the project, with the proper tree structure and access rights. So to create a project, simply create a new directory and ask symfony to make it a project.

For a PEAR installation, issue these commands:

```
> mkdir ~/myproject
> cd ~/myproject
> symfony init-project myproject
```

For an SVN installation, create a project with these commands:

```
> mkdir ~/myproject
> cd ~/myproject
> php /path/to/symfony/data/bin/symfony init-project myproject
```

The `symfony` command must always be called from the project's root directory (`myproject/` in the preceding examples), because all the tasks performed by this command are project-specific.

Symfony will create a directory structure that looks like this:

```
apps/
batch/
cache/
config/
data/
doc/
lib/
log/
plugins/
test/
web/
```

■Tip The `init-project` task adds a `symfony` script in the project root directory. This PHP script does the same as the `symfony` command installed by PEAR, so you can call `php symfony` instead of `symfony` if you don't have native command-line support (for SVN installations).

Creating the Application

The project is not yet ready to be viewed, because it requires at least one application. To initialize it, use the `symfony init-app` command and pass the name of the application as an argument:

```
> symfony init-app myapp
```

This will create a `myapp/` directory in the `apps/` folder of the project root, with a default application configuration and a set of directories ready to host the file of your website:

```
apps/
  myapp/
    config/
    i18n/
    lib/
    modules/
    templates/
```

Some PHP files corresponding to the front controllers of each default environment are also created in the project web directory:

```
web/
  index.php
  myapp_dev.php
```

   index.php is the *production front controller* of the new application. Because you created the first application of the project, symfony created a file called index.php instead of myapp.php (if you now add a new application called mynewapp, the new production front controller will be named mynewapp.php). To run your application in the development environment, call the front controller myapp_dev.php. You'll learn more about these environments in Chapter 5.

Configuring the Web Server

The scripts of the web/ directory are the entry points to the application. To be able to access them from the Internet, the web server must be configured. In your development server, as well as in a professional hosting solution, you probably have access to the Apache configuration and you can set up a virtual host. On a shared-host server, you probably have access only to an .htaccess file.

Setting Up a Virtual Host

Listing 3-1 is an example of Apache configuration, where a new virtual host is added in the httpd.conf file.

Listing 3-1. *Sample Apache Configuration, in apache/conf/httpd.conf*

```
<VirtualHost *:80>
  ServerName myapp.example.com
  DocumentRoot "/home/steve/myproject/web"
  DirectoryIndex index.php
  Alias /sf /$sf_symfony_data_dir/web/sf
  <Directory "/$sf_symfony_data_dir/web/sf">
    AllowOverride All
    Allow from All
  </Directory>
  <Directory "/home/steve/myproject/web">
    AllowOverride All
    Allow from All
  </Directory>
</VirtualHost>
```

   In the configuration in Listing 3-1, the /path/to/symfony/data placeholder must be replaced by the actual path. For example, for a PEAR installation in *nix, you should type something like this:

```
  Alias /sf /usr/local/lib/php/data/symfony/web/sf
```

Note The alias to the `web/sf/` directory is not mandatory. It allows Apache to find images, style sheets, and JavaScript files for the web debug toolbar, the admin generator, the default symfony pages, and the Ajax support. An alternative to this alias would be to create a symbolic link (symlink) or copy the `/path/to/symfony/data/web/sf/` directory to `myproject/web/sf/`.

Restart Apache, and that's it. Your newly created application can now be called and viewed through a standard web browser at the following URL:

```
http://localhost/myapp_dev.php/
```

You should see a congratulations page similar to the one shown earlier in Figure 3-1.

URL REWRITING

Symfony uses URL rewriting to display "smart URLs"—meaningful locations that display well on search engines and hide all the technical data from the user. You will learn more about this feature, called *routing*, in Chapter 9.

If your version of Apache is not compiled with the `mod_rewrite` module, check that you have the `mod_rewrite` Dynamic Shared Object (DSO) installed and the following lines in your `httpd.conf`:

```
AddModule mod_rewrite.c
LoadModule rewrite_module modules/mod_rewrite.so
```

For Internet Information Services (IIS), you will need `isapi/rewrite` installed and running. Check the symfony online documentation for a detailed IIS installation guide.

Configuring a Shared-Host Server

Setting up an application in a shared host is a little trickier, since the host usually has a specific directory layout that you can't change.

Caution Doing tests and development directly in a shared host is not a good practice. One reason is that it makes the application visible even if it is not finished, revealing its internals and opening large security breaches. Another reason is that the performance of shared hosts is often not sufficient to browse your application with the debug tools on efficiently. So you should not start your development with a shared-host installation, but rather build your application locally and deploy it to the shared host when it is finished. Chapter 16 will tell you more about deployment techniques and tools.

Let's imagine that your shared host requires that the web folder is named `www/` instead of `web/`, and that it doesn't give you access to the `httpd.conf` file, but only to an `.htaccess` file in the web folder.

In a symfony project, every path to a directory is configurable. Chapter 19 will tell you more about it, but in the meantime, you can still rename the web directory to www and have the application take it into account by changing the configuration, as shown in Listing 3-2. These lines are to be added to the end of the application config.php file.

Listing 3-2. *Changing the Default Directory Structure Settings, in apps/myapp/config/config.php*

```
$sf_root_dir = sfConfig::get('sf_root_dir');
sfConfig::add(array(
  'sf_web_dir_name' => $sf_web_dir_name = 'www',
  'sf_web_dir'      => $sf_root_dir.DIRECTORY_SEPARATOR.$sf_web_dir_name,
  'sf_upload_dir'   => $sf_root_dir.DIRECTORY_SEPARATOR.$sf_web_dir_name ➡
                      .DIRECTORY_SEPARATOR.sfConfig::get('sf_upload_dir_name'),
));
```

The project web root contains an .htaccess file by default. It is shown in Listing 3-3. Modify it as necessary to match your shared host requirements.

Listing 3-3. *Default .htaccess Configuration, Now in myproject/www/.htaccess*

```
Options +FollowSymLinks +ExecCGI

<IfModule mod_rewrite.c>
  RewriteEngine On

  # we skip all files with .something
  RewriteCond %{REQUEST_URI} \..+$
  RewriteCond %{REQUEST_URI} !\.html$
  RewriteRule .* - [L]

  # we check if the .html version is here (caching)
  RewriteRule ^$ index.html [QSA]
  RewriteRule ^([^.]+)$ $1.html [QSA]
  RewriteCond %{REQUEST_FILENAME} !-f

  # no, so we redirect to our front web controller
  RewriteRule ^(.*)$ index.php [QSA,L]
</IfModule>

# big crash from our front web controller
ErrorDocument 500 "<h2>Application error</h2>symfony application➡
 failed to start properly"
```

You should now be ready to browse your application. Check the congratulation page by requesting this URL:

```
http://www.example.com/myapp_dev.php/
```

OTHER SERVER CONFIGURATIONS

Symfony is compatible with other server configurations. You can, for instance, access a symfony application using an alias instead of a virtual host. You can also run a symfony application with an IIS server. There are as many techniques as there are configurations, and it is not the purpose of this book to explain them all.

To find directions for a specific server configuration, refer to the symfony wiki (http://www.symfony-project.com/trac/wiki), which contains many step-by-step tutorials.

Troubleshooting

If you encounter problems during the installation, try to make the best out of the errors or exceptions thrown to the shell or to the browser. They are often self-explanatory and may even contain links to specific resources on the Web about your issue.

Typical Problems

If you are still having problems getting symfony running, check the following:

- Some PHP installations come with both a PHP 4 and a PHP 5 command. In that case, the command line is probably php5 instead of php, so try calling php5 symfony instead of the symfony command. You may also need to add SetEnv PHP_VER 5 to your .htaccess configuration, or rename the scripts of the web/ directory from .php to .php5. The error thrown by a PHP 4 command line trying to access symfony looks like this:

```
Parse error, unexpected ',', expecting '(' in .../symfony.php on line 19.
```

- The memory limit, defined in the php.ini, must be set to 16M at least. The usual symptom for this problem is an error message when installing symfony via PEAR or using the command line.

```
Allowed memory size of 8388608 bytes exhausted
```

- The zend.ze1_compatibility_mode setting must be set to off in your php.ini. If it is not, trying to browse to one of the web scripts will produce an "implicit cloning" error:

```
Strict Standards: Implicit cloning object of class 'sfTimer' ➥
because of 'zend.ze1_compatibility_mode'
```

- The log/ and cache/ directories of your project must be writable by the web server. Attempts to browse a symfony application without these directory permissions will result in an exception:

```
sfCacheException [message] Unable to write cache file ➥
"/usr/myproject/cache/frontend/prod/config/config_config_handlers.yml.php"
```

- The include path of your system must include the path to the php command, and the include path of your php.ini must contain a path to PEAR (if you use PEAR).

- Sometimes, there is more than one php.ini on a server's file system (for instance, if you use the WAMP package), so it is difficult to know which php.ini is used. Make the setting changes described in the previous items in *all* the php.ini files that you can find.

■**Note** Although it is not mandatory, it is strongly advised, for performance reasons, to set the magic_quotes_gpc and register_globals settings to off in your php.ini.

Symfony Resources

You can check if your problem has already happened to someone else and find solutions in various places:

- The symfony *installation forum* (http://www.symfony-project.com/forum/) is full of installation questions about a given platform, environment, configuration, host, and so on.

- The archives of the *users mailing-list* (http://groups.google.fr/group/symfony-users) are also searchable. You may find similar experiences to your own there.

- The symfony *wiki* (http://www.symfony-project.com/trac/wiki#Installingsymfony) contains step-by-step tutorials, contributed by symfony users, about installation.

If you don't find any answer, try posing your question to the symfony community. You can post your query in the forum, the mailing list, or even drop to the #symfony IRC channel to get feedback from the most active members of the community.

Source Versioning

Once the setup of the application is done, starting a source versioning (or version control) process is recommended. Source versioning keeps track of all modifications in the code, gives access to previous releases, facilitates patching, and allows for efficient team work. Symfony natively supports CVS, although Subversion (http://subversion.tigris.org/) is recommended. The following examples show the commands for Subversion, and assume that you already have a Subversion server installed and that you wish to create a new repository for your project.

For Windows users, a recommended Subversion client is TortoiseSVN (http://tortoisesvn.tigris.org/). For more information about source versioning and the commands used here, consult the Subversion documentation.

The following example assumes that $SVNREP_DIR is defined as an environment variable. If you don't have it defined, you will need to substitute the actual location of the repository in place of $SVNREP_DIR.

So let's create the new repository for the myproject project:

```
> svnadmin create $SVNREP_DIR/myproject
```

Then the base structure (layout) of the repository is created with the trunk, tags, and branches directories with this pretty long command:

```
> svn mkdir -m "layout creation" file:///$SVNREP_DIR/myproject/trunk ➥
file:///$SVNREP_DIR/myproject/tags file:///$SVNREP_DIR/myproject/branches
```

This will be your first revision. Now you need to import the files of the project except the cache and log temporary files:

```
> cd ~/myproject
> rm -rf cache/*
> rm -rf log/*
> svn import -m "initial import" . file:///$SVNREP_DIR/myproject/trunk
```

Check the committed files by typing the following:

```
> svn ls file:///$SVNREP_DIR/myproject/trunk/
```

That seems good. Now the SVN repository has the reference version (and the history) of all your project files. This means that the files of the actual ~/myproject/ directory need to refer to the repository. To do that, first rename the myproject/ directory—you will erase it soon if everything works well—and do a checkout of the repository in a new directory:

```
> cd ~
> mv myproject myproject.origin
> svn co file:///$SVNREP_DIR/myproject/trunk myproject
> ls myproject
```

That's it. Now you can work on the files located in ~/myproject/ and commit your modifications to the repository. Don't forget to do some cleanup and erase the myproject.origin/ directory, which is now useless.

There is one remaining thing to set up. If you commit your working directory to the repository, you may copy some unwanted files, like the ones located in the cache and log directories of your project. So you need to specify an ignore list to SVN for this project. You also need to set full access to the cache/ and log/ directories again:

```
> cd ~/myproject
> chmod 777 cache
> chmod 777 log
> svn propedit svn:ignore log
> svn propedit svn:ignore cache
```

The default text editor configured for SVN should launch. If this doesn't happen, make Subversion use your preferred editor by typing this:

```
> export SVN_EDITOR=<name of editor>
> svn propedit svn:ignore log
> svn propedit svn:ignore cache
```

Now simply add all files from the subdirectories of myproject/ that SVN should ignore when committing:

```
*
```

Save and quit. You're finished.

Summary

To test and play with symfony on your local server, your best option for installation is definitely the sandbox, which contains a preconfigured symfony environment.

For a real development or in a production server, opt for the PEAR installation or the SVN checkout. This will install the symfony libraries, and you still need to initialize a project and an application. The last step of the application setup is the server configuration, which can be done in many ways. Symfony works perfectly fine with a virtual host, and it is the recommended solution.

If you have any problems during installation, you will find many tutorials and answers to frequently asked questions on the symfony website. If necessary, you can submit your problem to the symfony community, and you will get a quick and effective answer.

Once your project is initiated, it is a good habit to start a version-control process.

Now that you are ready to use symfony, it is time to see how to build a basic web application.

CHAPTER 4

■■■

The Basics of Page Creation

Curiously, the first tutorial that programmers follow when learning a new language or a framework is the one that displays "Hello, world!" on the screen. It is strange to think of the computer as something that can greet the whole world, since every attempt in the artificial intelligence field has so far resulted in poor conversational abilities. But symfony isn't dumber than any other program, and the proof is, you can create a page that says "Hello, <Your Name Here>" with it.

This chapter will teach you how to create a module, which is a structural element that groups pages. You will also learn how to create a page, which is divided into an action and a template, because of the MVC pattern. Links and forms are the basic web interactions; you will see how to insert them in a template and handle them in an action.

Creating a Module Skeleton

As Chapter 2 explained, symfony groups pages into modules. Before creating a page, you need to create a module, which is initially an empty shell with a file structure that symfony can recognize.

The symfony command line automates the creation of modules. You just need to call the init-module task with the application name and the module name as arguments. In the previous chapter, you created a myapp application. To add a mymodule module to this application, type the following commands:

```
> cd ~/myproject
> symfony init-module myapp mymodule
```

```
>> dir+      ~/myproject/apps/myapp/modules/mymodule
>> dir+      ~/myproject/apps/myapp/modules/mymodule/actions
>> file+     ~/myproject/apps/myapp/modules/mymodule/actions/actions.class.php
>> dir+      ~/myproject/apps/myapp/modules/mymodule/config
>> dir+      ~/myproject/apps/myapp/modules/mymodule/lib
>> dir+      ~/myproject/apps/myapp/modules/mymodule/templates
>> file+     ~/myproject/apps/myapp/modules/mymodule/templates/indexSuccess.php
>> dir+      ~/myproject/apps/myapp/modules/mymodule/validate
>> file+     ~/myproject/test/functional/myapp/mymoduleActionsTest.php
```

```
>> tokens    ~/myproject/test/functional/myapp/mymoduleActionsTest.php
>> tokens    ~/myproject/apps/myapp/modules/mymodule/actions/actions.class.php
>> tokens    ~/myproject/apps/myapp/modules/mymodule/templates/indexSuccess.php
```

Apart from the actions/, config/, lib/, templates/, and validate/ directories, this command created only three files. The one in the test/ folder concerns unit tests, and you don't need to bother with it until Chapter 15. The actions.class.php (shown in Listing 4-1) forwards to the default module congratulation page. The templates/indexSuccess.php file is empty.

Listing 4-1. *The Default Generated Action, in* actions/actions.class.php

```php
<?php

class mymoduleActions extends sfActions
{
  public function executeIndex()
  {
    $this->forward('default', 'module');
  }
}
```

■Note If you look at an actual actions.class.php file, you will find more than these few lines, including a lot of comments. This is because symfony recommends using PHP comments to document your project and prepares each class file to be compatible with the phpDocumentor tool (http://www.phpdoc.org/).

For each new module, symfony creates a default index action. It is composed of an action method called executeIndex and a template file called indexSuccess.php. The meanings of the execute prefix and Success suffix will be explained in Chapters 6 and 7, respectively. In the meantime, you can consider that this naming is a convention. You can see the corresponding page (reproduced in Figure 4-1) by browsing to the following URL:

```
http://localhost/myapp_dev.php/mymodule/index
```

The default index action will not be used in this chapter, so you can remove the executeIndex() method from the actions.class.php file, and delete the indexSuccess.php file from the templates/ directory.

■Note Symfony offers other ways to initiate a module than the command line. One of them is to create the directories and files yourself. In many cases, actions and templates of a module are meant to manipulate data of a given table. As the necessary code to create, retrieve, update, and delete records from a table is often the same, symfony provides a mechanism called *scaffolding* to generate this code for you. Refer to Chapter 14 for more information about this technique.

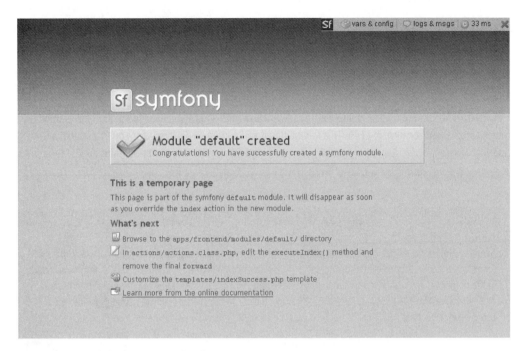

Figure 4-1. *The default generated index page*

Adding a Page

In symfony, the logic behind pages is stored in the action, and the presentation is in templates. Pages without logic (still) require an empty action.

Adding an Action

The "Hello, world!" page will be accessible through a `myAction` action. To create it, just add an `executeMyAction` method to the `mymoduleActions` class, as shown in Listing 4-2.

Listing 4-2. *Adding an Action Is Like Adding an Execute Method to the Action Class*

```php
<?php

class mymoduleActions extends sfActions
{
  public function executeMyAction()
  {
  }
}
```

The name of the action method is always `executeXxx()`, where the second part of the name is the action name with the first letter capitalized.

Now, if you request the following URL:

```
http://localhost/myapp_dev.php/mymodule/myAction
```

symfony will complain that the `myActionSuccess.php` template is missing. That's normal; in symfony, a page is always made of an action *and* a template.

■**Caution** URLs (not domain names) are case-sensitive, and so is symfony (even though the method names are case-insensitive in PHP). This means that if you add an `executemyaction()` method, or an `executeMyaction()`, and then you call `myAction` with the browser, symfony will return a 404 error.

URLS ARE PART OF THE RESPONSE

Symfony contains a *routing system* that allows you to have a complete separation between the actual action name and the form of the URL needed to call it. This allows for custom formatting of the URL as if it were part of the response. You are no longer limited by the file structure nor by the request parameters; the URL for an action can look like the phrase you want. For instance, the call to the `index` action of a module called `article` usually looks like this:

```
http://localhost/myapp_dev.php/article/index?id=123
```

This URL retrieves a given article from a database. In this example, it retrieves an article (with `id=123`) in the Europe section that specifically discusses finance in France. But the URL can be written in a completely different way with a simple change in the `routing.yml` configuration file:

```
http://localhost/articles/europe/france/finance.html
```

Not only is the resulting URL search engine-friendly, it is also significant for the user, who can then use the address bar as a pseudo command line to do custom queries, as in the following:

```
http://localhost/articles/tagged/finance+france+euro
```

Symfony knows how to parse *and* generate smart URLs for the user. The routing system automatically peels the request parameters from a smart URL and makes them available to the action. It also formats the hyperlinks included in the response so that they look "smart." You will learn more about this feature in Chapter 9.

Overall, this means that the way you name the actions of your applications should *not* be influenced by the way the URL used to call them should look, but by the actions' functions in the application. An action name explains what the action actually does, and it's often a verb in the infinitive form (like `show`, `list`, `edit`, and so on). Action names can be made totally invisible to the end user, so don't hesitate to use explicit action names (like `listByName` or `showWithComments`). You will economize on code comments to explain your action function, plus the code will be much easier to read.

Adding a Template

The action expects a template to render itself. A template is a file located in the `templates/` directory of a module, named by the action and the action termination. The default action termination is a "success," so the template file to be created for the `myAction` action is to be called `myActionSuccess.php`.

Templates are supposed to contain only presentational code, so keep as little PHP code in them as possible. As a matter of fact, a page displaying "Hello, world!" can have a template as simple as the one in Listing 4-3.

Listing 4-3. *The* `mymodule/templates/myActionSuccess.php` *Template*

```
<p>Hello, world!</p>
```

If you need to execute some PHP code in the template, you should avoid using the usual PHP syntax, as shown in Listing 4-4. Instead, write your templates using the PHP alternative syntax, as shown in Listing 4-5, to keep the code understandable for non-PHP programmers. Not only will the final code be correctly indented, but it will also help you keep the complex PHP code in the action, because only control statements (`if`, `foreach`, `while`, and so on) have an alternative syntax.

Listing 4-4. *The Usual PHP Syntax, Good for Actions, But Bad for Templates*

```
<p>Hello, world!</p>
<?php

if ($test)
{
  echo "<p>".time()."</p>";
}

?>
```

Listing 4-5. *The Alternative PHP Syntax, Good for Templates*

```
<p>Hello, world!</p>
<?php if ($test): ?>
<p><?php echo time(); ?></p>
<?php endif; ?>
```

■**Tip** A good rule of thumb to check if the template syntax is readable enough is that the file should not contain HTML code echoed by PHP or curly brackets. And most of the time, when opening a `<?php`, you will close it with `?>` in the same line.

Passing Information from the Action to the Template

The job of the action is to do all the complicated calculation, data retrieval, and tests, and to set variables for the template to be echoed or tested. Symfony makes the attributes of the action class (accessed via $this->variableName in the action) directly accessible to the template in the global namespace (via $variableName). Listings 4-6 and 4-7 show how to pass information from the action to the template.

Listing 4-6. *Setting an Action Attribute in the Action to Make It Available to the Template*

```php
<?php

class mymoduleActions extends sfActions
{
  public function executeMyAction()
  {
    $today = getdate();
    $this->hour = $today['hours'];
  }
}
```

Listing 4-7. *The Template Has Direct Access to the Action Attributes*

```php
<p>Hello, world!</p>
<?php if ($hour >= 18): ?>
<p>Or should I say good evening? It's already <?php echo $hour ?>.</p>
<?php endif; ?>
```

■**Note** The template already has access to a few pieces of data without the need of any variable setup in the action. Every template can call methods of the $sf_context, $sf_request, $sf_params, and $sf_user objects. They contain data related to the current context, request, request parameters, and session. You will soon learn how to use them efficiently.

Gathering Information from the User with Forms

Forms are a good way to get information from the user. Writing form and form elements in HTML can sometimes be cumbersome, especially when you want to be XHTML-compliant. You could include form elements in symfony templates the usual way, as shown in Listing 4-8, but symfony provides helpers that make this task easier.

Listing 4-8. *Templates Can Include Usual HTML Code*

```
<p>Hello, world!</p>
<?php if ($hour >= 18): ?>
<p>Or should I say good evening? It's already <?php echo $hour ?>.</p>
<?php endif; ?>
<form method="post" target="/myapp_dev.php/mymodule/anotherAction">
  <label for="name">What is your name?</label>
  <input type="text" name="name" id="name" value="" />
  <input type="submit" value="Ok" />
</form>
```

A *helper* is a PHP function defined by symfony that is meant to be used within templates. It outputs some HTML code and is faster to use than writing the actual HTML code by yourself. Using symfony helpers, you can have the same result as in Listing 4-8 with the code shown in Listing 4-9.

Listing 4-9. *It Is Faster and Easier to Use Helpers Than to Use HTML Tags*

```
<p>Hello, world!</p>
<?php if ($hour >= 18): ?>
<p>Or should I say good evening? It's already <?php echo $hour ?>.</p>
<?php endif; ?>
<?php echo form_tag('mymodule/anotherAction') ?>
  <?php echo label_for('name', 'What is your name?') ?>
  <?php echo input_tag('name') ?>
  <?php echo submit_tag('Ok') ?>
</form>
```

HELPERS ARE HERE TO HELP YOU

If, in the example in Listing 4-9, you think the helper version is not really faster to write than the HTML one, consider this one:

```
<?php
$card_list = array(
  'VISA' => 'Visa',
  'MAST' => 'MasterCard',
  'AMEX' => 'American Express',
  'DISC' => 'Discover');
echo select_tag('cc_type', options_for_select($card_list, 'AMEX'));
?>
```

This outputs the following HTML:

```
<select name="cc_type" id="cc_type">
  <option value="VISA">Visa</option>
  <option value="MAST">MasterCard</option>
  <option value="AMEX" selected="selected">American Express</option>
  <option value="DISC">Discover</option>
</select>
```

The benefit of helpers in templates is raw speed of coding, clarity of code, and concision. The only price to pay is the time to learn them, which will end when you finish this book, and the time to write `<?php echo ?>`, for which you should already have a shortcut in your favorite text editor. So you *could* not use the symfony helpers in templates and write HTML the way you always did, but this would be a great loss and much less fun.

Note that the use of the short opening tags (`<?=`, equivalent to `<?php echo`) is not recommended for professional web applications, since your production web server may be able to understand more than one scripting language and consequently get confused. Besides, the short opening tags do not work with the default PHP configuration and need server tweaking to be activated. Ultimately, when you have to deal with XML and validation, it falls short because `<?` has a special meaning in XML.

Form manipulation deserves a whole chapter of its own, since symfony provides many tools, mostly helpers, to make it easier. You will learn more about these helpers in Chapter 10.

Linking to Another Action

You already know that there is a total decoupling between an action name and the URL used to call it. So if you create a link to anotherAction in a template as in Listing 4-10, it will only work with the default routing. If you later decide to change the way the URLs look, then you will need to review all templates to change the hyperlinks.

Listing 4-10. *Hyperlinks, the Classic Way*

```
<a href="/myapp_dev.php/mymodule/anotherAction?name=anonymous">
  I never say my name
</a>
```

To avoid this hassle, you should always use the link_to() helper to create hyperlinks to your application's actions. Listing 4-11 demonstrates the use of the hyperlink helper.

Listing 4-11. *The link_to() Helper*

```
<p>Hello, world!</p>
<?php if ($hour >= 18): ?>
<p>Or should I say good evening? It's already <?php echo $hour ?>.</p>
<?php endif; ?>
```

```
<?php echo form_tag('mymodule/anotherAction') ?>
  <?php echo label_for('name', 'What is your name?') ?>
  <?php echo input_tag('name') ?>
  <?php echo submit_tag('Ok') ?>
  <?php echo link_to('I never say my name', ➥
 'mymodule/anotherAction?name=anonymous') ?>
</form>
```

The resulting HTML will be the same as previously, except that when you change your routing rules, all the templates will behave correctly and reformat the URLs accordingly.

The link_to() helper, like many other helpers, accepts another argument for special options and additional tag attributes. Listing 4-12 shows an example of an option argument and the resulting HTML. The option argument is either an associative array or a simple string showing key=value couples separated by blanks.

Listing 4-12. *Most Helpers Accept an Option Argument*

```
// Option argument as an associative array
<?php echo link_to('I never say my name', 'mymodule/anotherAction?name=anonymous',
  array(
    'class'    => 'special_link',
    'confirm'  => 'Are you sure?',
    'absolute' => true
)) ?>

// Option argument as a string
<?php echo link_to('I never say my name', 'mymodule/anotherAction?name=anonymous',
  'class=special_link confirm=Are you sure? absolute=true') ?>

// Both calls output the same
 => <a class="special_link" onclick="return confirm('Are you sure?');"
    href="http://localhost/myapp_dev.php/mymodule/anotherAction/name/anonymous">
    I never say my name</a>
```

Whenever you use a symfony helper that outputs an HTML tag, you can insert additional tag attributes (like the class attribute in the example in Listing 4-12) in the option argument. You can even write these attributes in the "quick-and-dirty" HTML 4.0 way (without double quotes), and symfony will output them in nicely formatted XHTML. That's another reason why helpers are faster to write than HTML.

■**Note** Because it requires an additional parsing and transformation, the string syntax is a little slower than the array syntax.

Like the form helpers, the link helpers are numerous and have many options. Chapter 9 will describe them in detail.

Getting Information from the Request

Whether the user sends information via a form (usually in a POST request) or via the URL (GET request), you can retrieve the related data from the action with the `getRequestParameter()` method of the `sfActions` object. Listing 4-13 shows how, in `anotherAction`, you retrieve the value of the `name` parameter.

Listing 4-13. *Getting Data from the Request Parameter in the Action*

```php
<?php

class mymoduleActions extends sfActions
{
  ...

  public function executeAnotherAction()
  {
    $this->name = $this->getRequestParameter('name');
  }
}
```

If the data manipulation is simple, you don't even need to use the action to retrieve the request parameters. The template has access to an object called `$sf_params`, which offers a `get()` method to retrieve the request parameters, just like the `getRequestParameter()` in the action.

If `executeAnotherAction()` were empty, Listing 4-14 shows how the `anotherActionSuccess.php` template would retrieve the same `name` parameter.

Listing 4-14. *Getting Data from the Request Parameter Directly in the Template*

```php
<p>Hello, <?php echo $sf_params->get('name') ?>!</p>
```

■Note Why not use the $_POST, $_GET, or $_REQUEST variables instead? Because then your URLs will be formatted differently (as in http://localhost/articles/europe/france/finance.html, without ? nor =), the usual PHP variables won't work anymore, and only the routing system will be able to retrieve the request parameters. And you may want to add input filtering to prevent malicious code injection, which is only possible if you keep all request parameters in one clean parameter holder.

The `$sf_params` object is more powerful than just giving a getter equivalent to an array. For instance, if you only want to test the existence of a request parameter, you can simply use the `$sf_params->has()` method instead of testing the actual value with `get()`, as in Listing 4-15.

Listing 4-15. *Testing the Existence of a Request Parameter in the Template*

```
<?php if ($sf_params->has('name')): ?>
  <p>Hello, <?php echo $sf_params->get('name') ?>!</p>
<?php else: ?>
  <p>Hello, John Doe!</p>
<?php endif; ?>
```

You may have already guessed that this can be written in a single line. As with most getter methods in symfony, both the getRequestParameter() method in the action and the $sf_params->get() method in the template (which, as a matter of fact, calls the same method on the same object) accept a second argument: the default value to be used if the request parameter is not present.

```
<p>Hello, <?php echo $sf_params->get('name', 'John Doe') ?>!</p>
```

Summary

In symfony, pages are composed of an *action* (a method in the actions/actions.class.php file prefixed with execute) and a *template* (a file in the templates/ directory, usually ending with Success.php). They are grouped in *modules*, according to their function in the application. Writing templates is facilitated by *helpers*, which are functions provided by symfony that return HTML code. And you need to think of the *URL* as a part of the response, which can be formatted as needed, so you should refrain for using any direct reference to the URL in action naming or request parameter retrieval.

Once you know these basic principles, you can already write a whole web application with symfony. But it would take you way too long, since almost every task you will have to achieve during the course of the application development is facilitated one way or another by some symfony feature . . . which is why the book doesn't stop now.

## CHAPTER 5

Configuring Symfony

To be simple and easy to use, symfony defines a few conventions, which should satisfy the most common requirements of standard applications without need for modification. However, using a set of simple and powerful configuration files, it is possible to customize almost everything about the way the framework and your application interact with each other. With these files, you will also be able to add specific parameters for your applications.

This chapter explains how the configuration system works:

- The symfony configuration is kept in files written in YAML, although you can always choose another format.

- Configuration files are at the project, application, and module levels in a project's directory structure.

- You can define several sets of configuration settings; in symfony, a set of configuration is called an *environment*.

- The values defined in the configuration files are available from the PHP code of your application.

- Additionally, symfony authorizes PHP code in YAML files and other tricks to make the configuration system even more flexible.

The Configuration System

Regardless of purpose, most web applications share a common set of characteristics. For instance, some sections can be restricted to a subset of users, or the pages can be decorated by a layout, or a form can be filled with the user input after a failed validation. A framework defines a structure for emulating these characteristics, and the developer can further tweak them by changing a configuration setting. This strategy saves a lot of development time, since many changes don't require a single line of code, even if there is a lot of code behind. It is also much more efficient, because it ensures such information can be maintained in a single and easily identifiable location.

However, this approach has two serious drawbacks:

- Developers end up writing endlessly complex XML files.

- In a PHP architecture, every request takes much longer to process.

Taking these disadvantages into account, symfony uses configuration files only for what they are best at doing. As a matter of fact, the ambition of the configuration system in symfony is to be:

Powerful: Almost every aspect that can be managed using configuration files is managed using configuration files.

Simple: Many aspects of configuration are not shown in a normal application, since they seldom need to be changed.

Easy: Configuration files are easy to read, to modify, and to create by the developer.

Customizable: The default configuration language is YAML, but it can be INI, XML, or whatever format the developer prefers.

Fast: The configuration files are never processed by the application but by the configuration system, which compiles them into a fast-processing chunk of code for the PHP server.

YAML Syntax and Symfony Conventions

For its configuration, symfony uses the YAML format by default, instead of more traditional INI or XML formats. YAML shows structure through indentation and is fast to write. Its advantages and basic rules were already described in Chapter 1. However, you need to keep a few conventions in mind when writing YAML files. This section introduces several of the most prominent conventions. For a complete dissertation on the topic, visit the YAML website ((http://www.yaml.org/).

First of all, *never use tabs* in YAML files; use spaces instead. YAML parsers can't understand files with tabs, so indent your lines with spaces (a double blank is the symfony convention for indentation), as shown in Listing 5-1.

Listing 5-1. *YAML Files Forbid Tabs*

```
# Never use tabs
all:
-> mail:
-> -> webmaster:  webmaster@example.com

# Use blanks instead
all:
  mail:
    webmaster: webmaster@example.com
```

If your parameters are *strings* starting or ending with spaces, enclose the value in single quotes. If a string parameter contains special characters, also enclose the value in single quotes, as shown in Listing 5-2.

Listing 5-2. *Nonstandard Strings Should Be Enclosed in Single Quotes*

```
error1: This field is compulsory
error2: ' This field is compulsory  '
error3: 'Don''t leave this field blank'   # Single quotes must be doubled
```

You can define long strings in multiple lines, and also multiple-line strings, with the special string headers (> and |) plus an additional indentation. Listing 5-3 demonstrates this convention.

Listing 5-3. *Defining Long and Multiline Strings*

```
accomplishment: >         # Folded style, introduced by >
  Mark set a major league # Each line break is folded to a space
  home run record in 1998. # Makes YAML more readable
stats: |                  # Literal style, introduced by |
  65 Home Runs            # All line breaks count
  0.278 Batting Average   # Indentation doesn't appear in the resulting string
```

To define a value as an *array*, enclose the elements in square brackets or use the expanded syntax with dashes, as shown in Listing 5-4.

Listing 5-4. *YAML Array Syntax*

```
# Shorthand syntax for arrays
players: [ Mark McGwire, Sammy Sosa, Ken Griffey ]

# Expanded syntax for arrays
players:
  - Mark McGwire
  - Sammy Sosa
  - Ken Griffey
```

To define a value as an *associative array*, or hash, enclose the elements in curly brackets and *always insert a space between the key and the value* in the key: value couple. You can also use the expanded syntax by adding indentation and a carriage return for every new key, as shown in Listing 5-5.

Listing 5-5. *YAML Associative Array Syntax*

```
# Incorrect syntax, blanks are missing after the colon
mail: {webmaster:webmaster@example.com,contact:contact@example.com}

# Correct shorthand syntax for associative arrays
mail: { webmaster: webmaster@example.com, contact: contact@example.com }

# Expanded syntax for associative arrays
mail:
  webmaster: webmaster@example.com
  contact:   contact@example.com
```

To give a *Boolean* value, use either on, 1, or true for a positive value and off, 0, or false for a negative one. Listing 5-6 shows the possible Boolean values.

Listing 5-6. *YAML Boolean Values Syntax*

```
true_values:   [ on, 1, true ]
false_values:  [ off, 0, false ]
```

Don't hesitate to add comments (starting with the hash mark, #) and extra spaces to values to make your YAML files more readable, as shown in Listing 5-7.

Listing 5-7. *YAML Comments Syntax and Value Alignment*

```
# This is a comment line
mail:
  webmaster: webmaster@example.com
  contact:   contact@example.com
  admin:     admin@example.com   # extra spaces allow nice alignment of values
```

In some symfony configuration files, you will sometimes see lines that start with a hash mark (and, as such, ignored by the YAML parsers) but look like usual settings lines. This is a symfony convention: the default configuration, inherited from other YAML files located in the symfony core, is repeated in commented lines in your application configuration, for your information. If you want to change the value of such a parameter, you need to uncomment the line first, as shown in Listing 5-8.

Listing 5-8. *Default Configuration Is Shown Commented*

```
# The cache is off by default
settings:
# cache: off

# If you want to change this setting, uncomment the line first
settings:
  cache: on
```

Symfony sometimes groups the parameter definitions into *categories*. All settings of a given category appear indented under the category header. Structuring long lists of key: value pairs by grouping them into categories improves the readability of the configuration. Category headers start with a dot (.). Listing 5-9 shows an example of categories.

Listing 5-9. *Category Headers Look Like Keys, But Start with a Dot*

```
all:
  .general:
    tax:       19.6

  mail:
    webmaster: webmaster@example.com
```

In this example, `mail` is a key and `general` is only a category header. Everything works as if the category header didn't exist, as shown in Listing 5-10. The `tax` parameter is actually a direct child of the `all` key.

Listing 5-10. *Category Headers Are Only There for Readability and Are Actually Ignored*

```
all:
  tax:          19.6

mail:
  webmaster:  webmaster@example.com
```

AND IF YOU DON'T LIKE YAML

YAML is just an interface to define settings to be used by PHP code, so the configuration defined in YAML files ends up being transformed into PHP. After browsing an application, check its cached configuration (in `cache/myapp/dev/config/`, for instance). You will see the PHP files corresponding to your YAML configuration. You will learn more about the configuration cache later in this chapter.

The good news is that if you don't want to use YAML files, you can still do what the configuration files do by hand, in PHP or via another format (XML, INT, and so on). Throughout this book, you will meet alternative ways to define configuration without YAML, and you will even learn to replace the symfony configuration handlers (in Chapter 19). If you use them wisely, these tricks will enable you to bypass configuration files or define your own configuration format.

Help, a YAML File Killed My App!

The YAML files are parsed into PHP hashes and arrays, and then the values are used in various parts of the application to modify the behavior of the view, the controller, or the model. Many times, when there is a problem in a YAML file, it is not detected until the value actually needs to be used. Moreover, the error or exception that is thrown then is usually not clearly related to the YAML configuration file.

If your application suddenly stops working after a configuration change, you should check that you didn't make any of the common mistakes of the inattentive YAML coder:

- You miss a space between a key and its value:

  ```
  key1:value1      # A space is missing after the :
  ```

- Keys in a sequence are not indented the same way:

  ```
  all:
    key1:  value1
     key2: value2   # Indentation is not the same as the other sequence members
    key3:  value3
  ```

- There is a reserved YAML character in a key or a value, without string delimiters:

  ```
  message: tell him: go way      # :, [, ], { and } are reserved in YAML
  message: 'tell him: go way'    # Correct syntax
  ```

- You are modifying a commented line:

  ```
  # key: value     # Will never be taken into account due to the leading #
  ```

- You set values with the same key name twice at the same level:

  ```
  key1: value1
  key2: value2
  key1: value3     # key1 is defined twice, the value is the last one defined
  ```

- You think that the setting takes a special type, while it is always a string, until you convert it:

  ```
  income: 12,345   # Until you convert it, this is still a string
  ```

Overview of the Configuration Files

Configuration is distributed into files, by subject. The files contain parameter definitions, or settings. Some of these parameters can be overridden at several levels (project, application, and module); some are specific to a certain level. The next chapters will deal with the configuration files related to their main topic, and Chapter 19 will deal with advanced configuration.

Project Configuration

There are a few project configuration files by default. Here are the files that can be found in the `myproject/config/` directory:

`config.php`: This is the very first file executed by any request or command. It contains the path to the framework files, and you can change it to use a different installation. If you add some `define` statements at the end of this file, the constants will be accessible from every application of the project. See Chapter 19 for advanced usage of this file.

`databases.yml`: This is where you define the access and connection settings to the database (host, login, password, database name, and so on). Chapter 8 will tell you more about it. It can also be overridden at the application level.

`properties.ini`: This file holds a few parameters used by the command line tool, including the project name and the connection settings for distant servers. See Chapter 16 for an overview of the features using this file.

`rsync_exclude.txt`: This file specifies which directories must be excluded from the synchronization between servers. It is discussed in Chapter 16.

`schema.yml` and `propel.ini`: These are data access configuration files used by Propel (symfony's ORM layer). They are used to make the Propel libraries work with the symfony classes and the data of your project. `schema.yml` contains a representation of the project's relational data model. `propel.ini` is automatically generated, so you probably do not need to modify it. If you don't use Propel, these files are not needed. Chapter 8 will tell you more about their use.

These files are mostly used by external components or by the command line, or they need to be processed even before any YAML parsing program can be loaded by the framework. That's why some of them don't use the YAML format.

Application Configuration

The main part of the configuration is the application configuration. It is defined in the front controller (in the web/ directory) for the main constants, in YAML files located in the application config/ directory, in i18n/ directories for the internationalization files, and in the framework files for invisible—although useful—additional application configuration.

Front Controller Configuration

The very first application configuration is actually found in the *front controller*, that is the very first script executed by a request. Take a look at the default web/index.php in Listing 5-11.

Listing 5-11. *The Default Production Front Controller*

```php
<?php

define('SF_ROOT_DIR',    dirname(__FILE__).'/..');
define('SF_APP',         'myapp');
define('SF_ENVIRONMENT', 'prod');
define('SF_DEBUG',       true);

require_once(SF_ROOT_DIR.DIRECTORY_SEPARATOR.'apps'.DIRECTORY_SEPARATOR. ➥
  SF_APP.DIRECTORY_SEPARATOR.'config'.DIRECTORY_SEPARATOR.'config.php');

sfContext::getInstance()->getController()->dispatch();
```

After defining the name of the application (myapp) and the environment (prod), the general configuration file is called before the dispatching. So a few useful constants are defined here:

SF_ROOT_DIR: Project root directory (normally, should remain at its default value, unless you change the file structure).

SF_APP: Application name in the project. Necessary to compute file paths.

SF_ENVIRONMENT: Environment name (prod, dev, or any other project-specific environment that you define). Will determine which configuration settings are to be used. Environments are explained later in this chapter.

SF_DEBUG: Activation of the debug mode (see Chapter 16 for details).

If you want to change one of these values, you probably need an additional front controller. The next chapter will tell you more about front controllers and how to create a new one.

THE ROOT DIRECTORY CAN BE ANYWHERE

Only the files and scripts located under the web root (the `web/` directory in a symfony project) are available from the outside. The front controller scripts, images, style sheets, and JavaScript files are public. All the other files must be outside the server web root—that means they can be anywhere else.

The non-public files of a project are accessed by the front controller from the `SF_ROOT_DIR` path. Classically, the root directory is one level up the `web/` directory. But you can choose a completely different structure. Imagine that your main directory structure is made of two directories, one public and one private:

```
symfony/    # Private area
  apps/
  batch/
  cache/
  ...
www/        # Public area
  images/
  css/
  js/
  index.php
```

In this case, the root directory is the `symfony/` directory. So the `index.php` front controller simply needs to define the `SF_ROOT_DIR` as follows for the application to work:

```
define('SF_ROOT_DIR', dirname(__FILE__).'/../symfony');
```

Chapter 19 will give you more information about how to tweak symfony to make it work on a specific directory structure.

Main Application Configuration

The main application configuration is stored in files located in the `myproject/apps/myapp/config/` directory:

app.yml: This file should contain the application-specific configuration; that is, global variables defining business or applicative logic specific to an application, which don't need to be stored in a database. Tax rates, shipping fares, and e-mail addresses are often stored in this file. It is empty by default.

config.php: This file bootstraps the application, which means that it does all the very basic initializations to allow the application to start. This is where you can customize your directory structure or add application-specific constants (Chapter 19 provides more details). It starts by including the project's config.php.

factories.yml: Symfony defines its own class to handle the view, the request, the response, the session, and so on. If you want to use your own classes instead, this is where you can specify them. Chapter 19 provides more information.

`filters.yml`: Filters are portions of code executed for every request. This file is where you define which filters are to be processed, and it can be overridden for each module. Chapter 6 discusses filters in more detail.

`logging.yml`: This file defines which level of detail must be recorded in the logs, to help you manage and debug your application. The use of this configuration is explained in Chapter 16.

`routing.yml`: The routing rules, which allow transforming unreadable and unbookmark-able URLs into "smart" and explicit ones, are stored in this file. For new applications, a few default rules exist. Chapter 9 is all about links and routing.

`settings.yml`: The main settings of a symfony application are defined in this file. This is where you specify if your application has internationalization, its default language, the request timeout and whether caching is turned on. With a one-line change in this file, you can shut down the application so you can perform maintenance or upgrade one of its components. The common settings and their use are described in Chapter 19.

`view.yml`: The structure of the default view (name of the layout, title, and meta tags; default style sheets and JavaScript files to be included; default content-type, and so on) is set in this file. It also defines the default value of the meta and title tags. Chapter 7 will tell you more about this file. These settings can be overridden for each module.

Internationalization Configuration

Internationalized applications can display pages in several languages. This requires specific configuration. There are two configuration places for internationalization:

`i18n.yml` of the application `config/` directory: This file defines general translation settings, such as the default culture for the translation, whether the translations come from files or a database, and their format.

Translation files in the application `i18n/` directory: These are basically dictionaries, giving a translation for each of the phrases used in the application templates so that the pages show translated text when the user switches language.

Note that the activation of the i18n features is set in the `settings.yml` file. You will find more information about these features in Chapter 13.

Additional Application Configuration

A second set of configuration files is in the symfony installation directory (in `$sf_symfony_data_dir/config/`) and doesn't appear in the configuration directory of your applications. The settings defined there are defaults that seldom need to be modified, or that are global to all projects. However, if you need to modify them, just create an empty file with the same name in your `myproject/apps/myapp/config/` directory, and override the settings you want to change. The settings defined in an application always have precedence over the ones defined in the framework. The following are the configuration files in the symfony installation `config/` directory:

autoload.yml: This file contains the settings of the autoloading feature. This feature exempts you from requiring custom classes in your code if they are located in specific directories. It is described in detail in Chapter 19.

constants.php: This file contains the default application file structure. To override the settings of this file, use the application config.php, as explained in Chapter 19.

core_compile.yml and bootstrap_compile.yml: These are lists of classes to be included to start an application (in bootstrap_compile.yml) and to process a request (in core_compile.yml). These classes are actually concatenated into an optimized PHP file without comments, which will accelerate the execution by minimizing the file access operations (one file is loaded instead of more than forty for each request). This is especially useful if you don't use a PHP accelerator. Optimization techniques are described in Chapter 18.

config_handlers.yml: This is where you can add or modify the handlers used to process each configuration file. Chapter 19 provides more details.

php.yml: This file checks that the variables of the php.ini file are properly defined and allows you to override them, if necessary. Check Chapter 19 for details.

Module Configuration

By default, a module has no specific configuration. But, if required, you can override some application-level settings for a given module. For instance, you might do this to change the HTML description of all the actions of a module, or to include a specific JavaScript file. You can also choose to add new parameters restricted to a specific module to preserve encapsulation.

As you may have guessed, module configuration files must be located in a myproject/apps/myapp/modules/mymodule/config/ directory. These files are as follows:

generator.yml: For modules generated according to a database table (scaffoldings and administrations), this file defines how the interface displays rows and fields, and which interactions are proposed to the user (filters, sorting, buttons, and so on). Chapter 14 will tell you more about it.

module.yml: This file contains custom parameters specific to a module (equivalent to the app.yml, but at the module level) and action configuration. Chapter 6 provides more details.

security.yml: This file sets access restrictions for actions. This is where you specify that a page can be viewed only by registered users or by a subset of registered users with special permissions. Chapter 6 will tell you more about it.

view.yml: This file contains configuration for the views of one or all of the actions of a module. It overrides the application view.yml and is described in Chapter 7.

Data validation files: Although located in the validate/ directory instead of the config/ one, the YAML data validation files, used to control the data entered in forms, are also module configuration files. You will learn how to use them in Chapter 10.

Most module configuration files offer the ability to define parameters for all the views or all the actions of a module, or for a subset of them.

TOO MANY FILES?

You might be overwhelmed by the number of configuration files present in the application. But please keep the following in mind:

- Most of the time, you don't need to change the configuration, since the default conventions match the most common requirements.

- Each configuration file is related to a particular feature, and the next chapters will detail their use one by one. When you focus on a single file, you can see clearly what it does and how it is organized.

- For professional web development, the default configuration is often not completely adapted. The configuration files allow for an easy modification of the symfony mechanisms without code. Imagine the amount of PHP code necessary to achieve the same amount of control.

- If all the configuration were located in one file, not only would the file be completely unreadable, but you could not redefine configuration at several levels (see the "Configuration Cascade" section later in this chapter).

The configuration system is one of the great strengths of symfony, because it makes symfony usable for almost every kind of web application, and not only for the ones for which the framework was originally designed.

Environments

During the course of application development, you will probably need to keep several sets of configuration in parallel. For instance, you will need to have the connection settings for your tests database available during development, and the ones for your real data available for production. To answer the need of concurrent configurations, symfony offers different environments.

What Is an Environment?

An application can run in various *environments*. The different environments share the same PHP code (apart from the front controller), but can have completely different configurations. For each application, symfony provides three default environments: production (prod), test (test), and development (dev). You're also free to add as many custom environments as you wish.

So basically, *environments and configuration are synonyms*. For instance, a test environment will log alerts and errors, while a prod environment will only log errors. Cache acceleration is often deactivated in the dev environment, but activated in the test and prod environments. The dev and test environments may need test data, stored in a database distinct from the one used in the production environment. So the database configuration will be different between the two environments. All environments can live together on the same machine, although a production server generally contains only the prod environment.

In the dev environment, the logging and debugging settings are all enabled, since maintenance is more important than performance. On the contrary, the prod environment has settings optimized for performance by default, so the production configuration turns off many features. A good rule of thumb is to navigate in the development environment until you are satisfied with the feature you are working on, and then switch to the production environment to check its speed.

The test environment differs from the dev and prod environment in other ways. You interact with this environment solely through the command line for the purpose of functional testing and batch scripting. Consequently, the test environment is close to the production one, but it is not accessed through a web browser. It simulates the use of cookies and other HTTP specific components.

To change the environment in which you're browsing your application, just change the front controller. Until now, you have seen only the development environment, since the URLs used in the example called the development front controller:

```
http://localhost/myapp_dev.php/mymodule/index
```

However, if you want to see how the application reacts in production, call the production front controller instead:

```
http://localhost/index.php/mymodule/index
```

If your web server has mod_rewrite enabled, you can even use the custom symfony rewriting rules, written in web/.htaccess. They define the production front controller as the default execution script and allow for URLs like this:

```
http://localhost/mymodule/index
```

ENVIRONMENTS AND SERVERS

Don't mix up the notions of environment and server. In symfony, different environments are different configurations, and correspond to a front controller (the script that executes the request). Different servers correspond to different domain names in the URL.

```
http://localhost/myapp_dev.php/mymodule/index

              ----------  -----------
                server     environment
```

Usually, developers work on applications in a development server, disconnected from the Internet and where all the server and PHP configuration can be changed at will. When the time comes for releasing the application to production, the application files are transferred to the production server and made accessible to the end users.

This means that many environments are available on each server. For instance, you can run in the production environment even on your development server. However, most of the time, only the production environment should be accessible in the production server, to avoid public visibility of server configuration and security risks.

To add a new environment, you don't need to create a directory or to use the symfony CLI. Simply create a new front controller and change the environment name definition in it. This environment inherits all the default configuration plus the settings that are common to all environments. The next chapter will show you how to do this.

Configuration Cascade

The same setting can be defined more than once, in different places. For instance, you may want to set the mime-type of your pages to text/html for all of the application, except for the pages of an rss module, which will need a text/xml mime-type. Symfony gives you the ability to write the first setting in myapp/config/view.yml and the second in myapp/modules/rss/config/view.yml. The configuration system knows that a setting defined at the module level must override a setting defined at the application level.

In fact, there are several configuration levels in symfony:

- Granularity levels:

  - The *default* configuration located in the framework

  - The global configuration for the whole *project* (in myproject/config/)

  - The local configuration for an *application* of the project (in myproject/apps/myapp/config/)

  - The local configuration restricted to a *module* (in myproject/apps/myapp/modules/mymodule/config/)

- Environment levels:

  - Specific to one environment

  - For all environments

Of all the properties that can be customized, many are environment-dependent. Consequently, many YAML configuration files are divided by environment, plus a tail section for all environments. The result is that typical symfony configuration looks like Listing 5-12.

Listing 5-12. *The Structure of Symfony Configuration Files*

```
# Production environment settings
prod:
  ...

# Development environment settings
dev:
  ...

# Test environment settings
test:
  ...

# Custom environment settings
myenv:
  ...
```

```
# Settings for all environments
all:
  ...
```

In addition, the framework itself defines default values in files that are not located in the project tree structure, but in the $sf_symfony_data_dir/config/ directory of your symfony installation. The *default* configuration is set in these files as shown in Listing 5-13. These settings are inherited by all applications.

Listing 5-13. *The Default Configuration, in* $sf_symfony_data_dir/config/settings.yml

```
# Default settings:
default:
  default_module:      default
  default_action:      index
  ...
```

These default definitions are repeated in the project, application, and module configuration files as comments, as shown in Listing 5-14, so that you know that some parameters are defined by default and that they can be modified.

Listing 5-14. *The Default Configuration, Repeated for Information, in* myapp/config/settings.yml

```
#all:
#   default_module:      default
#   default_action:      index
  ...
```

This means that a property can be defined several times, and the actual value results from a definition cascade. A parameter definition in a *named environment* has precedence over the same parameter definition for *all* environments, which has precedence over a definition in the *default* configuration. A parameter definition at the *module* level has precedence over the same parameter definition at the *application* level, which has precedence over a definition at the *project* level. This can be wrapped up in the following priority list:

1. Module

2. Application

3. Project

4. Specific environment

5. All environments

6. Default

The Configuration Cache

Parsing YAML and dealing with the configuration cascade at runtime represent a significant overhead for each request. Symfony has a built-in configuration cache mechanism designed to speed up requests.

The configuration files, whatever their format, are processed by some special classes, called handlers, that transform them into fast-processing PHP code. In the development environment, the handlers check the configuration for changes at each request, to promote interactivity. They parse the recently modified files so that you can see a change in a YAML file immediately. But in the production environment, the processing occurs once during the first request, and then the processed PHP code is stored in the cache for subsequent requests. The performance is guaranteed, since every request in production will just execute some well-optimized PHP code.

For instance, if the `app.yml` file contains this:

```
all:                    # Setting for all environments
  mail:
    webmaster:          webmaster@example.com
```

then the file `config_app.yml.php`, located in the `cache/` folder of your project, will contain this:

```php
<?php

sfConfig::add(array(
  'app_mail_webmaster' => 'webmaster@example.com',
));
```

As a consequence, most of the time, the YAML files aren't even parsed by the framework, which relies on the configuration cache instead. However, in the development environment, symfony will systematically compare the dates of modification of the YAML files and the cached files, and reprocess only the ones that have changed since the previous request.

This presents a major advantage over many PHP frameworks, where configuration files are compiled at every request, even in production. Unlike Java, PHP doesn't share an execution context between requests. For other PHP frameworks, keeping the flexibility of XML configuration files requires a major performance hit to process all the configuration at every request. This is not the case in symfony. Thanks to the cache system, the overhead caused by configuration is very low.

There is an important consequence of this mechanism. If you change the configuration in the production environment, you need to force the reparsing of all the configuration files for your modification to be taken into account. For that, you just need to *clear the cache*, either by deleting the content of the `cache/` directory or, more easily, by calling the `clear-cache` symfony task:

```
> symfony clear-cache
```

Accessing the Configuration from Code

All the configuration files are eventually transformed into PHP, and many of the settings they contain are automatically used by the framework, without further intervention. However, you sometimes need to access some of the settings defined in the configuration files from your code (in actions, templates, custom classes, and so on). The settings defined in settings.yml, app.yml, module.yml, logging.yml, and i18n.yml are available through a special class called sfConfig.

The sfConfig Class

You can access settings from within the application code through the sfConfig class. It is a registry for configuration parameters, with a simple getter class method, accessible from every part of the code:

```
// Retrieve a setting
parameter = sfConfig::get('param_name', $default_value);
```

Note that you can also define, or override, a setting from within PHP code:

```
// Define a setting
sfConfig::set('param_name', $value);
```

The parameter name is the concatenation of several elements, separated by underscores, in this order:

- A prefix related to the configuration file name (sf_ for settings.yml, app_ for app.yml, mod_ for module.yml, sf_i18n_ for i18n.yml, and sf_logging_ for logging.yml)

- The parent keys (if defined), in lowercase

- The name of the key, in lowercase

The environment is not included, since your PHP code will have access only to the values defined for the environment in which it's executed.

For instance, if you need to access the values defined in the app.yml file shown in Listing 5-15, you will need the code shown in Listing 5-16.

Listing 5-15. *Sample app.yml Configuration*

```
all:
  version:      1.5
  .general:
    tax:        19.6
  default_user:
    name:       John Doe
  mail:
    webmaster:  webmaster@example.com
    contact:    contact@example.com
dev:
  mail:
    webmaster:  dummy@example.com
    contact:    dummy@example.com
```

Listing 5-16. *Accessing Configuration Settings in PHP in the dev Environment*

```
echo sfConfig::get('app_version');
 => '1.5'
echo sfConfig::get('app_tax');    // Remember that category headers are ignored
 => '19.6'
echo sfConfig::get('app_default_user_name);
 => 'John Doe'
echo sfConfig::get('app_mail_webmaster');
 => 'dummy@example.com'
echo sfConfig::get('app_mail_contact');
 => 'dummy@example.com'
```

So symfony configuration settings have all the advantages of PHP constants, but without the disadvantages, since the value can be changed.

On that account, the settings.yml file, where you can set the framework settings for an application, is the equivalent to a list of sfConfig::set() calls. Listing 5-17 is interpreted as shown in Listing 5-18.

Listing 5-17. *Extract of settings.yml*

```
all:
  .settings:
    available:          on
    path_info_array:    SERVER
    path_info_key:      PATH_INFO
    url_format:         PATH
```

Listing 5-18. *What Symfony Does When Parsing settings.yml*

```
sfConfig::add(array(
  'sf_available' => true,
  'sf_path_info_array' => 'SERVER',
  'sf_path_info_key' => 'PATH_INFO',
  'sf_url_format' => 'PATH',
));
```

Refer to Chapter 19 for the meanings of the settings found in the settings.yml file.

Custom Application Settings and app.yml

Most of the settings related to the features of an application should be stored in the app.yml file, located in the myproject/apps/myapp/config/ directory. This file is environment-dependent and empty by default. Put in every setting that you want to be easily changed, and use the sfConfig class to access these settings from your code. Listing 5-19 shows an example.

Listing 5-19. *Sample app.yml to Define Credit Card Operators Accepted for a Given Site*

```
all:
  creditcards:
    fake:              off
    visa:              on
    americanexpress:   on

dev:
  creditcards:
    fake:              on
```

To know if the `fake` credit cards are accepted in the current environment, get the value of:

```
sfConfig::get('app_creditcards_fake');
```

■**Tip** Each time you are tempted to define a constant or a setting in one of your scripts, think about if it would be better located in the `app.yml` file. This is a very convenient place to store all application settings.

When your need for custom parameters becomes hard to handle with the `app.yml` syntax, you may need to define a syntax of your own. In that case, you can store the configuration in a new file, interpreted by a new configuration handler. Refer to Chapter 19 for more information about configuration handlers.

Tips for Getting More from Configuration Files

There are a few last tricks to learn before writing your own YAML files. They will allow you to avoid configuration duplication and to deal with your own YAML formats.

Using Constants in YAML Configuration Files

Some configuration settings rely on the value of other settings. To avoid setting the same value twice, symfony supports *constants* in YAML files. On encountering a setting name (one that can be accessed by `sfConfig::get()`) in capital letters enclosed in % signs, the configuration handlers replace them with their current value. See Listing 5-20 for an example.

Listing 5-20. *Using Constants in YAML Files, Example from autoload.yml*

```
autoload:
  symfony:
    name:         symfony
    path:         %SF_SYMFONY_LIB_DIR%
    recursive:    on
    exclude:      [vendor]
```

The path parameter will take the value returned by sfConfig::get('sf_symfony_lib_dir'). If you want one configuration file to rely on another, you need to make sure that the file you rely on is already parsed (look in the symfony source to find out the order in which the configuration files are parsed). app.yml is one of the last files parsed, so you may rely on others in it.

Using Scriptable Configuration

It may happen that your configuration relies on external parameters (such as a database or another configuration file). To deal with these particular cases, the symfony configuration files are parsed as PHP files before being passed to the YAML parser. It means that *you can put PHP code in YAML files*, as in Listing 5-21.

Listing 5-21. *YAML Files Can Contain PHP*

```
all:
  translation:
    format:  <?php echo sfConfig::get('sf_i18n') == true ? 'xliff' : 'none' ?>
```

But be aware that the configuration is parsed very early in the life of a request, so you will not have any symfony built-in methods or functions to help you.

■**Caution** In the production environment, the configuration is cached, so the configuration files are parsed (and executed) only once after the cache is cleared.

Browsing Your Own YAML File

Whenever you want to read a YAML file directly, you can use the sfYaml class. It is a YAML parser that can turn a YAML file into a PHP associative array. Listing 5-22 presents a sample YAML file, and Listing 5-23 shows you how to parse it.

Listing 5-22. *Sample test.yml File*

```
house:
  family:
    name:     Doe
    parents:  [John, Jane]
    children: [Paul, Mark, Simone]
  address:
    number:   34
    street:   Main Street
    city:     Nowheretown
    zipcode:  12345
```

Listing 5-23. *Using the* sfYaml *Class to Turn a YAML File into an Associative Array*

```
$test = sfYaml::load('/path/to/test.yml');
print_r($test);
```

```
Array(
  [house] => Array(
    [family] => Array(
      [name] => Doe
      [parents] => Array(
        [0] => John
        [1] => Jane
      )
      [children] => Array(
        [0] => Paul
        [1] => Mark
        [2] => Simone
      )
    )
    [address] => Array(
      [number] => 34
      [street] => Main Street
      [city] => Nowheretown
      [zipcode] => 12345
    )
  )
)
```

Summary

The symfony configuration system uses the YAML language to be simple and readable. The ability to deal with multiple *environments* and to set parameters through a *definition cascade* offers versatility to the developer. Some of the configuration can be accessed from within the code via the sfConfig object, especially the application settings stored in the app.yml file.

Yes, symfony does have a lot of configuration files, but this approach makes it more adaptable. Remember that you don't need to bother with them unless your application requires a high level of customization.

The Core Architecture

CHAPTER 6

■■■

Inside the Controller Layer

In symfony, the controller layer, which contains the code linking the business logic and the presentation, is split into several components that you use for different purposes:

- The *front controller* is the unique entry point to the application. It loads the configuration and determines the action to execute.

- *Actions* contain the applicative logic. They check the integrity of the request and prepare the data needed by the presentation layer.

- The *request, response,* and *session* objects give access to the request parameters, the response headers, and the persistent user data. They are used very often in the controller layer.

- *Filters* are portions of code executed for every request, before or after the action. For example, the security and validation filters are commonly used in web applications. You can extend the framework by creating your own filters.

This chapter describes all these components, but don't be intimidated by their number. For a basic page, you will probably need to write only a few lines in the action class, and that's all. The other controller components will be of use only in specific situations.

The Front Controller

All web requests are handled by a single front controller, which is the unique entry point to the whole application in a given environment.

When the front controller receives a request, it uses the routing system to match an action name and a module name with the URL typed (or clicked) by the user. For instance, the following request URL calls the `index.php` script (that's the front controller) and will be understood as a call to the action `myAction` of the module `mymodule`:

```
http://localhost/index.php/mymodule/myAction
```

If you are not interested in symfony's internals, that's all that you need to know about the front controller. It is an indispensable component of the symfony MVC architecture, but you will seldom need to change it. So you can jump to the next section unless you really want to know about the guts of the front controller.

The Front Controller's Job in Detail

The front controller does the dispatching of the request, but that means a little more than just determining the action to execute. In fact, it executes the code that is common to all actions, including the following:

1. Define the core constants.

2. Locate the symfony libraries.

3. Load and initiate the core framework classes.

4. Load the configuration.

5. Decode the request URL to determine the action to execute and the request parameters.

6. If the action does not exist, redirect to the 404 error action.

7. Activate filters (for instance, if the request needs authentication).

8. Execute the filters, first pass.

9. Execute the action and render the view.

10. Execute the filters, second pass.

11. Output the response.

The Default Front Controller

The default front controller, called index.php and located in the web/ directory of the project, is a simple PHP file, as shown in Listing 6-1.

Listing 6-1. *The Default Production Front Controller*

```
<?php

define('SF_ROOT_DIR',    realpath(dirname(__FILE__).'/..'));
define('SF_APP',         'myapp');
define('SF_ENVIRONMENT', 'prod');
define('SF_DEBUG',       false);

require_once(SF_ROOT_DIR.DIRECTORY_SEPARATOR.'apps'.DIRECTORY_SEPARATOR ➥
  .SF_APP.DIRECTORY_SEPARATOR.'config'.DIRECTORY_SEPARATOR.'config.php');

sfContext::getInstance()->getController()->dispatch();
```

The constants definition corresponds to the first step described in the previous section. Then the front controller includes the application config.php, which takes care of steps 2 through 4. The call to the dispatch() method of the sfController object (which is the core controller object of the symfony MVC architecture) dispatches the request, taking care of steps 5 through 7. The last steps are handled by the filter chain, as explained later in this chapter.

Calling Another Front Controller to Switch the Environment

One front controller exists per environment. As a matter of fact, it is the very existence of a front controller that defines an environment. The environment is defined in the SF_ENVIRONMENT constant.

To change the environment in which you're browsing your application, just choose another front controller. The default front controllers available when you create a new application with the symfony init-app task are index.php for the production environment and myapp_dev.php for the development environment (provided that your application is called myapp). The default mod_rewrite configuration will use index.php when the URL doesn't contain a front controller script name. So both of these URLs display the same page (mymodule/index) in the production environment:

```
http://localhost/index.php/mymodule/index
http://localhost/mymodule/index
```

and this URL displays that same page in the development environment:

```
http://localhost/myapp_dev.php/mymodule/index
```

Creating a new environment is as easy as creating a new front controller. For instance, you may need a staging environment to allow your customers to test the application before going to production. To create this staging environment, just copy web/myapp_dev.php into web/myapp_staging.php, and change the value of the SF_ENVIRONMENT constant to staging. Now, in all the configuration files, you can add a new staging: section to set specific values for this environment, as shown in Listing 6-2.

Listing 6-2. *Sample app.yml with Specific Settings for the Staging Environment*

```
staging:
  mail:
    webmaster:    dummy@mysite.com
    contact:      dummy@mysite.com
all:
  mail:
    webmaster:    webmaster@mysite.com
    contact:      contact@mysite.com
```

If you want to see how the application reacts in this new environment, call the related front controller:

```
http://localhost/myapp_staging.php/mymodule/index
```

Batch Files

You may want to execute a script from the command line (or via a cron table) with access to all the symfony classes and features, for instance to launch batch e-mail jobs or to periodically update your model through a process-intensive calculation. For such a script, you need to include the same lines as in a front controller at the beginning. Listing 6-3 shows an example of the beginning of a batch script.

Listing 6-3. *Sample Batch Script*

```php
<?php

define('SF_ROOT_DIR',    realpath(dirname(__FILE__).'/..'));
define('SF_APP',         'myapp');
define('SF_ENVIRONMENT', 'prod');
define('SF_DEBUG',       false);

require_once(SF_ROOT_DIR.DIRECTORY_SEPARATOR.'apps'.DIRECTORY_SEPARATOR ➥
  .SF_APP.DIRECTORY_SEPARATOR.'config'.DIRECTORY_SEPARATOR.'config.php');

// add code here
```

You can see that the only missing line is the call to the `dispatch()` method of the `sfController` object, which can be used only with a web server, not in a batch process. Defining an application and an environment gives you access to a specific configuration. Including the application `config.php` initiates the context and the autoloading.

■Tip The symfony CLI offers an `init-batch` task, which automatically creates a skeleton similar to the one in Listing 6-3 in the `batch/` directory. Just pass it an application name, an environment name, and a batch name as arguments.

Actions

The actions are the heart of an application, because they contain all the application's logic. They use the model and define variables for the view. When you make a web request in a symfony application, the URL defines an action and the request parameters.

The Action Class

Actions are methods named `executeActionName` of a class named `moduleNameActions` inheriting from the `sfActions` class, and grouped by modules. The action class of a module is stored in an `actions.class.php` file, in the module's `actions/` directory.

Listing 6-4 shows an example of an `actions.class.php` file with only an index action for the whole `mymodule` module.

Listing 6-4. *Sample Action Class, in* apps/myapp/modules/mymodule/actions/actions.class.php

```php
class mymoduleActions extends sfActions
{
  public function executeIndex()
  {

  }
}
```

■**Caution** Even if method names are not case-sensitive in PHP, they are in symfony. So don't forget that the action methods must start with a lowercase `execute`, followed by the exact action name with the first letter capitalized.

In order to request an action, you need to call the front controller script with the module name and action name as parameters. By default, this is done by appending the couple `module_name/action_name` to the script. This means that the action defined in Listing 6-4 can be called by this URL:

`http://localhost/index.php/mymodule/index`

Adding more actions just means adding more `execute` methods to the `sfActions` object, as shown in Listing 6-5.

Listing 6-5. *Action Class with Two Actions, in* `myapp/modules/mymodule/actions/actions.class.php`

```
class mymoduleActions extends sfActions
{
  public function executeIndex()
  {
    ...
  }

  public function executeList()
  {
    ...
  }
}
```

If the size of an action class grows too much, you probably need to do some refactoring and move some code to the model layer. Actions should often be kept short (not more than a few lines), and all the business logic should usually be in the model.

Still, the number of actions in a module can be important enough to lead you to split it in two modules.

SYMFONY CODING STANDARDS

In the code examples given in this book, you probably noticed that the opening and closing curly braces ({ and }) occupy one line each. This standard makes the code easier to read.

Among the other coding standards of the framework, indentation is always done by two blank spaces; tabs are not used. This is because tabs have a different space value according to the text editor you use, and because code with mixed tab and blank indentation is impossible to read.

Core and generated symfony PHP files do not end with the usual `?>` closing tag. This is because it is not really needed, and because it can create problems in the output if you ever have blanks after this tag.

And if you really pay attention, you will see that a line never ends with a blank space in symfony. The reason, this time, is more prosaic: lines ending with blanks look ugly in Fabien's text editor.

Alternative Action Class Syntax

An alternative action syntax is available to dispatch the actions in separate files, one file per action. In this case, each action class extends sfAction (instead of sfActions) and is named actionNameAction. The actual action method is simply named execute. The file name is the same as the class name. This means that the equivalent of Listing 6-5 can be written with the two files shown in Listings 6-6 and 6-7.

Listing 6-6. *Single Action File, in myapp/modules/mymodule/actions/indexAction.class.php*

```
class indexAction extends sfAction
{
  public function execute()
  {
    ...
  }
}
```

Listing 6-7. *Single Action File, in myapp/modules/mymodule/actions/listAction.class.php*

```
class listAction extends sfAction
{
  public function execute()
  {
    ...
  }
}
```

Retrieving Information in the Action

The action class offers a way to access controller-related information and the core symfony objects. Listing 6-8 demonstrates how to use them.

Listing 6-8. *sfActions Common Methods*

```
class mymoduleActions extends sfActions
{
  public function executeIndex()
  {
    // Retrieving request parameters
    $password   = $this->getRequestParameter('password');

    // Retrieving controller information
    $moduleName = $this->getModuleName();
    $actionName = $this->getActionName();
```

```
// Retrieving framework core objects
$request      = $this->getRequest();
$userSession  = $this->getUser();
$response     = $this->getResponse();
$controller   = $this->getController();
$context      = $this->getContext();

// Setting action variables to pass information to the template
$this->setVar('foo', 'bar');
$this->foo = 'bar';              // Shorter version

  }
}
```

THE CONTEXT SINGLETON

You already saw, in the front controller, a call to sfContext::getInstance(). In an action, the getContext() method returns the same singleton. It is a very useful object that stores a reference to all the symfony core objects related to a given request, and offers an accessor for each of them:

- sfController: The controller object (->getController())

- sfRequest: The request object (->getRequest())

- sfResponse: The response object (->getResponse())

- sfUser: The user session object (->getUser())

- sfDatabaseConnection: The database connection (->getDatabaseConnection())

- sfLogger: The logger object (->getLogger())

- sfI18N: The internationalization object (->getI18N())

You can call the sfContext::getInstance() singleton from any part of the code.

Action Termination

Various behaviors are possible at the conclusion of an action's execution. The value returned by the action method determines how the view will be rendered. Constants of the sfView class are used to specify which template is to be used to display the result of the action.

If there is a *default view* to call (this is the most common case), the action should end as follows:

```
return sfView::SUCCESS;
```

Symfony will then look for a template called actionNameSuccess.php. This is defined as the default action behavior, so if you omit the return statement in an action method, symfony will also look for an actionNameSuccess.php template. Empty actions will also trigger that behavior. See Listing 6-9 for examples of successful action termination.

Listing 6-9. *Actions That Will Call the* indexSuccess.php *and* listSuccess.php *Templates*

```
public function executeIndex()
{
  return sfView::SUCCESS;
}

public function executeList()
{
}
```

If there is an *error view* to call, the action should end like this:

```
return sfView::ERROR;
```

Symfony will then look for a template called actionNameError.php.
To call a *custom view*, use this ending:

```
return 'MyResult';
```

Symfony will then look for a template called actionNameMyResult.php.

If there is no view to call—for instance, in the case of an action executed in a batch process—
the action should end as follows:

```
return sfView::NONE;
```

No template will be executed in that case. It means that you can bypass completely the
view layer and output HTML code directly from an action. As shown in Listing 6-10, symfony
provides a specific renderText() method for this case. This can be useful when you need
extreme responsiveness of the action, such as for Ajax interactions, which will be discussed in
Chapter 11.

Listing 6-10. *Bypassing the View by Echoing the Response and Returning* sfView::NONE

```
public function executeIndex()
{
  echo "<html><body>Hello, World!</body></html>";

  return sfView::NONE;
}

// Is equivalent to
public function executeIndex()
{
  return $this->renderText("<html><body>Hello, World!</body></html>");
}
```

In some cases, you need to send an empty response but with some headers defined in it
(especially the X-JSON header). Define the headers via the sfResponse object, discussed in the
next chapter, and return the sfView::HEADER_ONLY constant, as shown in Listing 6-11.

Listing 6-11. *Escaping View Rendering and Sending Only Headers*

```
public function executeRefresh()
{
  $output = '[["title","My basic letter"],["name","Mr Brown"]]';
  $this->getResponse()->setHttpHeader("X-JSON", '('.$output.')');

  return sfView::HEADER_ONLY;
}
```

If the action must be rendered by a specific template, ignore the return statement and use the setTemplate() method instead.

```
$this->setTemplate('myCustomTemplate');
```

Skipping to Another Action

In some cases, the action execution ends by requesting a new action execution. For instance, an action handling a form submission in a POST request usually redirects to another action after updating the database. Another example is an action alias: the index action is often a way to display a list, and actually forwards to a list action.

The action class provides two methods to execute another action:

- If the action forwards the call to another action:

  ```
  $this->forward('otherModule', 'index');
  ```

- If the action results in a web redirection:

  ```
  $this->redirect('otherModule/index');
  $this->redirect('http://www.google.com/');
  ```

■**Note** The code located after a forward or a redirect in an action is never executed. You can consider that these calls are equivalent to a return statement. They throw an sfStopException to stop the execution of the action; this exception is later caught by symfony and simply ignored.

The choice between a redirect or a forward is sometimes tricky. To choose the best solution, keep in mind that a forward is internal to the application and transparent to the user. As far as the user is concerned, the displayed URL is the same as the one requested. In contrast, a redirect is a message to the user's browser, involving a new request from it and a change in the final resulting URL.

If the action is called from a submitted form with method="post", you should always do a redirect. The main advantage is that if the user refreshes the resulting page, the form will not be submitted again; in addition, the back button works as expected by displaying the form and not an alert asking the user if he wants to resubmit a POST request.

There is a special kind of forward that is used very commonly. The forward404() method forwards to a "page not found" action. This method is often called when a parameter necessary to the action execution is not present in the request (thus detecting a wrongly typed URL). Listing 6-12 shows an example of a show action expecting an id parameter.

Listing 6-12. *Use of the forward404() Method*

```
public function executeShow()
{
  $article = ArticlePeer::retrieveByPK($this->getRequestParameter('id'));
  if (!$article)
  {
    $this->forward404();
  }
}
```

■**Tip** If you are looking for the error 404 action and template, you will find them in the $sf_symfony_ data_dir/modules/default/ directory. You can customize this page by adding a new default module to your application, overriding the one located in the framework, and by defining an error404 action and an error404Success template inside. Alternatively, you can set the error_404_module and error_404_ action constants in the settings.yml file to use an existing action.

Experience shows that, most of the time, an action makes a redirect or a forward after testing something, such as in Listing 6-12. That's why the sfActions class has a few more methods, named forwardIf(), forwardUnless(), forward404If(), forward404Unless(), redirectIf(), and redirectUnless(). These methods simply take an additional parameter representing a condition that triggers the execution if tested true (for the *xxx*If() methods) or false (for the *xxx*Unless() methods), as illustrated in Listing 6-13.

Listing 6-13. *Use of the forward404If() Method*

```
// This action is equivalent to the one shown in Listing 6-12
public function executeShow()
{
  $article = ArticlePeer::retrieveByPK($this->getRequestParameter('id'));
  $this->forward404If(!$article);
}

// So is this one
public function executeShow()
{
  $article = ArticlePeer::retrieveByPK($this->getRequestParameter('id'));
  $this->forward404Unless($article);
}
```

Using these methods will not only keep your code short, but it will also make it more readable.

> ■**Tip** When the action calls `forward404()` or its fellow methods, symfony throws an `sfError404Exception` that manages the 404 response. This means that if you need to display a 404 message from somewhere where you don't want to access the controller, you can just throw a similar exception.

Repeating Code for Several Actions of a Module

The convention to name actions `executeActionName()` (in the case of an `sfActions` class) or `execute()` (in the case of an `sfAction` class) guarantees that symfony will find the action method. It gives you the ability to add other methods of your own that will not be considered as actions, as long as they don't start with `execute`.

There is another useful convention for when you need to repeat several statements in each action *before* the actual action execution. You can then extract them into the `preExecute()` method of your action class. You can probably guess how to repeat statements *after* every action is executed: wrap them in a `postExecute()` method. The syntax of these methods is shown in Listing 6-14.

Listing 6-14. *Using preExecute, postExecute, and Custom Methods in an Action Class*

```
class mymoduleActions extends sfActions
{
  public function preExecute()
  {
    // The code inserted here is executed at the beginning of each action call
    ...
  }

  public function executeIndex()
  {
    ...
  }

  public function executeList()
  {
    ...
    $this->myCustomMethod();  // Methods of the action class are accessible
  }

  public function postExecute()
  {
    // The code inserted here is executed at the end of each action call
    ...
  }
```

```
  protected function myCustomMethod()
  {
    // You can also add your own methods, as long as they don't start with "execute"
    // In that case, it's better to declare them as protected or private
    ...
  }
}
```

Accessing the Request

You're familiar with the getRequestParameter('myparam') method, used to retrieve the value of a request parameter by its name. As a matter of fact, this method is a proxy for a chain of calls to the request's parameter holder getRequest()->getParameter('myparam'). The action class has access to the request object, called sfWebRequest in symfony, and to all its methods, via the getRequest() method. Table 6-1 lists the most useful sfWebRequest methods.

Table 6-1. *Methods of the sfWebRequest Object*

Name	Function	Sample Output
Request Information		
getMethod()	Request method	Returns sfRequest::GET or sfRequest::POST constants
getMethodName()	Request method name	'POST'
getHttpHeader('Server')	Value of a given HTTP header	'Apache/2.0.59 (Unix) DAV/2 PHP/5.1.6'
getCookie('foo')	Value of a named cookie	'bar'
isXmlHttpRequest()*	Is it an Ajax request?	true
isSecure()	Is it an SSL request?	true
Request Parameters		
hasParameter('foo')	Is a parameter present in the request?	true
getParameter('foo')	Value of a named parameter	'bar'
getParameterHolder()->getAll()	Array of all request parameters	
URI-Related Information		
getUri()	Full URI	'http://localhost/ myapp_dev.php/mymodule/ myaction'
getPathInfo()	Path info	'/mymodule/myaction'
getReferer()**	Referrer	'http://localhost/ myapp_dev.php/'
getHost()	Host name	'localhost'

Table 6-1. *Methods of the sfWebRequest Object*

Name	Function	Sample Output
getScriptName()	Front controller path and name	'myapp_dev.php'
Client Browser Information		

getLanguages()	Array of accepted languages	Array(
		  [0] => fr
		  [1] => fr_FR
		  [2] => en_US
		  [3] => en
		)

getCharsets()	Array of accepted charsets	Array(
		  [0] => ISO-8859-1
		  [1] => UTF-8
		  [2] => *
		)

getAcceptableContentType()	Array of accepted content types	Array(
		  [0] => text/xml
		  [1] => text/html

*Works only with prototype

**Sometimes blocked by proxies

The sfActions class offers a few proxies to access the request methods more quickly, as shown in Listing 6-15.

Listing 6-15. *Accessing the sfRequest Object Methods from an Action*

```
class mymoduleActions extends sfActions
{
  public function executeIndex()
  {
    $hasFoo = $this->getRequest()->hasParameter('foo');
    $hasFoo = $this->hasRequestParameter('foo');  // Shorter version
    $foo    = $this->getRequest()->getParameter('foo');
    $foo    = $this->getRequestParameter('foo');  // Shorter version
  }
}
```

For multipart requests to which users attach files, the sfWebRequest object provides a means to access and move these files, as shown in Listing 6-16.

Listing 6-16. *The sfWebRequest Object Knows How to Handle Attached Files*

```
class mymoduleActions extends sfActions
{
  public function executeUpload()
  {
```

```
    if ($this->getRequest()->hasFiles())
    {
      foreach ($this->getRequest()->getFileNames() as $fileName)
      {
        $fileSize  = $this->getRequest()->getFileSize($fileName);
        $fileType  = $this->getRequest()->getFileType($fileName);
        $fileError = $this->getRequest()->hasFileError($fileName);
        $uploadDir = sfConfig::get('sf_upload_dir');
        $this->getRequest()->moveFile('file', $uploadDir.'/'.$fileName);
      }
    }
  }
}
```

You don't have to worry about whether your server supports the $_SERVER or the $_ENV variables, or about default values or server-compatibility issues—the sfWebRequest methods do it all for you. Besides, their names are so evident that you will no longer need to browse the PHP documentation to find out how to get information from the request.

User Session

Symfony automatically manages user sessions and is able to keep persistent data between requests for users. It uses the built-in PHP session-handling mechanisms and enhances them to make them more configurable and easier to use.

Accessing the User Session

The session object for the current user is accessed in the action with the getUser() method and is an instance of the sfUser class. This class contains a parameter holder that allows you to store any user attribute in it. This data will be available to other requests until the end of the user session, as shown in Listing 6-17. User attributes can store any type of data (strings, arrays, and associative arrays). They can be set for every individual user, even if that user is not identified.

Listing 6-17. *The sfUser Object Can Hold Custom User Attributes Existing Across Requests*

```
class mymoduleActions extends sfActions
{
  public function executeFirstPage()
  {
    $nickname = $this->getRequestParameter('nickname');

    // Store data in the user session
    $this->getUser()->setAttribute('nickname', $nickname);
  }
```

```
public function executeSecondPage()
{
  // Retrieve data from the user session with a default value
  $nickname = $this->getUser()->getAttribute('nickname', 'Anonymous Coward');
}
}
```

■**Caution** You can store objects in the user session, but it is strongly discouraged. This is because the session object is serialized between requests and stored in a file. When the session is deserialized, the class of the stored objects must already be loaded, and that's not always the case. In addition, there can be "stalled" objects if you store Propel objects.

Like many getters in symfony, the getAttribute() method accepts a second argument, specifying the default value to be used when the attribute is not defined. To check whether an attribute has been defined for a user, use the hasAttribute() method. The attributes are stored in a parameter holder that can be accessed by the getAttributeHolder() method. It allows for easy cleanup of the user attributes with the usual parameter holder methods, as shown in Listing 6-18.

Listing 6-18. *Removing Data from the User Session*

```
class mymoduleActions extends sfActions
{
  public function executeRemoveNickname()
  {
    $this->getUser()->getAttributeHolder()->remove('nickname');
  }

  public function executeCleanup()
  {
    $this->getUser()->getAttributeHolder()->clear();
  }
}
```

The user session attributes are also available in the templates by default via the $sf_user variable, which stores the current sfUser object, as shown in Listing 6-19.

Listing 6-19. *Templates Also Have Access to the User Session Attributes*

```
<p>
  Hello, <?php echo $sf_user->getAttribute('nickname') ?>
</p>
```

Note If you need to store information just for the duration of the current request—for instance, to pass information through a chain of action calls—you may prefer the sfRequest class, which also has getAttribute() and setAttribute() methods. Only the attributes of the sfUser object are persistent between requests.

Flash Attributes

A recurrent problem with user attributes is the cleaning of the user session once the attribute is not needed anymore. For instance, you may want to display a confirmation after updating data via a form. As the form-handling action makes a redirect, the only way to pass information from this action to the action it redirects to is to store the information in the user session. But once the confirmation message is displayed, you need to clear the attribute; otherwise, it will remain in the session until it expires.

The flash attribute is an ephemeral attribute that you can define and forget, knowing that it will disappear after the very next request and leave the user session clean for the future. In your action, define the flash attribute like this:

```
$this->setFlash('attrib', $value);
```

The template will be rendered and delivered to the user, who will then make a new request to another action. In this second action, just get the value of the flash attribute like this:

```
$value = $this->getFlash('attrib');
```

Then forget about it. After delivering this second page, the attrib flash attribute will be flushed. And even if you don't require it during this second action, the flash will disappear from the session anyway.

If you need to access a flash attribute from a template, use the $sf_flash object:

```
<?php if ($sf_flash->has('attrib')): ?>
  <?php echo $sf_flash->get('attrib') ?>
<?php endif; ?>
```

or just:

```
<?php echo $sf_flash->get('attrib') ?>
```

Flash attributes are a clean way of passing information to the very next request.

Session Management

Symfony's session-handling feature completely masks the client and server storage of the session IDs to the developer. However, if you want to modify the default behaviors of the session-management mechanisms, it is still possible. This is mostly for advanced users.

On the client side, sessions are handled by cookies. The symfony session cookie is called symfony, but you can change its name by editing the factories.yml configuration file, as shown in Listing 6-20.

Listing 6-20. *Changing the Session Cookie Name, in apps/myapp/config/factories.yml*

```
all:
  storage:
    class: sfSessionStorage
    param:
      session_name: my_cookie_name
```

■Tip The session is started (with the PHP function `session_start()`) only if the `auto_start` parameter is set to `true` in `factories.yml` (which is the case by default). If you want to start the user session manually, disable this setting of the storage factory.

Symfony's session handling is based on PHP sessions. This means that if you want the client-side management of sessions to be handled by URL parameters instead of cookies, you just need to change the use_trans_sid setting in your php.ini. Be aware that this is not recommended.

```
session.use_trans_sid = 1
```

On the server side, symfony stores user sessions in files by default. You can store them in your database by changing the value of the class parameter in factories.yml, as shown in Listing 6-21.

Listing 6-21. *Changing the Server Session Storage, in apps/myapp/config/factories.yml*

```
all:
  storage:
    class: sfMySQLSessionStorage
    param:
      db_table: SESSION_TABLE_NAME       # Name of the table storing the sessions
      database: DATABASE_CONNECTION      # Name of the database connection to use
```

The available session storage classes are sfMySQLSessionStorage, sfPostgreSQLSessionStorage, and sfPDOSessionStorage; the latter is preferred. The optional database setting defines the database connection to be used; symfony will then use databases.yml (see Chapter 8) to determine the connection settings (host, database name, user, and password) for this connection.

Session expiration occurs automatically after sf_timeout seconds. This constant is 30 minutes by default and can be modified for each environment in the settings.yml configuration file, as shown in Listing 6-22.

Listing 6-22. *Changing Session Lifetime, in apps/myapp/config/settings.yml*

```
default:
  .settings:
    timeout:      1800          # Session lifetime in seconds
```

Action Security

The ability to execute an action can be restricted to users with certain privileges. The tools provided by symfony for this purpose allow the creation of secure applications, where users need to be authenticated before accessing some features or parts of the application. Securing an application requires two steps: declaring the security requirements for each action and logging in users with privileges so that they can access these secure actions.

Access Restriction

Before being executed, every action passes by a special filter that checks if the current user has the privileges to access the requested action. In symfony, privileges are composed of two parts:

- *Secure* actions require users to be authenticated.

- *Credentials* are named security privileges that allow organizing security by group.

Restricting access to an action is simply made by creating and editing a YAML configuration file called security.yml in the module config/ directory. In this file, you can specify the security requirements that users must fulfill for each action or for all actions. Listing 6-23 shows a sample security.yml.

Listing 6-23. *Setting Access Restrictions, in apps/myapp/modules/mymodule/config/security.yml*

```
read:
  is_secure:   off      # All users can request the read action

update:
  is_secure:   on       # The update action is only for authenticated users

delete:
  is_secure:   on       # Only for authenticated users
  credentials: admin    # With the admin credential

all:
  is_secure:   off      # off is the default value anyway
```

Actions are not secure by default, so when there is no security.yml or no mention of an action in it, actions are accessible by everyone. If there is a security.yml, symfony looks for the name of the requested action and, if it exists, checks the fulfillment of the security requirements. What happens when a user tries to access a restricted action depends on his credentials:

- If the user is authenticated and has the proper credentials, the action is executed.

- If the user is not identified, he will be redirected to the default *login* action.

- If the user is identified but doesn't have the proper credentials, he will be redirected to the default *secure* action, shown in Figure 6-1.

The default login and secure pages are pretty simple, and you will probably want to customize them. You can configure which actions are to be called in case of insufficient privileges in the application settings.yml by changing the value of the properties shown in Listing 6-24.

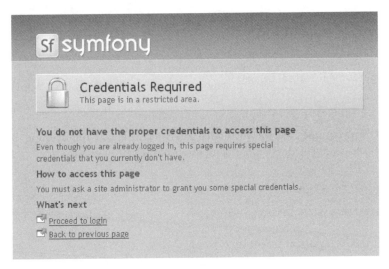

Figure 6-1. *The default secure action page*

Listing 6-24. *Default Security Actions Are Defined in* apps/myapp/config/security.yml

```
all:
  .actions:
    login_module:       default
    login_action:       login

    secure_module:      default
    secure_action:      secure
```

Granting Access

To get access to restricted actions, users need to be authenticated and/or to have certain credentials. You can extend a user's privileges by calling methods of the sfUser object. The authenticated status of the user is set by the setAuthenticated() method. Listing 6-25 shows a simple example of user authentication.

Listing 6-25. *Setting the Authenticated Status of a User*

```
class myAccountActions extends sfActions
{
  public function executeLogin()
  {
```

```
    if ($this->getRequestParameter('login') == 'foobar')
    {
      $this->getUser()->setAuthenticated(true);
    }
  }

  public function executeLogout()
  {
    $this->getUser()->setAuthenticated(false);
  }
}
```

Credentials are a bit more complex to deal with, since you can check, add, remove, and clear credentials. Listing 6-26 describes the credential methods of the sfUser class.

Listing 6-26. *Dealing with User Credentials in an Action*

```
class myAccountActions extends sfActions
{
  public function executeDoThingsWithCredentials()
  {
    $user = $this->getUser();

    // Add one or more credentials
    $user->addCredential('foo');
    $user->addCredentials('foo', 'bar');

    // Check if the user has a credential
    echo $user->hasCredential('foo');                     =>    true

    // Check if the user has one of the credentials
    echo $user->hasCredential(array('foo', 'bar'));       =>    true

    // Check if the user has both credentials
    echo $user->hasCredential(array('foo', 'bar'), true); =>    true

    // Remove a credential
    $user->removeCredential('foo');
    echo $user->hasCredential('foo');                     =>    false

    // Remove all credentials (useful in the logout process)
    $user->clearCredentials();
    echo $user->hasCredential('bar');                     =>    false
  }
}
```

If a user has the 'foo' credential, that user will be able to access the actions for which the security.yml requires that credential. Credentials can also be used to display only authorized content in a template, as shown in Listing 6-27.

Listing 6-27. *Dealing with User Credentials in a Template*

```
<ul>
  <li><?php echo link_to('section1', 'content/section1') ?></li>
  <li><?php echo link_to('section2', 'content/section2') ?></li>
  <?php if ($sf_user->hasCredential('section3')): ?>
  <li><?php echo link_to('section3', 'content/section3') ?></li>
  <?php endif; ?>
</ul>
```

As for the authenticated status, credentials are often given to users during the login process. This is why the sfUser object is often extended to add login and logout methods, in order to set the security status of users in a central place.

■**Tip** Among the symfony plug-ins, the sfGuardPlugin extends the session class to make login and logout easy. Refer to Chapter 17 for more information.

Complex Credentials

The YAML syntax used in the security.yml file allows you to restrict access to users having a combination of credentials, using either AND-type or OR-type associations. With such a combination, you can build a complex workflow and user privilege management system—for instance, a content management system (CMS) back-office accessible only to users with the admin credential, where articles can be edited only by users with the editor credential and published only by the ones with the publisher credential. Listing 6-28 shows this example.

Listing 6-28. *Credentials Combination Syntax*

```
editArticle:
  credentials: [ admin, editor ]            # admin AND editor

publishArticle:
  credentials: [ admin, publisher ]         # admin AND publisher

userManagement:
  credentials: [[ admin, superuser ]]       # admin OR superuser
```

Each time you add a new level of square brackets, the logic swaps between AND and OR. So you can create very complex credential combinations, such as this:

```
credentials: [[root, [supplier, [owner, quasiowner]], accounts]]
           # root OR (supplier AND (owner OR quasiowner)) OR accounts
```

Validation and Error-Handling Methods

Validating the action input—mostly request parameters—is a repetitive and tedious task. Symfony offers a built-in request validation system, using methods of the action class.

Let's start with an example. When a user makes a request for myAction, symfony always looks for a method called validateMyAction() first. If it is found, then symfony executes it. The return value of this validation method determines the next method to be executed: if it returns true, then executeMyAction() is executed; otherwise, handleErrorMyAction() is executed. And, if in the latter case, handleErrorMyAction() doesn't exist, symfony looks for a generic handleError() method. If that doesn't exist either, it simply returns sfView::ERROR to render the myActionError.php template. Figure 6-2 depicts this process.

Figure 6-2. *The validation process*

So the key to validation is to respect the naming conventions for the action methods:

- validateActionName is the validation method, returning true or false. It is the first method looked for when the action ActionName is requested. If it doesn't exist, the action method is executed directly.

- handleErrorActionName is the method called when the validation method fails. If it doesn't exist, the Error template is displayed.

- executeActionName is the action method. It must exist for all actions.

Listing 6-29 shows an example of an action class with validation methods. Whether the validation passes or fails in this example, the myActionSuccess.php template will be executed, but not with the same parameters.

Listing 6-29. *Sample Validation Methods*

```
class mymoduleActions extends sfActions
{
  public function validateMyAction()
  {
    return ($this->getRequestParameter('id') > 0);
  }

  public function handleErrorMyAction()
  {
    $this->message = "Invalid parameters";

    return sfView::SUCCESS;
  }

  public function executeMyAction()
  {
    $this->message = "The parameters are correct";
  }
}
```

You can put any code you want in the validate() methods. Just make sure they return either true or false. As it is a method of the sfActions class, it has access to the sfRequest and sfUser objects as well, which can be really useful for input and context validation.

You could use this mechanism to implement form validation (that is, control the values entered by the user in a form before processing it), but this is the type of repetitive task for which symfony provides automated tools, as described in Chapter 10.

Filters

The security process can be understood as a filter by which all requests must pass before executing the action. According to some tests executed in the filter, the processing of the request is modified—for instance, by changing the action executed (default/secure instead of the requested action in the case of the security filter). Symfony extends this idea to *filter classes*. You can specify any number of filter classes to be executed before the action execution or before the response rendering, and do this for every request. You can see filters as a way to package some code, similar to preExecute() and postExecute(), but at a higher level (for a whole application instead of for a whole module).

The Filter Chain

Symfony actually sees the processing of a request as a chain of filters. When a request is received by the framework, the first filter (which is always the sfRenderingFilter) is executed. At some point, it calls the next filter in the chain, then the next, and so on. When the last filter (which is always sfExecutionFilter) is executed, the previous filter can finish, and so on back to the rendering filter. Figure 6-3 illustrates this idea with a sequence diagram, using an artificially small filter chain (the real one contains more filters).

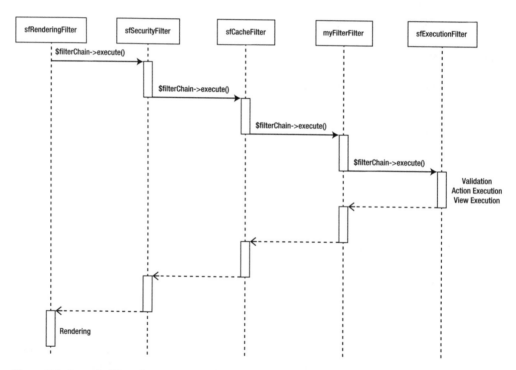

Figure 6-3. *Sample filter chain*

This process justifies the structure of the filter classes. They all extend the sfFilter class, and contain one execute() method, expecting a $filterChain object as parameter. Somewhere in this method, the filter passes to the next filter in the chain by calling $filterChain->execute(). See Listing 6-30 for an example. So basically, filters are divided into two parts:

- The code before the call to $filterChain->execute() executes before the action execution.

- The code after the call to $filterChain->execute() executes after the action execution and before the rendering.

Listing 6-30. *Filter Class Struture*

```
class myFilter extends sfFilter
{
  public function execute ($filterChain)
  {
    // Code to execute before the action execution
    ...

    // Execute next filter in the chain
    $filterChain->execute();

    // Code to execute after the action execution, before the rendering
    ...
  }
}
```

The default filter chain is defined in an application configuration file called `filters.yml`, and is shown in Listing 6-31. This file lists the filters that are to be executed for every request.

Listing 6-31. *Default Filter Chain, in* `myapp/config/filters.yml`

```
rendering:  ~
web_debug:  ~
security:   ~

# Generally, you will want to insert your own filters here

cache:      ~
common:     ~
flash:      ~
execution:  ~
```

These declarations have no parameter (the tilde character, ~, means "null" in YAML), because they inherit the parameters defined in the symfony core. In the core, symfony defines class and param settings for each of these filters. For instance, Listing 6-32 shows the default parameters for the rendering filter.

Listing 6-32. *Default Parameters of the rendering Filter, in* `$sf_symfony_data_dir/config/` `filters.yml`

```
rendering:
  class: sfRenderingFilter   # Filter class
  param:                     # Filter parameters
    type: rendering
```

By leaving the empty value (~) in the application `filters.yml`, you tell symfony to apply the filter with the default settings defined in the core.

You can customize the filter chain in various ways:

- Disable some filters from the chain by adding an `enabled: off` parameter. For instance, to disable the web debug filter, write:

```
web_debug:
  enabled: off
```

  Do not remove an entry from the `filters.yml` to disable a filter; symfony would throw an exception in this case.

- Add your own declarations somewhere in the chain (usually after the `security` filter) to add a custom filter (as discussed in the next section). Be aware that the `rendering` filter must be the first entry, and the `execution` filter must be the last entry of the filter chain.

- Override the default class and parameters of the default filters (notably to modify the security system and use your own security filter).

Tip The `enabled: off` parameter works well to disable your own filters, but you can deactivate the default filters via the `settings.yml` file, by modifying the values of the `web_debug`, `use_security`, `cache`, and `use_flash` settings. This is because each of the default filters has a `condition` parameter that tests the value of these settings.

Building Your Own Filter

It is pretty simple to build a filter. Create a class definition similar to the one shown in Listing 6-30, and place it in one of the project's `lib/` folders to take advantage of the autoloading feature.

As an action can forward or redirect to another action and consequently relaunch the full chain of filters, you might want to restrict the execution of your own filters to the first action call of the request. The `isFirstCall()` method of the `sfFilter` class returns a Boolean for this purpose. This call only makes sense before the action execution.

These concepts are clearer with an example. Listing 6-33 shows a filter used to auto-log users with a specific `MyWebSite` cookie, which is supposedly created by the login action. It is a rudimentary but working way to implement the "remember me" feature offered in login forms.

Listing 6-33. *Sample Filter Class File, Saved in apps/myapp/lib/rememberFilter.class.php*

```
class rememberFilter extends sfFilter
{
  public function execute($filterChain)
  {
    // Execute this filter only once
    if ($this->isFirstCall())
    {
      // Filters don't have direct access to the request and user objects.
      // You will need to use the context object to get them
      $request = $this->getContext()->getRequest();
      $user    = $this->getContext()->getUser();
```

```
    if ($request->getCookie('MyWebSite'))
    {
      // sign in
      $user->setAuthenticated(true);
    }
  }

  // Execute next filter
  $filterChain->execute();
  }
}
```

In some cases, instead of continuing the filter chain execution, you will need to forward to a specific action at the end of a filter. sfFilter doesn't have a forward() method, but sfController does, so you can simply do that by calling the following:

```
return $this->getController()->forward('mymodule', 'myAction');
```

Note The sfFilter class has an initialize() method, executed when the filter object is created. You can override it in your custom filter if you need to deal with filter parameters (defined in filters.yml, as described next) in your own way.

Filter Activation and Parameters

Creating a filter file is not enough to activate it. You need to add your filter to the filter chain, and for that, you must declare the filter class in the filters.yml, located in the application or in the module config/ directory, as shown in Listing 6-34.

Listing 6-34. *Sample Filter Activation File, Saved in* apps/myapp/config/filters.yml

```
rendering: ~
web_debug: ~
security:  ~

remember:                   # Filters need a unique name
  class: rememberFilter
  param:
    cookie_name: MyWebSite
    condition:   %APP_ENABLE_REMEMBER_ME%

cache:    ~
common:   ~
flash:    ~
execution: ~
```

When activated, the filter is executed for each request. The filter configuration file can contain one or more parameter definitions under the `param` key. The filter class has the ability to get the value of these parameters with the `getParameter()` method. Listing 6-35 demonstrates how to get a filter parameter value.

Listing 6-35. *Getting the Parameter Value, in apps/myapp/lib/rememberFilter.class.php*

```
class rememberFilter extends sfFilter
{
  public function execute ($filterChain)
  {
      ...
      if ($request->getCookie($this->getParameter('cookie_name')))
      ...
  }
}
```

The `condition` parameter is tested by the filter chain to see if the filter must be executed. So your filter declarations can rely on an application configuration, just like the one in Listing 6-34. The remember filter will be executed only if your application `app.yml` shows this:

```
all:
  enable_remember_me: on
```

Sample Filters

The filter feature is useful to repeat code for every action. For instance, if you use a distant analytics system, you probably need to put a code snippet calling a distant tracker script in every page. You could put this code in the global layout, but then it would be active for all of the application. Alternatively, you could place it in a filter, such as the one shown in Listing 6-36, and activate it on a per-module basis.

Listing 6-36. *Google Analytics Filter*

```
class sfGoogleAnalyticsFilter extends sfFilter
{
  public function execute($filterChain)
  {
    // Nothing to do before the action
    $filterChain->execute();

    // Decorate the response with the tracker code
    $googleCode = '
<script src="http://www.google-analytics.com/urchin.js" type="text/javascript">
</script>
<script type="text/javascript">
  _uacct="UA-'.$this->getParameter('google_id').'";urchinTracker();
</script>';
```

```
    $response = $this->getContext()->getResponse();
    $response->setContent(str_ireplace('</body>', $googleCode.'</body>', ➥
      $response->getContent()));
  }
}
```

Be aware that this filter is not perfect, as it should not add the tracker on responses that are not HTML.

Another example would be a filter that switches the request to SSL if it is not already, to secure the communication, as shown in Listing 6-37.

Listing 6-37. *Secure Communication Filter*

```
class sfSecureFilter extends sfFilter
{
  public function execute($filterChain)
  {
    $context = $this->getContext();
    $request = $context->getRequest();
    if (!$request->isSecure())
    {
      $secure_url = str_replace('http', 'https', $request->getUri());
      return $context->getController()->redirect($secure_url);
      // We don't continue the filter chain
    }
    else
    {
      // The request is already secure, so we can continue
      $filterChain->execute();
    }
  }
}
```

Filters are used extensively in plug-ins, as they allow you to extend the features of an application globally. Refer to Chapter 17 to learn more about plug-ins, and see the online wiki (http://www.symfony-project.com/trac/wiki) for more filter examples.

Module Configuration

A few module behaviors rely on configuration. To modify them, you must create a module.yml file in the module's config/ directory and define settings on a per-environment basis (or under the all: header for all environments). Listing 6-38 shows an example of a module.yml file for the mymodule module.

Listing 6-38. *Module Configuration, in apps/myapp/modules/mymodule/config/module.yml*

```
all:                # For all environments
  enabled:    true
  is_internal: false
  view_name:  sfPhpView
```

The `enabled` parameter allows you to disable all actions of a module. All actions are redirected to the `module_disabled_module/module_disabled_action` action (as defined in `settings.yml`).

The `is_internal` parameter allows you to restrict the execution of all actions of a module to internal calls. For example, this is useful for mail actions that you must be able to call from another action, to send an e-mail message, but not from the outside.

The `view_name` parameter defines the view class. It must inherit from `sfView`. Overriding this value allows you to use other view systems, with other templating engines, such as Smarty.

Summary

In symfony, the controller layer is split into two parts: the *front controller*, which is the unique entry point to the application for a given environment, and the *actions*, which contain the page logic. An action has the ability to determine how its view will be executed, by returning one of the `sfView` constants. Inside an action, you can manipulate the different elements of the context, including the *request* object (`sfRequest`) and the current *user session* object (`sfUser`).

Combining the power of the session object, the action object, and the security configuration provides a complete *security system*, with access restriction and credentials. Special `validate()` and `handleError()` methods in actions allow handling of *request validation*. And if the `preExecute()` and `postExecute()` methods are made for reusability of code inside a module, the *filters* authorize the same reusability for all the applications by making controller code executed for every request.

■ ■ ■

## CHAPTER 7

Inside the View Layer

The *view* is responsible for rendering the output correlated to a particular action. In symfony, the view consists of several parts, with each part designed to be easily modified by the person who usually works with it.

- Web designers generally work on the *templates* (the presentation of the current action data) and on the *layout* (containing the code common to all pages). These are written in HTML with small embedded chunks of PHP, which are mostly calls to *helpers*.

- For reusability, developers usually package template code fragments into *partials* or *components*. They use *slots* and *component slots* to affect more than one zone of the layout. Web designers can work on these template fragments as well.

- Developers focus on the YAML *view configuration* file (setting the properties of the response and other interface elements) and on the *response* object. When dealing with variables in the templates, the risks of cross-site scripting must not be ignored, and a good comprehension of *output escaping* techniques is required to safely record user data.

But whatever your role is, you will find useful tools to speed up the tedious job of presenting the results of the action. This chapter covers all of these tools.

Templating

Listing 7-1 shows a typical symfony template. It contains some HTML code and some basic PHP code, usually calls to *variables* defined in the action (via $this->name = 'foo';) and *helpers*.

Listing 7-1. *A Sample indexSuccess.php Template*

```
<h1>Welcome</h1>
<p>Welcome back, <?php echo $name ?>!</p>
<ul>What would you like to do?
   <li><?php echo link_to('Read the last articles', 'article/read') ?></li>
   <li><?php echo link_to('Start writing a new one', 'article/write') ?></li>
</ul>
```

As explained in Chapter 4, the alternative PHP syntax is preferable for templates to make them readable for non-PHP developers. You should keep PHP code to a minimum in templates, since these files are the ones used to design the GUI of the application, and are sometimes created and maintained by another team, specialized in presentation but not in application logic. Keeping the logic inside the action also makes it easier to have several templates for a single action, without any code duplication.

Helpers

Helpers are PHP functions that return HTML code and can be used in templates. In Listing 7-1, the `link_to()` function is a helper. Sometimes, helpers are just time-savers, packaging code snippets frequently used in templates. For instance, you can easily imagine the function definition for this helper:

```
<?php echo input_tag('nickname') ?>
 => <input type="text" name="nickname" id="nickname" value="" />
```

It should look like Listing 7-2.

Listing 7-2. *Sample Helper Definition*

```
function input_tag($name, $value = null)
{
  return '<input type="text" name="'.$name.'" id="'.$name.'" ➥
    value="'.$value.'" />';
}
```

As a matter of fact, the `input_tag()` function built into symfony is a little more complicated than that, as it accepts a third parameter to add other attributes to the `<input>` tag. You can check its complete syntax and options in the online API documentation (http://www.symfony-project.com/api/symfony.html).

Most of the time, helpers carry intelligence and save you long and complex coding:

```
<?php echo auto_link_text('Please visit our website www.example.com') ?>
 => Please visit our website <a href="http://www.example.com">www.example.com</a>
```

Helpers facilitate the process of writing templates and produce the best possible HTML code in terms of performance and accessibility. You can always use plain HTML, but helpers are usually faster to write.

■**Tip** You may wonder why the helpers are named according to the underscore syntax rather than the camelCase convention, used everywhere else in symfony. This is because helpers are *functions*, and all the core PHP functions use the underscore syntax convention.

Declaring Helpers

The symfony files containing helper definitions are not autoloaded (since they contain functions, not classes). Helpers are grouped by purpose. For instance, all the helper functions dealing with text are defined in a file called TextHelper.php, called the Text *helper group*. So if you need to use a helper in a template, you must load the related helper group earlier in the template by declaring it with the use_helper() function. Listing 7-3 shows a template using the auto_link_text() helper, which is part of the Text helper group.

Listing 7-3. *Declaring the Use of a Helper*

```
// Use a specific helper group in this template
<?php echo use_helper('Text') ?>
...
<h1>Description</h1>
<p><?php echo auto_link_text($description) ?></p>
```

■Tip If you need to declare more than one helper group, add more arguments to the use_helper() call. For instance, to load both the Text and the Javascript helper groups in a template, call <?php echo ➥ use_helper('Text', 'Javascript') ?>.

A few helpers are available by default in every template, without need for declaration. These are helpers of the following helper groups:

Helper: Required for helper inclusion (the use_helper() function is, in fact, a helper itself)

Tag: Basic tag helper, used by almost every helper

Url: Links and URL management helpers

Asset: Helpers populating the HTML <head> section, and providing easy links to external assets (images, JavaScript, and style sheet files)

Partial: Helpers allowing for inclusion of template fragments

Cache: Manipulation of cached code fragments

Form: Form input helpers

The list of the standard helpers, loaded by default for every template, is configurable in the settings.yml file. So if you know that you will not use the helpers of the Cache group, or that you will always use the ones of the Text group, modify the standard_helpers setting accordingly. This will speed up your application a bit. You cannot remove the first four helper groups in the preceding list (Helper, Tag, Url, and Asset), because they are compulsory for the templating engine to work properly. Consequently, they don't even appear in the list of standard helpers.

■Tip If you ever need to use a helper outside a template, you can still load a helper group from anywhere by calling sfLoader::loadHelpers($helpers), where $helpers is a helper group name or an array of helper group names. For instance, if you want to use auto_link_text() in an action, you need to call sfLoader::loadHelpers('Text') first.

Frequently Used Helpers

You will learn about some helpers in detail in later chapters, in relation with the feature they are helping. Listing 7-4 gives a brief list of the default helpers that are used a lot, together with the HTML code they return.

Listing 7-4. *Common Default Helpers*

```
// Helper group
<?php echo use_helper('HelperName') ?>
<?php echo use_helper('HelperName1', 'HelperName2', 'HelperName3') ?>

// Tag group
<?php echo tag('input', array('name' => 'foo', 'type' => 'text')) ?>
<?php echo tag('input', 'name=foo type=text') ?>  // Alternative options syntax
 => <input name="foo" type="text" />
<?php echo content_tag('textarea', 'dummy content', 'name=foo') ?>
 => <textarea name="foo">dummy content</textarea>

// Url group
<?php echo link_to('click me', 'mymodule/myaction') ?>
=> <a href="/route/to/myaction">click me</a>  // Depends on the routing settings

// Asset group
<?php echo image_tag('myimage', 'alt=foo size=200x100') ?>
 => <img src="/images/myimage.png" alt="foo" width="200" height="100"/>
<?php echo javascript_include_tag('myscript') ?>
 => <script language="JavaScript" type="text/javascript" src="/js/myscript.js"> ➥
    </script>
<?php echo stylesheet_tag('style') ?>
 => <link href="/stylesheets/style.css" media="screen" rel="stylesheet" ➥
        type="text/css" />
```

There are many other helpers in symfony, and it would take a full book to describe all of them. The best reference for helpers is the online API documentation (http://www.symfony-project.com/api/symfony.html), where all the helpers are well documented, with their syntax, options, and examples.

Adding Your Own Helpers

Symfony ships with a lot of helpers for various purposes, but if you don't find what you need in the API documentation, you will probably want to create a new helper. This is very easy to do.

Helper functions (regular PHP functions returning HTML code) should be saved in a file called FooBarHelper.php, where FooBar is the name of the helper group. Store the file in the apps/myapp/lib/helper/ directory (or in any helper/ directory created under one of the lib/ folders of your project) so it can be found automatically by the use_helper('FooBar') helper for inclusion.

▓**Tip** This system even allows you to override the existing symfony helpers. For instance, to redefine all the helpers of the Text helper group, just create a TextHelper.php file in your apps/myapp/lib/helper/ directory. Whenever you call use_helper('Text'), symfony will use your helper group rather than its own. But be careful: as the original file is not even loaded, you must redefine *all* the functions of a helper group to override it; otherwise, some of the original helpers will not be available at all.

Page Layout

The template shown in Listing 7-1 is not a valid XHTML document. The DOCTYPE definition and the <html> and <body> tags are missing. That's because they are stored somewhere else in the application, in a file called layout.php, which contains the page layout. This file, also called the *global template*, stores the HTML code that is common to all pages of the application to avoid repeating it in every template. The content of the template is integrated into the layout, or, if you change the point of view, the layout "decorates" the template. This is an application of the *decorator design pattern*, illustrated in Figure 7-1.

▓**Tip** For more information about the decorator and other design patterns, see *Patterns of Enterprise Application Architecture* by Martin Fowler (Addison-Wesley, ISBN: 0-32112-742-0).

Figure 7-1. *Decorating a template with a layout*

Listing 7-5 shows the default page layout, located in the application templates/ directory.

Listing 7-5. *Default Layout, in* myproject/apps/myapp/templates/layout.php

```
<!DOCTYPE html PUBLIC "-//W3C//DTD XHTML 1.0 Transitional//EN" ➥
  "http://www.w3.org/TR/2000/REC-xhtml1-20000126/DTD/xhtml1-transitional.dtd">
<html xmlns="http://www.w3.org/1999/xhtml" xml:lang="en" lang="en">
<head>
  <?php echo include_http_metas() ?>
  <?php echo include_metas() ?>
  <?php echo include_title() ?>
  <link rel="shortcut icon" href="/favicon.ico" />
</head>
<body>

<?php echo $sf_data->getRaw('sf_content') ?>

</body>
</html>
```

The helpers called in the <head> section grab information from the response object and the
view configuration. The <body> tag outputs the result of the template. With this layout, the
default configuration, and the sample template in Listing 7-1, the processed view looks like
Listing 7-6.

Listing 7-6. *The Layout, the View Configuration, and the Template Assembled*

```
<!DOCTYPE html PUBLIC "-//W3C//DTD XHTML 1.0 Transitional//EN" ➥
  "http://www.w3.org/TR/2000/REC-xhtml1-20000126/DTD/xhtml1-transitional.dtd">
<html xmlns="http://www.w3.org/1999/xhtml" xml:lang="en" lang="en">
<head>
  <meta http-equiv="content-type" content="text/html; charset=utf-8" />
  <meta name="title" content="symfony project" />
  <meta name="robots" content="index, follow" />
  <meta name="description" content="symfony project" />
  <meta name="keywords" content="symfony, project" />
  <title>symfony project</title>
  <link rel="stylesheet" type="text/css" href="/css/main.css" />
  <link rel="shortcut icon" href="/favicon.ico">
</head>
<body>

<h1>Welcome</h1>
<p>Welcome back, <?php echo $name ?>!</p>
<ul>What would you like to do?
  <li><?php echo link_to('Read the last articles', 'article/read') ?></li>
  <li><?php echo link_to('Start writing a new one', 'article/write') ?></li>
</ul>

</body>
</html>
```

The global template can be entirely customized for each application. Add in any HTML code you need. This layout is often used to hold the site navigation, logo, and so on. You can even have more than one layout, and decide which layout should be used for each action. Don't worry about JavaScript and style sheet inclusion for now; the "View Configuration" section later in this chapter shows how to handle that.

Template Shortcuts

In templates, a few symfony variables are always available. These shortcuts give access to the most commonly needed information in templates, through the core symfony objects:

$sf_context: The whole context object (instance of sfContext)

$sf_request: The request object (instance of sfRequest)

$sf_params: Parameters of the request

$sf_user: The current user session object (instance of sfUser)

The previous chapter detailed useful methods of the sfRequest and sfUser objects. You can actually call these methods in templates through the $sf_request and $sf_user variables. For instance, if the request includes a total parameter, its value is available in the template with the following:

```
// Long version
<?php echo $sf_request->getParameter('total'); ?>

// Shorter version
<?php echo $sf_params->get('total'); ?>

// Equivalent to the following action code
echo $this->getRequestParameter('total');
```

Code Fragments

You may often need to include some HTML or PHP code in several pages. To avoid repeating that code, the PHP include() statement will suffice most of the time.

For instance, if many of the templates of your application need to use the same fragment of code, save it in a file called myFragment.php in the global template directory (myproject/apps/myapp/templates/) and include it in your templates as follows:

```
<?php include(sfConfig::get('sf_app_template_dir').'/myFragment.php') ?>
```

But this is not a very clean way to package a fragment, mostly because you can have different variable names between the fragment and the various templates including it. In addition, the symfony cache system (described in Chapter 12) has no way to detect an include, so the fragment cannot be cached independently from the template. Symfony provides three alternative types of intelligent code fragments to replace includes:

- If the logic is lightweight, you will just want to include a template file having access to some data you pass to it. For that, you will use a *partial*.

- If the logic is heavier (for instance, if you need to access the data model and/or modify the content according to the session), you will prefer to separate the presentation from the logic. For that, you will use a *component*.

- If the fragment is meant to replace a specific part of the layout, for which default content may already exist, you will use a *slot*.

Note Another code fragment type, called a *component slot*, is to be used when the nature of the fragment depends on the context (for instance, if the fragment needs to be different for the actions of a given module). Component slots are described later in this chapter.

The inclusion of these fragments is achieved by helpers of the `Partial` group. These helpers are available from any symfony template, without initial declaration.

Partials

A partial is a reusable chunk of template code. For instance, in a publication application, the template code displaying an article is used in the article detail page, and also in the list of the best articles and the list of latest articles. This code is a perfect candidate for a partial, as illustrated in Figure 7-2.

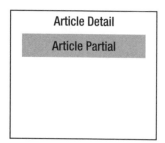
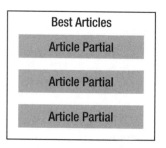
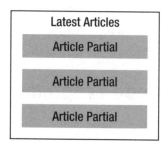

Figure 7-2. *Reusing partials in templates*

Just like templates, partials are files located in the `templates/` directory, and they contain HTML code with embedded PHP. A partial file name always starts with an underscore (_), and that helps to distinguish partials from templates, since they are located in the same `templates/` folders.

A template can include partials whether it is in the same module, in another module, or in the global `templates/` directory. Include a partial by using the `include_partial()` helper, and specify the module and partial name as a parameter (but omit the leading underscore and the trailing `.php`), as described in Listing 7-7.

Listing 7-7. *Including a Partial in a Template of the mymodule Module*

```
// Include the myapp/modules/mymodule/templates/_mypartial1.php partial
// As the template and the partial are in the same module,
// you can omit the module name
<?php include_partial('mypartial1') ?>

// Include the myapp/modules/foobar/templates/_mypartial2.php partial
// The module name is compulsory in that case
<?php include_partial('foobar/mypartial2') ?>

// Include the myapp/templates/_mypartial3.php partial
// It is considered as part of the 'global' module
<?php include_partial('global/mypartial3') ?>
```

Partials have access to the usual symfony helpers and template shortcuts. But since partials can be called from anywhere in the application, they do not have automatic access to the variables defined in the action calling the templates that includes them, unless passed explicitly as an argument. For instance, if you want a partial to have access to a $total variable, the action must hand it to the template, and then the template to the helper as a second argument of the include_partial() call, as shown in Listings 7-8, 7-9, and 7-10.

Listing 7-8. *The Action Defines a Variable, in mymodule/actions/actions.class.php*

```
class mymoduleActions extends sfActions
{
  public function executeIndex()
  {
    $this->total = 100;
  }
}
```

Listing 7-9. *The Template Passes the Variable to the Partial, in mymodule/templates/indexSuccess.php*

```
<p>Hello, world!</p>
<?php include_partial('mypartial', array('mytotal' => $total)) ?>
```

Listing 7-10. *The Partial Can Now Use the Variable, in mymodule/templates/_mypartial.php*

```
<p>Total: <?php echo $mytotal ?></p>
```

■**Tip** All the helpers so far were called by `<?php echo functionName() ?>`. The partial helper, however, is simply called by `<?php include_partial() ?>`, without echo, to make it behave similar to the regular PHP include() statement. If you ever need a function that returns the content of a partial without actually displaying it, use get_partial() instead. All the include_ helpers described in this chapter have a get_ counterpart that can be called together with an echo statement.

Components

In Chapter 2, the first sample script was split into two parts to separate the logic from the presentation. Just like the MVC pattern applies to actions and templates, you may need to split a partial into a logic part and a presentation part. In such a case, you should use a component.

A component is like an action, except it's much faster. The logic of a component is kept in a class inheriting from sfComponents, located in an action/components.class.php file. Its presentation is kept in a partial. Methods of the sfComponents class start with the word execute, just like actions, and they can pass variables to their presentation counterpart in the same way that actions can pass variables. Partials that serve as presentation for components are named by the component (without the leading execute, but with an underscore instead). Table 7-1 compares the naming conventions for actions and components.

Table 7-1. *Action and Component Naming Conventions*

Convention	Actions	Components
Logic file	actions.class.php	components.class.php
Logic class extends	sfActions	sfComponents
Method naming	executeMyAction()	executeMyComponent()
Presentation file naming	myActionSuccess.php	_myComponent.php

■**Tip** Just as you can separate actions files, the sfComponents class has an sfComponent counterpart that allows for single component files with the same type of syntax.

For instance, suppose you have a sidebar displaying the latest news headlines for a given subject, depending on the user's profile, which is reused in several pages. The queries necessary to get the news headlines are too complex to appear in a simple partial, so they need to be moved to an action-like file—a component. Figure 7-3 illustrates this example.

For this example, shown in Listings 7-11 and 7-12, the component will be kept in its own module (called news), but you can mix components and actions in a single module if it makes sense from a functional point of view.

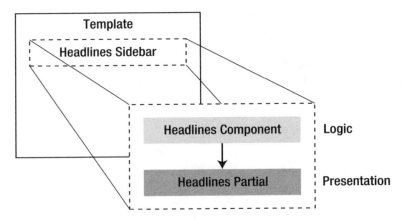

Figure 7-3. *Using components in templates*

Listing 7-11. *The Components Class, in modules/news/actions/components.class.php*

```php
<?php

class newsComponents extends sfComponents
{
  public function executeHeadlines()
  {
    $c = new Criteria();
    $c->addDescendingOrderByColumn(NewsPeer::PUBLISHED_AT);
    $c->setLimit(5);
    $this->news = NewsPeer::doSelect($c);
  }
}
```

Listing 7-12. *The Partial, in modules/news/templates/_headlines.php*

```php
<div>
  <h1>Latest news</h1>
  <ul>
  <?php foreach($news as $headline): ?>
    <li>
      <?php echo $headline->getPublishedAt() ?>
      <?php echo link_to($headline->getTitle(), ➥
                         'news/show?id='.$headline->getId()) ?>
    </li>
  <?php endforeach ?>
  </ul>
</div>
```

Now, every time you need the component in a template, just call this:

```php
<?php include_component('news', 'headlines') ?>
```

Just like the partials, components accept additional parameters in the shape of an associative array. The parameters are available to the partial under their name, and in the component via the $this object. See Listing 7-13 for an example.

Listing 7-13. *Passing Parameters to a Component and Its Template*

```php
// Call to the component
<?php include_component('news', 'headlines', array('foo' => 'bar')) ?>

// In the component itself
echo $this->foo;
 => 'bar'

// In the _headlines.php partial
echo $foo;
 => 'bar'
```

You can include components in components, or in the global layout, as in any regular template. Like actions, components' execute methods can pass variables to the related partial and have access to the same shortcuts. But the similarities stop there. A component doesn't handle security or validation, cannot be called from the Internet (only from the application itself), and doesn't have various return possibilities. That's why a component is faster to execute than an action.

Slots

Partials and components are great for reusability. But in many cases, code fragments are required to fill a layout with more than one dynamic zone. For instance, suppose that you want to add some custom tags in the <head> section of the layout, depending on the content of the action. Or, suppose that the layout has one major dynamic zone, which is filled by the result of the action, plus a lot of other smaller ones, which have a default content defined in the layout but can be overridden at the template level.

For these situations, the solution is a slot. Basically, a slot is a placeholder that you can put in any of the view elements (in the layout, a template, or a partial). Filling this placeholder is just like setting a variable. The filling code is stored globally in the response, so you can define it anywhere (in the layout, a template, or a partial). Just make sure to define a slot before including it, and remember that the layout is executed after the template (this is the decoration process), and the partials are executed when they are called in a template. Does it sound too abstract? Let's see an example.

Imagine a layout with one zone for the template and two slots: one for the sidebar and the other for the footer. The slot values are defined in the templates. During the decoration process, the layout code wraps the template code, and the slots are filled with the previously defined values, as illustrated in Figure 7-4. The sidebar and the footer can then be contextual to the main action. This is like having a layout with more than one "hole."

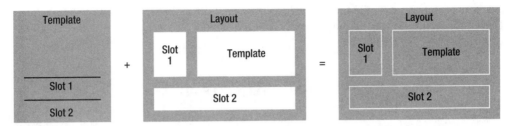

Figure 7-4. *Layout slots defined in a template*

Seeing some code will clarify things further. To include a slot, use the include_slot() helper. The has_slot() helper returns true if the slot has been defined before, providing a fallback mechanism as a bonus. For instance, define a placeholder for a 'sidebar' slot in the layout and its default content as shown in Listing 7-14.

Listing 7-14. *Including a 'sidebar' Slot in the Layout*

```
<div id="sidebar">
<?php if (has_slot('sidebar'): ?>
  <?php include_slot('sidebar') ?>
<?php else: ?>
  <!-- default sidebar code -->
  <h1>Contextual zone</h1>
  <p>This zone contains links and information
  relative to the main content of the page.</p>
<?php endif; ?>
</div>
```

Each template has the ability to define the contents of a slot (actually, even partials can do it). As slots are meant to hold HTML code, symfony offers a convenient way to define them: just write the slot code between a call to the slot() and end_slot() helpers, as in Listing 7-15.

Listing 7-15. *Overriding the 'sidebar' Slot Content in a Template*

```
...
<?php slot('sidebar') ?>
  <!-- custom sidebar code for the current template-->
  <h1>User details</h1>
  <p>name:  <?php echo $user->getName() ?></p>
  <p>email: <?php echo $user->getEmail() ?></p>
<?php end_slot() ?>
```

The code between the slot helpers is executed in the context of the template, so it has access to all the variables that were defined in the action. Symfony will automatically put the result of this code in the response object. It will not be displayed in the template, but made available for future include_slot() calls, like the one in Listing 7-14.

Slots are very useful to define zones meant to display contextual content. They can also be used to add HTML code to the layout for certain actions only. For instance, a template displaying the list of the latest news might want to add a link to an RSS feed in the `<head>` part of the layout. This is achieved simply by adding a `'feed'` slot in the layout and overriding it in the template of the list.

WHERE TO FIND TEMPLATE FRAGMENTS

People working on templates are usually web designers, who may not know symfony very well and may have difficulties finding template fragments, since they can be scattered all over the application. These few guidelines will make them more comfortable with the symfony templating system.

First of all, although a symfony project contains many directories, all the layouts, templates, and template fragments files reside in directories named `templates/`. So as far as a web designer is concerned, a project structure can be reduced to something like this:

```
myproject/
  apps/
    application1/
      templates/        # Layouts for application 1
      modules/
        module1/
          templates/    # Templates and partials for module 1
        module2/
          templates/    # Templates and partials for module 2
        module3/
          templates/    # Templates and partials for module 3
```

All other directories can be ignored.

When meeting an `include_partial()`, web designers just need to understand that only the first argument is important. This argument's pattern is `module_name/partial_name`, and that means that the presentation code is to be found in `modules/module_name/templates/_partial_name.php`.

For the `include_component()` helper, module name and partial name are the first two arguments. As for the rest, a general idea about what helpers are and which helpers are the most common in templates should be enough to start designing templates for symfony applications.

View Configuration

In symfony, a view consists of two distinct parts:

- The HTML presentation of the action result (stored in the template, in the layout, and in the template fragments)

- All the rest, including the following:

  - Meta declarations: Keywords, description, or cache duration.

  - Page title: Not only does it help users with several browser windows open to find yours, but it is also very important for search sites' indexing.

- File inclusions: JavaScript and style sheet files.

- Layout: Some actions require a custom layout (pop-ups, ads, and so on) or no layout at all (such as Ajax actions).

In the view, all that is not HTML is called *view configuration*, and symfony provides two ways to manipulate it. The usual way is through the view.yml configuration file. It can be used whenever the values don't depend on the context or on database queries. When you need to set dynamic values, the alternative method is to set the view configuration via the sfResponse object attributes directly in the action.

■**Note** If you ever set a view configuration parameter both via the sfResponse object and via the view.yml file, the sfResponse definition takes precedence.

The view.yml File

Each module can have one view.yml file defining the settings of its views. This allows you to define view settings for a whole module and per view in a single file. The first-level keys of the view.yml file are the module view names. Listing 7-16 shows an example of view configuration.

Listing 7-16. *Sample Module-Level view.yml*

```
editSuccess:
  metas:
    title: Edit your profile

editError:
  metas:
    title: Error in the profile edition

all:
  stylesheets: [my_style]
  metas:
    title: My website
```

■**Caution** Be aware that the main keys in the view.yml file are view names, not action names. As a reminder, a view name is composed of an action name and an action termination. For instance, if the edit action returns sfView::SUCCESS (or returns nothing at all, since it is the default action termination), then the view name is editSuccess.

The default settings for the module are defined under the `all:` key in the *module* view.yml. The default settings for all the application views are defined in the *application* view.yml. Once again, you recognize the configuration cascade principle:

- In apps/myapp/modules/mymodule/config/view.yml, the per-view definitions apply only to one view and override the module-level definitions.

- In apps/myapp/modules/mymodule/config/view.yml, the `all:` definitions apply to all the actions of the module and override the application-level definitions.

- In apps/myapp/config/view.yml, the `default:` definitions apply to all modules and all actions of the application.

Tip Module-level view.yml files don't exist by default. The first time you need to adjust a view configuration parameter for a module, you will have to create an empty view.yml in its config/ directory.

After seeing the default template in Listing 7-5 and an example of a final response in Listing 7-6, you may wonder where the header values come from. As a matter of fact, they are the default view settings, defined in the application view.yml and shown in Listing 7-17.

Listing 7-17. *Default Application-Level View Configuration, in apps/myapp/config/view.yml*

```
default:
  http_metas:
    content-type: text/html

  metas:
    title:        symfony project
    robots:       index, follow
    description:  symfony project
    keywords:     symfony, project
    language:     en

  stylesheets:    [main]

  javascripts:    [ ]

  has_layout:     on
  layout:         layout
```

Each of these settings will be described in detail in the "View Configuration Settings" section.

The Response Object

Although part of the view layer, the response object is often modified by the action. Actions can access the symfony response object, called sfResponse, via the getResponse() method. Listing 7-18 lists some of the sfResponse methods often used from within an action.

Listing 7-18. *Actions Have Access to the sfResponse Object Methods*

```
class mymoduleActions extends sfActions
{
  public function executeIndex()
  {
    $response = $this->getResponse();

    // HTTP headers
    $response->setContentType('text/xml');
    $response->setHttpHeader('Content-Language', 'en');
    $response->setStatusCode(403);
    $response->addVaryHttpHeader('Accept-Language');
    $response->addCacheControlHttpHeader('no-cache');

    // Cookies
    $response->setCookie($name, $content, $expire, $path, $domain);

    // Metas and page headers
    $response->addMeta('robots', 'NONE');
    $response->addMeta('keywords', 'foo bar');
    $response->setTitle('My FooBar Page');
    $response->addStyleSheet('custom_style');
    $response->addJavaScript('custom_behavior');
  }
}
```

In addition to the setter methods shown here, the sfResponse class has getters that return the current value of the response attributes.

The header setters are very powerful in symfony. Headers are sent as late as possible (in the sfRenderingFilter), so you can alter them as much as you want and as late as you want. They also provide very useful shortcuts. For instance, if you don't specify a charset when you call setContentType(), symfony automatically adds the default charset defined in the settings.yml file.

```
$response->setContentType('text/xml');
echo $response->getContentType();
 => 'text/xml; charset=utf-8'
```

The status code of responses in symfony is compliant with the HTTP specification. Exceptions return a status 500, pages not found return a status 404, normal pages return a status 200, pages not modified can be reduced to a simple header with status code 304 (see Chapter 12 for details), and so on. But you can override these defaults by setting your own status code in the action with the setStatusCode() response method. You can specify a custom code and a custom message, or simply a custom code—in which case, symfony will add the most common message for this code.

```
$response->setStatusCode(404, 'This page no longer exists');
```

■**Tip** Before sending the headers, symfony normalizes their names. So you don't need to bother about writing content-language instead of Content-Language in a call to setHttpHeader(), as symfony will understand the former and automatically transform it to the latter.

View Configuration Settings

You may have noticed that there are two kinds of view configuration settings:

- The ones that have a unique value (the value is a string in the view.yml file and the response uses a set method for those)

- The ones with multiple values (for which view.yml uses arrays and the response uses an add method)

Keep in mind that the configuration cascade erases the unique value settings but piles up the multiple values settings. This will become more apparent as you progress through this chapter.

Meta Tag Configuration

The information written in the <meta> tags in the response is not displayed in a browser but is useful for robots and search engines. It also controls the cache settings of every page. Define these tags under the http_metas: and metas: keys in view.yml, as in Listing 7-19, or with the addHttpMeta() and addMeta() response methods in the action, as in Listing 7-20.

Listing 7-19. *Meta Definition As Key: Value Pairs in* view.yml

```
http_metas:
  cache-control: public

metas:
  description:   Finance in France
  keywords:      finance, France
```

Listing 7-20. *Meta Definition As Response Settings in the Action*

```
$this->getResponse()->addHttpMeta('cache-control', 'public');
$this->getResponse()->addMeta('description', 'Finance in France');
$this->getResponse()->addMeta('keywords', 'finance, France');
```

Adding an existing key will replace its current content by default. For HTTP meta tags, you can add a third parameter and set it to false to have the addHttpMeta() method (as well as the setHttpHeader()) append the value to the existing one, rather than replacing it.

```
$this->getResponse()->addHttpMeta('accept-language', 'en');
$this->getResponse()->addHttpMeta('accept-language', 'fr', false);
echo $this->getResponse()->getHttpHeader('accept-language');
 => 'en, fr'
```

In order to have these meta tags appear in the final document, the include_http_metas()
and include_metas() helpers must be called in the <head> section (this is the case in the default
layout; see Listing 7-5). Symfony automatically aggregates the settings from all the view.yml
files (including the default one shown in Listing 7-17) and the response attribute to output
proper <meta> tags. The example in Listing 7-19 ends up as shown in Listing 7-21.

Listing 7-21. *Meta Tags Output in the Final Page*

```
<meta http-equiv="content-type" content="text/html; charset=utf-8" />
<meta http-equiv="cache-control" content="public" />
<meta name="robots" content="index, follow" />
<meta name="description" content="Finance in France" />
<meta name="keywords" content="finance, France" />
```

As a bonus, the HTTP header of the response is also impacted by the http-metas: definition,
even if you don't have any include_http_metas() helpers in the layout, or if you have no layout
at all. For instance, if you need to send a page as plain text, define the following view.yml:

```
http_metas:
  content-type: text/plain

has_layout: false
```

Title Configuration

The page title is a key part to search engine indexing. It is also very useful with modern browsers
that provide tabbed browsing. In HTML, the title is both a tag and meta information of the page, so
the view.yml file sees the title: key as a child of the metas: key. Listing 7-22 shows the title
definition in view.yml, and Listing 7-23 shows the definition in the action.

Listing 7-22. *Title Definition in view.yml*

```
indexSuccess:
  metas:
    title: Three little piggies
```

Listing 7-23. *Title Definition in the Action—Allows for Dynamic Titles*

```
$this->getResponse()->setTitle(sprintf('%d little piggies', $number));
```

In the <head> section of the final document, the title definition sets the <meta name="title">
tag if the include_metas() helper is present, and the <title> tag if the include_title() helper
is present. If both are included (as in the default layout of Listing 7-5), the title appears twice in
the document source (see Listing 7-6), which is harmless.

File Inclusion Configuration

Adding a specific style sheet or JavaScript file to a view is easy, as Listings 7-24 and 7-25 demonstrate.

Listing 7-24. *File Inclusion in* `view.yml`

```
indexSuccess:
  stylesheets: [mystyle1, mystyle2]
  javascripts: [myscript]
```

Listing 7-25. *File Inclusion in the Action*

```
$this->getResponse()->addStylesheet('mystyle1');
$this->getResponse()->addStylesheet('mystyle2');
$this->getResponse()->addJavascript('myscript');
```

In each case, the argument is a file name. If the file has a logical extension (.css for a style sheet and .js for a JavaScript file), you can omit it. If the file has a logical location (/css/ for a style sheet and /js/ for a JavaScript file), you can omit it as well. Symfony is smart enough to figure out the correct extension or location.

Unlike the meta and title definitions, the file inclusion definitions don't require any helper in the template or layout to be included. This means that the previous settings will output the HTML code of Listing 7-26, whatever the content of the template and the layout.

Listing 7-26. *File Inclusion Result—No Need for a Helper Call in the Layout*

```
<head>
...
<link rel="stylesheet" type="text/css" media="screen" href="/css/mystyle1.css" />
<link rel="stylesheet" type="text/css" media="screen" href="/css/mystyle2.css" />
<script language="javascript" type="text/javascript" src="/js/myscript.js">
</script>
</head>
```

■Note Style sheet and JavaScript inclusions in the response are performed by a filter called sfCommonFilter. It looks for a <head> tag in the response, and adds the <link> and <script> just before the closing </head>. This means that the inclusion can't take place if there is no <head> tag in your layout or templates.

Remember that the configuration cascade principle applies, so any file inclusion defined in the application view.yml makes it appear in every page of the application. Listings 7-27, 7-28, and 7-29 demonstrate this principle.

Listing 7-27. *Sample Application* view.yml

```
default:
  stylesheets: [main]
```

Listing 7-28. *Sample Module* view.yml

```
indexSuccess:
  stylesheets: [special]

all:
  stylesheets: [additional]
```

Listing 7-29. *Resulting indexSuccess View*

```
<link rel="stylesheet" type="text/css" media="screen" href="/css/main.css" />
<link rel="stylesheet" type="text/css" media="screen" href="/css/additional.css" />
<link rel="stylesheet" type="text/css" media="screen" href="/css/special.css" />
```

If you need to remove a file defined at a higher level, just add a minus sign (-) in front of the file name in the lower-level definition, as shown in Listing 7-30.

Listing 7-30. *Sample Module* view.yml *That Removes the Files Defined at the Application Level*

```
indexSuccess:
  stylesheets: [-main, special]

all:
  stylesheets: [additional]
```

To remove all style sheets or JavaScript files, use the following syntax:

```
indexSuccess:
  stylesheets: [-*]
  javascripts: [-*]
```

You can be more accurate and define an additional parameter to force the position where to include the file (first or last position):

```
// In the view.yml
indexSuccess:
  stylesheets: [special: { position: first }]

// In the action
$this->getResponse()->addStylesheet('special', 'first');
```

To specify media for a style sheet inclusion, you can change the default style sheet tag options, as shown in Listings 7-31, 7-32, and 7-33.

Listing 7-31. *Style Sheet Inclusion with Media in* `view.yml`

```
indexSuccess:
  stylesheets: [main, paper: { media: print }]
```

Listing 7-32. *Style Sheet Inclusion with Media in the Action*

```
$this->getResponse()->addStylesheet('paper', '', array('media' => 'print'));
```

Listing 7-33. *Resulting View*

```
<link rel="stylesheet" type="text/css" media="print" href="/css/paper.css" />
```

Layout Configuration

According to the graphical charter of your website, you may have several layouts. Classic websites have at least two: the default layout and the pop-up layout.

You have already seen that the default layout is myproject/apps/myapp/templates/ layout.php. Additional layouts must be added in the same global `templates/` directory. If you want a view to use a `myapp/templates/my_layout.php` file, use the syntax shown in Listing 7-34 in `view.yml` or in Listing 7-35 in the action.

Listing 7-34. *Layout Definition in* `view.yml`

```
indexSuccess:
  layout: my_layout
```

Listing 7-35. *Layout Definition in the Action*

```
$this->setLayout('my_layout');
```

Some views don't need any layout at all (for instance, plain text pages or RSS feeds). In that case, set `has_layout` to `false`, as shown in Listings 7-36 and 7-37.

Listing 7-36. *Layout Removal in* `view.yml`

```
indexSuccess:
  has_layout: false
```

Listing 7-37. *Layout Removal in the Action*

```
$this->setLayout(false);
```

■**Note** Ajax actions views have no layout by default.

Component Slots

Combining the power of view components and view configuration brings a new perspective to view development: the component slot system. It is an alternative to slots focusing on reusability and layer separation. So component slots are more structured than slots, but a little slower to execute.

Just like slots, component slots are named placeholders that you can declare in the view elements. The difference resides in the way the filling code is determined. For a slot, the code is set in another view element; for a component slot, the code results from the execution of a component, and the name of this component comes from the view configuration. You will understand component slots more clearly after seeing them in action.

To set a component slot placeholder, use the `include_component_slot()` helper. This function expects a label as a parameter. For instance, suppose that the `layout.php` file of the application contains a contextual sidebar. Listing 7-38 shows how the component slot helper would be included.

Listing 7-38. *Including a Component Slot with the Name* `'sidebar'`

```
...
<div id="sidebar">
  <?php include_component_slot('sidebar') ?>
</div>
```

Define the correspondence between the component slot label and a component name in the view configuration. For instance, set the default component for the `sidebar` component slot in the application `view.yml`, under the `components` header. The key is the component slot label; the value must be an array containing a module and a component name. Listing 7-39 shows an example.

Listing 7-39. *Defining the Default* `'sidebar'` *Slot Component, in* `myapp/config/view.yml`

```
default:
  components:
    sidebar:  [bar, default]
```

So when the layout is executed, the `sidebar` component slot is filled with the result of the `executeDefault()` method of the `barComponents` class located in the `bar` module, and this method will display the `_default.php` partial located in `modules/bar/templates/`.

The configuration cascade gives you the ability to override this setting for a given module. For instance, in a `user` module, you may want the contextual component to display the user name and the number of articles that the user published. In that case, specialize the sidebar slot setting in the module `view.yml`, as shown in Listing 7-40.

Listing 7-40. *Specializing the* `'sidebar'` *Slot Component, in* `myapp/modules/user/config/view.yml`

```
all:
  components:
    sidebar:  [bar, user]
```

The component definitions to handle this slot should look like the ones in Listing 7-41.

Listing 7-41. *Components Used by the* `'sidebar'` *Slot, in modules/bar/actions/ components.class.php*

```php
class barComponents extends sfComponents
{
  public function executeDefault()
  {
  }

  public function executeUser()
  {
    $current_user = $this->getUser()->getCurrentUser();
    $c = new Criteria();
    $c->add(ArticlePeer::AUTHOR_ID, $current_user->getId());
    $this->nb_articles = ArticlePeer::doCount($c);
    $this->current_user = $current_user;
  }
}
```

Listing 7-42 shows the views for these two components.

Listing 7-42. *Partials Used by the* `'sidebar'` *Slot Components, in modules/bar/templates/*

```php
// _default.php
<p>This zone contains contextual information.</p>

// _user.php
<p>User name: <?php echo $current_user->getName() ?></p>
<p><?php echo $nb_articles ?> articles published</p>
```

Component slots can be used for breadcrumbs, contextual navigations, and dynamic insertions of all kinds. As components, they can be used in the global layout and regular templates, or even in other components. The configuration setting the component of a slot is always taken from the configuration of the last action called.

If you need to suspend the use of a component slot for a given module, just declare an empty module/component for it, as shown in Listing 7-43.

Listing 7-43. *Disabling a Component Slot in* `view.yml`

```yaml
all:
  components:
    sidebar:  []
```

Output Escaping

When you insert dynamic data in a template, you must be sure about the data integrity. For instance, if data comes from forms filled in by anonymous users, there is a risk that it may include malicious scripts intended to launch cross-site scripting (XSS) attacks. You must be able to escape the output data, so that any HTML tag it contains becomes harmless.

As an example, suppose that a user fills an input field with the following value:

```
<script>alert(document.cookie)</script>
```

If you echo this value without caution, the JavaScript will execute on every browser and allow for much more dangerous attacks than just displaying an alert. This is why you must escape the value before displaying it, so that it becomes something like this:

```
&lt;script&gt;alert(document.cookie)&lt;/script&gt;
```

You could escape your output manually by enclosing every unsure value in a call to htmlentities(), but that approach would be very repetitive and error-prone. Instead, symfony provides a special system, called *output escaping*, which automatically escapes every variable output in a template. It is activated by a simple parameter in the application settings.yml.

Activating Output Escaping

Output escaping is configured globally for an application in the settings.yml file. Two parameters control the way that output escaping works: the *strategy* determines how the variables are made available to the view, and the *method* is the default escaping function applied to the data.

The next sections describe these settings in detail but, basically, all you need to do to activate output escaping is to set the escaping_strategy parameter to both instead of its default value bc, as shown in Listing 7-44.

Listing 7-44. *Activating Output Escaping, in myapp/config/settings.yml*

```
all:
  .settings:
    escaping_strategy: both
    escaping_method:   ESC_ENTITIES
```

This will add htmlentities() to all variable output by default. For instance, suppose that you define a test variable in an action as follows:

```
$this->test = '<script>alert(document.cookie)</script>';
```

With output escaping turned on, echoing this variable in the template will output the escaped data:

```
echo $test;
 => &gt;&lt;script&gt;alert(document.cookie)&lt;/script&gt;
```

Activating output escaping also gives access to an $sf_data variable in every template. It is a container object referencing all the escaped variables. So you can also output the test variable with the following:

```
echo $sf_data->get('test');
=> &gt;&lt;script&gt;alert(document.cookie)&lt;/script&gt;
```

■Tip The $sf_data object implements the Array interface, so instead of using the $sf_data->get ➥ ('myvariable'), you can retrieve escaped values by calling $sf_data['myvariable']. But it is not a real array, so functions like print_r() will not work as expected.

This object also gives you access to the unescaped, or raw, data. This is useful when a variable stores HTML code meant to be interpreted by the browser, provided that you trust this variable. Call the getRaw() method when you need to output the raw data.

```
echo $sf_data->getRaw('test');
 => <script>alert(document.cookie)</script>
```

You will have to access raw data each time you need variables containing HTML to be really interpreted as HTML. You can now understand why the default layout uses $sf_data->getRaw('sf_content') to include the template, rather than a simpler $sf_content, which breaks when output escaping is activated.

Escaping Strategy

The escaping_strategy setting determines the way variables are output by default. The following are the possible values:

bc (backward compatible mode): Variables are not escaped, but an escaped version of each variable is available through the $sf_data container. So the *data is raw by default*, unless you choose to use the escaped value via the $sf_data object. This is the default value, and you should be aware that with this strategy, your application is subject to XSS attack risks.

both: All variables are *escaped by default*. Values are also made available in the $sf_data container. This is the recommended strategy, since you will be at risk only if you voluntarily output raw data. In some cases, you will have to use unescaped data—for instance, if you output a variable that contains HTML with the intention that this HTML be rendered as such in the browser. So be aware that if you switch to this strategy with a partially developed application, some features may break. The best choice is to use this setting right from the beginning.

on: Values are available only in the $sf_data container. This is the most secure and fastest way to deal with escaping, because each time you output a variable, you must choose if you want to use the escaped version with get() or the raw version with getRaw(). So you are always aware of the possibility that data may be corrupted.

off: Turns off output escaping. The $sf_data container is not available in templates. You can choose to use this strategy rather than bc to speed up your application if you are sure that you will never need to access escaped data.

Escaping Helpers

Escaping helpers are functions returning an escaped version of their input. They can be provided as a default `escaping_method` in the `settings.yml` file or to specify an escaping method for a specific value in the view. The following escaping helpers are available:

ESC_RAW: Doesn't escape the value.

ESC_ENTITIES: Applies the PHP function `htmlentities()` to the input with `ENT_QUOTES` as the quote style.

ESC_JS: Escapes a value to be put into a JavaScript string that is going to be used as HTML. This is useful for escaping things where HTML is going to be dynamically changed using JavaScript.

ESC_JS_NO_ENTITIES: Escapes a value to be put into a JavaScript string but does not add entities. This is useful if the value is going to be displayed using a dialog box (for example, for a `myString` variable used in `javascript:alert(myString);`).

Escaping Arrays and Objects

Output escaping not only works for strings, but also for arrays and objects. Any values that are objects or arrays will pass on their escaped state to their children. Assuming your strategy is set to `both`, Listing 7-45 demonstrates the escaping cascade.

Listing 7-45. *Escaping Also Works for Arrays and Objects*

```
// Class definition
class myClass
{
  public function testSpecialChars($value = '')
  {
    return '<'.$value.'>';
  }
}

// In the action
$this->test_array = array('&', '<', '>');
$this->test_array_of_arrays = array(array('&'));
$this->test_object = new myClass();

// In the template
<?php foreach($test_array as $value): ?>
  <?php echo $value ?>
<?php enforeach; ?>
 => &amp; &lt; &gt;
<?php echo $test_array_of_arrays[0][0] ?>
 => &amp;
<?php echo $test_object->testSpecialChars('&') ?>
 => &lt;&amp;&gt;
```

As a matter of fact, the variables in the template are not of the type you might expect. The output escaping system "decorates" them and transforms them into special objects:

```
<?php echo get_class($test_array) ?>
 => sfOutputEscaperArrayDecorator
<?php echo get_class($test_object) ?>
 => sfOutputEscaperObjectDecorator
```

This explains why some usual PHP functions (like array_shift(), print_r(), and so on) don't work on escaped arrays anymore. But they can be still be accessed using [ ], be traversed using foreach, and they give back the right result with count() (count() works only with PHP 5.2 or later). And in templates, the data should be read-only anyway, so most access will be through the methods that do work.

You still have a way to retrieve the raw data through the $sf_data object. In addition, methods of escaped objects are altered to accept an additional parameter: an escaping method. So you can choose an alternative escaping method each time you display a variable in a template, or opt for the ESC_RAW helper to deactivate escaping. See Listing 7-46 for an example.

Listing 7-46. *Methods of Escaped Objects Accept an Additional Parameter*

```
<?php echo $test_object->testSpecialChars('&') ?>
=> &lt;&amp;&gt;
// The three following lines return the same value
<?php echo $test_object->testSpecialChars('&', ESC_RAW) ?>
<?php echo $sf_data->getRaw('test_object')->testSpecialChars('&') ?>
<?php echo $sf_data->get('test_object', ESC_RAW)->testSpecialChars('&') ?>
 => <&>
```

If you deal with objects in your templates, you will use the additional parameter trick a lot, since it is the fastest way to get raw data on a method call.

■**Caution** The usual symfony variables are also escaped when you turn on output escaping. So be aware that $sf_user, $sf_request, $sf_param, and $sf_context still work, but their methods return escaped data, unless you add ESC_RAW as a final argument to their method calls.

Summary

All kinds of tools are available to manipulate the presentation layer. The *templates* are built in seconds, thanks to *helpers*. The *layouts*, *partials*, *components*, and *component slots* bring both modularity and reusability. The *view configuration* takes advantage of the speed of YAML to handle (mostly) page headers. The *configuration cascade* exempts you from defining every setting for each view. For every modification of the presentation that depends on dynamic data, the action has access to the sfResponse object. And the view is secure from XSS attacks, thanks to the *output escaping* system.

■ ■ ■

## CHAPTER 8

Inside the Model Layer

Much of the discussion so far has been devoted to building pages, and processing requests and responses. But the business logic of a web application relies mostly on its data model. Symfony's default model component is based on an object/relational mapping layer known as the Propel project (http://propel.phpdb.org/). In a symfony application, you access data stored in a database and modify it through objects; you never address the database explicitly. This maintains a high level of abstraction and portability.

This chapter explains how to create an object data model, and the way to access and modify the data in Propel. It also demonstrates the integration of Propel in Symfony.

Why Use an ORM and an Abstraction Layer?

Databases are *relational*. PHP 5 and symfony are *object-oriented*. In order to most effectively access the database in an object-oriented context, an interface translating the object logic to the relational logic is required. As explained in Chapter 1, this interface is called an *object-relational mapping* (ORM), and it is made up of objects that give access to data and keep business rules within themselves.

The main benefit of an ORM is *reusability*, allowing the methods of a data object to be called from various parts of the application, even from different applications. The ORM layer also *encapsulates* the data logic—for instance, the calculation of a forum user rating based on how many contributions were made and how popular these contributions are. When a page needs to display such a user rating, it simply calls a method of the data model, without worrying about the details of the calculation. If the calculation changes afterwards, you will just need to modify the rating method in the model, leaving the rest of the application unchanged.

Using objects instead of records, and classes instead of tables, has another benefit: They allow you to add *new accessors* to your objects that don't necessarily match a column in a table. For instance, if you have a table called `client` with two fields named `first_name` and `last_name`, you might like to be able to require just a `Name`. In an object-oriented world, it is as easy as adding a new accessor method to the `Client` class, as in Listing 8-1. From the application point of view, there is no difference between the `FirstName`, `LastName`, and `Name` attributes of the `Client` class. Only the class itself can determine which attributes correspond to a database column.

Listing 8-1. *Accessors Mask the Actual Table Structure in a Model Class*

```
public function getName()
{
  return $this->getFirstName.' '.$this->getLastName();
}
```

All the repeated data-access functions and the business logic of the data itself can be kept in such objects. Suppose you have a ShoppingCart class in which you keep Items (which are objects). To get the full amount of the shopping cart for the checkout, write a custom method to encapsulate the actual calculation, as shown in Listing 8-2.

Listing 8-2. *Accessors Mask the Data Logic*

```
public function getTotal()
{
  $total = 0;
  foreach ($this->getItems() as $item)
  {
    $total += $item->getPrice() * $item->getQuantity();
  }

  return $total;
}
```

There is another important point to consider when building data-access procedures: Database vendors use different SQL syntax variants. Switching to another database management system (DBMS) forces you to rewrite part of the SQL queries that were designed for the previous one. If you build your queries using a database-independent syntax, and leave the actual SQL translation to a third-party component, you can switch database systems without pain. This is the goal of the *database abstraction* layer. It forces you to use a specific syntax for queries, and does the dirty job of conforming to the DBMS particulars and optimizing the SQL code.

The main benefit of an abstraction layer is *portability*, because it makes switching to another database possible, even in the middle of a project. Suppose that you need to write a quick prototype for an application, but the client hasn't decided yet which database system would best suit his needs. You can start building your application with SQLite, for instance, and switch to MySQL, PostgreSQL, or Oracle when the client is ready to decide. Just change one line in a configuration file, and it works.

Symfony uses Propel as the ORM, and Propel uses Creole for database abstraction. These two third-party components, both developed by the Propel team, are seamlessly integrated into symfony, and you can consider them as part of the framework. Their syntax and conventions, described in this chapter, were adapted so that they differ from the symfony ones as little as possible.

■**Note** In a symfony project, all the applications share the same model. That's the whole point of the project level: regrouping applications that rely on common business rules. This is the reason that the model is independent from the applications and the model files are stored in a `lib/model/` directory at the root of the project.

Symfony's Database Schema

In order to create the data object model that symfony will use, you need to translate whatever relational model your database has to an object data model. The ORM needs a description of the relational model to do the mapping, and this is called a *schema*. In a schema, you define the tables, their relations, and the characteristics of their columns.

Symfony's syntax for schemas uses the YAML format. The `schema.yml` files must be located in the `myproject/config/` directory.

■**Note** Symfony also understands the Propel native XML schema format, as described in the "Beyond the schema.yml: The schema.xml" section later in this chapter.

Schema Example

How do you translate a database structure into a schema? An example is the best way to understand it. Imagine that you have a `blog` database with two tables: `blog_article` and `blog_comment`, with the structure shown in Figure 8-1.

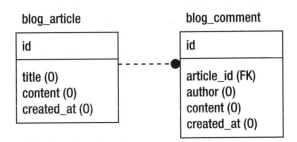

Figure 8-1. *A blog database table structure*

The related `schema.yml` file should look like Listing 8-3.

Listing 8-3. *Sample* `schema.yml`

```
propel:
  blog_article:
    _attributes: { phpName: Article }
    id:
    title:      varchar(255)
    content:    longvarchar
    created_at:
  blog_comment:
    _attributes: { phpName: Comment }
    id:
    article_id:
    author:     varchar(255)
    content:    longvarchar
    created_at:
```

Notice that the name of the database itself (`blog`) doesn't appear in the `schema.yml` file. Instead, the database is described under a *connection name* (`propel` in this example). This is because the actual connection settings can depend on the environment in which your application runs. For instance, when you run your application in the development environment, you will access a development database (maybe `blog_dev`), but with the same schema as the production database. The connection settings will be specified in the `databases.yml` file, described in the "Database Connections" section later in this chapter. The schema doesn't contain any detailed connection to settings, only a connection name, to maintain database abstraction.

Basic Schema Syntax

In a `schema.yml` file, the first key represents a *connection name*. It can contain several *tables*, each having a set of *columns*. According to the YAML syntax, the keys end with a colon, and the structure is shown through indentation (one or more spaces, but no tabulations).

A table can have special *attributes*, including the `phpName` (the name of the class that will be generated). If you don't mention a `phpName` for a table, symfony creates it based on the camelCase version of the table name.

■**Tip** The camelCase convention removes underscores from words, and capitalizes the first letter of inner words. The default camelCase versions of `blog_article` and `blog_comment` are `BlogArticle` and `BlogComment`. The name of this convention comes from the appearance of capitals inside a long word, suggestive of the humps of a camel.

A table contains columns. The column value can be defined in three different ways:

- If you define nothing, symfony will guess the best attributes according to the column name and a few conventions that will be described in the "Empty Columns" section later in this chapter. For instance, the `id` column in Listing 8-3 doesn't need to be defined. Symfony will make it an auto-incremented integer, primary key of the table. The `article_id` in the `blog_comment` table will be understood as a foreign key to the `blog_article` table (columns ending with `_id` are considered to be foreign keys, and the related table is automatically determined according to the first part of the column name). Columns called `created_at` are automatically set to the `timestamp` type. For all these columns, you don't need to specify any type. This is one of the reasons why `schema.yml` is so easy to write.

- If you define only one attribute, it is the column type. Symfony understands the usual column types: `boolean`, `integer`, `float`, `date`, `varchar(size)`, `longvarchar` (converted, for instance, to `text` in MySQL), and so on. For text content over 256 characters, you need to use the `longvarchar` type, which has no size (but cannot exceed 65KB in MySQL). Note that the `date` and `timestamp` types have the usual limitations of Unix dates and cannot be set to a date prior to 1970-01-01. As you may need to set older dates (for instance, for dates of birth), a format of dates "before Unix" can be used with `bu_date` and `bu_timestamp`.

- If you need to define other column attributes (like default value, required, and so on), you should write the column attributes as a set of `key: value`. This extended schema syntax is described later in the chapter.

Columns can also have a `phpName` attribute, which is the capitalized version of the name (`Id`, `Title`, `Content`, and so on) and doesn't need overriding in most cases.

Tables can also contain explicit foreign keys and indexes, as well as a few database-specific structure definitions. Refer to the "Extended Schema Syntax" section later in this chapter to learn more.

Model Classes

The schema is used to build the model classes of the ORM layer. To save execution time, these classes are generated with a command-line task called `propel-build-model`.

```
> symfony propel-build-model
```

Typing this command will launch the analysis of the schema and the generation of base data model classes in the `lib/model/om/` directory of your project:

- `BaseArticle.php`

- `BaseArticlePeer.php`

- `BaseComment.php`

- `BaseCommentPeer.php`

In addition, the actual data model classes will be created in `lib/model/`:

- `Article.php`

- `ArticlePeer.php`

- `Comment.php`

- `CommentPeer.php`

You defined only two tables, and you end up with eight files. There is nothing wrong, but it deserves some explanation.

Base and Custom Classes

Why keep two versions of the data object model in two different directories?

You will probably need to add custom methods and properties to the model objects (think about the `getName()` method in Listing 8-1). But as your project develops, you will also add tables or columns. Whenever you change the `schema.yml` file, you need to regenerate the object model classes by making a new call to `propel-build-model`. If your custom methods were written in the classes actually generated, they would be erased after each generation.

The `Base` classes kept in the `lib/model/om/` directory are the ones directly generated from the schema. *You should never modify them*, since every new build of the model will completely erase these files.

On the other hand, the custom object classes, kept in the `lib/model/` directory, actually inherit from the `Base` ones. When the `propel-build-model` task is called on an existing model, these classes are not modified. So this is where you can add custom methods.

Listing 8-4 presents an example of a custom model class as created by the first call to the `propel-build-model` task.

Listing 8-4. *Sample Model Class File, in* `lib/model/Article.php`

```php
<?php

class Article extends BaseArticle
{
}
```

It inherits all the methods of the `BaseArticle` class, but a modification in the schema will not affect it.

The mechanism of custom classes extending base classes allows you to start coding, even without knowing the final relational model of your database. The related file structure makes the model both *customizable* and *evolutionary*.

Object and Peer Classes

`Article` and `Comment` are *object classes* that represent a record in the database. They give access to the columns of a record and to related records. This means that you will be able to know the `title` of an article by calling a method of an `Article` object, as in the example shown in Listing 8-5.

Listing 8-5. *Getters for Record Columns Are Available in the Object Class*

```
$article = new Article();
...
$title = $article->getTitle();
```

`ArticlePeer` and `CommentPeer` are *peer classes*; that is, classes that contain static methods to operate on the tables. They provide a way to retrieve records from the tables. Their methods usually return an object or a collection of objects of the related object class, as shown in Listing 8-6.

Listing 8-6. *Static Methods to Retrieve Records Are Available in the Peer Class*

```
$articles = ArticlePeer::retrieveByPks(array(123, 124, 125));
// $articles is an array of objects of class Article
```

■**Note** From a data model point of view, there cannot be any peer *object*. That's why the methods of the peer classes are called with a : : (for static method call), instead of the usual -> (for instance method call).

So combining object and peer classes in a base and a custom version results in four classes generated per table described in the schema. In fact, there is a fifth class created in the `lib/model/map/` directory, which contains metadata information about the table that is needed for the runtime environment. But as you will probably never change this class, you can forget about it.

Accessing Data

In symfony, your data is accessed through objects. If you are used to the relational model and using SQL to retrieve and alter your data, the object model methods will likely look complicated. But once you've tasted the power of object orientation for data access, you will probably like it a lot.

But first, let's make sure we share the same vocabulary. Relational and object data model use similar concepts, but they each have their own nomenclature:

Relational	Object-Oriented
Table	Class
Row, record	Object
Field, column	Property

Retrieving the Column Value

When symfony builds the model, it creates one base object class for each of the tables defined in the schema.yml. Each of these classes comes with default constructors, accessors, and mutators based on the column definitions: The new, get*XXX*(), and set*XXX*() methods help to create objects and give access to the object properties, as shown in Listing 8-7.

Listing 8-7. *Generated Object Class Methods*

```
$article = new Article();
$article->setTitle('My first article');
$article->setContent('This is my very first article.\n Hope you enjoy it!');

$title   = $article->getTitle();
$content = $article->getContent();
```

■**Note** The generated object class is called Article, which is the phpName given to the blog_article table. If the phpName were not defined in the schema, the class would have been called BlogArticle. The accessors and mutators use a camelCase variant of the column names, so the getTitle() method retrieves the value of the title column.

To set several fields at one time, you can use the fromArray() method, also generated for each object class, as shown in Listing 8-8.

Listing 8-8. *The fromArray() Method Is a Multiple Setter*

```
$article->fromArray(array(
  'title'   => 'My first article',
  'content' => 'This is my very first article.\n Hope you enjoy it!',
));
```

Retrieving Related Records

The article_id column in the blog_comment table implicitly defines a foreign key to the blog_article table. Each comment is related to one article, and one article can have many comments. The generated classes contain five methods translating this relationship in an object-oriented way, as follows:

$comment->getArticle(): To get the related Article object

$comment->getArticleId(): To get the ID of the related Article object

$comment->setArticle($article): To define the related Article object

$comment->setArticleId($id): To define the related Article object from an ID

$article->getComments(): To get the related Comment objects

The getArticleId() and setArticleId() methods show that you can consider the article_id column as a regular column and set the relationships by hand, but they are not very interesting. The benefit of the object-oriented approach is much more apparent in the three other methods. Listing 8-9 shows how to use the generated setters.

Listing 8-9. *Foreign Keys Are Translated into a Special Setter*

```
$comment = new Comment();
$comment->setAuthor('Steve');
$comment->setContent('Gee, dude, you rock: best article ever!);

// Attach this comment to the previous $article object
$comment->setArticle($article);

// Alternative syntax
// Only makes sense if the object is already saved in the database
$comment->setArticleId($article->getId());
```

Listing 8-10 shows how to use the generated getters. It also demonstrates how to chain method calls on model objects.

Listing 8-10. *Foreign Keys Are Translated into Special Getters*

```
// Many to one relationship
echo $comment->getArticle()->getTitle();
 => My first article
echo $comment->getArticle()->getContent();
 => This is my very first article.
    Hope you enjoy it!

// One to many relationship
$comments = $article->getComments();
```

The getArticle() method returns an object of class Article, which benefits from the getTitle() accessor. This is much better than doing the join yourself, which may take a few lines of code (starting from the $comment->getArticleId() call).

The $comments variable in Listing 8-10 contains an array of objects of class Comment. You can display the first one with $comments[0] or iterate through the collection with foreach ➥ ($comments as $comment).

■**Note** Objects from the model are defined with a *singular name* by convention, and you can now understand why. The foreign key defined in the blog_comment table causes the creation of a getComments() method, named by adding an s to the Comment object name. If you gave the model object a plural name, the generation would lead to a method named getCommentss(), which doesn't make sense.

Saving and Deleting Data

By calling the new constructor, you created a new object, but not an actual record in the blog_article table. Modifying the object has no effect on the database either. In order to save the data into the database, you need to call the save() method of the object.

```
$article->save();
```

The ORM is smart enough to detect relationships between objects, so saving the $article object also saves the related $comment object. It also knows if the saved object has an existing counterpart in the database, so the call to save() is sometimes translated in SQL by an INSERT, and sometimes by an UPDATE. The primary key is automatically set by the save() method, so after saving, you can retrieve the new primary key with $article->getId().

■Tip You can check if an object is new by calling isNew(). And if you wonder if an object has been modified and deserves saving, call its isModified() method.

If you read comments to your articles, you might change your mind about the interest of publishing on the Internet. And if you don't appreciate the irony of article reviewers, you can easily delete the comments with the delete() method, as shown in Listing 8-11.

Listing 8-11. *Delete Records from the Database with the delete() Method on the Related Object*

```
foreach ($article->getComments() as $comment)
{
  $comment->delete();
}
```

■Tip Even after calling the delete() method, an object remains available until the end of the request. To determine if an object is deleted in the database, call the isDeleted() method.

Retrieving Records by Primary Key

If you know the primary key of a particular record, use the retrieveByPk() class method of the peer class to get the related object.

```
$article = ArticlePeer::retrieveByPk(7);
```

The schema.yml file defines the id field as the primary key of the blog_article table, so this statement will actually return the article that has id 7. As you used the primary key, you know that only one record will be returned; the $article variable contains an object of class Article.

In some cases, a primary key may consist of more than one column. In those cases, the retrieveByPK() method accepts multiple parameters, one for each primary key column.

You can also select multiple objects based on their primary keys, by calling the generated retrieveByPKs() method, which expects an array of primary keys as a parameter.

Retrieving Records with Criteria

When you want to retrieve more than one record, you need to call the doSelect() method of the peer class corresponding to the objects you want to retrieve. For instance, to retrieve objects of class Article, call ArticlePeer::doSelect().

The first parameter of the doSelect() method is an object of class Criteria, which is a simple query definition class defined without SQL for the sake of database abstraction.

An empty Criteria returns all the objects of the class. For instance, the code shown in Listing 8-12 retrieves all the articles.

Listing 8-12. *Retrieving Records by Criteria with doSelect()—Empty Criteria*

```
$c = new Criteria();
$articles = ArticlePeer::doSelect($c);

// Will result in the following SQL query
SELECT blog_article.ID, blog_article.TITLE, blog_article.CONTENT,
       blog_article.CREATED_AT
FROM   blog_article;
```

HYDRATING

The call to ::doSelect() is actually much more powerful than a simple SQL query. First, the SQL is optimized for the DBMS you choose. Second, any value passed to the Criteria is escaped before being integrated into the SQL code, which prevents SQL injection risks. Third, the method returns an array of objects, rather than a result set. The ORM automatically creates and populates objects based on the database result set. This process is called *hydrating*.

For a more complex object selection, you need an equivalent of the WHERE, ORDER BY, GROUP BY, and other SQL statements. The Criteria object has methods and parameters for all these conditions. For example, to get all comments written by Steve, ordered by date, build a Criteria as shown in Listing 8-13.

Listing 8-13. *Retrieving Records by Criteria with doSelect()—Criteria with Conditions*

```
$c = new Criteria();
$c->add(CommentPeer::AUTHOR, 'Steve');
$c->addAscendingOrderByColumn(CommentPeer::CREATED_AT);
$comments = CommentPeer::doSelect($c);

// Will result in the following SQL query
SELECT blog_comment.ARTICLE_ID, blog_comment.AUTHOR, blog_comment.CONTENT,
       blog_comment.CREATED_AT
```

```
FROM    blog_comment
WHERE   blog_comment.author = 'Steve'
ORDER BY blog_comment.CREATED_AT ASC;
```

The class constants passed as parameters to the add( ) methods refer to the property names. They are named after the capitalized version of the column names. For instance, to address the content column of the blog_article table, use the ArticlePeer::CONTENT class constant.

■**Note** Why use CommentPeer::AUTHOR instead of blog_comment.AUTHOR, which is the way it will be output in the SQL query anyway? Suppose that you need to change the name of the author field to contributor in the database. If you used blog_comment.AUTHOR, you would have to change it in every call to the model. On the other hand, by using CommentPeer::AUTHOR, you simply need to change the column name in the schema.yml file, keep phpName as AUTHOR, and rebuild the model.

Table 8-1 compares the SQL syntax with the Criteria object syntax.

Table 8-1. *SQL and Criteria Object Syntax*

SQL	Criteria
WHERE column = value	->add(column, value);
WHERE column <> value	->add(column, value, Criteria::NOT_EQUAL);
Other Comparison Operators	
> , <	Criteria::GREATER_THAN, Criteria::LESS_THAN
>=, <=	Criteria::GREATER_EQUAL, Criteria::LESS_EQUAL
IS NULL, IS NOT NULL	Criteria::ISNULL, Criteria::ISNOTNULL
LIKE, ILIKE	Criteria::LIKE, Criteria::ILIKE
IN, NOT IN	Criteria::IN, Criteria::NOT_IN
Other SQL Keywords	
ORDER BY column ASC	->addAscendingOrderByColumn(column);
ORDER BY column DESC	->addDescendingOrderByColumn(column);
LIMIT limit	->setLimit(limit)
OFFSET offset	->setOffset(offset)
FROM table1, table2 WHERE table1.col1 = table2.col2	->addJoin(col1, col2)
FROM table1 LEFT JOIN table2 ON table1.col1 = table2.col2	->addJoin(col1, col2, Criteria::LEFT_JOIN)
FROM table1 RIGHT JOIN table2 ON table1.col1 = table2.col2	->addJoin(col1, col2, Criteria::RIGHT_JOIN)

■**Tip** The best way to discover and understand which methods are available in generated classes is to look at the `Base` files in the `lib/model/om/` folder after generation. The method names are pretty explicit, but if you need more comments on them, set the `propel.builder.addComments` parameter to `true` in the `config/propel.ini` file and rebuild the model.

Listing 8-14 shows another example of `Criteria` with multiple conditions. It retrieves all the comments by Steve on articles containing the word "enjoy," ordered by date.

Listing 8-14. *Another Example of Retrieving Records by Criteria with doSelect()—Criteria with Conditions*

```
$c = new Criteria();
$c->add(CommentPeer::AUTHOR, 'Steve');
$c->addJoin(CommentPeer::ARTICLE_ID, ArticlePeer::ID);
$c->add(ArticlePeer::CONTENT, '%enjoy%', Criteria::LIKE);
$c->addAscendingOrderByColumn(CommentPeer::CREATED_AT);
$comments = CommentPeer::doSelect($c);

// Will result in the following SQL query
SELECT blog_comment.ID, blog_comment.ARTICLE_ID, blog_comment.AUTHOR,
       blog_comment.CONTENT, blog_comment.CREATED_AT
FROM   blog_comment, blog_article
WHERE  blog_comment.AUTHOR = 'Steve'
       AND blog_article.CONTENT LIKE '%enjoy%'
       AND blog_comment.ARTICLE_ID = blog_article.ID
ORDER BY blog_comment.CREATED_AT ASC
```

Just as SQL is a simple language that allows you to build very complex queries, the `Criteria` object can handle conditions with any level of complexity. But since many developers think first in SQL before translating a condition into object-oriented logic, the `Criteria` object may be difficult to comprehend at first. The best way to understand it is to learn from examples and sample applications. The symfony project website, for instance, is full of `Criteria` building examples that will enlighten you in many ways.

In addition to the `doSelect()` method, every peer class has a `doCount()` method, which simply counts the number of records satisfying the criteria passed as a parameter and returns the count as an integer. As there is no object to return, the hydrating process doesn't occur in this case, and the `doCount()` method is faster than `doSelect()`.

The peer classes also provide `doDelete()`, `doInsert()`, and `doUpdate()` methods, which all expect a `Criteria` as a parameter. These methods allow you to issue `DELETE`, `INSERT`, and `UPDATE` queries to your database. Check the generated peer classes in your model for more details on these Propel methods.

Finally, if you just want the first object returned, replace `doSelect()` with a `doSelectOne()` call. This may be the case when you know that a `Criteria` will return only one result, and the advantage is that this method returns an object rather than an array of objects.

■**Tip** When a doSelect() query returns a large number of results, you might want to display only a subset of it in your response. Symfony provides a pager class called sfPropelPager, which automates the pagination of results. Check the API documentation at http://www.symfony-project.com/api/symfony.html for more information and usage examples.

Using Raw SQL Queries

Sometimes, you don't want to retrieve objects, but want to get only synthetic results calculated by the database. For instance, to get the latest creation date of all articles, it doesn't make sense to retrieve all the articles and to loop on the array. You will prefer to ask the database to return only the result, because it will skip the object hydrating process.

On the other hand, you don't want to call the PHP commands for database management directly, because then you would lose the benefit of database abstraction. This means that you need to bypass the ORM (Propel) but not the database abstraction (Creole).

Querying the database with Creole requires that you do the following:

1. Get a *database connection*.

2. Build a *query string*.

3. Create a *statement* out of it.

4. Iterate on the *result set* that results from the statement execution.

If this looks like gibberish to you, the code in Listing 8-15 will probably be more explicit.

Listing 8-15. *Custom SQL Query with Creole*

```
$connection = Propel::getConnection();
$query = 'SELECT MAX(%s) AS max FROM %s';
$query = sprintf($query, ArticlePeer::CREATED_AT, ArticlePeer::TABLE_NAME);
$statement = $connnection->prepareStatement($query);
$resultset = $statement->executeQuery();
$resultset->next();
$max = $resultset->getInt('max');
```

Just like Propel selections, Creole queries are tricky when you first start using them. Once again, examples from existing applications and tutorials will show you the right way.

■**Caution** If you are tempted to bypass this process and access the database directly, you risk losing the security and abstraction provided by Creole. Doing it the Creole way is longer, but it forces you to use good practices that guarantee the performance, portability, and security of your application. This is especially true for queries that contain parameters coming from a untrusted source (such as an Internet user). Creole does all the necessary escaping and secures your database. Accessing the database directly puts you at risk of SQL-injection attacks.

Using Special Date Columns

Usually, when a table has a column called created_at, it is used to store a timestamp of the date when the record was created. The same applies to updated_at columns, which are to be updated each time the record itself is updated, to the value of the current time.

The good news is that symfony will recognize the names of these columns and handle their updates for you. You don't need to manually set the created_at and updated_at columns; they will automatically be updated, as shown in Listing 8-16. The same applies for columns named created_on and updated_on.

Listing 8-16. *created_at and updated_at Columns Are Dealt with Automatically*

```
$comment = new Comment();
$comment->setAuthor('Steve');
$comment->save();

// Show the creation date
echo $comment->getCreatedAt();
  => [date of the database INSERT operation]
```

Additionally, the getters for date columns accept a date format as an argument:

```
echo $comment->getCreatedAt('Y-m-d');
```

REFACTORING TO THE DATA LAYER

When developing a symfony project, you often start by writing the domain logic code in the actions. But the database queries and model manipulation should not be stored in the controller layer. So all the logic related to the data should be moved to the model layer. Whenever you need to do the same request in more than one place in your actions, think about transferring the related code to the model. It helps to keep the actions short and readable.

For example, imagine the code needed in a blog to retrieve the ten most popular articles for a given tag (passed as request parameter). This code should not be in an action, but in the model. In fact, if you need to display this list in a template, the action should simply look like this:

```
public function executeShowPopularArticlesForTag()
{
  $tag = TagPeer::retrieveByName($this->getRequestParameter('tag'));
  $this->foward404Unless($tag);
  $this->articles = $tag->getPopularArticles(10);
}
```

The action creates an object of class Tag from the request parameter. Then all the code needed to query the database is located in a ->getPopularArticles() method of this class. It makes the action more readable, and the model code can easily be reused in another action.

Moving code to a more appropriate location is one of the techniques of *refactoring*. If you do it often, your code will be easy to maintain and to understand by other developers. A good rule of thumb about when to do refactoring to the data layer is that the code of an action should rarely contain more than ten lines of PHP code.

Database Connections

The data model is independent from the database used, but you will definitely use a database. The minimum information required by symfony to send requests to the project database is the name, the access codes, and the type of database. These connection settings should be entered in the databases.yml file located in the config/ directory. Listing 8-17 shows an example of such a file.

Listing 8-17. *Sample Database Connection Settings, in* myproject/config/databases.yml

```
prod:
  propel:
    param:
      host:            mydataserver
      username:        myusername
      password:        xxxxxxxxxx

all:
  propel:
    class:             sfPropelDatabase
    param:
      phptype:         mysql     # Database vendor
      hostspec:        localhost
      database:        blog
      username:        login
      password:        passwd
      port:            80
      encoding:        utf-8     # Default charset for table creation
      persistent:      true      # Use persistent connections
```

The connection settings are environment-dependent. You can define distinct settings for the prod, dev, and test environments, or any other environment in your application. This configuration can also be overridden per application, by setting different values in an application-specific file, such as in apps/myapp/config/databases.yml. For instance, you can use this approach to have different security policies for a front-end and a back-end application, and define several database users with different privileges in your database to handle this.

For each environment, you can define many connections. Each connection refers to a schema being labeled with the same name. In the example in Listing 8-17, the propel connection refers to the propel schema in Listing 8-3.

The permitted values of the phptype parameter are the ones of the database systems supported by Creole:

- mysql

- sqlserver

- pgsql

- sqlite

- oracle

hostspec, database, username, and password are the usual database connection settings. They can also be written in a shorter way as a data source name (DSN). Listing 8-18 is equivalent to the all: section of Listing 8-17.

Listing 8-18. *Shorthand Database Connection Settings*

```
all:
  propel:
    class:        sfPropelDatabase
    param:
      dsn:        mysql://login:passwd@localhost/blog
```

If you use a SQLite database, the hostspec parameter must be set to the path of the database file. For instance, if you keep your blog database in data/blog.db, the databases.yml file will look like Listing 8-19.

Listing 8-19. *Database Connection Settings for SQLite Use a File Path As Host*

```
all:
  propel:
    class:        sfPropelDatabase
    param:
      phptype:  sqlite
      database: %SF_DATA_DIR%/blog.db
```

Extending the Model

The generated model methods are great but often not sufficient. As soon as you implement your own business logic, you need to extend it, either by adding new methods or by overriding existing ones.

Adding New Methods

You can add new methods to the empty model classes generated in the lib/model/ directory. Use $this to call methods of the current object, and use self:: to call static methods of the current class. Remember that the custom classes inherit methods from the Base classes located in the lib/model/om/ directory.

For instance, for the Article object generated based on Listing 8-3, you can add a magic __toString() method so that echoing an object of class Article displays its title, as shown in Listing 8-20.

Listing 8-20. *Customizing the Model, in* `lib/model/Article.php`

```php
<?php

class Article extends BaseArticle
{
  public function __toString()
  {
    return $this->getTitle();  // getTitle() is inherited from BaseArticle
  }
}
```

You can also extend the peer classes—for instance, to add a method to retrieve all articles ordered by creation date, as shown in Listing 8-21.

Listing 8-21. *Customizing the Model, in* `lib/model/ArticlePeer.php`

```php
<?php

class ArticlePeer extends BaseArticlePeer
{
  public static function getAllOrderedByDate()
  {
    $c = new Criteria();
    $c->addAscendingOrderByColumn(self:CREATED_AT);
    return self::doSelect($c);

  }
}
```

The new methods are available in the same way as the generated ones, as shown in Listing 8-22.

Listing 8-22. *Using Custom Model Methods Is Like Using the Generated Methods*

```php
foreach (ArticlePeer::getAllOrderedByDate() as $article)
{
  echo $article;      // Will call the magic __toString() method
}
```

Overriding Existing Methods

If some of the generated methods in the Base classes don't fit your requirements, you can still override them in the custom classes. Just make sure that you use the same method signature (that is, the same number of arguments).

For instance, the $article->getComments() method returns an array of Comment objects, in no particular order. If you want to have the results ordered by creation date, with the latest comment coming first, then override the getComments() method, as shown in Listing 8-23. Be aware that the original getComments() method (found in lib/model/om/BaseArticle.php) expects a criteria value and a connection value as parameters, so your function must do the same.

Listing 8-23. *Overriding Existing Model Methods, in* `lib/model/Article.php`

```php
public function getComments($criteria = null, $con = null )
{
  // Objects are passed by reference in PHP5, so to avoid modifying the original,
  // you must clone it
  $criteria = clone $criteria;
  $criteria->addDescendingOrderByColumn(ArticlePeer::CREATED_AT);

  return parent::getComments($criteria, $con);
}
```

The custom method eventually calls the one of the parent Base class, and that's good practice. However, you can completely bypass it and return the result you want.

Using Model Behaviors

Some model modifications are generic and can be reused. For instance, methods to make a model object sortable and an optimistic lock to prevent conflicts between concurrent object saving are generic extensions that can be added to many classes.

Symfony packages these extensions into *behaviors*. Behaviors are external classes that provide additional methods to model classes. The model classes already contain hooks, and symfony knows how to extend them by way of sfMixer (see Chapter 17 for details).

To enable behaviors in your model classes, you must modify one setting in the config/ propel.ini file:

```
propel.builder.AddBehaviors = true     // Default value is false
```

There is no behavior bundled by default in symfony, but they can be installed via plug-ins. Once a behavior plug-in is installed, you can assign the behavior to a class with a single line. For instance, if you install the sfPropelParanoidBehaviorPlugin in your application, you can extend an Article class with this behavior by adding the following at the end of the Article.class.php:

```php
sfPropelBehavior::add('Article', array(
  'paranoid' => array('column' => 'deleted_at')
));
```

After rebuilding the model, deleted Article objects will remain in the database, invisible to the queries using the ORM, unless you temporarily disable the behavior with sfPropelParanoidBehavior::disable().

Check the list of symfony plug-ins in the wiki to find behaviors (http://www.symfony-project. com/trac/wiki/SymfonyPlugins#Propelbehaviorplugins). Each has its own documentation and installation guide.

Extended Schema Syntax

A schema.yml file can be simple, as shown in Listing 8-3. But relational models are often complex. That's why the schema has an extensive syntax able to handle almost every case.

Attributes

Connections and tables can have specific attributes, as shown in Listing 8-24. They are set under an _attributes key.

Listing 8-24. *Attributes for Connections and Tables*

```
propel:
  _attributes:    { noXsd: false, defaultIdMethod: none, package: lib.model }
  blog_article:
    _attributes: { phpName: Article }
```

You may want your schema to be validated before code generation takes place. To do that, deactivate the noXSD attribute for the connection. The connection also supports the defaultIdMethod attribute. If none is provided, then the database's native method of generating IDs will be used—for example, autoincrement for MySQL, or sequences for PostgreSQL. The other possible value is none.

The package attribute is like a namespace; it determines the path where the generated classes are stored. It defaults to lib/model/, but you can change it to organize your model in subpackages. For instance, if you don't want to mix the core business classes and the classes defining a database-stored statistics engine in the same directory, then define two schemas with lib.model.business and lib.model.stats packages.

You already saw the phpName table attribute, used to set the name of the generated class mapping the table.

Tables that contain localized content (that is, several versions of the content, in a related table, for internationalization) also take two additional attributes (see Chapter 13 for details), as shown in Listing 8-25.

Listing 8-25. *Attributes for i18n Tables*

```
propel:
  blog_article:
    _attributes: { isI18N: true, i18nTable: db_group_i18n }
```

DEALING WITH MULTIPLE SCHEMAS

You can have more than one schema per application. Symfony will take into account every file ending with schema.yml or schema.xml in the config/ folder. If your application has many tables, or if some tables don't share the same connection, you will find this approach very useful.

Consider these two schemas:

```
// In config/business-schema.yml
propel:
  blog_article:
    _attributes: { phpName: Article }
    id:
    title: varchar(50)
```

```
// In config/stats-schema.yml
propel:
  stats_hit:
    _attributes: { phpName: Hit }
  id:
  resource: varchar(100)
  created_at:
```

Both schemas share the same connection (propel), and the `Article` and `Hit` classes will be generated under the same `lib/model/` directory. Everything happens as if you had written only one schema.

You can also have different schemas use different connections (for instance, `propel` and `propel_bis`, to be defined in `databases.yml`) and organize the generated classes in subdirectories:

```
// In config/business-schema.yml
propel:
  blog_article:
    _attributes: { phpName: Article, package: lib.model.business }
  id:
  title: varchar(50)
```

```
// In config/stats-schema.yml
propel_bis:
  stats_hit:
    _attributes: { phpName: Hit, package.lib.model.stat }
  id:
  resource: varchar(100)
  created_at:
```

Many applications use more than one schema. In particular, some plug-ins have their own schema and package to avoid messing with your own classes (see Chapter 17 for details).

Column Details

The basic syntax gives you two choices: let symfony deduce the column characteristics from its name (by giving an empty value) or define the type with one of the type keywords. Listing 8-26 demonstrates these choices.

Listing 8-26. *Basic Column Attributes*

```
propel:
  blog_article:
    id:                     # Let symfony do the work
    title: varchar(50)      # Specify the type yourself
```

But you can define much more for a column. If you do, you will need to define column settings as an associative array, as shown in Listing 8-27.

Listing 8-27. *Complex Column Attributes*

```
propel:
  blog_article:
    id:      { type: integer, required: true, ➥
               primaryKey: true, autoIncrement: true }
    name:    { type: varchar(50), default: foobar, index: true }
    group_id: { type: integer, foreignTable: db_group, ➥
               foreignReference: id, onDelete: cascade }
```

The column parameters are as follows:

type: Column type. The choices are boolean, tinyint, smallint, integer, bigint, double, float, real, decimal, char, varchar(size), longvarchar, date, time, timestamp, bu_date, bu_timestamp, blob, and clob.

required: Boolean. Set it to true if you want the column to be required.

default: Default value.

primaryKey: Boolean. Set it to true for primary keys.

autoIncrement: Boolean. Set it to true for columns of type integer that need to take an auto-incremented value.

sequence: Sequence name for databases using sequences for autoIncrement columns (for example, PostgreSQL and Oracle).

index: Boolean. Set it to true if you want a simple index or to unique if you want a unique index to be created on the column.

foreignTable: A table name, used to create a foreign key to another table.

foreignReference: The name of the related column if a foreign key is defined via foreignTable.

onDelete: Determines the action to trigger when a record in a related table is deleted. When set to setnull, the foreign key column is set to null. When set to cascade, the record is deleted. If the database engine doesn't support the set behavior, the ORM emulates it. This is relevant only for columns bearing a foreignTable and a foreignReference.

isCulture: Boolean. Set it to true for culture columns in localized content tables (see Chapter 13).

Foreign Keys

As an alternative to the foreignTable and foreignReference column attributes, you can add foreign keys under the _foreignKeys: key in a table. The schema in Listing 8-28 will create a foreign key on the user_id column, matching the id column in the blog_user table.

Listing 8-28. *Foreign Key Alternative Syntax*

```
propel:
  blog_article:
    id:
    title:   varchar(50)
    user_id: { type: integer }
    _foreignKeys:
      -
        foreignTable: blog_user
        onDelete:     cascade
        references:
          - { local: user_id, foreign: id }
```

The alternative syntax is useful for multiple-reference foreign keys and to give foreign keys a name, as shown in Listing 8-29.

Listing 8-29. *Foreign Key Alternative Syntax Applied to Multiple Reference Foreign Key*

```
  _foreignKeys:
    my_foreign_key:
      foreignTable:  db_user
      onDelete:      cascade
      references:
        - { local: user_id, foreign: id }
        - { local: post_id, foreign: id }
```

Indexes

As an alternative to the `index` column attribute, you can add indexes under the `_indexes:` key in a table. If you want to define unique indexes, you must use the `_uniques:` header instead. Listing 8-30 shows the alternative syntax for indexes.

Listing 8-30. *Indexes and Unique Indexes Alternative Syntax*

```
propel:
  blog_article:
    id:
    title:            varchar(50)
    created_at:
    _indexes:
      my_index:       [title, user_id]
    _uniques:
      my_other_index: [created_at]
```

The alternative syntax is useful only for indexes built on more than one column.

Empty Columns

When meeting a column with no value, symfony will do some magic and add a value of its own. See Listing 8-31 for the details added to empty columns.

Listing 8-31. *Column Details Deduced from the Column Name*

```
// Empty columns named id are considered primary keys
id:         { type: integer, required: true, primaryKey: true, autoIncrement: true }

// Empty columns named XXX_id are considered foreign keys
foobar_id: { type: integer, foreignTable: db_foobar, foreignReference: id }

// Empty columns named created_at, updated_at, created_on and updated_on
// are considered dates and automatically take the timestamp type
created_at: { type: timestamp }
updated_at: { type: timestamp }
```

For foreign keys, symfony will look for a table having the same phpName as the beginning of the column name, and if one is found, it will take this table name as the foreignTable.

I18n Tables

Symfony supports content internationalization in related tables. This means that when you have content subject to internationalization, it is stored in two separate tables: one with the invariable columns and another with the internationalized columns.

In a schema.yml file, all that is implied when you name a table foobar_i18n. For instance, the schema shown in Listing 8-32 will be automatically completed with columns and table attributes to make the internationalized content mechanism work. Internally, symfony will understand it as if it were written like Listing 8-33. Chapter 13 will tell you more about i18n.

Listing 8-32. *Implied i18n Mechanism*

```
propel:
  db_group:
    id:
    created_at:

  db_group_i18n:
    name:        varchar(50)
```

Listing 8-33. *Explicit i18n Mechanism*

```
propel:
  db_group:
    _attributes: { isI18N: true, i18nTable: db_group_i18n }
    id:
    created_at:
```

```
db_group_i18n:
  id:      { type: integer, required: true, primaryKey: true, ➥
             foreignTable: db_group, foreignReference: id, onDelete: cascade }
  culture: { isCulture: true, type: varchar(7), required: true, ➥
             primaryKey: true }
  name:    varchar(50)
```

Beyond the schema.yml: The schema.xml

As a matter of fact, the schema.yml format is internal to symfony. When you call a propel-command, symfony actually translates this file into a generated-schema.xml file, which is the type of file expected by Propel to actually perform tasks on the model.

The schema.xml file contains the same information as its YAML equivalent. For example, Listing 8-3 is converted to the XML file shown in Listing 8-34.

Listing 8-34. *Sample schema.xml, Corresponding to Listing 8-3*

```xml
<?xml version="1.0" encoding="UTF-8"?>
  <database name="propel" defaultIdMethod="native" noXsd="true" package="lib.model">
    <table name="blog_article" phpName="Article">
      <column name="id" type="integer" required="true" primaryKey="true" ➥
              autoIncrement="true" />
      <column name="title" type="varchar" size="255" />
      <column name="content" type="longvarchar" />
      <column name="created_at" type="timestamp" />
    </table>
    <table name="blog_comment" phpName="Comment">
      <column name="id" type="integer" required="true" primaryKey="true" ➥
              autoIncrement="true" />
      <column name="article_id" type="integer" />
      <foreign-key foreignTable="blog_article">
        <reference local="article_id" foreign="id"/>
      </foreign-key>
      <column name="author" type="varchar" size="255" />
      <column name="content" type="longvarchar" />
      <column name="created_at" type="timestamp" />
    </table>
  </database>
```

The description of the schema.xml format can be found in the documentation and the "Getting Started" sections of the Propel project website (http://propel.phpdb.org/docs/user_guide/chapters/appendices/AppendixB-SchemaReference.html).

The YAML format was designed to keep the schemas simple to read and write, but the trade-off is that the most complex schemas can't be described with a schema.yml file. On the other hand, the XML format allows for full schema description, whatever its complexity, and includes database vendor-specific settings, table inheritance, and so on.

Symfony actually understands schemas written in XML format. So if your schema is too complex for the YAML syntax, if you have an existing XML schema, or if you are already familiar with the Propel XML syntax, you don't have to switch to the symfony YAML syntax. Place your `schema.xml` in the project `config/` directory, build the model, and there you go.

PROPEL IN SYMFONY

All the details given in this chapter are not specific to symfony, but rather to Propel. Propel is the preferred object/relational abstraction layer for symfony, but you can choose an alternative one. However, symfony works more seamlessly with Propel, for the following reasons:

- All the object data model classes and the `Criteria` class are autoloading classes. As soon as you use them, symfony will include the right files, and you don't need to manually add the file inclusion statements.

- In symfony, Propel doesn't need to be launched nor initialized. When an object uses Propel, the library initiates by itself.

- Some symfony helpers use Propel objects as parameters to achieve high-level tasks (such as pagination or filtering).

- Propel objects allow rapid prototyping and generation of a backend for your application (Chapter 14 provides more details).

- The schema is faster to write through the `schema.yml` file.

  And, as Propel is independent of the database used, so is symfony.

Don't Create the Model Twice

The trade-off of using an ORM is that you must define the data structure twice: once for the database, and once for the object model. Fortunately, symfony offers command-line tools to generate one based on the other, so you can avoid duplicate work.

Building a SQL Database Structure Based on an Existing Schema

If you start your application by writing the `schema.yml` file, symfony can generate a SQL query that creates the tables directly from the YAML data model. To use the query, go to your root project directory and type this:

```
> symfony propel-build-sql
```

A `lib.model.schema.sql` file will be created in `myproject/data/sql/`. Note that the generated SQL code will be optimized for the database system defined in the `phptype` parameter of the `propel.ini` file.

You can use the `schema.sql` file directly to build the tables. For instance, in MySQL, type this:

```
> mysqladmin -u root -p create blog
> mysql -u root -p blog < data/sql/lib.model.schema.sql
```

The generated SQL is also helpful to rebuild the database in another environment, or to change to another DBMS. If the connection settings are properly defined in your `propel.ini`, you can even use the `symfony propel-insert-sql` command to do this automatically.

■**Tip** The command line also offers a task to populate your database with data based on a text file. See Chapter 16 for more information about the `propel-load-data` task and the YAML fixture files.

Generating a YAML Data Model from an Existing Database

Symfony can use the Creole database access layer to generate a `schema.yml` file from an existing database, thanks to *introspection* (the capability of databases to determine the structure of the tables on which they are operating). This can be particularly useful when you do reverse-engineering, or if you prefer working on the database before working on the object model.

In order to do this, you need to make sure that the project `propel.ini` file points to the correct database and contains all connection settings, and then call the `propel-build-schema` command:

```
> symfony propel-build-schema
```

A brand-new `schema.yml` file built from your database structure is generated in the `config/` directory. You can build your model based on this schema.

The schema-generation command is quite powerful and can add a lot of database-dependent information to your schema. As the YAML format doesn't handle this kind of vendor information, you need to generate an XML schema to take advantage of it. You can do this simply by adding an `xml` argument to the `build-schema` task:

```
> symfony propel-build-schema xml
```

Instead of generating a `schema.yml` file, this will create a `schema.xml` file fully compatible with Propel, containing all the vendor information. But be aware that generated XML schemas tend to be quite verbose and difficult to read.

THE PROPEL.INI CONFIGURATION

The `propel-build-sql` and `propel-build-schema` tasks don't use the connection settings defined in the `databases.yml` file. Rather, these tasks use the connection settings in another file, called `propel.ini` and stored in the project `config/` directory:

```
propel.database.createUrl = mysql://login:passwd@localhost
propel.database.url       = mysql://login:passwd@localhost/blog
```

This file contains other settings used to configure the Propel generator to make generated model classes compatible with symfony. Most settings are internal and of no interest to the user, apart from a few:

```
// Base classes are autoloaded in symfony
// Set this to true to use include_once statements instead
// (Small negative impact on performance)
propel.builder.addIncludes = false

// Generated classes are not commented by default
// Set this to true to add comments to Base classes
// (Small negative impact on performance)
propel.builder.addComments = false

// Behaviors are not handled by default
// Set this to true to be able to handle them
propel.builder.AddBehaviors = false
```

After you make a modification to the `propel.ini` settings, don't forget to rebuild the model so the changes will take effect.

Summary

Symfony uses Propel as the ORM and Creole as the database abstraction layer. It means that you must first describe the relational *schema* of your database in YAML before *generating the object model classes*. Then, at runtime, use the methods of the *object and peer classes* to retrieve information about a record or a set of records. You can override them and extend the model easily by adding methods to the *custom classes*. The connection settings are defined in a `databases.yml` file, which can support more than one connection. And the command line contains special tasks to avoid duplicate structure definition.

The model layer is the most complex of the symfony framework. One reason for this complexity is that data manipulation is an intricate matter. The related security issues are crucial for a website and should not be ignored. Another reason is that symfony is more suited for middle- to large-scale applications in an enterprise context. In such applications, the automations provided by the symfony model really represent a gain of time, worth the investment in learning its internals.

So don't hesitate to spend some time testing the model objects and methods to fully understand them. The solidity and scalability of your applications will be a great reward.

PART 3

Special Features

■ ■ ■

## CHAPTER 9

Links and the Routing System

Links and URLs deserve particular treatment in a web application framework. This is because the unique entry point of the application (the front controller) and the use of helpers in templates allow for a complete separation between the way URLs work and their appearance. This is called *routing*. More than a gadget, routing is a useful tool to make web applications even more user-friendly and secure. This chapter will tell you everything you need to know to handle URLs in your symfony applications:

- What the routing system is and how it works

- How to use link helpers in templates to enable routing of outgoing URLs

- How to configure the routing rules to change the appearance of URLs

You will also find a few tricks for mastering routing performance and adding finishing touches.

What Is Routing?

Routing is a mechanism that rewrites URLs to make them more user-friendly. But to understand why this is important, you must first take a few minutes to think about URLs.

URLs As Server Instructions

URLs carry information from the browser to the server required to enact an action as desired by the user. For instance, a traditional URL contains the file path to a script and some parameters necessary to complete the request, as in this example:

```
http://www.example.com/web/controller/article.php?id=123456&format_code=6532
```

This URL conveys information about the application's architecture and database. Developers usually hide the application's infrastructure in the interface (for instance, they choose page titles like "Personal profile page" rather than "QZ7.65"). Revealing vital clues to the internals of the application in the URL contradicts this effort and has serious drawbacks:

- The technical data appearing in the URL creates *potential security breaches.* In the preceding example, what happens if an ill-disposed user changes the value of the `id` parameter? Does this mean the application offers a direct interface to the database? Or what if the user tries other script names, like `admin.php`, just for fun? All in all, raw URLs offer an easy way to hack an application, and managing security is almost impossible with them.

- The unintelligibility of URLs makes them *disturbing* wherever they appear, and they dilute the impact of the surrounding content. And nowadays, URLs don't appear only in the address bar. They appear when a user hovers the mouse over a link, as well as in search results. When users look for information, you want to give them easily understandable clues regarding what they found, rather than a confusing URL such as the one shown in Figure 9-1.

Microsoft Office Clip Art and Media Home Page
Microsoft Office Clip Art and Media - Over 140000 clip art graphics, animations, photos, and sounds for use in **Microsoft** Office products.
office.**microsoft**.com/clipart/default.aspx?lc=en-us - 56k - 30 Aug 2006 -
Cached - Similar pages

Figure 9-1. *URLs appear in many places, such as in search results.*

- If one URL has to be changed (for instance, if a script name or one of its parameters is modified), *every link to this URL must be changed* as well. It means that modifications in the controller structure are heavyweight and expensive, which is not ideal in agile development.

And it could be much worse if symfony didn't use the *front controller* paradigm; that is, if the application contained many scripts accessible from the Internet, in many directories, such as these:

```
http://www.example.com/web/gallery/album.php?name=my%20holidays
http://www.example.com/web/weblog/public/post/list.php
http://www.example.com/web/general/content/page.php?name=about%20us
```

In this case, developers would need to match the URL structure with the file structure, resulting in a maintenance nightmare when either structure changed.

URLs As Part of the Interface

The idea behind routing is to consider the URL as *part of the interface.* The application can format a URL to bring information to the user, and the user can use the URL to access resources of the application.

This is possible in symfony applications, because the URL presented to the end user is unrelated to the server instruction needed to perform the request. Instead, it is related to the resource requested, and it can be formatted freely. For instance, symfony can understand the following URL and have it display the same page as the first URL shown in this chapter:

```
http://www.example.com/articles/finance/2006/activity-breakdown.html
```

The benefits are immense:

- URLs actually *mean something*, and they can help the users decide if the page behind a link contains what they expect. A link can contain additional details about the resource it returns. This is particularly useful for search engine results. Additionally, URLs sometimes appear without any mention of the page title (think about when you copy a URL in an e-mail message), and in this case, they must mean something on their own. See Figure 9-2 for an example of a user-friendly URL.

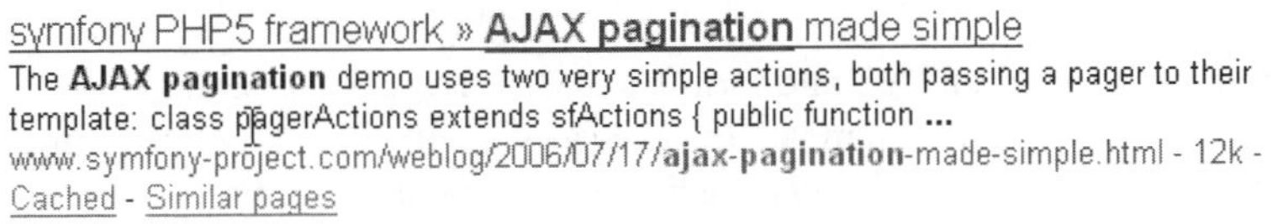

symfony PHP5 framework » **AJAX pagination** made simple
The **AJAX pagination** demo uses two very simple actions, both passing a pager to their
template: class pagerActions extends sfActions { public function ...
www.symfony-project.com/weblog/2006/07/17/**ajax-pagination**-made-simple.html - 12k -
Cached - Similar pages

Figure 9-2. *URLs can convey additional information about a page, like the publication date.*

- URLs written in paper documents are *easier to type and remember*. If your company website appears as `http://www.example.com/controller/web/index.jsp?id=ERD4` on your business card, it will probably not receive many visits.

- The URL can become a *command-line tool of its own*, to perform actions or retrieve information in an intuitive way. Applications offering such a possibility are faster to use for power users.

  ```
  // List of results: add a new tag to narrow the list of results
  http://del.icio.us/tag/symfony+ajax
  // User profile page: change the name to get another user profile
  http://www.askeet.com/user/francois
  ```

- You can change the URL formatting and the action name/parameters independently, with a single modification. It means that you can *develop first, and format the URLs afterwards*, without totally messing up your application.

- Even when you reorganize the internals of an application, the URLs can remain the same for the outside world. It makes *URLs persistent*, which is a must because it allows bookmarking on dynamic pages.

- Search engines tend to skip dynamic pages (ending with `.php`, `.asp`, and so on) when they index websites. So you can format URLs to have search engines think they are browsing static content, even when they meet a dynamic page, thus resulting in *better indexing* of your application pages.

- It is *safer*. Any unrecognized URL will be redirected to a page specified by the developer, and users cannot browse the web root file structure by testing URLs. The actual script name called by the request, as well as its parameters, is hidden.

The correspondence between the URLs presented to the user and the actual script name and request parameters is achieved by a *routing system*, based on patterns that can be modified through configuration.

■Note How about assets? Fortunately, the URLs of assets (images, style sheets, and JavaScript) don't appear much during browsing, so there is no real need for routing for those. In symfony, all assets are located under the `web/` directory, and their URL matches their location in the file system. However, you can manage dynamic assets (handled by actions) by using a generated URL inside the asset helper. For instance, to display a dynamically generated image, use `image_tag(url_for('captcha/image?key='.$key))`.

How It Works

Symfony disconnects the external URL and its internal URI. The correspondence between the two is made by the routing system. To make things easy, symfony uses a syntax for internal URIs very similar to the one of regular URLs. Listing 9-1 shows an example.

Listing 9-1. *External URL and Internal URI*

```
// Internal URI syntax
<module>/<action>[?param1=value1][&param2=value2][&param3=value3]...

// Example internal URI, which never appears to the end user
article/permalink?year=2006&subject=finance&title=activity-breakdown

// Example external URL, which appears to the end user
http://www.example.com/articles/finance/2006/activity-breakdown.html
```

The routing system uses a special configuration file, called `routing.yml`, in which you can define *routing rules*. Consider the rule shown in Listing 9-2. It defines a pattern that looks like `articles/*/*/*` and names the pieces of content matching the wildcards.

Listing 9-2. *A Sample Routing Rule*

```
article_by_title:
  url:    articles/:subject/:year/:title.html
  param:  { module: article, action: permalink }
```

Every request sent to a symfony application is first analyzed by the routing system (which is simple because every request in handled by a single front controller). The routing system looks for a match between the request URL and the patterns defined in the routing rules. If a match is found, the named wildcards become request parameters and are merged with the ones defined in the `param:` key. See how it works in Listing 9-3.

Listing 9-3. *The Routing System Interprets Incoming Request URLs*

```
// The user types (or clicks on) this external URL
http://www.example.com/articles/finance/2006/activity-breakdown.html
```

```
// The front controller sees that it matches the article_by_title rule
// The routing system creates the following request parameters
  'module'  => 'article'
  'action'  => 'permalink'
  'subject' => 'finance'
  'year'    => '2006'
  'title'   => 'activity-breakdown'
```

■Tip The `.html` extension of the external URL is a simple decoration and is ignored by the routing system. Its sole interest is to makes dynamic pages look like static ones. You will see how to activate this extension in the "Routing Configuration" section later in this chapter.

The request is then passed to the `permalink` action of the `article` module, which has all the required information in the request parameters to determine which article is to be shown.

But the mechanism also must work the other way around. For the application to show external URLs in its links, you must provide the routing system with enough data to determine which rule to apply to it. You also must not write hyperlinks directly with <a> tags—this would bypass routing completely—but with a special helper, as shown in Listing 9-4.

Listing 9-4. *The Routing System Formats Outgoing URLs in Templates*

```
// The url_for() helper transforms an internal URI into an external URL
<a href="<?php echo url_for('article/permalink?subject=finance&year=2006 ➧
&title=activity-breakdown') ?>">click here</a>

// The helper sees that the URI matches the article_by_title rule
// The routing system creates an external URL out of it
 => <a href="http://www.example.com/articles/finance/2006/ ➧
    activity-breakdown.html">click here</a>

// The link_to() helper directly outputs a hyperlink
// and avoids mixing PHP with HTML
<?php echo link_to(
  'click here',
  'article/permalink?subject=finance&year=2006&title=activity-breakdown'
) ?>

// Internally, link_to() will make a call to url_for() so the result is the same
 => <a href="http://www.example.com/articles/finance/2006/ ➧
    activity-breakdown.html">click here</a>
```

So *routing is a two-way mechanism,* and it works only if you use the `link_to()` helper to format *all* your links.

URL Rewriting

Before getting deeper into the routing system, one matter needs to be clarified. In the examples given in the previous section, there is no mention of the front controller (index.php or myapp_dev.php) in the internal URIs. The front controller, not the elements of the application, decides the environment. So all the links must be environment-independent, and the front controller name can *never* appear in internal URIs.

There is no script name in the examples of generated URLs either. This is because generated URLs don't contain any script name in the production environment by default. The no_script_name parameter of the settings.yml file precisely controls the appearance of the front controller name in generated URLs. Set it to off, as shown in Listing 9-5, and the URLs output by the link helpers will mention the front controller script name in every link.

Listing 9-5. *Showing the Front Controller Name in URLs, in* apps/myapp/settings.yml

```
prod:
  .settings
    no_script_name:  off
```

Now, the generated URLs will look like this:

http://www.example.com/**index.php**/articles/finance/2006/activity-breakdown.html

In all environments except the production one, the no_script_name parameter is set to off by default. So when you browse your application in the development environment, for instance, the front controller name always appears in the URLs.

http://www.example.com/**myapp_dev.php**/articles/finance/2006/activity-breakdown.html

In production, the no_script_name is set to on, so the URLs show only the routing information and are more user-friendly. No technical information appears.

http://www.example.com/articles/finance/2006/activity-breakdown.html

But how does the application know which front controller script to call? This is where *URL rewriting* comes in. The web server can be configured to call a given script when there is none in the URL.

In Apache, this is possible once you have the mod_rewrite extension activated. Every symfony project comes with an .htaccess file, which adds mod_rewrite settings to your server configuration for the web/ directory. The default content of this file is shown in Listing 9-6.

Listing 9-6. *Default Rewriting Rules for Apache, in* myproject/web/.htaccess

```
<IfModule mod_rewrite.c>
  RewriteEngine On

  # we skip all files with .something
  RewriteCond %{REQUEST_URI} \..+$
  RewriteCond %{REQUEST_URI} !\.html$
  RewriteRule .* - [L]
```

```
# we check if the .html version is here (caching)
RewriteRule ^$ index.html [QSA]
RewriteRule ^([^.]+)$ $1.html [QSA]
RewriteCond %{REQUEST_FILENAME} !-f

# no, so we redirect to our front web controller
RewriteRule ^(.*)$ index.php [QSA,L]
</IfModule>
```

The web server inspects the shape of the URLs it receives. If the URL does not contain a suffix and if there is no cached version of the page available (Chapter 12 covers caching), then the request is handed to index.php.

However, the web/ directory of a symfony project is shared among all the applications and environments of the project. It means that there is usually more than one front controller in the web directory. For instance, a project having a frontend and a backend application, and a dev and prod environment, contains four front controller scripts in the web/ directory:

```
index.php          // frontend in prod
frontend_dev.php   // frontend in dev
backend.php        // backend in prod
backend_dev.php    // backend in dev
```

The mod_rewrite settings can specify only one default script name. If you set no_script_name to on for all the applications and environments, all URLs will be interpreted as requests to the frontend application in the prod environment. This is why *you can have only one application with one environment taking advantage of the URL rewriting* for a given project.

■**Tip** There is a way to have more than one application with no script name. Just create subdirectories in the web root, and move the front controllers inside them. Change the SF_ROOT_DIR constants definition accordingly, and create the .htaccess URL rewriting configuration that you need for each application.

Link Helpers

Because of the routing system, you should use link helpers instead of regular <a> tags in your templates. Don't look at it as a hassle, but rather as an opportunity to keep your application clean and easy to maintain. Besides, link helpers offer a few very useful shortcuts that you don't want to miss.

Hyperlinks, Buttons, and Forms

You already know about the link_to() helper. It outputs an XHTML-compliant hyperlink, and it expects two parameters: the element that can be clicked and the internal URI of the resource to which it points. If, instead of a hyperlink, you want a button, use the button_to() helper. Forms also have a helper to manage the value of the action attribute. You will learn more about forms in the next chapter. Listing 9-7 shows some examples of link helpers.

Listing 9-7. *Link Helpers for `<a>`, `<input>`, and `<form>` Tags*

```
// Hyperlink on a string
<?php echo link_to('my article', 'article/read?title=Finance_in_France') ?>
 => <a href="/routed/url/to/Finance_in_France">my article</a>

// Hyperlink on an image
<?php echo link_to(image_tag('read.gif'), 'article/read?title=Finance_in_France') ?>
 => <a href="/routed/url/to/Finance_in_France"><img src="/images/read.gif" /></a>

// Button tag
<?php echo button_to('my article', 'article/read?title=Finance_in_France') ?>
 => <input value="my article" type="button" ➥
    onclick="document.location.href='/routed/url/to/Finance_in_France';" />

// Form tag
<?php echo form_tag('article/read?title=Finance_in_France') ?>
 => <form method="post" action="/routed/url/to/Finance_in_France" />
```

Link helpers can accept internal URIs as well as absolute URLs (starting with `http://`, and skipped by the routing system) and anchors. Note that in real-world applications, internal URIs are built with dynamic parameters. Listing 9-8 shows examples of all these cases.

Listing 9-8. *URLs Accepted by Link Helpers*

```
// Internal URI
<?php echo link_to('my article', 'article/read?title=Finance_in_France') ?>
 => <a href="/routed/url/to/Finance_in_France">my article</a>

// Internal URI with dynamic parameters
<?php echo link_to('my article', 'article/read?title='.$article->getTitle()) ?>

// Internal URI with anchors
<?php echo link_to('my article', 'article/read?title=Finance_in_France#foo') ?>
 => <a href="/routed/url/to/Finance_in_France#foo">my article</a>

// Absolute URL
<?php echo link_to('my article', 'http://www.example.com/foobar.html') ?>
 => <a href="http://www.example.com/foobar.html">my article</a>
```

Link Helper Options

As explained in Chapter 7, helpers accept an additional options argument, which can be an associative array or a string. This is true for link helpers, too, as shown in Listing 9-9.

Listing 9-9. *Link Helpers Accept Additional Options*

```
// Additional options as an associative array
<?php echo link_to('my article', 'article/read?title=Finance_in_France', array(
  'class'  => 'foobar',
  'target' => '_blank'
)) ?>

// Additional options as a string (same result)
<?php echo link_to('my article', 'article/read?title=Finance_in_France', ➥
  'class=foobar target=_blank') ?>
 => <a href="/routed/url/to/Finance_in_France" class="foobar" target="_blank"> ➥
    my article</a>
```

You can also add one of the symfony-specific options for link helpers: confirm and popup. The first one displays a JavaScript confirmation dialog box when the link is clicked, and the second opens the link in a new window, as shown in Listing 9-10.

Listing 9-10. *'confirm' and 'popup' Options for Link Helpers*

```
<?php echo link_to('delete item', 'item/delete?id=123', 'confirm=Are you sure?') ?>
 => <a onclick="return confirm('Are you sure?');"
       href="/routed/url/to/delete/123.html">add to cart</a>

<?php echo link_to('add to cart', 'shoppingCart/add?id=100', 'popup=true') ?>
 => <a onclick="window.open(this.href);return false;"
       href="/fo_dev.php/shoppingCart/add/id/100.html">add to cart</a>

<?php echo link_to('add to cart', 'shoppingCart/add?id=100', array(
  'popup' => array('Window title', 'width=310,height=400,left=320,top=0')
)) ?>
 => <a onclick="window.open(this.href,'Window title', ➥
              'width=310,height=400,left=320,top=0');return false;"
       href="/fo_dev.php/shoppingCart/add/id/100.html">add to cart</a>
```

These options can be combined.

Fake GET and POST Options

Sometimes web developers use GET requests to actually do a POST. For instance, consider the following URL:

```
http://www.example.com/index.php/shopping_cart/add/id/100
```

This request will change the data contained in the application, by adding an item to a shopping cart object, stored in the session or in a database. This URL can be bookmarked, cached, and indexed by search engines. Imagine all the nasty things that might happen to the database or to the metrics of a website using this technique. As a matter of fact, this request should be considered as a POST, because search engine robots do not do POST requests on indexing.

Symfony provides a way to transform a call to a link_to() or button_to() helper into an actual POST. Just add a post=true option, as shown in Listing 9-11.

Listing 9-11. *Making a Link Call a POST Request*

```
<?php echo link_to('go to shopping cart', 'shoppingCart/add?id=100', 'post=true') ?>
 => <a onclick="f = document.createElement('form'); document.body.appendChild(f);
              f.method = 'POST'; f.action = this.href; f.submit();return false;"
      href="/shoppingCart/add/id/100.html">go to shopping cart</a>
```

This <a> tag has an href attribute, and browsers without JavaScript support, such as search engine robots, will follow the link doing the default GET. So you must also restrict your action to respond only to the POST method, by adding something like the following at the beginning of the action:

```
$this->forward404If($request->getMethod() != sfRequest::POST);
```

Just make sure you don't use this option on links located in forms, since it generates its own <form> tag.

It is a good habit to tag as POST the links that actually post data.

Forcing Request Parameters As GET Variables

According to your routing rules, variables passed as parameters to a link_to() are transformed into patterns. If no rule matches the internal URI in the routing.yml file, the default rule transforms module/action?key=value into /module/action/key/value, as shown in Listing 9-12.

Listing 9-12. *Default Routing Rule*

```
<?php echo link_to('my article', 'article/read?title=Finance_in_France') ?>
=> <a href="/article/read/title/Finance_in_France">my article</a>
```

If you actually need to keep the GET syntax—to have request parameters passed under the ?key=value form—you should put the variables that need to be forced outside the URL parameter, in the query_string option. All the link helpers accept this option, as demonstrated in Listing 9-13.

Listing 9-13. *Forcing GET Variables with the query_string Option*

```
<?php echo link_to('my article', 'article/read?title=Finance_in_France', array(
  'query_string' => 'title=Finance_in_France'
)) ?>
=> <a href="/article/read?title=Finance_in_France">my article</a>
```

A URL with request parameters appearing as GET variables can be interpreted by a script on the client side, and by the $_GET and $_REQUEST variables on the server side.

ASSET HELPERS

Chapter 7 introduced the asset helpers `image_tag()`, `stylesheet_tag()`, and `javascript_include_tag()`, which allow you to include an image, a style sheet, or a JavaScript file in the response. The paths to such assets are not processed by the routing system, because they link to resources that are actually located under the public web directory.

You don't need to mention a file extension for an asset. Symfony automatically adds `.png`, `.js`, or `.css` to an image, JavaScript, or style sheet helper call. Also, symfony will automatically look for those assets in the `web/images/`, `web/js/`, and `web/css/` directories. Of course, if you want to include a specific file format or a file from a specific location, just use the full file name or the full file path as an argument. And don't bother to specify an `alt` attribute if your media file has an explicit name, since symfony will determine it for you.

```php
<?php echo image_tag('test') ?>
<?php echo image_tag('test.gif') ?>
<?php echo image_tag('/my_images/test.gif') ?>
 => <img href="/images/test.png" alt="Test" />
    <img href="/images/test.gif" alt="Test" />
    <img href="/my_images/test.gif" alt="Test" />
```

To fix the size of an image, use the `size` attribute. It expects a width and a height in pixels, separated by an x.

```php
<?php echo image_tag('test', 'size=100x20')) ?>
 => <img href="/images/test.png" alt="Test" width="100" height="20"/>
```

If you want the asset inclusion to be done in the `<head>` section (for JavaScript files and style sheets), you should use the `use_stylesheet()` and `use_javascript()` helpers in your templates, instead of the `_tag()` versions in the layout. They add the asset to the response, and these assets are included before the `</head>` tag is sent to the browser.

Using Absolute Paths

The link and asset helpers generate relative paths by default. To force the output to absolute paths, set the `absolute` option to `true`, as shown in Listing 9-14. This technique is useful for inclusions of links in an e-mail message, RSS feed, or API response.

Listing 9-14. *Getting Absolute URLs Instead of Relative URLs*

```php
<?php echo url_for('article/read?title=Finance_in_France') ?>
 => '/routed/url/to/Finance_in_France'
<?php echo url_for('article/read?title=Finance_in_France', true) ?>
 => 'http://www.example.com/routed/url/to/Finance_in_France'
```

```
<?php echo link_to('finance', 'article/read?title=Finance_in_France') ?>
 => <a href="/routed/url/to/Finance_in_France">finance</a>
<?php echo link_to('finance', 'article/read?title=Finance_in_France', ➥
 'absolute=true') ?>
 => <a href=" http://www.example.com/routed/url/to/Finance_in_France">finance</a>

// The same goes for the asset helpers
<?php echo image_tag('test', 'absolute=true') ?>
<?php echo javascript_include_tag('myscript', 'absolute=true') ?>
```

THE MAIL HELPER

Nowadays, e-mail-harvesting robots prowl about the Web, and you can't display an e-mail address on a website without becoming a spam victim within days. This is why symfony provides a `mail_to()` helper.

The `mail_to()` helper takes two parameters: the actual e-mail address and the string that should be displayed. Additional options accept an `encode` parameter to output something pretty unreadable in HTML, which is understood by browsers but not by robots.

```
<?php echo mail_to('myaddress@mydomain.com', 'contact') ?>
 => <a href="mailto:myaddress@mydomain.com">contact</a>
<?php echo mail_to('myaddress@mydomain.com', 'contact', 'encode=true') ?>
 => <a href="&#109;&#x61;... &#111;&#x6d;">&#x63;&#x74;... e&#115;&#x73;</a>
```

Encoded e-mail messages are composed of characters transformed by a random decimal and hexadecimal entity encoder. This trick stops most of the address-harvesting spambots for now, but be aware that the harvesting techniques evolve rapidly.

Routing Configuration

The routing system does two things:

- It interprets the external URL of incoming requests and transforms it into an internal URI, to determine the module/action and the request parameters.

- It formats the internal URIs used in links into external URLs (provided that you use the link helpers).

The conversion is based on a set of *routing rules*. These rules are stored in a `routing.yml` configuration file located in the application `config/` directory. Listing 9-15 shows the default routing rules, bundled with every symfony project.

Listing 9-15. *The Default Routing Rules, in* `myapp/config/routing.yml`

```
# default rules
homepage:
  url:   /
  param: { module: default, action: index }

default_symfony:
  url:   /symfony/:action/*
  param: { module: default }

default_index:
  url:   /:module
  param: { action: index }

default:
  url:   /:module/:action/*
```

Rules and Patterns

Routing rules are bijective associations between an external URL and an internal URI. A typical rule is made up of the following:

- A unique *label*, which is there for legibility and speed, and can be used by the link helpers

- A *pattern* to be matched (`url` key)

- An array of *request parameter* values (`param` key)

Patterns can contain wildcards (represented by an asterisk, *) and named wildcards (starting with a colon, :). A match to a named wildcard becomes a request parameter value. For instance, the `default` rule defined in Listing 9-15 will match any URL like /foo/bar, and set the `module` parameter to `foo` and the `action` parameter to `bar`. And in the `default_symfony` rule, `symfony` is a keyword and `action` is named wildcard parameter.

The routing system parses the `routing.yml` file *from the top to the bottom* and stops at the first match. This is why you must add your own rules on top of the default ones. For instance, the URL /foo/123 matches both of the rules defined in Listing 9-16, but symfony first tests `my_rule:`, and as that rule matches, it doesn't even test the `default:` one. The request is handled by the `mymodule/myaction` action with `bar` set to 123 (and not by the foo/123 action).

Listing 9-16. *Rules Are Parsed Top to Bottom*

```
my_rule:
  url:   /foo/:bar
  param: { module: mymodule, action: myaction }

# default rules
default:
  url:   /:module/:action/*
```

Note When a new action is created, it does not imply that you must create a routing rule for it. If the default module/action pattern suits you, then forget about the `routing.yml` file. If, however, you want to customize the action's external URL, add a new rule above the default one.

Listing 9-17 shows the process of changing the external URL format for an `article/read` action.

Listing 9-17. *Changing the External URL Format for an article/read Action*

```
<?php echo url_for('my article', 'article/read?id=123) ?>
 => /article/read/id/123        // Default formatting

// To change it to /article/123, add a new rule at the beginning
// of your routing.yml
article_by_id:
  url:    /article/:id
  param: { module: article, action: read }
```

The problem is that the `article_by_id` rule in Listing 9-17 breaks the default routing for all the other actions of the `article` module. In fact, a URL like `article/delete` will match this rule instead of the `default` one, and call the `read` action with `id` set to `delete` instead of the `delete` action. To get around this difficulty, you must add a pattern constraint so that the `article_by_id` rule matches only URLs where the `id` wildcard is an integer.

Pattern Constraints

When a URL can match more than one rule, you must refine the rules by adding constraints, or requirements, to the pattern. A requirement is a set of regular expressions that must be matched by the wildcards for the rule to match.

For instance, to modify the `article_by_id` rule so that it matches only URLs where the `id` parameter is an integer, add a line to the rule, as shown in Listing 9-18.

Listing 9-18. *Adding a Requirement to a Routing Rule*

```
article_by_id:
  url:    /article/:id
  param: { module: article, action: read }
  requirements: { id: \d+ }
```

Now an `article/delete` URL can't match the `article_by_id` rule anymore, because the `'delete'` string doesn't satisfy the requirements. Therefore, the routing system will keep on looking for a match in the following rules and finally find the `default` rule.

PERMALINKS

A good security guideline for routing is to hide primary keys and replace them with significant strings as much as possible. What if you wanted to give access to articles from their title rather than from their ID? It would make external URLs look like this:

```
http://www.example.com/article/Finance_in_France
```

To that extent, you need to create a new permalink action, which will use a slug parameter instead of an id one, and add a new rule for it:

```
article_by_id:
  url:          /article/:id
  param:        { module: article, action: read }
  requirements: { id: \d+ }

article_by_slug:
  url:          /article/:slug
  param:        { module: article, action: permalink }
```

The permalink action needs to determine the requested article from its title, so your model must provide an appropriate method.

```
public function executePermalink()
{
  $article = ArticlePeer::retrieveBySlug($this->getRequestParameter('slug');
  $this->forward404Unless($article);  // Display 404 if no article matches slug
  $this->article = $article;          // Pass the object to the template
}
```

You also need to replace the links to the read action in your templates with links to the permalink one, to enable correct formatting of internal URIs.

```
// Replace
<?php echo link_to('my article', 'article/read?id='.$article->getId()) ?>

// With
<?php echo link_to('my article', 'article/permalink?slug='.$article ➥
->getSlug()) ?>
```

Thanks to the requirements line, an external URL like /article/Finance_in_France matches the article_by_slug rule, even though the article_by_id rule appears first.

Note that as articles will be retrieved by slug, you should add an index to the slug column in the Article model description to optimize database performance.

Setting Default Values

You can give named wildcards a default value to make a rule work, even if the parameter is not defined. Set default values in the param: array.

For instance, the article_by_id rule doesn't match if the id parameter is not set. You can force it, as shown in Listing 9-19.

Listing 9-19. *Setting a Default Value for a Wildcard*

```
article_by_id:
  url:          /article/:id
  param:        { module: article, action: read, id: 1 }
```

The default parameters don't need to be wildcards found in the pattern. In Listing 9-20, the display parameter takes the value true, even if it is not present in the URL.

Listing 9-20. *Setting a Default Value for a Request Parameter*

```
article_by_id:
  url:          /article/:id
  param:        { module: article, action: read, id: 1, display: true }
```

If you look carefully, you can see that article and read are also default values for module and action variables not found in the pattern.

■**Tip** You can define a default parameter for all the routing rules by defining the sf_routing_default configuration parameter. For instance, if you want all the rules to have a theme parameter set to default by default, add the line sfConfig::set('sf_routing_defaults', array('theme' => 'default')); to your application's config.php.

Speeding Up Routing by Using the Rule Name

The link helpers accept a *rule label* instead of a module/action pair if the rule label is preceded by an at sign (@), as shown in Listing 9-21.

Listing 9-21. *Using the Rule Label Instead of the Module/Action*

```
<?php echo link_to('my article', 'article/read?id='.$article->getId()) ?>

// can also be written as
<?php echo link_to('my article', '@article_by_id?id='.$article->getId()) ?>
```

There are pros and cons to this trick. The advantages are as follows:

- The formatting of internal URIs is done much faster, since symfony doesn't have to browse all the rules to find the one that matches the link. In a page with a great number of routed hyperlinks, the boost will be noticeable if you use rule labels instead of module/action pairs.

- Using the rule label helps to abstract the logic behind an action. If you decide to change an action name but keep the URL, a simple change in the `routing.yml` file will suffice. All of the `link_to()` calls will still work without further change.

- The logic of the call is more apparent with a rule name. Even if your modules and actions have explicit names, it is often better to call `@display_article_by_slug` than `article/display`.

On the other hand, a disadvantage is that adding new hyperlinks becomes less self-evident, since you always need to refer to the `routing.yml` file to find out which label is to be used for an action.

The best choice depends on the project. In the long run, it's up to you.

■Tip During your tests (in the `dev` environment), if you want to check which rule was matched for a given request in your browser, develop the "logs and msgs" section of the web debug toolbar and look for a line specifying "matched route *XXX*." You will find more information about the web debug mode in Chapter 16.

Adding an .html Extension

Compare these two URLs:

```
http://myapp.example.com/article/Finance_in_France
http://myapp.example.com/article/Finance_in_France.html
```

Even if it is the same page, users and (robots) may see it differently because of the URL. The second URL evokes a deep and well-organized web directory of static pages, which is exactly the kind of websites that search engines know how to index.

To add a suffix to every external URL generated by the routing system, change the `suffix` value in the application `settings.yml`, as shown in Listing 9-22.

Listing 9-22. *Setting a Suffix for All URLs, in* `myapp/config/settings.yml`

```
prod:
  .settings
    suffix:         .html
```

The default suffix is set to a period (`.`), which means that the routing system doesn't add a suffix unless you specify it.

It is sometimes necessary to specify a suffix for a unique routing rule. In that case, write the suffix directly in the related `url:` line of the `routing.yml` file, as shown in Listing 9-23. Then the global suffix will be ignored.

Listing 9-23. *Setting a Suffix for One URL, in myapp/config/routing.yml*

```
article_list:
  url:          /latest_articles
  param:        { module: article, action: list }

article_list_feed:
  url:          /latest_articles.rss
  param:        { module: article, action: list, type: feed }
```

Creating Rules Without routing.yml

As is true of most of the configuration files, the routing.yml is a solution to define routing rules, but not the only one. You can define rules in PHP, either in the application config.php file or in the front controller script, but before the call to dispatch(), because this method determines the action to execute according to the present routing rules. Defining rules in PHP authorizes you to create dynamic rules, depending on configuration or other parameters.

The object that handles the routing rules is the sfRouting singleton. It is available from every part of the code by requiring sfRouting::getInstance(). Its prependRoute() method adds a new rule on top of the existing ones defined in routing.yml. It expects four parameters, which are the same as the parameters needed to define a rule: a route label, a pattern, an associative array of default values, and another associative array for requirements. For instance, the routing.yml rule definition shown in Listing 9-18 is equivalent to the PHP code shown in Listing 9-24.

Listing 9-24. *Defining a Rule in PHP*

```
sfRouting::getInstance()->prependRoute(
  'article_by_id',                                // Route name
  '/article/:id',                                 // Route pattern
  array('module' => 'article', 'action' => 'read'), // Default values
  array('id' => '\d+'),                           // Requirements
);
```

The sfRouting singleton has other useful methods for handling routes by hand: clearRoutes(), hasRoutes(), getRoutesByName(), and so on. Refer to the API documentation (http://www.symfony-project.com/api/symfony.html) to learn more.

■Tip Once you start to fully understand the concepts presented in this book, you can increase your understanding of the framework by browsing the online API documentation or, even better, the symfony source. Not all the tweaks and parameters of symfony can be described in this book. The online documentation, however, is limitless.

Dealing with Routes in Actions

If you need to retrieve information about the current route—for instance, to prepare a future "back to page *xxx*" link—you should use the methods of the sfRouting object. The URIs returned by the getCurrentInternalUri() method can be used in a call to a link_to() helper, as shown in Listing 9-25.

Listing 9-25. *Using sfRouting to Get Information About the Current Route*

```
// If you require a URL like
http://myapp.example.com/article/21

// Use the following in article/read action
$uri = sfRouting::getInstance()->getCurrentInternalUri();
 => article/read?id=21

$uri = sfRouting::getInstance()->getCurrentInternalUri(true);
 => @article_by_id?id=21

$rule = sfRouting::getInstance()->getCurrentRouteName();
 => article_by_id

// If you just need the current module/action names,
// remember that they are actual request parameters
$module = $this->getRequestParameter('module');
$action = $this->getRequestParameter('action');
```

If you need to transform an internal URI into an external URL in an action—just as url_for() does in a template—use the genUrl() method of the sfController object, as shown in Listing 9-26.

Listing 9-26. *Using sfController to Transform an Internal URI*

```
$uri = 'article/read?id=21';

$url = $this->getController()->genUrl($uri);
 => /article/21

$url = $this->getController()->genUrl($uri);
 => http://myapp.example.com/article/21
```

Summary

Routing is a *two-way mechanism* designed to allow *formatting of external URLs* so that they are more user-friendly. *URL rewriting* is required to allow the omission of the front controller name in the URLs of *one* of the applications of each project. You must use *link helpers* each time you need to output a URL in a template if you want the routing system to work both ways. The routing.yml file configures the *rules* of the routing system and uses an *order of precedence* and *rule requirements*. The settings.yml file contains additional settings concerning the presence of the *front controller name* and a possible *suffix* in external URLs.

CHAPTER 10

■■■

Forms

When writing templates, much of a developer's time is devoted to forms. Despite this, forms are generally poorly designed. Since much attention is required to deal with default values, formatting, validation, repopulation, and form handling in general, some developers tend to skim over some important details in the process. Accordingly, symfony devotes special attention to this topic. This chapter describes the tools that automate many of these requirements while speeding up forms development:

- The *form helpers* provide a faster way to write form inputs in templates, especially for complex elements such as dates, drop-down lists, and rich text.

- When a form is devoted to editing the properties of an object, the templating can be further accelerated by using *object form helpers*.

- The *YAML validation files* facilitate form validation and repopulation.

- *Validators* package the code required to validate input. Symfony bundles validators for the most common needs, and it is very easy to add custom validators.

Form Helpers

In templates, HTML tags of form elements are very often mixed with PHP code. Form helpers in symfony aim to simplify this task and to avoid opening `<?php echo` tags repeatedly in the middle of `<input>` tags.

Main Form Tag

As explained in the previous chapter, you must use the `form_tag()` helper to create a form, since it transforms the action given as a parameter into a routed URL. The second argument can support additional options—for instance, to change the default `method`, change the default `enctype`, or specify other attributes. Listing 10-1 shows examples.

Listing 10-1. *The form_tag() Helper*

```
<?php echo form_tag('test/save') ?>
 => <form method="post" action="/path/to/save">
```

```
<?php echo form_tag('test/save', 'method=get multipart=true class=simpleForm') ?>
 => <form method="get" enctype="multipart/form-data" class="simpleForm" ➡
    action="/path/to/save">
```

As there is no need for a closing form helper, you should use the HTML </form> tag, even if it doesn't look good in your source code.

Standard Form Elements

With form helpers, each element in a form is given an id attribute deduced from its name attribute by default. This is not the only useful convention. See Listing 10-2 for a full list of standard form helpers and their options.

Listing 10-2. *Standard Form Helpers Syntax*

```
// Text field (input)
<?php echo input_tag('name', 'default value') ?>
 => <input type="text" name="name" id="name" value="default value" />

// All form helpers accept an additional options parameter
// It allows you to add custom attributes to the generated tag
<?php echo input_tag('name', 'default value', 'maxlength=20') ?>
 => <input type="text" name="name" id="name" value="default value" ➡
    maxlength="20" />

// Long text field (text area)
<?php echo textarea_tag('name', 'default content', 'size=10x20') ?>
 => <textarea name="name" id="name" cols="10" rows="20">
        default content
    </textarea>

// Check box
<?php echo checkbox_tag('single', 1, true) ?>
<?php echo checkbox_tag('driverslicense', 'B', false) ?>
 => <input type="checkbox" name="single" id="single" value="1" ➡
    checked="checked" />
    <input type="checkbox" name="driverslicense" id="driverslicense" ➡
    value="B" />

// Radio button
<?php echo radiobutton_tag('status[]', 'value1', true) ?>
<?php echo radiobutton_tag('status[]', 'value2', false) ?>
 => <input type="radio" name="status[]" id="status_value1" value="value1" ➡
    checked="checked" />
    <input type="radio" name="status[]" id="status_value2" value="value2" />

// Dropdown list (select)
<?php echo select_tag('payment',
  '<option selected="selected">Visa</option>
```

```
    <option>Eurocard</option>
    <option>Mastercard</option>')
?>
 => <select name="payment" id="payment">
      <option selected="selected">Visa</option>
      <option>Eurocard</option>
      <option>Mastercard</option>
    </select>

// List of options for a select tag
<?php echo options_for_select(array('Visa', 'Eurocard', 'Mastercard'), 0) ?>
 => <option value="0" selected="selected">Visa</option>
    <option value="1">Eurocard</option>
    <option value="2">Mastercard</option>

// Dropdown helper combined with a list of options
<?php echo select_tag('payment', options_for_select(array(
  'Visa',
  'Eurocard',
  'Mastercard'
), 0)) ?>
 => <select name="payment" id="payment">
      <option value="0" selected="selected">Visa</option>
      <option value="1">Eurocard</option>
      <option value="2">Mastercard</option>
    </select>

// To specify option names, use an associative array
<?php echo select_tag('name', options_for_select(array(
  'Steve'  => 'Steve',
  'Bob'    => 'Bob',
  'Albert' => 'Albert',
  'Ian'    => 'Ian',
  'Buck'   => 'Buck'
), 'Ian')) ?>
 => <select name="name" id="name">
      <option value="Steve">Steve</option>
      <option value="Bob">Bob</option>
      <option value="Albert">Albert</option>
      <option value="Ian" selected="selected">Ian</option>
      <option value="Buck">Buck</option>
    </select>

// Dropdown list with multiple selection (selected values can be an array)
<?php echo select_tag('payment', options_for_select(
  array('Visa' => 'Visa', 'Eurocard' => 'Eurocard', 'Mastercard' => 'Mastercard'),
  array('Visa', 'Mastecard'),
), array('multiple' => true))) ?>
```

```
=> <select name="payment[]" id="payment" multiple="multiple">
      <option value="Visa" selected="selected">Visa</option>
      <option value="Eurocard">Eurocard</option>
      <option value="Mastercard">Mastercard</option>
   </select>
// Drop-down list with multiple selection (selected values can be an array)
<?php echo select_tag('payment', options_for_select(
  array('Visa' => 'Visa', 'Eurocard' => 'Eurocard', 'Mastercard' => 'Mastercard'),
  array('Visa', 'Mastecard')
), 'multiple=multiple') ?>
 => <select name="payment" id="payment" multiple="multiple">
      <option value="Visa" selected="selected">
      <option value="Eurocard">Eurocard</option>
      <option value="Mastercard" selected="selected">Mastercard</option>
   </select>


// Upload file field
<?php echo input_file_tag('name') ?>
 => <input type="file" name="name" id="name" value="" />


// Password field
<?php echo input_password_tag('name', 'value') ?>
 => <input type="password" name="name" id="name" value="value" />


// Hidden field
<?php echo input_hidden_tag('name', 'value') ?>
 => <input type="hidden" name="name" id="name" value="value" />


// Submit button (as text)
<?php echo submit_tag('Save') ?>
 => <input type="submit" name="submit" value="Save" />


// Submit button (as image)
<?php echo submit_image_tag('submit_img') ?>
 => <input type="image" name="submit" src="/images/submit_img.png" />
```

The submit_image_tag() helper uses the same syntax and has the same advantages as the image_tag().

■Note For radio buttons, the id attribute is not set by default to the value of the name attribute, but to a combination of the name and the value. That's because you need to have several radio button tags with the same name to obtain the automated "deselecting the previous one when selecting another" feature, and the id=name convention would imply having several HTML tags with the same id attribute in your page, which is strictly forbidden.

HANDLING FORM SUBMISSION

How do you retrieve the data submitted by users through forms? It is available in the request parameters, so the action only needs to call `$this->getRequestParameter($elementName)` to get the value.

A good practice is to use the same action to display *and* handle the form. According to the request method (GET or POST), either the form template is called or the form is handled and the request is redirected to another action.

```php
// In mymodule/actions/actions.class.php
public function executeEditAuthor()
{
  if ($this->getRequest()->getMethod() != sfRequest::POST)
  {
    // Display the form
    return sfView::SUCCESS;
  }
  else
  {
    // Handle the form submission
    $name = $this->getRequestParameter('name');
    ...
    $this->redirect('mymodule/anotheraction');
  }
}
```

For this to work, the form target must be the same action as the one displaying it.

```php
// In mymodule/templates/editAuthorSuccess.php
<?php echo form_tag('mymodule/editAuthor') ?>
```

...

Symfony offers specialized form helpers to do asynchronous requests in the background. The next chapter, which focuses on Ajax, provides more details.

Date Input Widgets

Forms are often used to retrieve dates. Dates in the wrong format are the main reason for form-submission failures. The `input_date_tag()` helper can assist the user in entering a date with an interactive JavaScript calendar, if you set the `rich` option to `true`, as shown in Figure 10-1.

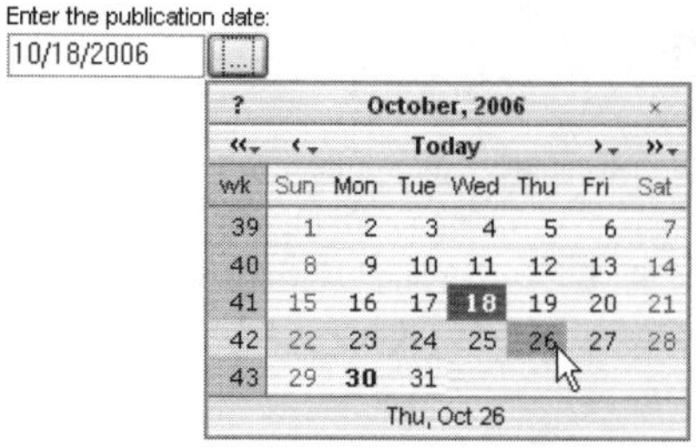

Enter the publication date:

Figure 10-1. *Rich date input tag*

If the rich option is omitted, the helper echoes three <select> tags populated with a range of months, days, and years. You can display these drop-downs separately by calling their helpers (select_day_tag(), select_month_tag(), and select_year_tag()). The default values of these elements are the current day, month, and year. Listing 10-3 shows the input date helpers.

Listing 10-3. *Input Date Helpers*

```
<?php echo input_date_tag('dateofbirth', '2005-05-03', 'rich=true') ?>
 => a text input tag together with a calendar widget

<?php echo select_day_tag('day', 1, 'include_custom=Choose a day') ?>
=> <select name="day" id="day">
      <option value="">Choose a day</option>
      <option value="1" selected="selected">01</option>
      <option value="2">02</option>
      ...
      <option value="31">31</option>
   </select>

<?php echo select_month_tag('month', 1, 'include_custom=Choose a month ➡
  use_short_month=true') ?>
=> <select name="month" id="month">
      <option value="">Choose a month</option>
      <option value="1" selected="selected">Jan</option>
      <option value="2">Feb</option>
      ...
      <option value="12">Dec</option>
   </select>

<?php echo select_year_tag('year', 2007, 'include_custom=Choose a year ➡
  year_end=2010') ?>
 => <select name="year" id="year">
      <option value="">Choose a year</option>
      <option value="2006">2006</option>
      <option value="2007" selected="selected">2007</option>
      ...
   </select>
```

The accepted date values for the `input_date_tag()` helper are the ones recognized by the `strtotime()` PHP function. Listing 10-4 shows which formats can be used, and Listing 10-5 shows the ones that must be avoided.

Listing 10-4. *Accepted Date Formats in Date Helpers*

```
// Work fine
<?php echo input_date_tag('test', '2006-04-01', 'rich=true') ?>
<?php echo input_date_tag('test', 1143884373, 'rich=true') ?>
<?php echo input_date_tag('test', 'now', 'rich=true') ?>
<?php echo input_date_tag('test', '23 October 2005', 'rich=true') ?>
<?php echo input_date_tag('test', 'next tuesday', 'rich=true') ?>
<?php echo input_date_tag('test', '1 week 2 days 4 hours 2 seconds', 'rich=true') ?>

// Return null
<?php echo input_date_tag('test', null, 'rich=true') ?>
<?php echo input_date_tag('test', '', 'rich=true') ?>
```

Listing 10-5. *Incorrect Date Formats in Date Helpers*

```
// Date zero = 01/01/1970
<?php echo input_date_tag('test', 0, 'rich=true') ?>

// Non-English date formats don't work
<?php echo input_date_tag('test', '01/04/2006', 'rich=true') ?>
```

Rich Text Editing

Rich text editing is also possible in a `<textarea>` tag, thanks to the integration of the TinyMCE and FCKEditor widgets. They provide a word-processor-like interface with buttons to format text as bold, italic, and other styles, as shown in Figure 10-2.

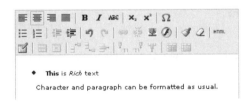

Figure 10-2. *Rich text editing*

Both widgets require manual installation. As the procedure is the same for the two widgets, only the TinyMCE rich text editing is described here. You need to download the editor from the project website (`http://tinymce.moxiecode.com/`) and unpack it in a temporary folder. Copy the `tinymce/jscripts/tiny_mce/` directory into your project `web/js/` directory, and define the path to the library in `settings.yml`, as shown in Listing 10-6.

Listing 10-6. *Setting Up the TinyMCE Library Path*

```
all:
  .settings:
    rich_text_js_dir:  js/tiny_mce
```

Once this is done, toggle the use of rich text editing in text areas by adding the `rich=true` option. You can also specify custom options for the JavaScript editor using the `tinymce_options` option. Listing 10-7 shows examples.

Listing 10-7. *Rich Text Area*

```
<?php echo textarea_tag('name', 'default content', 'rich=true size=10x20')) ?>
 => a rich text edit zone powered by TinyMCE
<?php echo textarea_tag('name', 'default content', 'rich=true size=10x20 ➥
  tinymce_options=language:"fr",theme_advanced_buttons2:"separator"')) ?>
=> a rich text edit zone powered by TinyMCE with custom parameters
```

Country and Language Selection

You may need to display a country selection field. But since country names are not the same in all languages, the options of a country drop-down list should vary according to the user culture (see Chapter 13 for more information about cultures). As shown in Listing 10-8, the `select_country_tag()` helper does it all for you: It internationalizes country names and uses the standard ISO country codes for values.

Listing 10-8. *Select Country Tag Helper*

```
<?php echo select_country_tag('country', 'AL') ?>
 => <select name="country" id="country">
      <option value="AF">Afghanistan</option>
      <option value="AL" selected="selected">Albania</option>
      <option value="DZ">Algeria</option>
      <option value="AS">American Samoa</option>
  ...
```

Similar to `select_country_tag()` helper, the `select_language_tag()` helper displays a list of languages, as shown in Listing 10-9.

Listing 10-9. *Select Language Tag Helper*

```
<?php echo select_language_tag('language', 'en') ?>
 => <select name="language" id="language">
      ...
      <option value="elx">Elamite</option>
      <option value="en" selected="selected">English</option>
      <option value="enm">English, Middle (1100-1500)</option>
      <option value="ang">English, Old (ca.450-1100)</option>
```

```
<option value="myv">Erzya</option>
<option value="eo">Esperanto</option>
...
```

Form Helpers for Objects

When form elements are used to edit the properties of an object, standard link helpers can become tedious to write. For instance, to edit the `telephone` attribute of a `Customer` object, you would write this:

```
<?php echo input_tag('telephone', $customer->getTelephone()) ?>
=> <input type="text" name="telephone" id="telephone" value="0123456789" />
```

To avoid repeating the attribute name, symfony provides an alternative *object form helper* for each form helper. An object form helper deduces the name and the default value of a form element from an object and a method name. The previous `input_tag()` is equivalent to this:

```
<?php echo object_input_tag($customer, 'getTelephone') ?>
=> <input type="text" name="telephone" id="telephone" value="0123456789" />
```

The economy might not look crucial for the `object_input_tag()`. However, every standard form helper has a corresponding object form helper, and they all share the same syntax. It makes generation of forms quite straightforward. That's why the object form helpers are used extensively in the scaffolding and generated administrations (see Chapter 14). Listing 10-10 lists the object form helpers.

Listing 10-10. *Object Form Helpers Syntax*

```
<?php echo object_input_tag($object, $method, $options) ?>
<?php echo object_input_date_tag($object, $method, $options) ?>
<?php echo object_input_hidden_tag($object, $method, $options) ?>
<?php echo object_textarea_tag($object, $method, $options) ?>
<?php echo object_checkbox_tag($object, $method, $options) ?>
<?php echo object_select_tag($object, $method, $options) ?>
<?php echo object_select_country_tag($object, $method, $options) ?>
<?php echo object_select_language_tag($object, $method, $options) ?>
```

There is no `object_password_tag()` helper, since it is a bad practice to give a default value to a password tag, based on something the user has previously entered.

■**Caution** Unlike the regular form helpers, the object form helpers are available only if you declare explicitly the use of the `Object` helper group in your template with `use_helper('Object')`.

The most interesting of all object form helpers are `objects_for_select()` and `object_select_tag()`, which concern drop-down lists.

Populating Drop-Down Lists with Objects

The options_for_select() helper, described previously with the other standard helpers, transforms a PHP associative array into an options list, as shown in Listing 10-11.

Listing 10-11. *Creating a List of Options Based on an Array with options_for_select()*

```
<?php echo options_for_select(array(
  '1' => 'Steve',
  '2' => 'Bob',
  '3' => 'Albert',
  '4' => 'Ian',
  '5' => 'Buck'
), 4) ?>
 => <option value="1">Steve</option>
    <option value="2">Bob</option>
    <option value="3">Albert</option>
    <option value="4" selected="selected">Ian</option>
    <option value="5">Buck</option>
```

Suppose that you already have an array of objects of class Author, resulting from a Propel query. If you want to build a list of options based on this array, you will need to loop on it to retrieve the id and the name of each object, as shown in Listing 10-12.

Listing 10-12. *Creating a List of Options Based on an Array of Objects with options_for_select()*

```
// In the action
$options = array();
foreach ($authors as $author)
{
  $options[$author->getId()] = $author->getName();
}
$this->options = $options;

// In the template
<?php echo options_for_select($options, 4) ?>
```

This kind of processing happens so often that symfony has a helper to automate it: objects_for_select(), which creates an option list based directly on an array of objects. The helper needs two additional parameters: the method names used to retrieve the value and the text contents of the <option> tags to be generated. So Listing 10-12 is equivalent to this simpler form:

```
<?php echo objects_for_select($authors, 'getId', 'getName', 4) ?>
```

That's smart and fast, but symfony goes even further, when you deal with foreign key columns.

Creating a Drop-Down List Based on a Foreign Key Column

The values a foreign key column can take are the primary key values of the foreign table records. If, for instance, the `article` table has an `author_id` column that is a foreign key to an `author` table, the possible values for this column are the `id` of all the records of the `author` table. Basically, a drop-down list to edit the author of an article would look like Listing 10-13.

Listing 10-13. *Creating a List of Options Based on a Foreign Key with* `objects_for_select()`

```
<?php echo select_tag('author_id', objects_for_select(
  AuthorPeer::doSelect(new Criteria()),
  'getId',
  '__toString()',
  $article->getAuthorId()
)) ?>
=> <select name="author_id" id="author_id">
     <option value="1">Steve</option>
     <option value="2">Bob</option>
     <option value="3">Albert</option>
     <option value="4" selected="selected">Ian</option>
     <option value="5">Buck</option>
   </select>
```

The `object_select_tag()` does all that by itself. It displays a drop-down list populated with the name of the possible records of the foreign table. The helper can guess the foreign table and foreign column from the schema, so its syntax is very concise. Listing 10-13 is equivalent to this:

```
<?php echo object_select_tag($article, 'getAuthorId') ?>
```

The `object_select_tag()` helper guesses the related peer class name (`AuthorPeer` in the example) based on the method name passed as a parameter. However, you can specify your own class by setting the `related_class` option in the third argument. The text content of the `<option>` tags is the record name, which is the result of the `__toString()` method of the object class (if `$author->__toString()` method is undefined, the primary key is used instead). In addition, the list of options is built from a `doSelect()` method with an empty criteria value; it returns all the records ordered by creation date. If you prefer to display only a subset of records with a specific ordering, create a method in the peer class returning this selection as an array of objects, and set it in the `peer_method` option. Lastly, you can add a blank option or a custom option at the top of the drop-down list by setting the `include_blank` and `include_custom` options. Listing 10-14 demonstrates these different options for the `object_select_tag()` helper.

Listing 10-14. *Options of the* `object_select_tag()` *Helper*

```
// Base syntax
<?php echo object_select_tag($article, 'getAuthorId') ?>
// Builds the list from AuthorPeer::doSelect(new Criteria())
```

```
// Change the peer class used to retrieve the possible values
<?php echo object_select_tag($article, 'getAuthorId', 'related_class=Foobar') ?>
// Builds the list from FoobarPeer::doSelect(new Criteria())

// Change the peer method used to retrieve the possible values
<?php echo object_select_tag($article, 'getAuthorId', ➡
  'peer_method=getMostFamousAuthors') ?>
// Builds the list from AuthorPeer::getMostFamousAuthors(new Criteria())

// Add an <option value=""> </option> at the top of the list
<?php echo object_select_tag($article, 'getAuthorId', 'include_blank=true') ?>

// Add an <option value="">Choose an author</option> at the top of the list
<?php echo object_select_tag($article, 'getAuthorId',
  'include_custom=Choose an author') ?>
```

Updating Objects

A form completely dedicated to editing object properties by using object helpers is easier to
handle in an action. For instance, if you have an object of class Author with name, age, and
address attributes, the form can be coded as shown in Listing 10-15.

Listing 10-15. *A Form with Only Object Helpers*

```
<?php echo form_tag('author/update') ?>
  <?php echo object_input_hidden_tag($author, 'getId') ?>
  Name: <?php echo object_input_tag($author, 'getName') ?><br />
  Age:  <?php echo object_input_tag($author, 'getAge') ?><br />
  Address: <br />
        <?php echo object_textarea_tag($author, 'getAddress') ?>
</form>
```

The update action of the author module, called when the form is submitted, can simply
update the object with the fromArray() modifier generated by Propel, as shown in Listing 10-16.

Listing 10-16. *Handling a Form Submission Based on Object Form Helpers*

```
public function executeUpdate ()
{
  $author = AuthorPeer::retrieveByPk($this->getRequestParameter('id'));
  $this->forward404Unless($author);

  $author->fromArray($this->getRequest()->getParameterHolder()->getAll(), ➡
    AuthorPeer::TYPE_FIELDNAME);
  $author->save();

  return $this->redirect('/author/show?id='.$author->getId());
}
```

Form Validation

Chapter 6 explained how to use the validate*XXX*() methods in the action class to validate the request parameters. However, if you use this technique to validate a form submission, you will end up rewriting the same portion of code over and over. Symfony provides an alternative form-validation technique, relying on only a YAML file, instead of PHP code in the action class.

To demonstrate the form-validation features, let's first consider the sample form shown in Listing 10-17. It is a classic contact form, with name, email, age, and message fields.

Listing 10-17. *Sample Contact Form, in* `modules/contact/templates/indexSuccess.php`

```
<?php echo form_tag('contact/send') ?>
  Name:    <?php echo input_tag('name') ?><br />
  Email:   <?php echo input_tag('email') ?><br />
  Age:     <?php echo input_tag('age') ?><br />
  Message: <?php echo textarea_tag('message') ?><br />
  <?php echo submit_tag() ?>
</form>
```

The principle of form validation is that if a user enters invalid data and submits the form, the next page should show an error message. Let's define what valid data should be for the sample form, in plain English:

- The name field is required. It must be a text entry between 2 and 100 characters.

- The email field is required. It must be a text entry between 2 and 100 characters, and it must be a valid e-mail address.

- The age field is required. It must be an integer between 0 and 120.

- The message field is required.

You could define more complex validation rules for the contact form, but these are just fine for a demonstration of the validation possibilities.

■**Note** Form validation can occur on the server side and/or on the client side. The server-side validation is compulsory to avoid corrupting a database with wrong data. The client-side validation is optional, though it greatly enhances the user experience. The client-side validation is to be done with custom JavaScript.

Validators

You can see that the name and email fields in the example share common validation rules. Some validation rules appear so often in web forms that symfony packages the PHP code that implements them into *validators*. A validator is simple class that provides an execute() method. This method expects the value of a field as parameter, and returns true if the value is valid and false otherwise.

Symfony ships with several validators (described in the "Standard Symfony Validators" section later in this chapter), but let's focus on the sfStringValidator for now. This validator checks that an input is a string, and that its size is between two specified character amounts (defined when calling the initialize() method). That's exactly what is required to validate the name field. Listing 10-18 shows how to use this validator in a validation method.

Listing 10-18. *Validating Request Parameters with Reusable Validators, in* modules/contact/action/actions.class.php

```php
public function validateSend()
{
  $name = $this->getRequestParameter('name');

  // The name field is required
  if (!$name)
  {
    $this->getRequest()->setError('name', 'The name field cannot be left blank');

    return false;
  }

  // The name field must be a text entry between 2 and 100 characters
  $myValidator = new sfStringValidator();
  $myValidator->initialize($this->getContext(), array(
    'min'       => 2,
    'min_error' => 'This name is too short (2 characters minimum)',
    'max'       => 100,
    'max_error' => 'This name is too long. (100 characters maximum)',
  ));
  if (!$myValidator->execute($name))
  {
    return false;
  }

  return true;
}
```

If a user submits the form in Listing 10-17 with the value a in the name field, the execute() method of the sfStringValidator will return false (because the string length is less than the minimum of two characters). The validateSend() method will then fail, and the handleErrorSend() method will be called instead of the executeSend() method.

■**Tip** The setError() method of the sfRequest method gives information to the template so that it can display an error message (as explained in the "Displaying the Error Messages in the Form" section later in this chapter). The validators set the errors internally, so you can define different errors for the different cases of nonvalidation. That's the purpose of the min_error and max_error initialization parameters of the sfStringValidator.

All the rules defined in the example can be translated into validators:

- name: sfStringValidator (min=2, max=100)

- email: sfStringValidator (min=2, max=100) and sfEmailValidator

- age: sfNumberValidator (min=0, max=120)

The fact that a field is required is not handled by a validator.

Validation File

You could easily implement the validation of the contact form with validators in the validateSend() method PHP, but that would imply repeating a lot of code. Symfony offers an alternative way to define validation rules for a form, and it involves YAML. For instance, Listing 10-19 shows the translation of the name field validation rules, and its results are equivalent to those of Listing 10-18.

Listing 10-19. *Validation File, in modules/contact/validate/send.yml*

```
fields:
  name:
    required:
      msg:       The name field cannot be left blank
    sfStringValidator:
      min:       2
      min_error: This name is too short (2 characters minimum)
      max:       100
      max_error: This name is too long. (100 characters maximum)
```

In a validation file, the fields header lists the fields that need to be validated, if they are required, and the validators that should be tested on them when a value is present. The parameters of each validator are the same as those you would use to initialize the validator manually. A field can be validated by as many validators as necessary.

> **■Note** The validation process doesn't stop when a validator fails. Symfony tests all the validators and declares the validation failed if at least one of them fails. And even if some of the rules of the validation file fail, symfony will still look for a `validateXXX()` method and execute it. So the two validation techniques are complementary. The advantage is that, in a form with multiple failures, all the error messages are shown.

Validation files are located in the module `validate/` directory, and named by the action they must validate. For example, Listing 10-19 must be stored in a file called `validate/send.yml`.

Redisplaying the Form

By default, symfony looks for a `handleErrorSend()` method in the action class whenever the validation process fails, or displays the `sendError.php` template if the method doesn't exist.

The usual way to inform the user of a failed validation is to display the form again with an error message. To that purpose, you need to override the `handleErrorSend()` method and end it with a redirection to the action that displays the form (in the example, `module/index`), as shown in Listing 10-20.

Listing 10-20. *Displaying the Form Again, in modules/contact/actions/actions.class.php*

```
class ContactActions extends sfActions
{
  public function executeIndex()
  {
    // Display the form
  }

  public function handleErrorSend()
  {
    $this->forward('contact', 'index');
  }

  public function executeSend()
  {
    // Handle the form submission
  }
}
```

If you choose to use the same action to display the form and handle the form submission, then the `handleErrorSend()` method can simply return `sfView::SUCCESS` to redisplay the form from `sendSuccess.php`, as shown in Listing 10-21.

Listing 10-21. *A Single Action to Display and Handle the Form, in* modules/contact/actions/
actions.class.php

```
class ContactActions extends sfActions
{
  public function executeSend()
  {
    if ($this->getRequest()->getMethod() != sfRequest::POST)
    {
      // Prepare data for the template

      // Display the form
      return sfView::SUCCESS;
    }
    else
    {
      // Handle the form submission

      ...

      $this->redirect('mymodule/anotheraction');
    }
  }
  public function handleErrorSend()
  {
    // Prepare data for the template

    // Display the form
    return sfView::SUCCESS;
  }
}
```

The logic necessary to prepare the data can be refactored into a protected method of the
action class, to avoid repeating it in the executeSend() and handleErrorSend() methods.

With this new configuration, when the user types an invalid name, the form is displayed
again, but the entered data is lost and no error message explains the reason of the failure. To
address the last issue, you must modify the template that displays the form, to insert error
messages close to the faulty field.

Displaying the Error Messages in the Form

The error messages defined as validator parameters are added to the request when a field fails
validation (just as you can add an error manually with the setError() method, as in Listing 10-18).
The sfRequest object provides two useful methods to retrieve the error message: hasError()
and getError(), which each expect a field name as parameter. In addition, you can display an
alert at the top of the form to draw attention to the fact that one or many of the fields contain
invalid data with the hasErrors() method. Listings 10-22 and 10-23 demonstrate how to use
these methods.

Listing 10-22. *Displaying Error Messages at the Top of the Form, in* `templates/indexSuccess.php`

```php
<?php if ($sf_request->hasErrors()): ?>
  <p>The data you entered seems to be incorrect.
  Please correct the following errors and resubmit:</p>
  <ul>
  <?php foreach($sf_request->getErrors() as $name => $error): ?>
    <li><?php echo $name ?>: <?php echo $error ?></li>
  <?php endforeach; ?>
  </ul>
<?php endif; ?>
```

Listing 10-23. *Displaying Error Messages Inside the Form, in* `templates/indexSuccess.php`

```php
<?php echo form_tag('contact/send') ?>
  <?php if ($sf_request->hasError('name')): ?>
    <?php echo $sf_request->getError('name') ?> <br />
  <?php endif; ?>
  Name:    <?php echo input_tag('name') ?><br />
  ...
  <?php echo submit_tag() ?>
</form>
```

The conditional use of the getError() method in Listing 10-23 is a bit long to write. That's why symfony offers a form_error() helper to replace it, provided that you declare the use of its helper group, Validation. Listing 10-24 replaces Listing 10-23 by using this helper.

Listing 10-24. *Displaying Error Messages Inside the Form, the Short Way*

```php
<?php use_helper('Validation') ?>
<?php echo form_tag('contact/send') ?>

           <?php echo form_error('name') ?><br />
  Name:    <?php echo input_tag('name') ?><br />
  ...
  <?php echo submit_tag() ?>
</form>
```

The form_error() helper adds a special character before and after each error message to make the messages more visible. By default, the character is an arrow pointing down (corresponding to the ↓ entity), but you can change it in the settings.yml file:

```yaml
all:
  .settings:
    validation_error_prefix:    ' &darr; '
    validation_error_suffix:    '  &darr;'
```

In case of failed validation, the form now displays errors correctly, but the data entered by the user is lost. You need to repopulate the form to make it really user-friendly.

Repopulating the Form

As the error handling is done through the forward() method (shown in Listing 10-20), the original request is still accessible, and the data entered by the user is in the request parameters. So you could repopulate the form by adding default values to each field, as shown in Listing 10-25.

Listing 10-25. *Setting Default Values to Repopulate the Form When Validation Fails, in* templates/indexSuccess.php

```
<?php use_helper('Validation') ?>
<?php echo form_tag('contact/send') ?>
          <?php echo form_error('name') ?><br />
  Name:   <?php echo input_tag('name', $sf_params->get('name')) ?><br />
          <?php echo form_error('email') ?><br />
  Email:  <?php echo input_tag('email', $sf_params->get('email')) ?><br />
          <?php echo form_error('age') ?><br />
  Age:    <?php echo input_tag('age', $sf_params->get('age')) ?><br />
          <?php echo form_error('message') ?><br />
  Message: <?php echo textarea_tag('message', $sf_params->get('message')) ?><br />
  <?php echo submit_tag() ?>
</form>
```

But once again, this is quite tedious to write. Symfony provides an alternative way of triggering repopulation for all the fields of a form, directly in the YAML validation file, without changing the default values of the elements. Just enable the fillin: feature for the form, with the syntax described in Listing 10-26.

Listing 10-26. *Activating* fillin *to Repopulate the Form When Validation Fails, in* validate/send.yml

```
fillin:
  enabled: true  # Enable the form repopulation
  param:
    name: test  # Form name, not needed if there is only one form in the page
    skip_fields:  [email] # Do not repopulate these fields
    exclude_types: [hidden, password] # Do not repopulate these field types
    check_types:  [text, checkbox, radio, password, hidden] # Do repopulate these
```

By default, the automatic repopulation works for text inputs, check boxes, radio buttons, text areas, and select components (simple and multiple), but it does not repopulate password or hidden tags. The fillin feature doesn't work for file tags.

■**Note** The fillin feature works by parsing the response content in XML just before sending it to the user. If the response is not a valid XHTML document, fillin might not work.

You might want to transform the values entered by the user before writing them back in a form input. Escaping, URL rewriting, transformation of special characters into entities, and all the other transformations that can be called through a function can be applied to the fields of your form if you define the transformation under the converters: key, as shown in Listing 10-27.

Listing 10-27. *Converting Input Before fillin, in validate/send.yml*

```
fillin:
  enabled: true
  param:
    name: test
    converters:          # Converters to apply
      htmlentities:      [first_name, comments]
      htmlspecialchars: [comments]
```

Standard Symfony Validators

Symfony contains some standard validators that can be used for your forms:

- sfStringValidator

- sfNumberValidator

- sfEmailValidator

- sfUrlValidator

- sfRegexValidator

- sfCompareValidator

- sfPropelUniqueValidator

- sfFileValidator

- sfCallbackValidator

Each has a default set of parameters and error messages, but you can easily override them through the initialize() validator method or in the YAML file. The following sections describe the validators and show usage examples.

String Validator

sfStringValidator allows you to apply string-related constraints to a parameter.

```
sfStringValidator:
  values:       [foo, bar]
  values_error: The only accepted values are foo and bar
  insensitive:  false # If true, comparison with values is case insensitive
  min:          2
  min_error:    Please enter at least 2 characters
  max:          100
  max_error:    Please enter less than 100 characters
```

Number Validator

sfNumberValidator verifies if a parameter is a number and allows you to apply size constraints.

```
sfNumberValidator:
  nan_error:   Please enter an integer
  min:         0
  min_error:   The value must be more than zero
  max:         100
  max_error:   The value must be less than 100
```

E-Mail Validator

sfEmailValidator verifies if a parameter contains a value that qualifies as an e-mail address.

```
sfEmailValidator:
  strict:      true
  email_error: This email address is invalid
```

RFC822 defines the format of e-mail addresses. However, it is more permissive than the generally accepted format. For instance, me@localhost is a valid e-mail address according to the RFC, but you probably don't want to accept it. When the strict parameter is set to true (its default value), only e-mail addresses matching the pattern name@domain.extension are valid. When set to false, RFC822 is used as a rule.

URL Validator

sfUrlValidator checks if a field is a correct URL.

```
sfUrlValidator:
  url_error:   This URL is invalid
```

Regular Expression Validator

sfRegexValidator allows you to match a value against a Perl-compatible regular expression pattern.

```
sfRegexValidator:
  match:       No
  match_error: Posts containing more than one URL are considered as spam
  pattern:     /http.*http/si
```

The match parameter determines if the request parameter must match the pattern to be valid (value Yes) or match the pattern to be invalid (value No).

Compare Validator

sfCompareValidator checks the equality of two different request parameters. It is very useful for password checks.

```
fields:
  password1:
    required:
      msg:       Please enter a password
  password2:
    required:
      msg:       Please retype the password
    sfCompareValidator:
      check:    password1
      compare_error: The two passwords do not match
```

The check parameter contains the name of the field that the current field must match to be valid.

Propel Unique Validator

sfPropelUniqueValidator validates that the value of a request parameter doesn't already exist in your database. It is very useful for unique indexes.

```
fields:
  nickname:
    sfPropelUniqueValidator:
      class:      User
      column:     login
      unique_error: This login already exists. Please choose another one.
```

In this example, the validator will look in the database for a record of class User where the login column has the same value as the field to validate.

File Validator

sfFileValidator applies format (an array of mime-types) and size constraints to file upload fields.

```
fields:
  image:
    required:
      msg:       Please upload an image file
    file:        True
    sfFileValidator:
      mime_types:
        - 'image/jpeg'
        - 'image/png'
        - 'image/x-png'
        - 'image/pjpeg'
      mime_types_error: Only PNG and JPEG images are allowed
      max_size:        512000
      max_size_error:  Max size is 512Kb
```

Be aware that the file attribute must be set to True for the field, and the template must declare the form as multipart.

Callback Validator

sfCallbackValidator delegates the validation to a third-party callable method or function to do the validation. The callable method or function must return true or false.

```
fields:
  account_number:
    sfCallbackValidator:
      callback:      is_integer
      invalid_error: Please enter a number.
  credit_card_number:
    sfCallbackValidator:
      callback:      [myTools, validateCreditCard]
      invalid_error: Please enter a valid credit card number.
```

The callback method or function receives the value to be validated as a first parameter. This is very useful when you want to reuse existing methods of functions, rather than create a full validator class.

■**Tip** You can also write your own validators, as described in the "Creating a Custom Validator" section later in this chapter.

Named Validators

If you see that you need to repeat a validator class and its settings, you can package it under a *named validator*. In the example of the contact form, the email field needs the same sfStringValidator parameters as the name field. So you can create a myStringValidator named validator to avoid repeating the same settings twice. To do so, add a myStringValidator label under the validators: header, and set the class and param keys with the details of the named validator you want to package. You can then use the named validator just like a regular one in the fields section, as shown in Listing 10-28.

Listing 10-28. *Reusing Named Validators in a Validation File, in validate/send.yml*

```
validators:
  myStringValidator:
    class: sfStringValidator
    param:
      min:       2
      min_error: This field is too short (2 characters minimum)
      max:       100
      max_error: This field is too long (100 characters maximum)
```

```
fields:
  name:
    required:
      msg:        The name field cannot be left blank
    myStringValidator:
  email:
    required:
      msg:        The email field cannot be left blank
    myStringValidator:
    sfEmailValidator:
      email_error:  This email address is invalid
```

Restricting the Validation to a Method

By default, the validators set in a validation file are run when the action is called with the POST method. You can override this setting globally or field by field by specifying another value in the methods key, to allow a different validation for different methods, as shown in Listing 10-29.

Listing 10-29. *Defining When to Test a Field, in* validate/send.yml

```
methods:        [post]     # This is the default setting

fields:
  name:
    required:
      msg:        The name field cannot be left blank
    myStringValidator:
  email:
    methods:      [post, get] # Overrides the global methods settings
    required:
      msg:        The email field cannot be left blank
    myStringValidator:
    sfEmailValidator:
      email_error:  This email address is invalid
```

What Does a Validation File Look Like?

So far, you have seen only bits and pieces of a validation file. When you put everything together, the validation rules find a clear translation in YAML. Listing 10-30 shows the complete validation file for the sample contact form, corresponding to all the rules defined earlier in the chapter.

Listing 10-30. *Sample Complete Validation File*

```
fillin:
  enabled:      true
```

```
validators:
  myStringValidator:
    class: sfStringValidator
    param:
      min:        2
      min_error: This field is too short (2 characters minimum)
      max:        100
      max_error: This field is too long (100 characters maximum)

fields:
  name:
    required:
      msg:        The name field cannot be left blank
    myStringValidator:
  email:
    required:
      msg:        The email field cannot be left blank
    myStringValidator:
    sfEmailValidator:
      email_error:  This email address is invalid
  age:
    sfNumberValidator
      nan_error:    Please enter an integer
      min:          0
      min_error:    "You're not even born. How do you want to send a message?"
      max:          120
      max_error:    "Hey, grandma, aren't you too old to surf on the Internet?"
  message:
    required:
      msg:        The message field cannot be left blank
```

Complex Validation

The validation file satisfies most needs, but when the validation is very complex, it might not be sufficient. In this case, you can still return to the validate*XXX*() method in the action, or find the solution to your problem in the following sections.

Creating a Custom Validator

Each validator is a class that extends the sfValidator class. If the validator classes shipped with symfony are not suitable for your needs, you can easily create a new one, in any of the lib/ directories where it can be autoloaded. The syntax is quite simple: The execute() method of the validator is called when the validator is executed. You can also define default settings in the initialize() method.

The execute() method receives the value to validate as the first parameter and the error message to throw as the second parameter. Both are passed as references, so you can modify the error message from within the method.

The `initialize()` method receives the context singleton and the array of parameters from the YAML file. It must first call the `initialize()` method of its parent `sfValidator` class, and then set the default values.

Every validator has a parameter holder accessible by `$this->getParameterHolder()`.

For instance, if you want to build an `sfSpamValidator` to check if a string is not spam, add the code shown in Listing 10-31 to an `sfSpamValidator.class.php` file. It checks if the `$value` contains more than `max_url` times the string `'http'`.

Listing 10-31. *Creating a Custom Validator, in* `lib/sfSpamValidator.class.php`

```php
class sfSpamValidator extends sfValidator
{
  public function execute (&$value, &$error)
  {
    // For max_url=2, the regexp is /http.*http/is
    $re = '/'.implode('.*', array_fill(0, $this ➡
        ->getParameter('max_url') + 1, 'http')).'/is';

    if (preg_match($re, $value))
    {
      $error = $this->getParameter('spam_error');

      return false;
    }

    return true;
  }

  public function initialize ($context, $parameters = null)
  {
    // Initialize parent
    parent::initialize($context);

    // Set default parameters value
    $this->setParameter('max_url', 2);
    $this->setParameter('spam_error', 'This is spam');

    // Set parameters
    $this->getParameterHolder()->add($parameters);

    return true;
  }
}
```

As soon as the validator is added to an autoloadable directory (and the cache cleared), you can use it in your validation files, as shown in Listing 10-32.

Listing 10-32. *Using a Custom Validator, in* `validate/send.yml`

```
fields:
  message:
    required:
      msg:            The message field cannot be left blank
    sfSpamValidator:
      max_url:        3
      spam_error:     Leave this site immediately, you filthy spammer!
```

Using Array Syntax for Form Fields

PHP allows you to use an array syntax for the form fields. When writing your own forms, or when using the ones generated by the Propel administration (see Chapter 14), you may end up with HTML code that looks like Listing 10-33.

Listing 10-33. *Form with Array Syntax*

```
<label for="story[title]">Title:</label>
<input type="text" name="story[title]" id="story[title]" value="default value"
    size="45" />
```

Using the input name as is (with brackets) in a validation file will throw a parsed-induced error. The solution here is to replace square brackets [ ] with curly brackets { } in the `fields` section, as shown in Listing 10-34, and symfony will take care of the conversion of the names sent to the validators afterwards.

Listing 10-34. *Validation File for a Form with Array Syntax*

```
fields:
  story{title}:
    required:    Yes
```

Executing a Validator on an Empty Field

You may need to execute a validator on a field that is not required, on an empty value. For instance, this happens with a form where the user can (but may not) want to change his password, and in this case, a confirmation password must be entered. See the example in Listing 10-35.

Listing 10-35. *Sample Validation File for a Form with Two Password Fields*

```
fields:
  password1:
  password2:
    sfCompareValidator:
      check:          password1
      compare_error: The two passwords do not match
```

The validation process executes as follows:

- If password1 == null and password2 == null:
  - The required test passes.
  - Validators are not run.
  - The form is valid.
- If password2 == null while password1 is not null:
  - The required test passes.
  - Validators are not run.
  - The form is valid.

You may want to execute your password2 validator *if* password1 is not null. Fortunately, the symfony validators handle this case, thanks to the group parameter. When a field is in a group, its validator will execute if it is not empty and if one of the fields of the same group is not empty.

So, if you change the configuration to that shown in Listing 10-36, the validation process behaves correctly.

Listing 10-36. *Sample Validation File for a Form with Two Password Fields and a Group*

```
fields:c
  password1:
    group:          password_group
  password2:
    group:          password_group
    sfCompareValidator:
      check:        password1
      compare_error: The two passwords do not match
```

The validation process now executes as follows:

- If password1 == null and password2 == null:
  - The required test passes.
  - Validators are not run.
  - The form is valid.
- If password1 == null and password2 == 'foo':
  - The required test passes.
  - password2 is not null, so its validator is executed, and it fails.
  - An error message is thrown for password2.

- If `password1` == `'foo'` and `password2` == `null`:
  - The `required` test passes.
  - `password1` is `not null`, so the validator for `password2`, which is in the same group, is executed, and it fails.
  - An error message is thrown for `password2`.
- If `password1` == `'foo'` and `password2` == `'foo'`:
  - The `required` test passes.
  - `password2` is `not null`, so its validator is executed, and it passes.
  - The form is valid.

Summary

Writing forms in symfony templates is facilitated by the standard *form helpers* and their smart options. When you design a form to edit the properties of an object, the *object form helpers* simplify the task a great deal. The *validation files, validation helpers,* and *repopulation feature* reduce the work necessary to build a robust and user-friendly server control on the value of a field. And even the most complex validation needs can be handled, either by writing a *custom validator* or by creating a `validateXXX()` method in the action class.

■■■

## CHAPTER 11

Ajax Integration

Interactions on the client side, complex visual effects, and asynchronous communication are common in Web 2.0 applications. All those require JavaScript, but coding it by hand is often cumbersome and time-consuming to debug. Fortunately, symfony automates many of the common uses of JavaScript in the templates with a complete set of helpers. Many of the client-side behaviors can even be coded without a single line of JavaScript. Developers only need to worry about the effect they want to achieve, and symfony will deal with complex syntax and compatibility issues.

This chapter describes the tools provided by symfony to facilitate client-side scripting:

- Basic JavaScript helpers output standards-compliant `<script>` tags in symfony templates, to update a Document Object Model (DOM) element or trigger a script with a link.

- Prototype is a JavaScript library integrated in symfony, which speeds up client-side scripting development by adding new functions and methods to the JavaScript core.

- Ajax helpers allow the user to update some parts of a page by clicking a link, submitting a form, or modifying a form element.

- The many options of these helpers provide even greater flexibility and power, notably by the use of callback functions.

- Script.aculo.us is another JavaScript library, also integrated in symfony, which adds dynamic visual effects to enhance the interface and the user experience.

- JavaScript Object Notation (JSON) is a standard used to communicate between a server and a client script.

- Complex client-side interactions, combining all the aforementioned elements, are possible in symfony applications. Autocompletion, drag-and-drop, sortable lists, and editable text can all be implemented with a single line of PHP—a call to a symfony helper.

Basic JavaScript Helpers

JavaScript has long been considered as having little real use in professional web applications due to the lack of cross-browser compatibility. Today, the compatibility issues are (mostly) solved, and some robust libraries allow you to program complex interactions in JavaScript without the need for countless lines of code and lost hours of debugging. The most popular advance is called Ajax, which is discussed in the "Ajax Helpers" section later in this chapter.

Paradoxically, you will see very little JavaScript code in this chapter. This is because symfony has an original approach to client-side scripting: It packages and abstracts JavaScript behaviors into helpers, so your templates end up showing no JavaScript code at all. For the developer, adding a behavior to an element in the page takes one line of PHP, but this helper call does output JavaScript code, and inspecting the generated responses will reveal all the encapsulated complexity. The helpers deal with browser consistency, complex limit cases, extensibility, and so on, so the amount of JavaScript code they contain can be quite important. Therefore, this chapter will teach you how *not* to use JavaScript to achieve effects that you use to build with JavaScript.

All of the helpers described here are available in templates, provided that you declare the use of the `Javascript` helper group.

```
<?php use_helper('Javascript') ?>
```

As you'll soon learn, some of these helpers output HTML code, and some of them output JavaScript code.

JavaScript in Templates

In XHTML, *JavaScript code blocks* must be enclosed within CDATA declarations. But pages requiring multiple JavaScript code blocks can soon become tedious to write. That's why symfony provides a `javascript_tag()` helper, which transforms a string into an XHTML-compliant `<script>` tag. Listing 11-1 demonstrates using this helper.

Listing 11-1. *Inserting JavaScript with the `javascript_tag()` Helper*

```
<?php echo javascript_tag("
  function foobar()
  {
  ...
  }
") ?>
 => <script type="text/javascript">
    //<![CDATA[
      function foobar()
      {
        ...
      }
    //]]>
    </script>
```

But the most common use of JavaScript, more than code blocks, is in a *hyperlink* that triggers a particular script. The `link_to_function()` helper does exactly that, as shown in Listing 11-2.

Listing 11-2. *Triggering JavaScript by a Link with the* `link_to_function()` *Helper*

```
<?php echo link_to_function('Click me!', "alert('foobar')") ?>
 => <a href="#" onClick="alert('foobar'); return none;">Click me!</a>
```

As with the `link_to()` helper, you can add options to the `<a>` tag in the third argument.

■**Note** Just as the `link_to()` helper has a `button_to()` brother, you can trigger JavaScript from a
button (`<input type="button">`) by calling the `button_to_function()` helper. And if you prefer a
clickable image, just call `link_to_function(image_tag('myimage'), "alert('foobar')")`.

Updating a DOM Element

One common task in dynamic interfaces is the update of an element in the page. This is something that you usually write as shown in Listing 11-3.

Listing 11-3. *Updating an Element in JavaScript*

```
<div id="indicator">Data processing beginning</div>
<?php echo javascript_tag("
  document.getElementById("indicator").innerHTML =
    "<strong>Data processing complete</strong>";
") ?>
```

Symfony provides a helper that produces JavaScript, not HTML, for this purpose, and it's called `update_element_function()`. Listing 11-4 shows its use.

Listing 11-4. *Updating an Element in JavaScript with the* `update_element_function()` *Helper*

```
<div id="indicator">Data processing beginning</div>
<?php echo javascript_tag(
  update_element_function('indicator', array(
    'content'  => "<strong>Data processing complete</strong>",
  ))
) ?>
```

You might be wondering why this helper is particularly useful, since it's at least as long as the actual JavaScript code. It's really a matter of readability. For instance, you might want to insert content before or after an element, remove an element instead of just updating it, or even do nothing according to a certain condition. In such cases, the JavaScript code becomes somewhat messier, but the `update_element_function()` keeps the template very readable, as you can see in Listing 11-5.

Listing 11-5. *Options of the* update_element_function() *Helper*

```
// Insert content just after the 'indicator' element
update_element_function('indicator', array(
  'position' => 'after',
  'content'  => "<strong>Data processing complete</strong>",
));

// Remove the element before the 'indicator', and only if $condition is true
update_element_function('indicator', array(
  'action'   => $condition ? 'remove' : 'empty',
  'position' => 'before',
))
```

The helper makes your templates easier to understand than any JavaScript code, and you have a single syntax for similar behaviors. That's also why the helper name is so long: It makes the code self-sufficient, without the need of extra comments.

Graceful Degradation

The <noscript> tag allows you to specify some HTML code that is displayed only by browsers that do not have JavaScript support. Symfony complements this with a helper that works the other way around: It qualifies some code so that only browsers that actually support JavaScript execute it. The if_javascript() and end_if_javascript() helpers facilitate the creation of applications that degrade gracefully, as demonstrated in Listing 11-6.

Listing 11-6. *Using the* if_javascript() *Helper to Allow Graceful Degradation*

```
<?php if_javascript(); ?>
  <p>You have JavaScript enabled.</p>
<?php end_if_javascript(); ?>

<noscript>
  <p>You don't have JavaScript enabled.</p>
</noscript>
```

■**Note** You don't need to include echo when calling the if_javascript() and end_if_javascript() helpers.

Prototype

Prototype is a great JavaScript library that extends the possibilities of the client scripting language, adds the missing functions you've always dreamed of, and offers new mechanisms to manipulate the DOM. The project website is http://prototype.conio.net/.

The Prototype files are bundled with the symfony framework and accessible in every new symfony project, in `web/sf/prototype/`. This means that you can use Prototype by adding the following code to your action:

```
$prototypeDir = sfConfig::get('sf_prototype_web_dir');
$this->getResponse()->addJavascript($prototypeDir.'/js/prototype');
```

or by adding it in the `view.yml` file:

```
all:
  javascripts: [%SF_PROTOTYPE_WEB_DIR%/js/prototype]
```

■Note Since the symfony Ajax helpers, described in the next section, rely on Prototype, the Prototype library is already included automatically as soon as you use one of them. It means that you won't need to manually add the Prototype JavaScript to your response if your template calls a _remote helper.

Once the Prototype library is loaded, you can take advantage of all the new functions it adds to the JavaScript core. This book's purpose is not to describe them all, but you will easily find good documentation about Prototype on the Web, including at the following websites:

- Particletree: `http://particletree.com/features/quick-guide-to-prototype/`

- Sergio Pereira: `http://www.sergiopereira.com/articles/prototype.js.html`

- Script.aculo.us: `http://wiki.script.aculo.us/scriptaculous/show/Prototype`

One of the functions Prototype adds to JavaScript is the dollar function, $(). Basically, this function is a simple shortcut to `document.getElementById()`, but a little more powerful. See Listing 11-7 for an example of its use.

Listing 11-7. *Using the $() Function to Get an Element by ID in JavaScript*

```
node = $('elementID');

// Means the same as
node = document.getElementById('elementID');

// It can also retrieve more than one element at a time
// And in this case the result is an array of DOM elements
nodes = $('firstDiv', 'secondDiv');
```

Prototype also provides a function that the JavaScript core really lacks, which returns an array of all the DOM elements that have the class passed as argument:

```
nodes = document.getElementByClassName('myclass');
```

However, you will seldom use it, because Prototype provides an even more powerful function called double dollar, $$(). This function returns an array of DOM elements based on a CSS selector. So the previous call can also be written as follows:

```
nodes = $$('.myclass');
```

Thanks to the power of CSS selectors, you can parse the DOM by class, ID, and parent-child and previous-next relationships even more easily than you would with an XPath expression. You can even access elements with a complex selector combining all these:

```
nodes = $$('body div#main ul li.last img > span.legend');
```

One last example of the syntax enhancements provided by Prototype is the each array iterator. It provides the same concision as in PHP, added to the ability to define anonymous functions and closures in JavaScript. You will probably use it a lot if you code JavaScript by hand.

```
var vegetables = ['Carrots', 'Lettuce', 'Garlic'];
vegetables.each(function(food) { alert('I love ' + food); });
```

Because programming in JavaScript with Prototype is much more fun than doing it by hand, and because it is also part of symfony, you should really spend a few minutes to read the related documentation.

Ajax Helpers

What if you wanted to update an element in the page, not with JavaScript as in Listing 11-5, but with a PHP script executed by the server? This would give you the opportunity to change part of the page according to a server response. The remote_function() helper does exactly that, as demonstrated in Listing 11-8.

Listing 11-8. *Using the remote_function() Helper*

```
<div id="myzone"></div>
<?php echo javascript_tag(
  remote_function(array(
    'update'  => 'myzone',
    'url'     => 'mymodule/myaction',
  ))
) ?>
```

■**Note** The url parameter can contain either an internal URI (module/action?key1=value1&...) or a routing rule name, just as in a regular url_for().

When called, this script will update the element of id myzone with the response or the request of the mymodule/myaction action. This kind of interaction is called *Ajax*, and it's the heart of highly interactive web applications. Here is how Wikipedia (`http://en.wikipedia.org/wiki/AJAX`) describes it:

> *Ajax makes web pages feel more responsive by exchanging small amounts of data with the server behind the scenes, so that the entire web page does not have to be reloaded each time the user makes a change. This is meant to increase the web page's interactivity, speed, and usability.*

Ajax relies on `XMLHttpRequest`, a JavaScript object that behaves like a hidden frame, which you can update from a server request and reuse to manipulate the rest of your web page. This object is quite low level, and different browsers deal with it in different ways, so handling Ajax requests manually usually means writing long portions of code. Fortunately, Prototype encapsulates all the code necessary to deal with Ajax and provides a simpler `Ajax` object, and symfony relies on this object. This is why the Prototype library is automatically loaded once you use an Ajax helper in a template.

■**Caution** The Ajax helpers won't work if the URL of the remote action doesn't belong to the *same domain* as the current page. This restriction exists for security reasons, and relies on browsers limitations that cannot be bypassed.

An Ajax interaction is made up of three parts: a caller (a link, a button, a form, a clock, or any control that the user manipulates to launch the action), a server action, and a zone in the page to display the response of the action. You can build more complex interactions if the remote action returns data to be processed by a javascript function on the client side. Symfony provides multiple helpers to insert Ajax interaction in your templates, all containing the word `remote` in their name. They also share a common syntax—an associative array with all the Ajax parameters in it. Be aware that the Ajax helpers output HTML code, not JavaScript.

HOW ABOUT AJAX ACTIONS?

Actions called as remote functions are regular actions. They follow routing, can determine the view to render the response with their `return`, pass variables to the templates, and alter the model just like other actions. However, when called through Ajax, actions return `true` to the following call:

```
$isAjax = $this->getIsXmlHttpRequest();
```

Symfony knows that an action is in an Ajax context and can adapt the response processing accordingly. Therefore, by default, Ajax actions don't include the web debug toolbar in the development environment. Also, they skip the decoration process (their template is not included in a layout by default). If you want an Ajax view to be decorated, you need to specify explicitly `has_layout: true` for this view in the module `view.yml` file.

One more thing: Because responsiveness is crucial in Ajax interactions, if the response is not too complex, it might be a good idea to avoid creating a view and instead return the response directly from the action. So you can use the `renderText()` method in the action to skip the template and boost Ajax requests.

Ajax Link

Ajax links form a large share of the Ajax interactions available in Web 2.0 applications. The link_to_remote() helper outputs a link that calls, not surprisingly, a remote function. The syntax is very similar to that of link_to() (except that the second parameter is the associative array of Ajax options), as shown in Listing 11-9.

Listing 11-9. *Ajax Link with the link_to_remote() Helper*

```
<div id="feedback"></div>
<?php echo link_to_remote('Delete this post', array(
    'update' => 'feedback',
    'url'    => 'post/delete?id='.$post->getId(),
)) ?>
```

In this example, clicking the 'Delete this post' link will issue a call to the post/delete action in the background. The response returned by the server will appear in the element of id feedback. This process is illustrated in Figure 11-1.

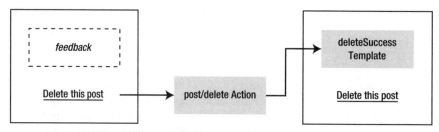

Figure 11-1. *Triggering a remote update with a hyperlink*

You can use an image instead of a string to bear the link, use a rule name instead of an internal module/action URL, and add options to the <a> tag in a third argument, as shown in Listing 11-10.

Listing 11-10. *Options of the link_to_remote() Helper*

```
<div id="emails"></div>
<?php echo link_to_remote(image_tag('refresh'), array(
    'update' => 'emails',
    'url'    => '@list_emails',
), array(
    'class' => 'ajax_link',
)) ?>
```

Ajax-Driven Forms

Web forms typically call another action, but this causes the whole page to be refreshed. The correspondence of the link_to_function() for a form would be that the form submission only

updates an element in the page with the server response. This is what the form_remote_tag()
helper does, and its syntax is demonstrated in Listing 11-11.

Listing 11-11. *Ajax Form with the form_remote_tag() Helper*

```
<div id="item_list"></div>
<?php echo form_remote_tag(array(
    'update'    => 'item_list',
    'url'       => 'item/add',
)) ?>
  <label for="item">Item:</label>
  <?php echo input_tag('item') ?>
  <?php echo submit_tag('Add') ?>
</form>
```

A form_remote_tag() opens a <form>, just like the regular form_tag() helper. Submitting
this form will issue a POST request to the item/add action in the background, with the item field
as a request parameter. The response will replace the contents of the item_list element, as
illustrated in Figure 11-2. Close an Ajax form with a regular </form> closing tag.

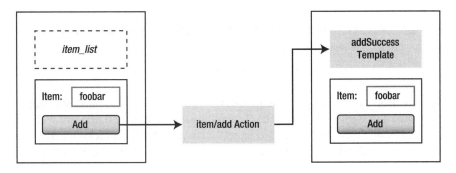

Figure 11-2. *Triggering a remote update with a form*

■**Caution** Ajax forms can't be multipart. This is a limitation of the XMLHttpRequest object. This means
you can't handle file uploads via an Ajax form. There are workarounds though—for instance, using a hidden
iframe instead of an XMLHttpRequest (see an implementation at http://www.air4web.com/files/
upload/).

If you want to allow a form to work in both page mode and Ajax mode, the best solution is
to define it like a regular form, but to provide, in addition to the normal submit button, a
second button (<input type="button" />) to submit the form in Ajax. Symfony calls this button
submit_to_remote(). This will help you build Ajax interactions that degrade gracefully. See an
example in Listing 11-12.

Listing 11-12. *A Form with Regular and Ajax Submission*

```
<div id="item_list"></div>
<?php echo form_tag('@item_add_regular') ?>
  <label for="item">Item:</label>
  <?php echo input_tag('item') ?>
  <?php if_javascript(); ?>
    <?php echo submit_to_remote('ajax_submit', 'Add in Ajax', array(
        'update'   => 'item_list',
        'url'      => '@item_add',
    )) ?>
  <?php end_if_javascript(); ?>
  <noscript>
    <?php echo submit_tag('Add') ?>
  </noscript>
</form>
```

Another example of combined use of remote and regular submit tags is a form that edits an article. It can offer a preview button in Ajax and a publish button that does a regular submission.

Note When the user presses the Enter key, the form is submitted using the action defined in the main `<form>` tag—in this example, a regular action.

Modern forms can also react not only when submitted, but also when the value of a field is being updated by a user. In symfony, you use the `observe_field()` helper for that. Listing 11-13 shows an example of using this helper to build a suggestion feature: Each character typed in an item field triggers an Ajax call refreshing the `item_suggestion` element in the page.

Listing 11-13. *Calling a Remote Function When a Field Value Changes with* `observe_field()`

```
<?php echo form_tag('@item_add_regular') ?>
  <label for="item">Item:</label>
  <?php echo input_tag('item') ?>
  <div id="item_suggestion"></div>
  <?php echo observe_field('item', array(
      'update'   => 'item_suggestion',
      'url'      => '@item_being_typed',
  )) ?>
  <?php echo submit_tag('Add') ?>
</form>
```

The module/action written in the `@item_being_typed` rule will be called each time the user changes the value of the observed field (`item`), even without submitting the form. The action will be able to get the current `item` value from the `value` request parameter. If you want to pass something other than the value of the observed field, you can specify it as a JavaScript expression in the `with` parameter. For instance, if you want the action to get a `param` parameter, write the `observe_field()` helper as shown in Listing 11-14.

Listing 11-14. *Passing Your Own Parameters to the Remote Action with the with Option*

```php
<?php echo observe_field('item', array(
    'update'  => 'item_suggestion',
    'url'     => '@item_being_typed',
    'with'    => "'param=' + value",
)) ?>
```

Note that this helper doesn't output an HTML element, but instead outputs a behavior for the element passed as a parameter. You will see more examples of JavaScript helpers assigning behaviors later in this chapter.

If you want to observe all the fields of a form, you should use the observe_form() helper, which calls a remote function each time one of the form fields is modified.

Periodically Calling Remote Functions

Last but not least, the periodically_call_remote() helper is an Ajax interaction triggered every few seconds. It is not attached to an HTML control, but runs transparently in the background, as a behavior of the whole page. This can be of great use to track the position of the mouse, autosave the content of a large text area, and so on. Listing 11-15 shows an example of using this helper.

Listing 11-15. *Periodically Calling a Remote Function with periodically_call_remote()*

```php
<div id="notification"></div>
<?php echo periodically_call_remote(array(
    'frequency' => 60,
    'update'    => 'notification',
    'url'       => '@watch',
    'with'      => "'param=' + $('mycontent').value",
)) ?>
```

If you don't specify the number of seconds (frequency) to wait between two calls to the remote function, the default value of 10 seconds is used. Note that the with parameter is evaluated in JavaScript, so you can use Prototype functions in it, such as the dollar function, $().

Remote Call Parameters

All the Ajax helpers described in the previous sections can take other parameters, in addition to the update and url parameters. The associative array of Ajax parameters can alter and tweak the behavior of the remote calls and the processing of their response.

Updating Distinct Elements According to the Response Status

If the remote action fails, the remote helpers can choose to update another element than the one updated by a successful response. To that purpose, just split the value of the update parameter into an associative array, and set different values for the element to update in cases of success and failure. This is of great use if, for instance, there are many Ajax interactions in a page and one error feedback zone. Listing 11-16 demonstrates handling a conditional update.

Listing 11-16. *Handling a Conditional Update*

```
<div id="error"></div>
<div id="feedback"></div>
<p>Hello, World!</p>
<?php echo link_to_remote('Delete this post', array(
    'update'   => array('success' => 'feedback', 'failure' => 'error')
    'url'      => 'post/delete?id='.$post->getId(),
)) ?>
```

■**Tip** Only HTTP error codes (500, 404, and all codes not in the 2*XX* range) will trigger the failure update, not the actions returning sfView::ERROR. So if you want to make an action return an Ajax failure, it must call $this->getResponse()->setStatusCode(404) or similar.

Updating an Element According to Position

Just as with the update_element_function() helper, you can specify the element to update as relative to a specific element by adding a position parameter. Listing 11-17 shows an example.

Listing 11-17. *Using the Position Parameter to Change the Response Location*

```
<div id="feedback"></div>
<p>Hello, World!</p>
<?php echo link_to_remote('Delete this post', array(
    'update'   => 'feedback',
    'url'      => 'post/delete?id='.$post->getId(),
    'position' => 'after',
)) ?>
```

This will insert the response of the Ajax call *after* the feedback element; that is, between the <div> and the <p>. With this method, you can do several Ajax calls and see the responses accumulate after the update element.

The position parameter can take the following values:

before: Before the element

after: After the element

top: At the top of the content of the element

bottom: At the bottom of the content of the element

Updating an Element According to a Condition

A remote call can take an additional parameter to allow confirmation by the user before actually submitting the XMLHttpRequest, as shown in Listing 11-18.

Listing 11-18. *Using the Confirm Parameter to Ask for a Confirmation Before Calling the Remote Function*

```
<div id="feedback"></div>
<?php echo link_to_remote('Delete this post', array(
    'update'  => 'feedback',
    'url'     => 'post/delete?id='.$post->getId(),
    'confirm' => 'Are you sure?',
)) ?>
```

A JavaScript dialog box showing "Are you sure?" will pop up when the user clicks the link, and the post/delete action will be called only if the user confirms his choice by clicking OK.

The remote call can also be conditioned by a test performed on the browser side (in JavaScript), if you provide a condition parameter, as shown in Listing 11-19.

Listing 11-19. *Conditionally Calling the Remote Function According to a Test on the Client Side*

```
<div id="feedback"></div>
<?php echo link_to_remote('Delete this post', array(
    'update'    => 'feedback',
    'url'       => 'post/delete?id='.$post->getId(),
    'condition' => "$('elementID') == true",
)) ?>
```

Determining the Ajax Request Method

By default, Ajax requests are made with the POST method. If you want to make an Ajax call that doesn't modify data, or if you want to display a form that has built-in validation as the result of an Ajax call, you might need to change the Ajax request method to GET. The method option alters the Ajax request method, as shown in Listing 11-20.

Listing 11-20. *Changing the Ajax Request Method*

```
<div id="feedback"></div>
<?php echo link_to_remote('Delete this post', array(
    'update'  => 'feedback',
    'url'     => 'post/delete?id='.$post->getId(),
    'method'  => 'get',
)) ?>
```

Authorizing Script Execution

If the response code of the Ajax call (the code sent by the server, inserted in the update element) contains JavaScript, you might be surprised to see that these scripts are not executed by default. This is to reduce remote attack risks and to allow script execution only when the developer knows for sure what code is in the response.

That's why you need to declare explicitly the ability to execute scripts in remote responses, with the script option. Listing 11-21 gives an example of an Ajax call declaring that JavaScript from the remote response can be executed.

Listing 11-21. *Authorizing Script Execution in the Ajax Response*

```
<div id="feedback"></div>
// If the response of the post/delete action contains JavaScript,
// allow it to be executed by the browser
<?php echo link_to_remote('Delete this post', array(
    'update' => 'feedback',
    'url'    => 'post/delete?id='.$post->getId(),
    'script' => true,
)) ?>
```

If the remote template contains Ajax helpers (such as remote_function()), be aware that these PHP functions generate JavaScript code, and they won't execute unless you add the 'script' => true option.

■**Note** Even if you enable script execution for the remote response, you won't actually see the scripts in the remote code, if you use a tool to check the generated code. The scripts will execute but will not appear in the code. Although peculiar, this behavior is perfectly normal.

Creating Callbacks

One important drawback of Ajax interactions is that they are invisible to the user until the zone to update is actually updated. This means that in cases of a slow network or server failure, users may believe that their action was taken into account, when it actually was not processed. This is why it is important to *notify the user* of the events of an Ajax interaction.

By default, each remote request is an asynchronous process during which various JavaScript callbacks can be triggered (for progress indicators and the like). All callbacks have access to the request object, which holds the underlying XMLHttpRequest. The callbacks correspond to the events of any Ajax interaction:

before: Before request is initiated

after: Immediately after request is initiated and before loading

loading: When the remote response is being loaded by the browser

loaded: When the browser has finished loading the remote response

interactive: When the user can interact with the remote response, even though it has not finished loading

success: When the XMLHttpRequest is completed, and the HTTP status code is in the 2*XX* range

failure: When the XMLHttpRequest is completed, and the HTTP status code is not in the 2*XX* range

404: When the request returns a 404 status

complete: When the XMLHttpRequest is complete (fires after success or failure, if they are present)

For instance, it is very common to show a *loading indicator* when a remote call is initiated, and to hide it once the response is received. To achieve that, simply add loading and complete parameters to the Ajax call, as shown in Listing 11-22.

Listing 11-22. *Using Ajax Callbacks to Show and Hide an Activity Indicator*

```
<div id="feedback"></div>
<div id="indicator">Loading...</div>
<?php echo link_to_remote('Delete this post', array(
    'update'   => 'feedback',
    'url'      => 'post/delete?id='.$post->getId(),
    'loading'  => "Element.show('indicator')",
    'complete' => "Element.hide('indicator')",
)) ?>
```

The show and hide methods, as well as the JavaScript Element object, are other useful additions of Prototype.

Creating Visual Effects

Symfony integrates the visual effects of the script.aculo.us library, to allow you to do more than show and hide <div> elements in your web pages. You will find good documentation on the effects syntax in the wiki at http://script.aculo.us/. Basically, the library provides JavaScript objects and functions that manipulate the DOM in order to achieve complex visual effects. See a few examples in Listing 11-23. Since the result is a visual animation of certain areas in a web page, it is recommended that you test the effects yourself to understand what they really do. The script.aculo.us website offers a gallery where you can get an idea of the dynamic effects.

Listing 11-23. *Visual Effects in JavaScript with Script.aculo.us*

```
// Highlights the element 'my_field'
Effect.Highlight('my_field', { startcolor:'#ff99ff', endcolor:'#999999' })

// Blinds down an element
Effect.BlindDown('id_of_element');

// Fades away an element
Effect.Fade('id_of_element', { transition: Effect.Transitions.wobble })
```

Symfony encapsulates the JavaScript Effect object in a helper called visual_effect(), still part of the Javascript helper group. It outputs JavaScript that can be used in a regular link, as shown in Listing 11-24.

Listing 11-24. *Visual Effects in Templates with the* `visual_effect()` *Helper*

```
<div id="secret_div" style="display:none">I was here all along!</div>
<?php echo link_to_function(
  'Show the secret div',
  visual_effect('appear', 'secret_div')
) ?>
// Will make a call to Effect.Appear('secret_div')
```

The visual_effects() helper can also be used in the Ajax callbacks, as shown in Listing 11-25, which displays an activity indicator like Listing 11-22, but is visually more satisfactory. The indicator element appears progressively when the Ajax call starts, and it fades progressively when the response arrives. In addition, the feedback element is highlighted after being updated by the remote call, to draw the user's attention to this part of the window.

Listing 11-25. *Visual Effects in Ajax Callbacks*

```
<div id="feedback"></div>
<div id="indicator" style="display: none">Loading...</div>
<?php echo link_to_remote('Delete this post', array(
    'update'   => 'feedback',
    'url'      => 'post/delete?id='.$post->getId(),
    'loading'  => visual_effect('appear', 'indicator'),
    'complete' => visual_effect('fade', 'indicator').
                  visual_effect('highlight', 'feedback'),
)) ?>
```

Notice how you can combine visual effects by concatenating them in a callback.

JSON

JavaScript Object Notation (JSON) is a lightweight data-interchange format. Basically, it is nothing more than a JavaScript hash (see an example in Listing 11-26) used to carry object information. But JSON has two great benefits for Ajax interactions: It is easy to read in JavaScript, and it can reduce the size of a web response.

Listing 11-26. *A Sample JSON Object in JavaScript*

```
var myJsonData = {"menu": {
  "id": "file",
  "value": "File",
  "popup": {
    "menuitem": [
      {"value": "New", "onclick": "CreateNewDoc()"},
      {"value": "Open", "onclick": "OpenDoc()"},
      {"value": "Close", "onclick": "CloseDoc()"}
    ]
  }
}}
```

If an Ajax action needs to return structured data to the caller page for further JavaScript processing, JSON is a good format for the response. This is very useful if, for instance, *one Ajax call is to update several elements* in the caller page.

For instance, imagine a caller page that looks like Listing 11-27. It has two elements that may need to be updated. One remote helper could update only one of the elements of the page (either the title or the name), but not both.

Listing 11-27. *Sample Template for Multiple Ajax Updates*

```
<h1 id="title">Basic letter</h1>
<p>Dear <span id="name">name_here</span>,</p>
<p>Your e-mail was received and will be answered shortly.</p>
<p>Sincerely,</p>
```

To update both, imagine that the Ajax response can be a JSON header containing the following array:

```
[["title", "My basic letter"], ["name", "Mr Brown"]]
```

Then the remote call can easily interpret this response and update several fields in a row, with a little help from JavaScript. The code in Listing 11-28 shows what could be added to the template of Listing 11-27 to achieve this effect.

Listing 11-28. *Updating More Than One Element from a Remote Response*

```
<?php echo link_to_remote('Refresh the letter', array(
  'url'      => 'publishing/refresh',
  'complete' => 'updateJSON(request, json)'
)) ?>

<?php echo javascript_tag("
function updateJSON(request, json)
{
  var nbElementsInResponse = json.length;
  for (var i = 0; i < nbElementsInResponse; i++)
  {
    Element.update(json[i][0], json[i][1]);
  }
}
") ?>
```

The complete callback has access to the json header of the response and can pass it to a third-party function. This custom updateJSON() function iterates over the JSON header and for each member of the array, updates the element named by the first parameter with the content of the second parameter.

Listing 11-29 shows how the publishing/refresh action can return a JSON response.

Listing 11-29. *Sample Action Returning a JSON Header*

```
class publishingActions extends sfActions
{
  public function executeRefresh()
  {
    $output = '[["title", "My basic letter"], ["name", "Mr Brown"]]';
    $this->getResponse()->setHttpHeader("X-JSON", '('.$output.')');

    return sfView::HEADER_ONLY;
  }
}
```

The HTTP protocol allows JSON to be stored in a response header. As the response doesn't have any content, the action sends it immediately as a header only. This bypasses the view layer entirely and is as fast as a ->renderText(), but with an even smaller response.

■**Caution** There is a severe limitation to the approach shown in Listing 11-29: the maximum size of HTTP headers. There is no official limitation, but large headers may not be well transferred or interpreted by a browser. This means that if your JSON array is large, the remote action should return a normal response, with the JSON as a JavaScript array.

JSON has become a standard among web applications. Web services often propose responses in JSON rather than XML to allow service integration in the client (mashup), rather than on the server. So if you wonder which format to use for communication between your server and a JavaScript function, JSON is probably your best bet.

■**Tip** Since version 5.2, PHP offers two functions, json_encode() and json_decode(), that allow you to convert an array between the PHP syntax and the JSON syntax, and vice versa (http://www.php.net/manual/en/ref.json.php). These facilitate the integration of JSON arrays and Ajax in general.

Performing Complex Interactions with Ajax

Among the symfony Ajax helpers, you will also find some tools that build up complex interactions with a single call. They allow you to enhance the user experience by desktop-application-like interactions (drag-and-drop, autocompletion, and live editing) without the need for complex JavaScript. The following sections describe the helpers for complex interactions and show simple examples. Additional parameters and tweaks are described in the script.aculo.us documentation.

■**Caution** If complex interactions are possible, they need extra time for presentation tweaking to make them feel natural. Use them only when you are sure that they enhance the user experience. Avoid them when there is a risk that they will disorient users.

Autocompletion

A text-input component that shows a list of words matching the user's entry while the user types is called an autocompletion. With a single helper called input_auto_complete_tag(), you can achieve this effect, provided that the remote action returns a response formatted as an HTML item list similar to the example shown in Listing 11-30.

Listing 11-30. *Example of a Response Compatible with the Autocomplete Tag*

```
<ul>
  <li>suggestion1</li>
  <li>suggestion2</li>
  ...
</ul>
```

Insert the helper in a template as you would do with a regular text input, following the example shown in Listing 11-31.

Listing 11-31. *Using the Autocomplete Tag Helper in a Template*

```
<?php echo form_tag('mymodule/myaction') ?>
  Find an author by name:
  <?php echo input_auto_complete_tag('author', 'default name',
    'author/autocomplete',
    array('autocomplete' => 'off'),
    array('use_style'    => true)
  ) ?>
  <?php echo submit_tag('Find') ?>
</form>
```

This will call the author/autocomplete action each time the user types a character in the author field. It's up to you to design the action so that it determines a list of possible matches according to the author request parameter and returns them in a format similar to Listing 11-30. The helper will then display the list under the author tag, and clicking one of the suggestions or selecting it with the keyboard will complete the input, as shown in Figure 11-3.

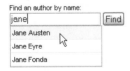

Figure 11-3. *An autocompletion example*

The third argument of the input_auto_complete_tag() helper can take the following parameters:

use_style: Styles the response list automatically.

frequency: Frequency of the periodical call (defaults to 0.4s).

tokens: To allow tokenized incremental autocompletion. For instance, if you set this parameter to , and if the user entered jane, george, the action would receive only the value 'george'.

■**Note** The input_auto_complete_tag() helper, like the following ones, also accepts the usual remote helper options described earlier in this chapter. In particular, it is a good habit to set loading and complete visual effects for a better user experience.

Drag-and-Drop

The ability to grab an element with the mouse, move it, and release it somewhere else is familiar in desktop applications but rarer in web browsers. This is because coding such behavior in plain JavaScript is very complicated. Fortunately, it requires only one line in symfony.

The framework provides two helpers, draggable_element() and drop_receiving_element(), that can be seen as behavior modifiers; they add observers and abilities to the element they address. Use them to declare an element as *draggable* or as a *receiving element* for draggable elements. A *draggable element* can be grabbed by clicking it with the mouse. Until the mouse button is released, the element can be moved, or dragged, across the window. A *receiving element* calls a remote function when a *draggable* element is released on it. Listing 11-32 demonstrates this type of interaction with a shopping cart receiving element.

Listing 11-32. *Draggable Elements and Drop-Receiving Elements in a Shopping Cart*

```
<ul id="items">
  <li id="item_1" class="food">Carrot</li>
  <?php echo draggable_element('item_1', array('revert' => true)) ?>
  <li id="item_2" class="food">Apple</li>
  <?php echo draggable_element('item_2', array('revert' => true)) ?>
  <li id="item_3" class="food">Orange</li>
  <?php echo draggable_element('item_3', array('revert' => true)) ?>
</li>
<div id="cart">
  <p>Your cart is empty</p>
  <p>Drag items here to add them to your cart</p>
</div>
```

```php
<?php echo drop_receiving_element('cart', array(
  'url'        => 'cart/add',
  'accept'     => 'food',
  'update'     => 'cart',
)) ?>
```

Each of the items of the unordered list can be grabbed by the mouse and dragged across the window. When released, they return to their original position. When released over the cart element, it triggers a remote call to the cart/add action. The action will be able to determine which item was dropped in the cart element by looking at the id request parameter. So Listing 11-32 simulates a real shopping session: You grab items and release them in the cart, and then proceed to checkout.

■**Tip** In Listing 11-32, the helpers are written just after the element they modify, but that is not a requirement. You could very well group all the draggable_element() and drop_receiving_element() helpers at the end of the template. The important thing is the first argument of the helper call, which specifies the identifier of the element to receive the behavior.

The draggable_element() helper accepts the following parameters:

revert: If set to true, the element will return to its original location when released. It can also be an arbitrary function reference, called when the drag ends.

ghosting: Clones the element and drags the clone, leaving the original in place until the clone is dropped.

snap: If set to false, no snapping occurs. Otherwise, the draggable can be dragged only to the intersections of a grid of interval x and y, and in this case, it takes the form xy or [x,y] or function(x,y){ return [x,y] }.

The drop_receiving_element() helper accepts the following parameters:

accept: A string or an array of strings describing CSS classes. The element will accept only draggable elements that have one or more of these CSS classes.

hoverclass: CSS class added to the element when the user drags an accepted draggable element over it.

Sortable Lists

Another possibility offered by draggable elements is the ability to sort a list by moving its items with the mouse. The sortable_element() helper adds the sortable behavior to an item, and Listing 11-33 is a good example of implementing this feature.

Listing 11-33. *Sortable List Example*

```
<p>What do you like most?</p>
<ul id="order">
  <li id="item_1" class="sortable">Carrots</li>
  <li id="item_2" class="sortable">Apples</li>
  <li id="item_3" class="sortable">Oranges</li>
  // Nobody likes Brussel sprouts anyway
  <li id="item_4">Brussel sprouts</li>
</ul>
<div id="feedback"></div>
<?php echo sortable_element('order', array(
  'url'    => 'item/sort',
  'update' => 'feedback',
  'only'   => 'sortable';
)) ?>
```

By the magic of the sortable_element() helper, the <ul> element is made *sortable*, which means that its children can be reordered by drag-and-drop. Each time the user drags an item and releases it to reorder the list, an Ajax request is made with the following parameters:

```
POST /sf_sandbox/web/frontend_dev.php/item/sort HTTP/1.1
  order[]=1&order[]=3&order[]=2&_=
```

The full ordered list is passed as an array (with the format order[$rank]=$id, the $order starting at 0, and the $id based on what comes after the underscore (_) in the list element id property). The id property of the sortable element (order in the example) is used to name the array of parameters.

The sortable_element() helper accepts the following parameters:

only: A string or an array of strings describing CSS classes. Only the child elements of the sortable element with this class can be moved.

hoverclass: CSS class added to the element when the mouse is hovered over it.

overlap: Set it to horizontal if the items are displayed inline, and to vertical (the default value) when there is one item per line (as in the example).

tag: If the list to order is not a set of <li> elements, you must define which child elements of the sortable element are to be made draggable (for instance, div or dl).

Edit in Place

More and more web applications allow users to edit the contents of pages directly on the page, without the need to redisplay the content in a form. The principle of the interaction is simple. A block of text is highlighted when the user hovers the mouse over it. If the user clicks inside the block, the plain text is converted into a text area filled with the text of the block, and a save button appears. The user can edit the text inside the text area, and once he saves it, the text area disappears and the text is displayed in plain form. With symfony, you can add this *editable* behavior to an element with the input_in_place_editor_tag() helper. Listing 11-34 demonstrates using this helper.

Listing 11-34. *Editable Text Example*

```
<div id="edit_me">You can edit this text</div>
<?php echo input_in_place_editor_tag('edit_me', 'mymodule/myaction', array(
  'cols'         => 40,
  'rows'         => 10,
)) ?>
```

When the user clicks the editable text, it is replaced by a text input area filled with the text, which can be edited. When the form is submitted, the `mymodule/myaction` action is called in Ajax with the edited value set as the `value` parameter. The result of the action updates the editable element. It is very fast to write and very powerful.

The `input_in_place_editor_tag()` helper accepts the following parameters:

`cols` and `rows`: The size of the text input area that appears for editing (it becomes a `<textarea>` if `rows` is more than 1).

`loadTextURL`: The URI of an action that is called to display the text to edit. This is useful if the content of the editable element uses special formatting and if you want the user to edit the text without formatting.

`save_text` and `cancel_text`: The text on the save link (defaults to "ok") and on the cancel link (defaults to "cancel").

Summary

If you are tired of writing JavaScript in your templates to get client-side behaviors, the *JavaScript helpers* offer a simple alternative. Not only do they automate the *basic link behavior* and *element update*, but they also provide a way to develop *Ajax interactions* in a snap. With the help of the powerful *syntax enhancements* provided by Prototype and the great *visual effects* provided by script.aculo.us, even *complex interactions* take no more than a few lines to write.

And since making a highly interactive application is as easy as making static pages with symfony, you can consider that almost all desktop applications interactions are now available in web applications.

CHAPTER 12

■■■

Caching

One of the ways to speed up an application is to store chunks of generated HTML code, or even full pages, for future requests. This technique is known as *caching*, and it can be managed on the server side and on the client side.

Symfony offers a flexible server-caching system. It allows saving the full response, the result of an action, a partial, or a template fragment into a file, through a very intuitive setup based on YAML files. When the underlying data changes, you can easily clear selective parts of the cache with the command line or special action methods. Symfony also provides an easy way to control the client-side cache through HTTP 1.1 headers. This chapter deals with all these subjects, and gives you a few tips on monitoring the improvements that caching can bring to your applications.

Caching the Response

The principle of HTML caching is simple: Part or all of the HTML code that is sent to a user upon a request can be reused for a similar request. This HTML code is stored in a special place (the cache/ folder in symfony), where the front controller will look for it before executing an action. If a cached version is found, it is sent without executing the action, thus greatly speeding up the process. If no cached version is found, the action is executed, and its result (the view) is stored in the cache folder for future requests.

As all the pages may contain dynamic information, the HTML cache is disabled by default. It is up to the site administrator to enable it in order to improve performance.

Symfony handles three different types of HTML caching:

- Cache of an action (with or without the layout)

- Cache of a partial, a component, or a component slot

- Cache of a template fragment

The first two types are handled with YAML configuration files. Template fragment caching is managed by calls to helper functions in the template.

Global Cache Settings

For each application of a project, the HTML cache mechanism can be enabled or disabled (the default), per environment, in the `cache` setting of the `settings.yml` file. Listing 12-1 demonstrates enabling the cache.

Listing 12-1. *Activating the Cache, in* `myapp/config/settings.yml`

```
dev:
  .settings:
    cache:            on
```

Caching an Action

Actions displaying static information (not depending on database or session-dependent data) or actions reading information from a database but without modifying it (typically, GET requests) are often ideal for caching. Figure 12-1 shows which elements of the page are cached in this case: either the action result (its template) or the action result together with the layout.

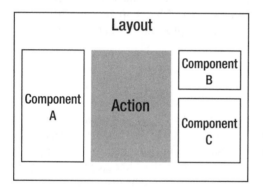
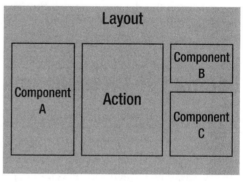

Action Cache   **Action** Cache **with Layout**

Figure 12-1. *Caching an action*

For instance, consider a `user/list` action that returns the list of all users of a website. Unless a user is modified, added, or removed (and this matter will be discussed later in the "Removing Items from the Cache" section), this list always displays the same information, so it is a good candidate for caching.

Cache activation and settings, action by action, are defined in a `cache.yml` file located in the module `config/` directory. See Listing 12-2 for an example.

Listing 12-2. *Activating the Cache for an Action, in* `myapp/modules/user/config/cache.yml`

```
list:
  enabled:      on
  with_layout:  false    # Default value
  lifetime:     86400    # Default value
```

This configuration stipulates that the cache is on for the list action, and that the layout will not be cached with the action (which is the default behavior). It means that even if a cached version of the action exists, the layout (together with its partials and components) is still executed. If the with_layout setting is set to true, the layout is cached with the action and not executed again.

To test the cache settings, call the action in the development environment from your browser.

```
http://myapp.example.com/myapp_dev.php/user/list
```

You will notice a border around the action area in the page. The first time, the area has a blue header, showing that it did not come from the cache. Refresh the page, and the action area will have a yellow header, showing that it did come from the cache (with a notable boost in response time). You will learn more about the ways to test and monitor caching later in this chapter.

■**Note** Slots are part of the template, and caching an action will also store the value of the slots defined in this action's template. So the cache works natively for slots.

The caching system also works for pages with arguments. The user module may have, for instance, a show action that expects an id argument to display the details of a user. Modify the cache.yml file to enable the cache for this action as well, as shown in Listing 12-3.

In order to organize your cache.yml, you can regroup the settings for all the actions of a module under the all: key, also shown in Listing 12-3.

Listing 12-3. *A Full* cache.yml *Example, in* myapp/modules/user/config/cache.yml

```
list:
  enabled:    on
show:
  enabled:    on

all:
  with_layout: false    # Default value
  lifetime:    86400     # Default value
```

Now, every call to the user/show action with a different id argument creates a new record in the cache. So the cache for this:

```
http://myapp.example.com/user/show/id/12
```

will be different than the cache for this:

```
http://myapp.example.com/user/show/id/25
```

■**Caution** Actions called with a POST method or with GET parameters are not cached.

The with_layout setting deserves a few more words. It actually determines what kind of data is stored in the cache. For the cache without layout, only the result of the template execution and the action variables are stored in the cache. For the cache with layout, the whole response object is stored. This means that *the cache with layout is much faster than the cache without it.*

If you can functionally afford it (that is, if the layout doesn't rely on session-dependent data), you should opt for the cache with layout. Unfortunately, the layout often contains some dynamic elements (for instance, the name of the user who is connected), so action cache without layout is the most common configuration. However, RSS feeds, pop-ups, and pages that don't depend on cookies can be cached with their layout.

Caching a Partial, Component, or Component Slot

Chapter 7 explained how to reuse code fragments across several templates, using the include_partial() helper. A *partial* is as easy to cache as an action, and its cache activation follows the same rules, as shown in Figure 12-2.

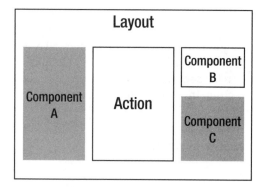

Figure 12-2. *Caching a partial, component, or component slot*

For instance, Listing 12-4 shows how to edit the cache.yml file to enable the cache on a _my_partial.php partial located in the user module. Note that the with_layout setting doesn't make sense in this case.

Listing 12-4. *Caching a Partial, in myapp/modules/user/config/cache.yml*

```
_my_partial:
  enabled:    on
list:
  enabled:    on
...
```

Now all the templates using this partial won't actually execute the PHP code of the partial, but will use the cached version instead.

```
<?php include_partial('user/my_partial') ?>
```

Just as for actions, partial caching is also relevant when the result of the partial depends on parameters. The cache system will store as many versions of a template as there are different values of parameters.

```
<?php include_partial('user/my_other_partial', array('foo' => 'bar')) ?>
```

■Tip The *action* cache is more powerful than the *partial* cache, since when an action is cached, the template is not even executed; if the template contains calls to partials, these calls are not performed. Therefore, partial caching is useful only if you don't use action caching in the calling action or for partials included in the layout.

A little reminder from Chapter 7: A *component* is a light action put on top of a partial, and a *component slot* is a component for which the action varies according to the calling actions. These two inclusion types are very similar to partials, and support caching in the same way. For instance, if your global layout includes a component called day with include_ ➥ component('general/day') in order to show the current date, set the cache.yml file of the general module as follows to enable the cache on this component:

```
_day:
  enabled: on
```

When caching a component or a partial, you must decide whether to store a single version for all calling templates or a version for each template. By default, a component is stored independently of the template that calls it. But contextual components, such as a component that displays a different sidebar with each action, should be stored as many times as there are templates calling it. The caching system can handle this case, provided that you set the contextual parameter to true, as follows:

```
_day:
  contextual: true
  enabled:   on
```

■Note Global components (the ones located in the application templates/ directory) can be cached, provided that you declare their cache settings in the *application* cache.yml.

Caching a Template Fragment

Action caching applies to only a subset of actions. For the other actions—those that update data or display session-dependent information in the template—there is still room for cache improvement but in a different way. Symfony provides a third cache type, which is dedicated to template fragments and enabled directly inside the template. In this mode, the action is always executed, and the template is split into executed fragments and fragments in the cache, as illustrated in Figure 12-3.

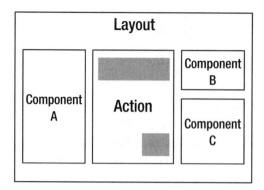

Fragment Cache

Figure 12-3. *Caching a template fragment*

For instance, you may have a list of users that shows a link of the last-accessed user, and this information is dynamic. The cache() helper defines the parts of a template that are to be put in the cache. See Listing 12-5 for details on the syntax.

Listing 12-5. *Using the cache() Helper, in myapp/modules/user/templates/listSuccess.php*

```
<!-- Code executed each time -->
<?php echo link_to('last accessed user', 'user/show?id='.$last_accessed_user_id) ?>

<!-- Cached code -->
<?php if (!cache('users')): ?>
  <?php foreach ($users as $user): ?>
    <?php echo $user->getName() ?>
  <?php endforeach; ?>
  <?php cache_save() ?>
<?php endif; ?>
```

Here's how it works:

- If a cached version of the fragment named 'users' is found, it is used to replace the code between the <?php if (!cache($unique_fragment_name)): ?> and the <?php endif; ?> lines.

- If not, the code between these lines is processed and saved in the cache, identified with the unique fragment name.

The code not included between such lines is always processed and not cached.

■**Caution** The action (list in the example) must not have caching enabled, since this would bypass the whole template execution and ignore the fragment cache declaration.

The speed boost of using the template fragment cache is not as significant as with the action cache, since the action is always executed, the template is partially processed, and the layout is always used for decoration.

You can declare additional fragments in the same template; however, you need to give each of them a unique name so that the symfony cache system can find them afterwards.

As with actions and components, cached fragments can take a lifetime in seconds as a second argument of the call to the cache() helper.

```
<?php if (!cache('users', 43200)): ?>
```

The default cache lifetime (86400 seconds, or one day) is used if no parameter is given to the helper.

■**Tip** Another way to make an action cacheable is to insert the variables that make it vary into the action's routing pattern. For instance, if a home page displays the name of the connected user, it cannot be cached unless the URL contains the user nickname. Another example is for internationalized applications: If you want to enable caching on a page that has several translations, the language code must somehow be included in the URL pattern. This trick will multiply the number of pages in the cache, but it can be of great help to speed up heavily interactive applications.

Configuring the Cache Dynamically

The cache.yml file is one way to define cache settings, but it has the inconvenience of being invariant. However, as usual in symfony, you can use plain PHP rather than YAML, and that allows you to configure the cache dynamically.

Why would you want to change the cache settings dynamically? A good example is a page that is different for authenticated users and for anonymous ones, but the URL remains the same. Imagine an article/show page with a rating system for articles. The rating feature is disabled for anonymous users. For those users, rating links trigger the display of a login form. This version of the page can be cached. On the other hand, for authenticated users, clicking a rating link makes a POST request and creates a new rating. This time, the cache must be disabled for the page so that symfony builds it dynamically.

The right place to define dynamic cache settings is in a filter executed before the sfCacheFilter. Indeed, the cache is a filter in symfony, just like the web debug toolbar and the security features. In order to enable the cache for the article/show page only if the user is not authenticated, create a conditionalCacheFilter in the application lib/ directory, as shown in Listing 12-6.

Listing 12-6. *Configuring the Cache in PHP, in* myapp/lib/conditionalCacheFilter.class.php

```php
class conditionalCacheFilter extends sfFilter
{
  public function execute($filterChain)
  {
    $context = $this->getContext();
    if (!$context->getUser()->isAuthenticated())
    {
      foreach ($this->getParameter('pages') as $page)
      {
        $context->getViewCacheManager()->addCache($page['module'], $page['action'], ➥
array('lifeTime' => 86400));
      }
    }

    // Execute next filter
    $filterChain->execute();
  }
}
```

You must register this filter in the filters.yml file before the sfCacheFilter, as shown in Listing 12-7.

Listing 12-7. *Registering Your Custom Filter, in* myapp/config/filters.yml

```yaml
...
security: ~

conditionalCache:
  class: conditionalCacheFilter
  param:
    pages:
      - { module: article, action: show }

cache: ~
...
```

Clear the cache (to autoload the new filter class), and the conditional cache is ready. It will enable the cache of the pages defined in the pages parameter only for users who are not authenticated.

The addCache() method of the sfViewCacheManager object expects a module name, an action name, and an associative array with the same parameters as the ones you would define in a cache.yml file. For instance, if you want to define that the article/show action must be cached with the layout and with a lifetime of 3600 seconds, then write the following:

```
$context->getViewCacheManager()->addCache('article', 'show', array(
  'withLayout' => true,
  'lifeTime'   => 3600,
));
```

ALTERNATIVE CACHING STORAGE

By default, the symfony cache system stores data in files on the web server hard disk. You may want to store cache in memory (for instance, via memcache) or in a database (notably if you want to share your cache among several servers or speed up cache removal). You can easily alter symfony's default cache storage system because the cache class used by the symfony view cache manager is defined in factories.yml.

The default view cache storage factory is the sfFileCache class:

```
view_cache:
    class: sfFileCache
    param:
        automaticCleaningFactor: 0
        cacheDir:                %SF_TEMPLATE_CACHE_DIR%
```

You can replace the class with your own cache storage class or with one of the symfony alternative classes (sfSQLiteCache for instance). The parameters defined under the param key are passed to the initialize() method of your class as an associative array. Any view cache storage class must implement all methods found in the abstract sfCache class. Refer to the API documentation (http://www.symfony-project.com/api/symfony.html) for more information on this subject.

Using the Super Fast Cache

Even a cached page involves some PHP code execution. For such a page, symfony still loads the configuration, builds the response, and so on. If you are really sure that a page is not going to change for a while, you can bypass symfony completely by putting the resulting HTML code directly into the web/ folder. This works thanks to the Apache mod_rewrite settings, provided that your routing rule specifies a pattern ending without a suffix or with .html.

You can do this by hand, page by page, with a simple command-line call:

```
> curl http://myapp.example.com/user/list.html > web/user/list.html
```

After that, every time that the user/list action is requested, Apache finds the corresponding list.html page and bypasses symfony completely. The trade-off is that you can't control the page cache with symfony anymore (lifetime, automatic deletion, and so on), but the speed gain is very impressive.

Alternatively, you can use the sfSuperCache symfony plug-in, which automates the process and supports lifetime and cache clearing. Refer to Chapter 17 for more information about plug-ins.

OTHER SPEEDUP TACTICS

In addition to the HTML cache, symfony has two other cache mechanisms, which are completely automated and transparent to the developer. In the production environment, the *configuration* and the *template translations* are cached in files stored in the `myproject/cache/config/` and `myproject/cache/i18n/` directories without any intervention.

PHP accelerators (eAccelerator, APC, XCache, and so on), also called *opcode caching modules*, increase performance of PHP scripts by caching them in a compiled state, so that the overhead of code parsing and compiling is almost completely eliminated. This is particularly effective for the Propel classes, which contain a great amount of code. These accelerators are compatible with symfony and can easily triple the speed of an application. They are recommended in production environments for any symfony application with a large audience.

With a PHP accelerator, you can manually *store persistent data in memory*, to avoid doing the same processing for each request, with the `sfProcessCache` class. And if you want to store the result of a CPU-intensive function in a file, you will probably use the `sfFunctionCache` object. Refer to Chapter 18 for more information about these mechanisms.

Removing Items from the Cache

If the scripts or the data of your application change, the cache will contain outdated information. To avoid incoherence and bugs, you can remove parts of the cache in many different ways, according to your needs.

Clearing the Entire Cache

The `clear-cache` task of the symfony command line erases the cache (HTML, configuration, and i18n cache). You can pass it arguments to erase only a subset of the cache, as shown in Listing 12-8. Remember to call it only from the root of a symfony project.

Listing 12-8. *Clearing the Cache*

```
// Erase the whole cache
> symfony clear-cache

// Short syntax
> symfony cc

// Erase only the cache of the myapp application
> symfony clear-cache myapp

// Erase only the HTML cache of the myapp application
> symfony clear-cache myapp template

// Erase only the configuration cache of the myapp application
> symfony clear-cache myapp config
```

Clearing Selective Parts of the Cache

When the database is updated, the cache of the actions related to the modified data must be cleared. You could clear the whole cache, but that would be a waste for all the existing cached actions that are unrelated to the model change. This is where the remove() method of the sfViewCacheManager object applies. It expects an internal URI as argument (the same kind of argument you would provide to a link_to()), and removes the related action cache.

For instance, imagine that the update action of the user module modifies the columns of a User object. The cached versions of the list and show actions need to be cleared, or else the old versions, which contain erroneous data, are displayed. To handle this, use the remove() method, as shown in Listing 12-9.

Listing 12-9. *Clearing the Cache for a Given Action, in* modules/user/actions/actions.class.php

```
public function executeUpdate()
{
  // Update a user
  $user_id = $this->getRequestParameter('id');
  $user = UserPeer::retrieveByPk($user_id);
  $this->foward404Unless($user);
  $user->setName($this->getRequestParameter('name'));
  ...
  $user->save();

  // Clear the cache for actions related to this user
  $cacheManager = $this->getContext()->getViewCacheManager();
  $cacheManager->remove('user/list');
  $cacheManager->remove('user/show?id='.$user_id);
  ...
}
```

Removing cached partials, components, and component slots is a little trickier. As you can pass them any type of parameter (including objects), it is almost impossible to identify their cached version after the fact. Let's focus on partials, as the explanation is the same for the other template components. Symfony identifies a cached partial with a special prefix (sf_cache_partial), the name of the module, and the name of the partial, plus a hash of all the parameters used to call it, as follows:

```
// A partial called by
<?php include_partial('user/my_partial', array('user' => $user) ?>

// Is identified in the cache as
/sf_cache_partial/user/_my_partial/sf_cache_key/bf41dd9c84d59f3574a5da244626dcc8
```

In theory, you could remove a cached partial with the remove() method if you knew the value of the parameters hash used to identify it, but this is very impracticable. Fortunately, if you add a sf_cache_key parameter to the include_partial() helper call, you can identify the partial in the cache with something that you know. As you can see in Listing 12-10, clearing a single cached partial—for instance, to clean up the cache from the partial based on a modified User—becomes easy.

Listing 12-10. *Clearing Partials from the Cache*

```php
<?php include_partial('user/my_partial', array(
  'user'        => $user,
  'sf_cache_key' => $user->getId()
) ?>

// Is identified in the cache as
/sf_cache_partial/user/_my_partial/sf_cache_key/12

// Clear _my_partial for a specific user in the cache with $cacheManager->re-
move('@sf_cache_partial?module=user&action=_my_partial&sf_cache_key=' ➥
.$user->getId());
```

You cannot use this method to clear all occurrences of a partial in the cache. You will learn how to clear these in the "Clearing the Cache Manually" section later in this chapter.

To clear template fragments, use the same remove() method. The key identifying the fragment in the cache is composed of the same sf_cache_partial prefix, the module name, the action name, and the sf_cache_key (the unique name of the cache fragment included by the cache() helper). Listing 12-11 shows an example.

Listing 12-11. *Clearing Template Fragments from the Cache*

```php
<!-- Cached code -->
<?php if (!cache('users')): ?>
  ... // Whatever
  <?php cache_save() ?>
<?php endif; ?>

// Is identified in the cache as
/sf_cache_partial/user/list/sf_cache_key/users

// Clear it with
$cacheManager->remove('@sf_cache_partial?module=user&action=list&sf_cache_key=users');
```

SELECTIVE CACHE CLEARING CAN DAMAGE YOUR BRAIN

The trickiest part of the cache-clearing job is to determine which actions are influenced by a data update.

For instance, imagine that the current application has a publication module where publications are listed (list action) and described (show action), along with the details of their author (an instance of the User class). Modifying one User record will affect all the descriptions of the user's publications and the list of publications. This means that you need to add to the update action of the user module, something like this:

```
$c = new Criteria();
$c->add(PublicationPeer::AUTHOR_ID, $this->getRequestParameter('id'));
$publications = PublicationPeer::doSelect($c);

$cacheManager = sfContext::getInstance()->getViewCacheManager();
foreach ($publications as $publication)
{
  $cacheManager->remove('publication/show?id='.$publication->getId());
}
$cacheManager->remove('publication/list');
```

When you start using the HTML cache, you need to keep a clear view of the dependencies between the model and the actions, so that new errors don't appear because of a misunderstood relationship. Keep in mind that all the actions that modify the model should probably contain a bunch of calls to the `remove()` method if the HTML cache is used somewhere in the application.

And, if you don't want to damage your brain with too difficult an analysis, you can always clear the whole cache each time you update the database . . .

Cache Directory Structure

The `cache/` directory of your application has the following structure:

```
cache/                   # sf_root_cache_dir
  [APP_NAME]/            # sf_base_cache_dir
    [ENV_NAME]/          # sf_cache_dir
      config/            # sf_config_cache_dir
      i18n/              # sf_i18n_cache_dir
      modules/           # sf_module_cache_dir
      template/          # sf_template_cache_dir
        [HOST_NAME]/
          all/
```

Cached templates are stored under the `[HOST_NAME]` directory (where dots are replaced by underscores for compatibility with file systems), in a directory structure corresponding to their URL. For instance, the template cache of a page called with:

```
http://www.myapp.com/user/show/id/12
```

is stored in:

```
cache/myapp/prod/template/www_myapp_com/all/user/show/id/12.cache
```

You should not write file paths directly in your code. Instead, you can use the file path constants. For instance, to retrieve the absolute path to the `template/` directory of the current application in the current environment, use `sfConfig::get('sf_template_cache_dir')`.

Knowing this directory structure will help you deal with manual cache clearing.

Clearing the Cache Manually

Clearing the cache across applications can be a problem. For instance, if an administrator modifies a record in the user table in a backend application, all the actions depending on this user in the frontend application need to be cleared from the cache. The remove() method expects an internal URI, but applications don't know other application's routing rules (applications are isolated from each other), so you cannot use the remove() method to clear the cache of another application.

The solution is to manually remove the files from the cache/ directory, based on a file path. For instance, if the backend application needs to clear the cache of the user/show action in the frontend application for the user of id 12, it can use the following:

```
$sf_root_cache_dir = sfConfig::get('sf_root_cache_dir');
$cache_dir = $sf_root_cache_dir.'/frontend/prod/template/www_myapp_com/all';
unlink($cache_dir.'/user/show/id/12.cache');
```

But this is not very satisfactory. This command will erase only the cache of the current environment, and it forces you to write the environment name and the current host name in the file path. To bypass these limitations, you can use the sfToolkit::clearGlob() method. It takes a file pattern as a parameter and accepts wildcards. For instance, you can clear the same cache files as in the preceding example, regardless of host and environment, with this:

```
$cache_dir = $sf_root_cache_dir.'/frontend/*/template/*/all';
sfToolkit::clearGlob($cache_dir.'/user/show/id/12.cache');
```

This method is also of great use when you need to erase a cached action regardless of certain parameters. For instance, if your application handles several languages, you may have chosen to insert the language code in all URLs. So the link to a user profile page should look like this:

```
http://www.myapp.com/en/user/show/id/12
```

To remove the cached profile of the user having an id of 12 in all languages, you can simply do this:

```
sfToolkit::clearGlob($cache_dir.'/*/user/show/id/12.cache');
```

Testing and Monitoring Caching

HTML caching, if not properly handled, can create incoherence in displayed data. Each time you disable the cache for an element, you should test it thoroughly and monitor the execution boost to tweak it.

Building a Staging Environment

The caching system is prone to new errors in the production environment that can't be detected in the development environment, since the HTML cache is disabled by default in development. If you enable the HTML cache for some actions, you should add a new environment, called staging in this section, with the same settings as the prod environment (thus, with cache enabled) but with web_debug set to on.

To set it up, edit the `settings.yml` file of your application and add the lines shown in Listing 12-12 at the top.

Listing 12-12. *Settings for a staging Environment, in* `myapp/config/settings.yml`

```
staging:
  .settings:
    web_debug:  on
    cache:      on
```

In addition, create a new front controller by copying the production one (probably `myproject/web/index.php`) to a new `myapp_staging.php`. Edit it to change the `SF_ENVIRONMENT` and `SF_DEBUG` values, as follows:

```
define('SF_ENVIRONMENT', 'staging');
define('SF_DEBUG',        true);
```

That's it—you have a new environment. Use it by adding the front controller name after the domain name:

```
http://myapp.example.com/myapp_staging.php/user/list
```

■**Tip** Instead of copying an existing one, you can create a new front controller with the `symfony` command line. For instance, to create a `staging` environment for the `myapp` application, called `myapp_staging.php` and where `SF_DEBUG` is `true`, just call `symfony init-controller myapp staging myapp_` ➥ `staging.php true`.

Monitoring Performance

Chapter 16 will explore the web debug toolbar and its contents. However, as this toolbar offers valuable information about cached elements, here is a brief description of its cache features.

When you browse to a page that contains cacheable elements (action, partials, fragments, and so on), the web debug toolbar (in the top-right corner of the window) shows an ignore cache button (a green, rounded arrow), as shown in Figure 12-4. This button reloads the page and forces the processing of cached elements. Be aware that it does not clear the cache.

The last number on the right side of the debug toolbar is the duration of the request execution. If you enable cache on a page, this number should decrease the second time you load the page, since symfony uses the data from the cache instead of reprocessing the scripts. You can easily monitor the cache improvements with this indicator.

Figure 12-4. *Web debug toolbar for pages using caching*

The debug toolbar also shows the number of database queries executed during the processing of the request, and the detail of the durations per category (click the total duration to display the detail). Monitoring this data, in conjunction with the total duration, will help you do fine measures of the performance improvements brought by the cache.

Benchmarking

The debug mode greatly decreases the speed of your application, since a lot of information is logged and made available to the web debug toolbar. So the processed time displayed when you browse in the staging environment is not representative of what it will be in production, where the debug mode is turned off.

To get a better view of the process time of each request, you should use *benchmarking tools*, like Apache Bench or JMeter. These tools allow load testing and provide two important pieces of information: the average loading time of a specific page and the maximum capacity of your server. The average loading time data is very useful for monitoring performance improvements due to cache activation.

Identifying Cache Parts

When the web debug toolbar is enabled, the cached elements are identified in a page with a red frame, each having a cache information box on the top left, as shown in Figure 12-5. The box has a blue background if the element has been executed, or a yellow background if it comes from the cache. Clicking the cache information link displays the identifier of the cache element, its lifetime, and the elapsed time since its last modification. This will help you identify problems when dealing with out-of-context elements, to see when the element was created and which parts of a template you can actually cache.

Figure 12-5. *Identification for cached elements in a page*

HTTP 1.1 and Client-Side Caching

The HTTP 1.1 protocol defines a bunch of headers that can be of great use to further speed up an application by controlling the browser's cache system.

The HTTP 1.1 specifications of the World Wide Web Consortium (W3C, http://www.w3.org/Protocols/rfc2616/rfc2616-sec14.html) describe these headers in detail. If an action has caching enabled, and it uses the with_layout option, it can use one or more of the mechanisms described in the following sections.

Even if some of the browsers of your website's users may not support HTTP 1.1, there is no risk in using the HTTP 1.1 cache features. A browser receiving headers that it doesn't understand simply ignores them, so you are advised to set up the HTTP 1.1 cache mechanisms.

In addition, HTTP 1.1 headers are also understood by proxies and caching servers. Even if a user's browser doesn't understand HTTP 1.1, there can be a proxy in the route of the request to take advantage of it.

Adding an ETag Header to Avoid Sending Unchanged Content

When the ETag feature is enabled, the web server adds to the response a special header containing a signature of the response itself.

```
ETag: 1A2Z3E4R5T6Y7U
```

The user's browser will store this signature, and send it again together with the request the next time it needs the same page. If the new signature shows that the page didn't change since the first request, the browser doesn't send the response back. Instead, it just sends a 304: Not modified header. It saves CPU time (if gzipping is enabled for example) and bandwidth (page transfer) for the server, and time (page transfer) for the client. Overall, pages in a cache with an ETag are even faster to load than pages in a cache without an ETag.

In symfony, you enable the ETag feature for the whole application in settings.yml. Here is the default ETag setting:

```
all:
  .settings:
    etag: on
```

For actions in a cache with layout, the response is taken directly from the cache/ directory, so the process is even faster.

Adding a Last-Modified Header to Avoid Sending Still Valid Content

When the server sends the response to the browser, it can add a special header to specify when the data contained in the page was last changed:

```
Last-Modified: Sat, 23 Nov 2006 13:27:31 GMT
```

Browsers can understand this header and, when requesting the page again, add an If-Modified header accordingly:

```
If-Modified-Since: Sat, 23 Nov 2006 13:27:31 GMT
```

The server can then compare the value kept by the client and the one returned by its application. If they match, the server returns a 304: Not modified header, saving bandwidth and CPU time, just as with ETags.

In symfony, you can set the Last-Modified response header just as you would for another header. For instance, you can use it like this in an action:

```
$this->getResponse()->setHttpHeader('Last-Modified', $this->getResponse() ➥
->getDate($timestamp));
```

This date can be the actual date of the last update of the data used in the page, given from your database or your file system. The getDate() method of the sfResponse object converts a timestamp to a formatted date in the format needed for the Last-Modified header (RFC1123).

Adding Vary Headers to Allow Several Cached Versions of a Page

Another HTTP 1.1 header is Vary. It defines which parameters a page depends on, and is used by browsers and proxies to build cache keys. For example, if the content of a page depends on cookies, you can set its Vary header as follows:

```
Vary: Cookie
```

Most often, it is difficult to enable caching on actions because the page may vary according to the cookie, the user language, or something else. If you don't mind expanding the size of your cache, set the Vary header of the response properly. This can be done for the whole application or on a per-action basis, using the cache.yml configuration file or the sfResponse related method as follows:

```
$this->getResponse()->addVaryHttpHeader('Cookie');
$this->getResponse()->addVaryHttpHeader('User-Agent');
$this->getResponse()->addVaryHttpHeader('Accept-Language');
```

Symfony will store a different version of the page in the cache for each value of these parameters. This will increase the size of the cache, but whenever the server receives a request matching these headers, the response is taken from the cache instead of being processed. This is a great performance tool for pages that vary only according to request headers.

Adding a Cache-Control Header to Allow Client-Side Caching

Up to now, even by adding headers, the browser keeps sending requests to the server even if it holds a cached version of the page. You can avoid that by adding Cache-Control and Expires headers to the response. These headers are disabled by default in PHP, but symfony can override this behavior to avoid unnecessary requests to your server.

As usual, you trigger this behavior by calling a method of the sfResponse object. In an action, define the maximum time a page should be cached (in seconds):

```
$this->getResponse()->addCacheControlHttpHeader('max_age=60');
```

You can also specify under which conditions a page may be cached, so that the provider's cache does not keep a copy of private data (like bank account numbers):

```
$this->getResponse()->addCacheControlHttpHeader('private=True');
```

Using Cache-Control HTTP directives, you get the ability to fine-tune the various cache mechanisms between your server and the client's browser. For a detailed review of these directives, see the W3C Cache-Control specifications.

One last header can be set through symfony: the Expires header:

```
$this->getResponse()->setHttpHeader('Expires', $this->getResponse() ➥
->getDate($timestamp));
```

■**Caution** The major consequence of turning on the Cache-Control mechanism is that your server logs won't show all the requests issued by the users, but only the ones actually received. If the performance gets better, the apparent popularity of the site may decrease in the statistics.

Summary

The cache system provides variable *performance boosts* according to the cache type selected. From the best gain to the least, the cache types are as follows:

- Super cache

- Action cache with layout

- Action cache without layout

- Fragment cache in the template

In addition, partials and components can be cached as well.

If changing data in the model or in the session forces you to *erase the cache* for the sake of coherence, you can do it with a *fine granularity* for optimum performance—erase only the elements that have changed, and keep the others.

Remember to *test* all the pages where caching is enabled with extra care, as new bugs may appear if you cache the wrong elements or if you forget to clear the cache when you update the underlying data. A *staging* environment, dedicated to cache testing, is of great use for that purpose.

Finally, make the best of the *HTTP 1.1* protocol with symfony's advanced cache-tweaking features, which will involve the client in the caching task and provide even more performance gains.

## CHAPTER 13

I18N and L10N

If you ever developed an international application, you know that dealing with every aspect of text translation, local standards, and localized content can be a nightmare. Fortunately, symfony natively automates all the aspects of internationalization.

As it is a long word, developers often refer to *internationalization* as i18n (count the letters in the word to know why). *Localization* is referred to as l10n. They cover two different aspects of multilingual web applications.

An *internationalized application* contains several versions of the same content in various languages or formats. For instance, a webmail interface can offer the same service in several languages; only the interface changes.

A *localized application* contains distinct information according to the country from which it is browsed. Think about the contents of a news portal: When browsed from the United States, it displays the latest headlines about the United States, but when browsed from France, the headlines concern the French news. So an l10n application not only provides content translation, but the content can be different from one localized version to another.

All in all, dealing with i18n and l10n means that the application can take care of the following:

- Text translation (interface, assets, and content)

- Standards and formats (dates, amounts, numbers, and so on)

- Localized content (many versions of a given object according to a country)

This chapter covers the way symfony deals with those elements and how you can use it to develop internationalized and localized applications.

User Culture

All the built-in i18n features in symfony are based on a parameter of the user session called the *culture*. The culture is the combination of the country and the language of the user, and it determines how the text and culture-dependent information are displayed. Since it is serialized in the user session, the culture is persistent between pages.

Setting the Default Culture

By default, the culture of new users is the default_culture. You can change this setting in the i18n.yml configuration file, as shown in Listing 13-1.

Listing 13-1. *Setting the Default Culture, in myapp/config/i18n.yml*

```
all:
  default_culture:    fr_FR
```

Note During development, you might be surprised that a culture change in the i18n.yml file doesn't change the current culture in the browser. That's because the session already has a culture from previous pages. If you want to see the application with the new default culture, you need to clear the domain cookies or restart your browser.

Keeping both the language and the country in the culture is necessary because you may have a different French translation for users from France, Belgium, or Canada, and a different Spanish content for users from Spain or Mexico. The language is coded in two lowercase characters, according to the ISO 639-1 standard (for instance, en for English). The country is coded in two uppercase characters, according to the ISO 3166-1 standard (for instance, GB for Great Britain).

Changing the Culture for a User

The user culture can be changed during the browsing session—for instance, when a user decides to switch from the English version to the French version of the application, or when a user logs in to the application and uses the language stored in his preferences. That's why the sfUser class offers getter and setter methods for the user culture. Listing 13-2 shows how to use these methods in an action.

Listing 13-2. *Setting and Retrieving the Culture in an Action*

```
// Culture setter
$this->getUser()->setCulture('en_US');

// Culture getter
$culture = $this->getUser()->getCulture();
 => en_US
```

CULTURE IN THE URL

When using symfony's localization and internationalization features, pages tend to have different versions for a single URL—it all depends on the user session. This prevents you from caching or indexing your pages in a search engine.

One solution is to make the culture appear in every URL, so that translated pages can be seen as different URLs to the outside world. In order to do that, add the `:sf_culture` token in every rule of your application `routing.yml`:

```
page:
  url: /:sf_culture/:page
  requirements: { sf_culture: (?:fr|en|de) }
  params: ...

article:
  url: /:sf_culture/:year/:month/:day/:slug
  requirements: { sf_culture: (?:fr|en|de) }
  params: ...
```

To avoid manually setting the `sf_culture` request parameter in every `link_to()`, symfony automatically adds the user culture to the default routing parameters. It also works inbound because symfony will automatically change the user culture if the `sf_culture` parameter is found in the URL.

Determining the Culture Automatically

In many applications, the user culture is defined during the first request, based on the browser preferences. Users can define a list of accepted languages in their browser, and this data is sent to the server with each request, in the `Accept-Language` HTTP header. You can retrieve it in symfony through the `sfRequest` object. For instance, to get the list of preferred languages of a user in an action, type this:

```
$languages = $this->getRequest()->getLanguages();
```

The HTTP header is a string, but symfony automatically parses it and converts it into an array. So the preferred language of the user is accessible with `$languages[0]` in the preceding example.

It can be useful to automatically set the user culture to the preferred browser languages in a site home page or in a filter for all pages.

Caution The `Accept-Language` HTTP header is not very reliable information, since users rarely know how to modify it in their browser. Most of the time, the preferred browser language is the language of the interface, and browsers are not available in all languages. If you decide to set the culture automatically according to the browser preferred language, make sure you provide a way for the user to choose an alternate language.

Standards and Formats

The internals of a web application don't care about cultural particularities. Databases, for instance, use international standards to store dates, amounts, and so on. But when data is sent to or retrieved from users, a conversion needs to be made. Users won't understand timestamps, and they will prefer to declare their mother language as Français instead of French. So you will need assistance to do the conversion automatically, based on the user culture.

Outputting Data in the User's Culture

Once the culture is defined, the helpers depending on it will automatically have proper output. For instance, the `format_number()` helper automatically displays a number in a format familiar to the user, according to its culture, as shown in Listing 13-3.

Listing 13-3. *Displaying a Number for the User's Culture*

```php
<?php use_helper('Number') ?>

<?php $sf_user->setCulture('en_US') ?>
<?php echo format_number(12000.10) ?>
 => '12,000.10'

<?php $sf_user->setCulture('fr_FR') ?>
<?php echo format_number(12000.10) ?>
 => '12 000,10'
```

You don't need to explicitly pass the culture to the helpers. They will look for it themselves in the current session object. Listing 13-4 lists helpers that take into account the user culture for their output.

Listing 13-4. *Culture-Dependent Helpers*

```php
<?php use_helper('Date') ?>

<?php echo format_date(time()) ?>
 => '9/14/06'

<?php echo format_datetime(time()) ?>
 => 'September 14, 2006 6:11:07 PM CEST'

<?php use_helper('Number') ?>

<?php echo format_number(12000.10) ?>
 => '12,000.10'

<?php echo format_currency(1350, 'USD') ?>
 => '$1,350.00'
```

```php
<?php use_helper('I18N') ?>

<?php echo format_country('US') ?>
 => 'United States'

<?php format_language('en') ?>
 => 'English'

<?php use_helper('Form') ?>

<?php echo input_date_tag('birth_date', mktime(0, 0, 0, 9, 14, 2006)) ?>
 => input type="text" name="birth_date" id="birth_date" value="9/14/06" size="11" />

<?php echo select_country_tag('country', 'US') ?>
 => <select name="country" id="country"><option value="AF">Afghanistan</option>

    ...
    <option value="GB">United Kingdom</option>
    <option value="US" selected="selected">United States</option>
    <option value="UM">United States Minor Outlying Islands</option>
    <option value="UY">Uruguay</option>

    ...
    </select>
```

The date helpers can accept an additional format parameter to force a culture-independent display, but you shouldn't use it if your application is internationalized.

Getting Data from a Localized Input

If it is necessary to show data in the user's culture, as for retrieving data, you should, as much as possible, push users of your application to input already internationalized data. This approach will save you from trying to figure out how to convert data with varying formats and uncertain locality. For instance, who might enter a monetary value with comma separators in an input box?

You can frame the user input format either by hiding the actual data (as in a select_country_tag()) or by separating the different components of complex data into several simple inputs.

For dates, however, this is often not possible. Users are used to entering dates in their cultural format, and you need to be able to convert such data to an internal (and international) format. This is where the sfI18N class applies. Listing 13-5 demonstrates how this class is used.

Listing 13-5. *Getting a Date from a Localized Format in an Action*

```php
$date= $this->getRequestParameter('birth_date');
$user_culture = $this->getUser()->getCulture();

// Getting a timestamp
$timestamp = sfI18N::getTimestampForCulture($date, $user_culture);

// Getting a structured date
list($d, $m, $y) = sfI18N::getDateForCulture($date, $user_culture);
```

Text Information in the Database

A localized application offers different content according to the user's culture. For instance, an online shop can offer products worldwide at the same price, but with a custom description for every country. This means that the database must be able to store different versions of a given piece of data, and for that, you need to design your schema in a particular way and use culture each time you manipulate localized model objects.

Creating Localized Schema

For each table that contains some localized data, you should split the table in two parts: one table that does not have any i18n column, and the other one with only the i18n columns. The two tables are to be linked by a one-to-many relationship. This setup lets you add more languages when required without changing your model. Let's consider an example using a Product table.

First, create tables in the schema.yml file, as shown in Listing 13-6.

Listing 13-6. *Sample Schema for i18n Data, in config/schema.yml*

```
my_connection:
  my_product:
    _attributes: { phpName: Product, isI18N: true, i18nTable: my_product_i18n }
    id:          { type: integer, required: true, primaryKey: true,
                   autoincrement: true }
    price:       { type: float }

  my_product_i18n:
    _attributes: { phpName: ProductI18n }
    id:          { type: integer, required: true, primaryKey: true,
                   foreignTable: my_product, foreignReference: id }
    culture:     { isCulture: true, type: varchar, size: 7, required: true,
                   primaryKey: true }
    name:        { type: varchar, size: 50 }
```

Notice the isI18N and i18nTable attributes in the first table, and the special culture column in the second. All these are symfony-specific Propel enhancements.

The symfony automations can make this much faster to write. If the table containing internationalized data has the same name as the main table with _i18n as a suffix, and they are related with a column named id in both tables, you can omit the id and culture columns in the _i18n table as well as the specific i18n attributes for the main table; symfony will infer them. It means that symfony will see the schema in Listing 13-7 as the same as the one in Listing 13-6.

Listing 13-7. *Sample Schema for i18n Data, Short Version, in* `config/schema.yml`

```
my_connection:
  my_product:
    _attributes: { phpName: Product }
    id:
    price:         float
  my_product_i18n:
    _attributes: { phpName: ProductI18n }
    name:          varchar(50)
```

Using the Generated I18n Objects

Once the corresponding object model is built (don't forget to call `symfony propel-build-model` and clear the cache with a `symfony cc` after each modification of the `schema.yml`), you can use your `Product` class with i18n support as if there were only one table, as shown in Listing 13-8.

Listing 13-8. *Dealing with i18n Objects*

```
$product = ProductPeer::retrieveByPk(1);
$product->setCulture('fr');
$product->setName('Nom du produit');
$product->save();

$product->setCulture('en');
$product->setName('Product name');
$product->save();

echo $product->getName();
 => 'Product name'

$product->setCulture('fr');
echo $product->getName();
 => 'Nom du produit'
```

If you'd rather not have to remember to change the culture each time you use an i18n object, you can also change the `hydrate()` method in the object class. See an example in Listing 13-9.

Listing 13-9. *Overriding the* `hydrate()` *Method to Set the Culture, in* `myproject/lib/model/` `Product.php`

```
public function hydrate(ResultSet $rs, $startcol = 1)
{
  parent::hydrate($rs, $startcol);
  $this->setCulture(sfContext::getInstance()->getUser()->getCulture());
}
```

As for queries with the peer objects, you can restrict the results to objects having a translation for the current culture by using the `doSelectWithI18n` method, instead of the usual `doSelect`, as shown in Listing 13-10. In addition, it will create the related i18n objects at the same time as the regular ones, resulting in a reduced number of queries to get the full content (refer to Chapter 18 for more information about this method's positive impacts on performance).

Listing 13-10. *Retrieving Objects with an i18n Criteria*

```
$c = new Criteria();
$c->add(ProductPeer::PRICE, 100, Criteria::LESS_THAN);
$products = ProductPeer::doSelectWithI18n($c, $culture);
// The $culture argument is optional
// The current user culture is used if no culture is given
```

So basically, you should never have to deal with the i18n objects directly, but instead pass the culture to the model (or let it guess it) each time you do a query with the regular objects.

Interface Translation

The user interface needs to be adapted for i18n applications. Templates must be able to display labels, messages, and navigation in several languages but with the same presentation. Symfony recommends that you build your templates with the default language, and that you provide a translation for the phrases used in your templates in a dictionary file. That way, you don't need to change your templates each time you modify, add, or remove a translation.

Configuring Translation

The templates are not translated by default, which means that you need to activate the template translation feature in the `settings.yml` file prior to everything else, as shown in Listing 13-11.

Listing 13-11. *Activating Interface Translation, in* `myapp/config/settings.yml`

```
all:
  .settings:
    i18n: on
```

Using the Translation Helper

Let's say that you want to create a website in English and French, with English being the default language. Before even thinking about having the site translated, you probably wrote the templates something like the example shown in Listing 13-12.

Listing 13-12. *A Single-Language Template*

```
Welcome to our website. Today's date is <?php echo format_date(date()) ?>
```

For symfony to translate the phrases of a template, they must be identified as text to be translated. This is the purpose of the __() helper (two underscores), a member of the I18N helper group. So all your templates need to enclose the phrases to translate in such function calls. Listing 13-12, for example, can be modified to look like Listing 13-13 (as you will see in the "Handling Complex Translation Needs" section later in this chapter, there is an even better way to call the translation helper in this example).

Listing 13-13. *A Multiple-Language-Ready Template*

```php
<?php use_helper('I18N') ?>

<?php echo __('Welcome to our website.') ?>
<?php echo __("Today's date is ") ?>
<?php echo format_date(date()) ?>
```

■**Tip** If your application uses the I18N helper group for every page, it is probably a good idea to include it in the standard_helpers setting in the settings.yml file, so that you avoid repeating use_helper('I18N') for each template.

Using Dictionary Files

Each time the __() function is called, symfony looks for a translation of its argument in the dictionary of the current user's culture. If it finds a corresponding phrase, the translation is sent back and displayed in the response. So the user interface translation relies on a dictionary file.

The dictionary files are written in the XML Localization Interchange File Format (XLIFF), named according to the pattern messages.[*language code*].xml, and stored in the application i18n/ directory.

XLIFF is a standard format based on XML. As it is well known, you can use third-party translation tools to reference all text in your website and translate it. Translation firms know how to handle such files and to translate an entire site just by adding a new XLIFF translation.

■**Tip** In addition to the XLIFF standard, symfony also supports several other translation back-ends for dictionaries: gettext, MySQL, SQLite, and Creole. Refer to the API documentation for more information about configuring these back-ends.

Listing 13-14 shows an example of the XLIFF syntax with the messages.fr.xml file necessary to translate Listing 13-13 into French.

Listing 13-14. *An XLIFF Dictionary, in* `myapp/i18n/messages.fr.xml`

```
<?xml version="1.0" ?>
<xliff version="1.0">
  <file orginal="global" source-language="en_US" datatype="plaintext">
    <body>
      <trans-unit id="1">
        <source>Welcome to our website.</source>
        <target>Bienvenue sur notre site web.</target>
      </trans-unit>
      <trans-unit id="2">
        <source>Today's date is </source>
        <target>La date d'aujourd'hui est </target>
      </trans-unit>
    </body>
  </file>
</xliff>
```

The `source-language` attribute must always contain the full ISO code of your default culture. Each translation is written in a `trans-unit` tag with a unique `id` attribute.

With the default user culture (set to en_US), the phrases are not translated and the raw arguments of the `__()` calls are displayed. The result of Listing 13-13 is then similar to Listing 13-12. However, if the culture is changed to fr_FR or fr_BE, the translations from the `messages.fr.xml` file are displayed instead, and the result looks like Listing 13-15.

Listing 13-15. *A Translated Template*

```
Bienvenue sur notre site web. La date d'aujourd'hui est
<?php echo format_date(date()) ?>
```

If additional translations need to be done, simply add a new `messages.XX.xml` translation file in the same directory.

Managing Dictionaries

If your `messages.XX.xml` file becomes too long to be readable, you can always split the translations into several dictionary files, named by theme. For instance, you can split the `messages.fr.xml` file into these three files in the application i18n/ directory:

- `navigation.fr.xml`
- `terms_of_service.fr.xml`
- `search.fr.xml`

Note that as soon as a translation is not to be found in the default `messages.XX.xml` file, you must declare which dictionary is to be used each time you call the `__()` helper, using its third argument. For instance, to output a string that is translated in the `navigation.fr.xml` dictionary, write this:

```
<?php echo __('Welcome to our website', null, 'navigation') ?>
```

Another way to organize translation dictionaries is to split them by module. Instead of writing a single messages.*XX*.xml file for the whole application, you can write one in each modules/[*module_name*]/i18n/ directory. It makes modules more independent from the application, which is necessary if you want to reuse them, such as in plug-ins (see Chapter 17).

Handling Other Elements Requiring Translation

The following are other elements that may require translation:

- Images, text documents, or any other type of *assets* can also vary according to the user culture. The best example is a piece of text with a special typography that is actually an image. For these, you can create subdirectories named after the user culture:

  ```
  <?php echo image_tag($sf_user->getCulture().'/myText.gif') ?>
  ```

- *Error messages* from validation files are automatically output by a __(), so you just need to add their translation to a dictionary to have them translated.

- The *default symfony pages* (page not found, internal server error, restricted access, and so on) are in English and must be rewritten in an i18n application. You should probably create your own default module in your application and use __() in its templates. Refer to Chapter 19 to see how to customize these pages.

Handling Complex Translation Needs

Translation only makes sense if the __() argument is a full sentence. However, as you sometimes have formatting or variables mixed with words, you could be tempted to cut sentences into several chunks, thus calling the helper on senseless phrases. Fortunately, the __() helper offers a replacement feature based on tokens, which will help you to have a meaningful dictionary that is easier to handle by translators. As with HTML formatting, you can leave it in the helper call as well. Listing 13-16 shows an example.

Listing 13-16. *Translating Sentences That Contain Code*

```
// Base example
Welcome to all the <b>new</b> users.<br />
There are <?php echo count_logged() ?> persons logged.

// Bad way to enable text translation
<?php echo __('Welcome to all the') ?>
<b><?php echo __('new') ?></b>
<?php echo __('users') ?>.<br />
<?php echo __('There are') ?>
<?php echo count_logged() ?>
<?php echo __('persons logged') ?>

// Good way to enable text translation
<?php echo __('Welcome to all the <b>new</b> users') ?> <br />
<?php echo __('There are %1% persons logged', array('%1%' => count_logged())) ?>
```

In this example, the token is %1%, but it can be anything, since the replacement function used by the translation helper is strtr().

One of the common problems with translation is the use of the *plural form*. According to the number of results, the text changes but not in the same way according to the language. For instance, the last sentence in Listing 13-16 is not correct if count_logged() returns 0 or 1. You could do a test on the return value of this function and choose which sentence to use accordingly, but that would represent a lot of code. Additionally, different languages have different grammar rules, and the declension rules of plural can be quite complex. As this problem is very common, symfony provides a helper to deal with it, called format_number_choice(). Listing 13-17 demonstrates how to use this helper.

Listing 13-17. *Translating Sentences Depending on the Value of Parameters*

```
<?php echo format_number_choice(
  '[0]Nobody is logged|[1]There is 1 person logged|(1,+Inf]There are ➥
  %1% persons logged', array('%1%' => count_logged()), count_logged()) ?>
```

The first argument is the multiple possibilities of text. The second argument is the replacement pattern (as with the __() helper) and is optional. The third argument is the number on which the test is made to determine which text is taken.

The message/string choices are separated by the pipe (|) character followed by an array of acceptable values, using the following syntax:

[1,2]: Accepts values between 1 and 2, inclusive

(1,2): Accepts values between 1 and 2, excluding 1 and 2

{1,2,3,4}: Only values defined in the set are accepted

[-Inf,0): Accepts values greater or equal to negative infinity and strictly less than 0

Any nonempty combinations of the delimiters of square brackets and parentheses are acceptable.

The message will need to appear explicitly in the XLIFF file for the translation to work properly. Listing 13-18 shows an example.

Listing 13-18. *XLIFF Dictionary for a format_number_choice() Argument*

```
...
<trans-unit id="3">
  <source>[0]Nobody is logged|[1]There is 1 person logged|(1,+Inf]There are ➥
  %1% persons logged</source>
  <target>[0]Personne n'est connecté|[1]Une personne est connectée|(1,+Inf]Il ➥
  y a %1% personnes en ligne</target>
</trans-unit>
...
```

A FEW WORDS ABOUT CHARSETS

Dealing with internationalized content in templates often leads to problems with charsets. If you use a localized charset, you will need to change it each time the user changes culture. In addition, the templates written in a given charset will not display the characters of another charset properly.

This is why, as soon as you deal with more than one culture, *all your templates must be saved in UTF-8*, and the layout must declare the content with this charset. You won't have any unpleasant surprises if you always work with UTF-8, and you will save yourself from a big headache.

Symfony applications rely on one central setting for the charset, in the `settings.yml` file. Changing this parameter will change the `content-type` header of all responses.

```
all:
  .settings:
    charset: utf-8
```

Calling the Translation Helper Outside a Template

Not all the text that is displayed in a page comes from templates. That's why you often need to call the __() helper in other parts of your application: actions, filters, model classes, and so on. Listing 13-19 shows how to call the helper in an action by retrieving the current instance of the I18N object through the context singleton.

Listing 13-19. *Calling __() in an Action*

```
$this->getContext()->getI18N()->__($text, $args, 'messages');
```

Summary

Handling internationalization and localization in web applications is painless if you know how to deal with the *user culture*. The *helpers* automatically take it into account to output correctly formatted data, and the *localized content from the database* is seen as if it were part of a simple table. As for the interface translation, the __() helper and *XLIFF dictionary* ensure that you will have maximum versatility with minimum work.

PART 4

Development Tools

CHAPTER 14

■■■

Generators

Many applications are based on data stored in a database and offer an interface to access it. Symfony automates the repetitive task of creating a module providing data manipulation capabilities based on a Propel object. If your object model is properly defined, symfony can even generate an entire site administration automatically. This chapter will tell you of the two generators bundled in symfony: scaffolding and administration generator. The latter relies on a special configuration file with a complete syntax, so most of this chapter describes the various possibilities of the administration generator.

Code Generation Based on the Model

In a web application, data access operations can be categorized as one of the following:

- Creation of a record

- Retrieval of records

- Update of a record (and modification of its columns)

- Deletion of a record

These operations are so common that they have a dedicated acronym: *CRUD*. Many pages can be reduced to one of them. For instance, in a forum application, the list of latest posts is a retrieve operation, and the reply to a post corresponds to a create operation.

The basic actions and templates that implement the CRUD operations for a given table are repeatedly created in web applications. In symfony, the model layer contains enough information to allow generating the CRUD operations code, so as to speed up the early part of the development or the back-end interfaces.

All the code generation tasks based on the model create *an entire module*, and result from a single call to the symfony command line in the shape of the following:

```
> symfony <TASK_NAME> <APP_NAME> <MODULE_NAME> <CLASS_NAME>
```

The code generation tasks are `propel-init-crud`, `propel-generate-crud`, and `propel-init-admin`.

Scaffolding and Administration

During application development, code generation can be used for two distinct purposes:

A *scaffolding* is the basic structure (actions and templates) required to operate CRUD on a given table. The code is minimal, since it is meant to serve as a guideline for further development. It is a starting base that must be adapted to match your logic and presentation requirements. Scaffoldings are mostly used during the development phase, to provide a web access to a database, to build a prototype, or to bootstrap a module primarily based on a table.

An *administration* is a sophisticated interface for data manipulation, dedicated to back-end administration. Administrations differ from scaffoldings because their code is not meant to be modified manually. They can be customized, extended, or assembled through configuration or inheritance. Their presentation is important, and they take advantage of additional features such as sorting, pagination, and filtering. An administration can be created and handed over to the client as a finished part of the software product.

The symfony command line uses the word *crud* to designate a scaffolding, and *admin* for an administration.

Initiating or Generating Code

Symfony offers two ways to generate code: either by inheritance (`init`) or by code generation (`generate`).

You can *initiate* a module, that is, create empty classes that inherit from the framework. This masks the PHP code of the actions and the templates to avoid them from being modified. This is useful if your data structure is not final, or if you just need a quick interface to a database to manipulate records. The code executed at runtime is not located in your application, but in the cache. The command-line tasks for this kind of generation start with `propel-init-`.

Initiated action code is empty. For instance, an initiated `article` module has actions looking like this:

```
class articleActions extends autoarticleActions
{
}
```

On the other hand, you can also *generate* the code of the actions and the templates so that it can be modified. The resulting module is therefore independent from the classes of the framework, and cannot be altered using configuration files. The command-line tasks for this kind of generation start with `propel-generate-`.

As the scaffoldings are built to serve as a base for further developments, it is often best to *generate* a scaffolding. On the other hand, an administration should be easy to update through a change in the configuration, and it should remain usable even if the data model changes. That's why administrations are *initiated* only.

Example Data Model

Throughout this chapter, the listings will demonstrate the capabilities of the symfony generators based on a simple example, which will remind you of Chapter 8. This is the well-known example of the weblog application, containing two `Article` and `Comment` classes. Listing 14-1 shows its schema, illustrated in Figure 14-1.

Listing 14-1. *schema.yml of the Example Weblog Application*

```
propel:
  blog_article:
    _attributes: { phpName: Article }
    id:
    title:      varchar(255)
    content:    longvarchar
    created_at:
  blog_comment:
    _attributes: { phpName: Comment }
    id:
    article_id:
    author:     varchar(255)
    content:    longvarchar
    created_at:
```

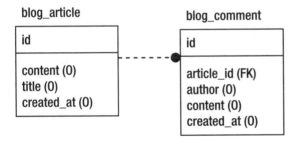

Figure 14-1. *Example data model*

There is no particular rule to follow during the schema creation to allow code generation. Symfony will use the schema as is and interpret its attributes to generate a scaffolding or an administration.

■**Tip** To get the most out of this chapter, you need to actually do the examples. You will get a better understanding of what symfony generates and what can be done with the generated code if you have a view of every step described in the listings. So you are invited to create a data structure such as the one described previously, to create a database with a `blog_article` and a `blog_comment` table, and to populate this database with sample data.

Scaffolding

Scaffolding is of great use in the early days of application development. With a single command, symfony creates an entire module based on the description of a given table.

Generating a Scaffolding

To generate the scaffolding for an `article` module based on the `Article` model class, type the following:

```
> symfony propel-generate-crud myapp article Article
```

Symfony reads the definition of the `Article` class in the `schema.yml` and creates a set of templates and actions based on it, in the `myapp/modules/article/` directory.

The generated module contains three views. The `list` view, which is the default view, displays the rows of the `blog_article` table when browsing to `http://localhost/myapp_dev.php/article` as reproduced in Figure 14-2.

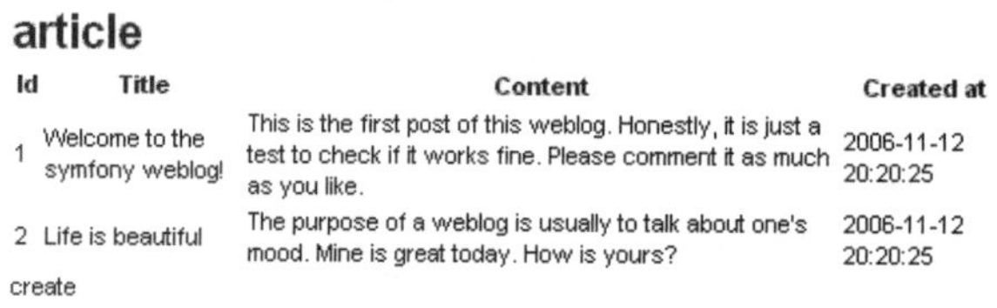

article

Id	Title	Content	Created at
1	Welcome to the symfony weblog!	This is the first post of this weblog. Honestly, it is just a test to check if it works fine. Please comment it as much as you like.	2006-11-12 20:20:25
2	Life is beautiful	The purpose of a weblog is usually to talk about one's mood. Mine is great today. How is yours?	2006-11-12 20:20:25

create

Figure 14-2. *list view of the article module*

Clicking an article identifier displays the `show` view. The details of one row appear in a single page, as in Figure 14-3.

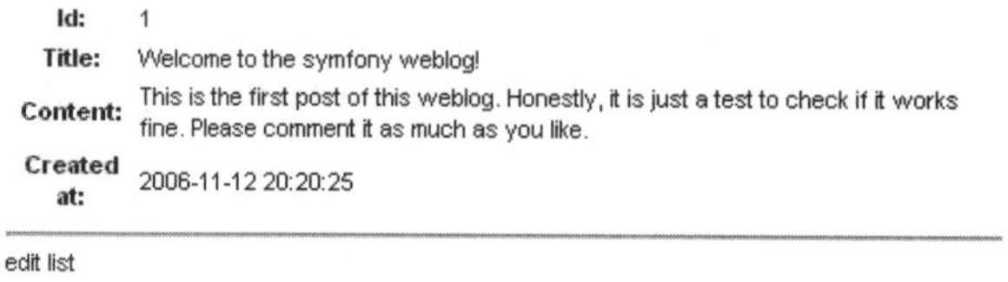

Id:	1
Title:	Welcome to the symfony weblog!
Content:	This is the first post of this weblog. Honestly, it is just a test to check if it works fine. Please comment it as much as you like.
Created at:	2006-11-12 20:20:25

edit list

Figure 14-3. *show view of the article module*

Editing an article by clicking the edit link, or creating a new article by clicking the create link in the `list` view, displays the `edit` view, reproduced in Figure 14-4.

Using this module, you can create new articles, and modify or delete existing ones. The generated code is a good base for further developments. Listing 14-2 lists the generated actions and templates of the new module.

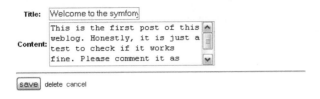

Figure 14-4. *edit view of the article module*

Listing 14-2. *Generated CRUD Elements, in myapp/modules/article/*

```
// In actions/actions.class.php
index          // Forwards to the list action below
list           // Displays the list of all the records of the table
show           // Displays the lists of all columns of a record
edit           // Displays a form to modify the columns of a record
update         // Action called by the edit action form
delete         // Deletes a record
create         // Creates a new record


// In templates/
editSuccess.php  // Record edition form (edit view)
listSuccess.php  // List of all records (list view)
showSuccess.php  // Detail of one record (show view)
```

The logic of these actions and templates is quite simple and explicit, and so rather than reproduce and explain it all, Listing 14-3 gives just a sneak peek on the generated action class.

Listing 14-3. *Generated Action Class, in myapp/modules/article/actions/actions.class.php*

```php
class articleActions extends sfActions
{
  public function executeIndex()
  {
    return $this->forward('article', 'list');
  }

  public function executeList()
  {
    $this->articles = ArticlePeer::doSelect(new Criteria());
  }

  public function executeShow()
  {
    $this->article = ArticlePeer::retrieveByPk($this->getRequestParameter('id'));
    $this->forward404Unless($this->article);
  }
  ...
```

Modify the generated code to fit your requirements, repeat the CRUD generation for all the tables that you want to interact with, and you have a basic working application. Generating a scaffolding really bootstraps development; let symfony do the dirty job for you and focus on the interface and specifics.

Initiating a Scaffolding

Initiating a scaffolding is mostly useful when you need to check that you can access the data in the database. It is fast to build and also fast to delete once you're sure that everything works fine.

To initiate a Propel scaffolding that will create an `article` module to deal with the records of the `Article` model class name, type the following:

```
> symfony propel-init-crud myapp article Article
```

You can then access the `list` view using the default action:

```
http://localhost/myapp_dev.php/article
```

The resulting pages are exactly the same as for a generated scaffolding. You can use them as a simple web interface to the database.

If you check the newly created `actions.class.php` in the `article` module, you will see that it is empty: Everything is inherited from an auto-generated class. The same goes for the templates: There is no template file in the `templates/` directory. The code behind the initiated actions and templates is the same as for a generated scaffolding, but lies only in the application cache (`myproject/cache/myapp/prod/module/autoArticle/`).

During application development, developers initiate scaffoldings to interact with the data, regardless of interface. The code is not meant to be customized; an initiated scaffolding can be seen as a simple alternative to PHPmyadmin to manage data.

Administration

Symfony can generate more advanced modules, still based on model class definitions from the `schema.yml` file, for the back-end of your applications. You can create an entire site administration with only generated administration modules. The examples of this section will describe administration modules added to a `backend` application. If your project doesn't have a `backend` application, create its skeleton now by calling the `init-app` task:

```
> symfony init-app backend
```

Administration modules interpret the model by way of a special configuration file called `generator.yml`, which can be altered to extend all the generated components and the module look and feel. Such modules benefit from the usual module mechanisms described in previous chapters (layout, validation, routing, custom configuration, autoloading, and so on). You can also override the generated action or templates, in order to integrate your own features into the generated administration, but `generator.yml` should take care of the most common requirements and restrict the use of PHP code only to the very specific.

Initiating an Administration Module

With symfony, you build an administration on a per-module basis. A module is generated based on a Propel object using the `propel-init-admin` task, which uses syntax similar to that used to initiate a scaffolding:

```
> symfony propel-init-admin backend article Article
```

This call is enough to create an `article` module in the `backend` application based on the `Article` class definition, and is accessible by the following:

```
http://localhost/backend.php/article
```

The look and feel of a generated module, illustrated in Figures 14-5 and 14-6, is sophisticated enough to make it usable out of the box for a commercial application.

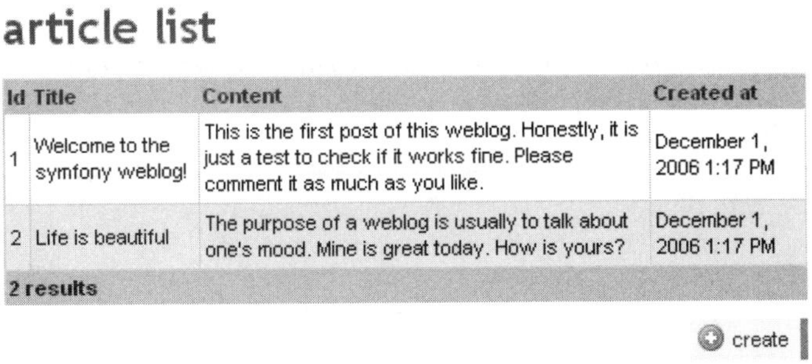

article list

Id	Title	Content	Created at
1	Welcome to the symfony weblog!	This is the first post of this weblog. Honestly, it is just a test to check if it works fine. Please comment it as much as you like.	December 1, 2006 1:17 PM
2	Life is beautiful	The purpose of a weblog is usually to talk about one's mood. Mine is great today. How is yours?	December 1, 2006 1:17 PM
2 results			

    ⊕ create |

Figure 14-5. *list view of the article module in the backend application*

edit article

Title:	Welcome to the symfony \
Content:	This is the first post of this weblog. Honestly, it is just a test to check if it works fine. Please comment it as much as you like.
Created at:	12/1/06

    ▦ list | ⊘ save | ⊘ save and add |

⊖ delete |

Figure 14-6. *edit view of the article module in the backend application*

The difference between the interface of the scaffolding and the one of the administration may not look significant now, but the configurability of the administration will allow you to enhance the basic layout with many additional features without a line of PHP.

■Note Administration modules can only be initiated (not generated).

A Look at the Generated Code

The code of the Article administration module, in the apps/backend/modules/article/ directory, is empty because it is only initiated. The best way to review the generated code of this module is to interact with it using the browser, and then check the contents of the cache/ folder. Listing 14-4 lists the generated actions and the templates found in the cache.

Listing 14-4. *Generated Administration Elements, in cache/backend/ENV/modules/article/*

```
// In actions/actions.class.php
create          // Forwards to edit
delete          // Deletes a record
edit            // Displays a form to modify the fields of a record
                // And handles the form submission
index           // Forwards to list
list            // Displays the list of all the records of the table
save            // Forwards to edit

// In templates/
_edit_actions.php
_edit_footer.php
_edit_form.php
_edit_header.php
_edit_messages.php
_filters.php
_list.php
_list_actions.php
_list_footer.php
_list_header.php
_list_messages.php
_list_td_actions.php
_list_td_stacked.php
_list_td_tabular.php
_list_th_stacked.php
_list_th_tabular.php
editSuccess.php
listSuccess.php
```

This shows that a generated administration module is composed mainly of two views, `edit` and `list`. If you have a look at the code, you will find it to be very modular, readable, and extensible.

Introducing the generator.yml Configuration File

The main difference between scaffoldings and administrations (apart from the fact that administration-generated modules don't have a `show` action) is that an administration relies on parameters found in the `generator.yml` YAML configuration file. To see the default configuration of a newly created administration module, open the `generator.yml` file, located in the `backend/modules/article/config/generator.yml` directory and reproduced in Listing 14-5.

Listing 14-5. *Default Generator Configuration, in backend/modules/article/config/generator.yml*

```
generator:
  class:           sfPropelAdminGenerator
  param:
    model_class:   Article
    theme:         default
```

This configuration is enough to generate the basic administration. Any customization is added under the `param` key, after the `theme` line (which means that all lines added at the bottom of the `generator.yml` file must at least start with four blank spaces to be properly indented). Listing 14-6 shows a typical customized `generator.yml`.

Listing 14-6. *Typical Complete Generator Configuration*

```
generator:
  class:           sfPropelAdminGenerator
  param:
    model_class:   Article
    theme:         default

    fields:
      author_id:   { name: Article author }

    list:
      title:       List of all articles
      display:     [title, author_id, category_id]
      fields:
        published_on: { params: date_format='dd/MM/yy' }
      layout:      stacked
      params:      |
        %%is_published%%<strong>%%=title%%</strong><br /><em>by %%author%%
        in %%category%% (%%published_on%%)</em><p>%%content_summary%%</p>
      filters:     [title, category_id, author_id, is_published]
      max_per_page: 2
```

```
edit:
  title:          Editing article "%%title%%"
  display:
    "Post":       [title, category_id, content]
    "Workflow":   [author_id, is_published, created_on]
  fields:
    category_id:  { params: disabled=true }
    is_published: { type: plain}
    created_on:   { type: plain, params: date_format='dd/MM/yy' }
    author_id:    { params: size=5 include_custom=>> Choose an author << }
    published_on: { credentials: [[admin, superdamin]] }
    content:      { params: rich=true tinymce_options=height:150 }
```

The following sections explain in detail all the parameters that can be used in this configuration file.

Generator Configuration

The generator configuration file is very powerful, allowing you to alter the generated administration in many ways. But such capabilities come with a price: The overall syntax description is long to read and learn, making this chapter one of the longest in this book. The symfony website proposes an additional resource that will help you learn this syntax: the administration generator cheat sheet, reproduced in Figure 14-7. Download it from http://www.symfony-project.com/uploads/assets/sfAdminGeneratorRefCard.pdf, and keep it close to you when you read the following examples of this chapter.

The examples of this section will tweak the article administration module, as well as the comment administration module, based on the Comment class definition. Create the latter with the propel-init-admin task:

```
> symfony propel-init-admin backend comment Comment
```

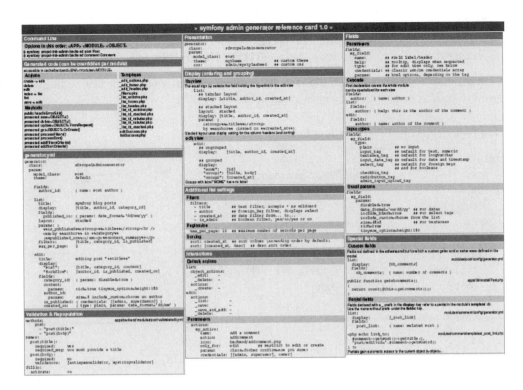

Figure 14-7. *The administration generator cheat sheet*

Fields

By default, the columns of the list view and the fields of the edit view are the columns defined in schema.yml. With generator.yml, you can choose which fields are displayed, which ones are hidden, and add fields of your own—even if they don't have a direct correspondence in the object model.

Field Settings

The administration generator creates a field for each column in the schema.yml file. Under the fields key, you can modify the way each field is displayed, formatted, etc. For instance, the field settings shown in Listing 14-7 define a custom label class and input type for the title field, and a label and a tooltip for the content field. The following sections will describe in detail how each parameter works.

Listing 14-7. *Setting a Custom Label for a Column*

```
generator:
  class:          sfPropelAdminGenerator
  param:
    model_class:    Article
    theme:          default
```

```
fields:
  title:        { name: Article Title, type: textarea_tag, params: class=foo }
  content:      { name: Body, help: Fill in the article body }
```

In addition to this default definition for all the views, you can override the field settings for a given view (list and edit), as demonstrated in Listing 14-8.

Listing 14-8. *Overriding Global Settings View per View*

```
generator:
  class:          sfPropelAdminGenerator
  param:
    model_class:    Article
    theme:          default

    fields:
      title:        { name: Article Title }
      content:      { name: Body }

    list:
      fields:
        title:        { name: Title }

    edit:
      fields:
        content:      { name: Body of the article }
```

This is a general principle: Any settings that are set for the whole module under the fields key can be overridden by view-specific (list and edit) areas that follow.

Adding Fields to the Display

The fields that you define in the fields section can be displayed, hidden, ordered, and grouped in various ways for each view. The display key is used for that purpose. For instance, to arrange the fields of the comment module, use the code of Listing 14-9.

Listing 14-9. *Choosing the Fields to Display, in* modules/comment/config/generator.yml

```
generator:
  class:              sfPropelAdminGenerator
  param:
    model_class:      Comment
    theme:            default

    fields:
      article_id:     { name: Article }
      created_at:     { name: Published on }
      content:        { name: Body }

    list:
      display:        [id, article_id, content]

    edit:
      display:
        NONE:         [article_id]
        Editable:     [author, content, created_at]
```

The list will then display three columns, as in Figure 14-8, and the edit form will display four fields, assembled in two groups, as in Figure 14-9.

comment list

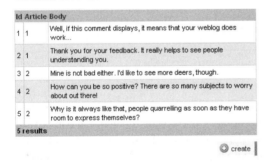

Figure 14-8. *Custom column setting in the* list *view of the* comment *module*

Figure 14-9. *Grouping fields in the edit view of the comment module*

So you can use the display setting in two ways:

- To select the columns to display and the order in which they appear, put the fields in a simple array—as in the previous list view.

- To group fields, use an associative array with the group name as a key, or NONE for a group with no name. The value is still an array of ordered column names.

■**Tip** By default, the primary key columns never appear in either view.

Custom Fields

As a matter of fact, the fields configured in generator.yml don't even need to correspond to actual columns defined in the schema. If the related class offers a custom getter, it can be used as a field for the list view; if there is a getter and/or a setter, it can also be used in the edit view. For instance, you can extend the Article model with a getNbComments() method similar to the one in Listing 14-10.

Listing 14-10. *Adding a Custom Getter in the Model, in lib/model/Article.class.php*

```
public function getNbComments()
{
  return $this->countComments();
}
```

Then nb_comments is available as a field in the generated module (notice that the getter uses a camelCase version of the field name), as in Listing 14-11.

Listing 14-11. *Custom Getters Provide Additional Columns for Administration Modules, in* backend/modules/article/config/generator.yml

```
generator:
  class:            sfPropelAdminGenerator
  param:
    model_class:    Article
    theme:          default

    list:
      display:      [id, title, nb_comments, created_at]
```

The resulting list view of the article module is shown in Figure 14-10.

article list

Figure 14-10. *Custom field in the list view of the article module*

Custom fields can even return HTML code to display more than raw data. For instance, you can extend the Comment class with a getArticleLink() method as in Listing 14-12.

Listing 14-12. *Adding a Custom Getter Returning HTML, in* lib/model/Comment.class.php

```
public function getArticleLink()
{
  return link_to($this->getArticle()->getTitle(),
                'article/edit?id='.$this->getArticleId());
}
```

You can use this new getter as a custom field in the comment/list view with the same syntax as in Listing 14-11. See the example in Listing 14-13, and the result in Figure 14-11, where the HTML code output by the getter (a hyperlink to the article) appears in the second column instead of the article primary key.

Listing 14-13. *Custom Getters Returning HTML Can Also Be Used As Additional Columns,* in modules/comment/config/generator.yml

```
generator:
  class:            sfPropelAdminGenerator
  param:
    model_class:    Comment
    theme:          default
```

```
list:
    display:        [id, article_link, content]
```

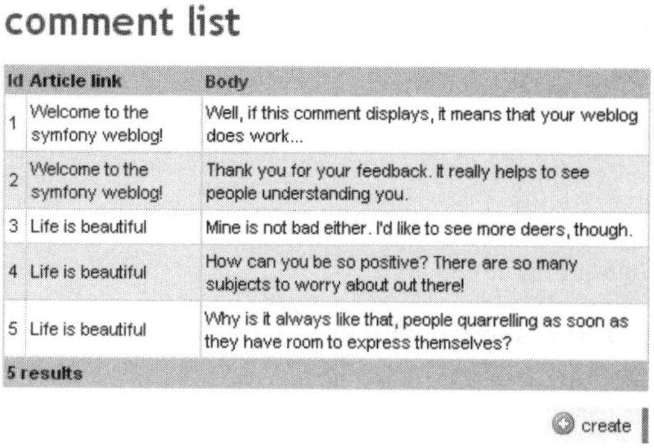

comment list

Id	Article link	Body
1	Welcome to the symfony weblog!	Well, if this comment displays, it means that your weblog does work...
2	Welcome to the symfony weblog!	Thank you for your feedback. It really helps to see people understanding you.
3	Life is beautiful	Mine is not bad either. I'd like to see more deers, though.
4	Life is beautiful	How can you be so positive? There are so many subjects to worry about out there!
5	Life is beautiful	Why is it always like that, people quarrelling as soon as they have room to express themselves?

5 results

⊕ create

Figure 14-11. *Custom field in the* list *view of the* comment *module*

Partial Fields

The code located in the model must be independent from the presentation. The example of the getArticleLink() method earlier doesn't respect this principle of layer separation, because some view code appears in the model layer. To achieve the same goal in a correct way, you'd better put the code that outputs HTML for a custom field in a *partial*. Fortunately, the administration generator allows it if you declare a field name prefixed by an underscore. In that case, the generator.yml file of Listing 14-13 is to be modified as in Listing 14-14.

Listing 14-14. *Partials Can Be Used As Additional Columns—Use the_ Prefix*

```
list:
    display:        [id, _article_link, created_at]
```

For this to work, an _article_link.php partial must be created in the modules/comment/templates/ directory, as in Listing 14-15.

Listing 14-15. *Example Partial for the* list *View, in* modules/comment/templates/_article_link.php

```php
<?php echo link_to($comment->getArticle()->getTitle(),
                   'article/edit?id='.$comment->getArticleId()) ?>
```

Notice that the partial template of a partial field has access to the current object through a variable named by the class ($comment in this example). For instance, for a module built for a class called UserGroup, the partial will have access to the current object through the $user_group variable.

The result is the same as in Figure 14-11, except that the layer separation is respected. If you get used to respecting the layer separation, you will end up with more maintainable applications.

If you need to customize the parameters of a partial field, do the same as for a normal field, under the `field` key. Just don't include the leading underscore (_) in the key—see an example in Listing 14-16.

Listing 14-16. *Partial Field Properties Can Be Customized Under the* `fields` *Key*

```
fields:
  article_link:   { name: Article }
```

If your partial becomes crowded with logic, you'll probably want to replace it with a component. Change the _ prefix to ~ and you can define a *component field*, as you can see in Listing 14-17.

Listing 14-17. *Components Can Be Used As Additional Columns—Use the* ~ *Prefix*

```
...
list:
  display:        [id, ~article_link, created_at]
```

In the generated template, this will result by a call to the `articleLink` component of the current module.

■Note Custom and partial fields can be used in the `list` view, the `edit` view, and for filters. If you use the same partial for several views, the context (`'list'`, `'edit'`, or `'filter'`) is stored in the `$type` variable.

View Customization

To change the `edit` and `list` views' appearance, you could be tempted to alter the templates. But because they are automatically generated, doing so isn't a very good idea. Instead, you should use the `generator.yml` configuration file, because it can do almost everything that you need without sacrificing modularity.

Changing the View Title

In addition to a custom set of fields, the `list` and `edit` pages can have a custom page title. For instance, if you want to customize the title of the `article` views, do as in Listing 14-18. The resulting `edit` view is illustrated in Figure 14-12.

Listing 14-18. *Setting a Custom Title for Each View, in* backend/modules/article/config/ generator.yml

```
list:
  title:          List of Articles
  ...
```

```
edit:
  title:          Body of article %%title%%
  display:        [content]
```

Body of article Welcome to the symfony weblog!

Content: This is the first post of this weblog.
          Honestly, it is just a test to check if it
          works fine. Please comment it as much
          as you like.

▦ list | ⊘ save | ⊘ save and add |

⊘ delete |

Figure 14-12. *Custom title in the edit view of the article module*

As the default titles use the class name, they are often good enough—provided that your model uses explicit class names.

■Tip In the string values of `generator.yml`, the value of a field can be accessed via the name of the field surrounded by %%.

Adding Tooltips

In the `list` and `edit` views, you can add tooltips to help describe the fields that are displayed. For instance, to add a tooltip to the `article_id` field of the `edit` view of the `comment` module, add a `help` property in the `fields` definition as in Listing 14-19. The result is shown in Figure 14-13.

Listing 14-19. *Setting a Tooltip in the edit View, in modules/comment/config/generator.yml*

```
edit:
  fields:
    ...
    article_id:   { help: The current comment relates to this article }
```

edit comment

Article: 1 ▾
            The current comment relates to this article

Figure 14-13. *Tooltip in the edit view of the comment module*

In the `list` view, tooltips are displayed in the column header; in the `edit` view, they appear under the input.

Modifying the Date Format

Dates can be displayed using a custom format as soon as you use the `date_format` param, as demonstrated in Listing 14-20.

Listing 14-20. *Formatting a Date in the* `list` *View*

```
list:
  fields:
    created_at:          { name: Published, params: date_format='dd/MM' }
```

It takes the same format parameter as the `format_date()` helper described in the previous chapter.

ADMINISTRATION TEMPLATES ARE I18N READY

All of the text found in the generated templates is automatically internationalized (i.e., enclosed in a call to the `__()` helper). This means that you can easily translate a generated administration by adding the translations of the phrases in an XLIFF file, in your `apps/myapp/i18n/` directory, as explained in the previous chapter.

List View–Specific Customization

The `list` view can display the details of a record in a tabular way, or with all the details stacked in one line. It also contains filters, pagination, and sorting features. These features can be altered by configuration, as described in the next sections.

Changing the Layout

By default, the hyperlink between the `list` view and the `edit` view is borne by the primary key column. If you refer back to Figure 14-11, you will see that the `id` column in the comment list not only shows the primary key of each comment, but also provides a hyperlink allowing users to access the `edit` view.

If you prefer the hyperlink to the detail of the record to appear on another column, prefix the column name by an equal sign (=) in the `display` key. Listing 14-21 shows how to remove the `id` from the displayed fields of the comment `list` and to put the hyperlink on the `content` field instead. Check Figure 14-14 for a screenshot.

Listing 14-21. *Moving the Hyperlink for the* `edit` *View in the* `list` *View, in* `modules/comment/config/generator.yml`

```
list:
  display:    [article_link, =content]
```

comment list

Article	Body
Welcome to the symfony weblog!	Well, if this comment displays, it means that your weblog does work...
Welcome to the symfony weblog!	Thank you for your feedback. It really helps to see people understanding you.
Life is beautiful	Mine is not bad either. I'd like to see more deers, though.
Life is beautiful	How can you be so positive? There are so many subjects to worry about out there!
Life is beautiful	Why is it always like that, people quarrelling as soon as they have room to express themselves?
5 results	

⊕ create |

Figure 14-14. *Moving the link to the edit view on another column, in the list view of the comment module*

By default, the list view uses the tabular layout, where the fields appear as columns, as shown previously. But you can also use the stacked layout and concatenate the fields into a single string that expands on the full length of the table. If you choose the stacked layout, you must set in the params key the pattern defining the value of each line of the list. For instance, Listing 14-22 defines a stacked layout for the list view of the comment module. The result appears in Figure 14-15.

Listing 14-22. *Using a stacked Layout in the list View, in modules/comment/config/generator.yml*

```
list:
  layout:  stacked
  params:  |
    %%=content%% <br />
    (sent by %%author%% on %%created_at%% about %%article_link%%)
  display:  [created_at, author, content]
```

comment list

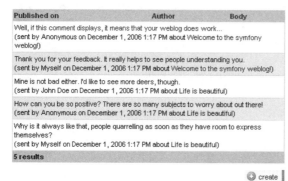

Figure 14-15. *Stacked layout in the list view of the comment module*

Notice that a tabular layout expects an array of fields under the display key, but a stacked layout uses the params key for the HTML code generated for each record. However, the display array is still used in a stacked layout to determine which column headers are available for the interactive sorting.

Filtering the Results

In a list view, you can add a set of filter interactions. With these filters, users can both display fewer results and get to the ones they want faster. Configure the filters under the filters key, with an array of field names. For instance, add a filter on the article_id, author, and created_at fields to the comment list view, as in Listing 14-23, to display a filter box similar to the one in Figure 14-16. You will need to add a __toString() method to the Article class (returning, for instance, the article title) for this to work.

Listing 14-23. *Setting the Filters in the list View, in modules/comment/config/generator.yml*

```
list:
  filters: [article_id, author, created_at]
  layout:  stacked
  params:  |
    %%=content%% <br />
    (sent by %%author%% on %%created_at%% about %%article_link%%)
  display: [created_at, author, content]
```

Figure 14-16. *Filters in the list view of the comment module*

The filters displayed by symfony depend on the column type:

- For text columns (like the author field in the comment module), the filter is a text input allowing text-based search with wildcards (*).

- For foreign keys (like the article_id field in the comment module), the filter is a drop-down list of the records of the related table. As for the regular object_select_tag(), the options of the drop-down list are the ones returned by the __toString() method of the related class.

- For date columns (like the created_at field in the comment module), the filter is a pair of rich date tags (text fields filled by calendar widgets), allowing the selection of a time interval.

- For Boolean columns, the filter is a drop-down list having true, false, and true or false options—the last value reinitializes the filter.

Just like you use partial fields in lists, you can also use *partial filters* to create a filter that symfony doesn't handle on its own. For instance, imagine a state field that may contain only two values (open and closed), but for some reason you store those values directly in the field instead of using a table relation. A simple filter on this field (of type string) would be a text-based search, but what you want is probably a drop-down list of values. That's easy to achieve with a partial filter. See Listing 14-24 for an example implementation.

Listing 14-24. *Using a Partial Filter*

```
// Define the partial, in templates/_state.php
<?php echo select_tag('filters[state]', options_for_select(array(
  '' => '',
  'open' => 'open',
  'closed' => 'closed',
), isset($filters['state']) ? $filters['state'] : '')) ?>

// Add the partial filter in the filter list, in config/generator.yml
  list:
    filters:        [date, _state]
```

Notice that the partial has access to a $filters variable, which is useful to get the current value of the filter.

There is one last option that can be very useful for looking for empty values. Imagine that you want to filter the list of comments to display only the ones that have no author. The problem is that if you leave the author filter empty, it will be ignored. The solution is to set the filter_is_empty field setting to true, as in Listing 14-25, and the filter will display an additional check box, which will allow you to look for empty values, as illustrated in Figure 14-17.

Listing 14-25. *Adding Filtering of Empty Values on the author Field in the list View*

```
  list:
    fields:
      author:   { filter_is_empty: true }
    filters:    [article_id, author, created_at]
```

Figure 14-17. *Allowing the filtering of empty author values*

Sorting the List

In a list view, the table headers are hyperlinks that can be used to reorder the list, as shown in Figure 14-18. These headers are displayed both in the tabular and stacked layouts. Clicking these links reloads the page with a sort parameter that rearranges the list order accordingly.

List of Articles

Id	Title	Nb comments	Created at
1	Welcome to the symfony weblog!	2	December 1, 2006 1:17 PM
2	Life is beautiful	3	December 1, 2006 1:17 PM
2 results			

⊕ create |

Figure 14-18. *Table headers of the list view are sort controls.*

You can reuse the syntax to point to a list directly sorted according to a column:

```
<?php echo link_to('Comment list by date', 'comment/list?sort=created_at ➥
&type=desc' ) ?>
```

You can also define a default sort order for the list view directly in the generator.yml file. The syntax follows the example given in Listing 14-26.

Listing 14-26. *Setting a Default Sort Field in the list View*

```
list:
  sort:   created_at
  # Alternative syntax, to specify a sort order
  sort:   [created_at, desc]
```

Note Only the fields that correspond to an actual column are transformed into sort controls—not the custom or partial fields.

Customizing the Pagination

The generated administration effectively deals with even large tables, because the list view uses pagination by default. When the actual number of rows in a table exceeds the number of maximum rows per page, pagination controls appear at the bottom of the list. For instance, Figure 14-19 shows the list of comments with six test comments in the table but a limit of five comments displayed per page. Pagination ensures a good performance, because only the displayed rows are effectively retrieved from the database, and a good usability, because even tables with millions of rows can be managed by an administration module.

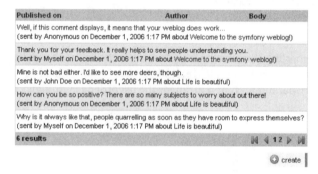

Figure 14-19. *Pagination controls appear on long lists.*

You can customize the number of records to be displayed in each page with the max_per_page parameter:

```
list:
  max_per_page:   5
```

Using a Join to Speed Up Page Delivery

By default, the administration generator uses a simple doSelect() to retrieve a list of records. But, if you use related objects in the list, the number of database queries required to display the list may rapidly increase. For instance, if you want to display the name of the article in a list of comments, an additional query is required for each post in the list to retrieve the related Article object. So you may want to force the pager to use a doSelectJoinXXX() method to optimize the number of queries. This can be specified with the peer_method parameter.

```
list:
  peer_method:    doSelectJoinArticle
```

Chapter 18 explains the concept of Join more extensively.

Edit View–Specific Customization

In an edit view, the user can modify the value of each column for a given record. Symfony determines the type of input to display according to the data type of the column. It then generates an `object_*_tag` helper, and passes that helper the object and the property to edit. For instance, if the article `edit` view configuration stipulates that the user can edit the `title` field:

```
edit:
  display: [title, ...]
```

then the `edit` page will display a regular text input tag to edit the `title` because this column is defined as a `varchar` type in the schema.

```
<?php echo object_input_tag($article, 'getTitle') ?>
```

Changing the Input Type

The default type-to-field conversion rules are as follows:

- A column defined as `integer`, `float`, `char`, `varchar(size)` appears in the `edit` view as an `object_input_tag()`.

- A column defined as `longvarchar` appears as an `object_textarea_tag()`.

- A foreign key column appears as an `object_select_tag()`.

- A column defined as `boolean` appears as an `object_checkbox_tag()`.

- A column defined as a `timestamp` or `date` appears as an `object_input_date_tag()`.

You may want to override these rules to specify a custom input type for a given field. To that extent, set the `type` parameter in the `fields` definition to a specific form helper name. As for the options of the generated `object_*_tag()`, you can change them with the `params` parameter. See an example in Listing 14-27.

Listing 14-27. *Setting a Custom Input Type and Params for the edit View*

```
generator:
  class:            sfPropelAdminGenerator
  param:
    model_class:    Comment
    theme:          default

    edit:
      fields:
                    ## Drop the input, just display plain text
        id:         { type: plain }
                    ## The input is not editable
        author:     { params: disabled=true }
                    ## The input is a textarea (object_textarea_tag)
        content:    { type: textarea_tag,
                      params: rich=true css=user.css tinymce_options=width:330 }
                    ## The input is a select (object_select_tag)
        article_id: { params: include_custom=Choose an article }
        ...
```

The params parameters are passed as options to the generated object_*_tag(). For instance, the params definition for the preceding article_id will produce in the template the following:

```
<?php echo object_select_tag($comment, 'getArticleId', 'related_class=Article',
        'include_custom=Choose an article') ?>
```

This means that all the options usually available in the form helpers can be customized in an edit view.

Handling Partial Fields

Partial fields can be used in edit views just like in list views. The difference is that you have to handle by hand, in the action, the update of the column according to the value of the request parameter sent by the partial field. Symfony knows how to handle the normal fields (corresponding to actual columns), but can't guess how to handle the inputs you may include in partial fields.

For instance, imagine an administration module for a User class where the available fields are id, nickname, and password. The site administrator must be able to change the password of a user upon request, but the edit view must not display the value of the password field for security reasons. Instead, the form should display an empty password input that the site administrator can fill to change the value. The generator settings for such an edit view are then similar to Listing 14-28.

Listing 14-28. *Including a Partial Field in the edit View*

```
edit:
  display:      [id, nickname, _newpassword]
  fields:
    newpassword:  { name: Password, help: Enter a password to change it,
                    leave the field blank to keep the current one }
```

The templates/_newpassword.php partial contains something like this:

```
<?php echo input_password_tag('newpassword', '') ?>
```

Notice that this partial uses a simple form helper, not an object form helper, since it is not desirable to retrieve the password value from the current User object to populate the form input—which could disclose the user password.

Now, in order to use the value from this control to update the object in the action, you need to extend the updateUserFromRequest() method in the action. To do that, create a method with the same name in the action class file with the custom behavior for the input of the partial field, as in Listing 14-29.

Listing 14-29. *Handling a Partial Field in the Action, in modules/user/actions/actions.class.php*

```
class userActions extends sfActions
{
  protected function updateUserFromRequest()
  {
    // Handle the input of the partial field
```

```
    $password = $this->getRequestParameter('newpassword');

    if ($password)
    {
      $this->user->setPassword($password);
    }

    // Let symfony handle the other fields
    parent::updateUserFromRequest();
  }
}
```

Dealing with Foreign Keys

If your schema defines table relationships, the generated administration modules take advantage of it and offer even more automated controls, thus greatly simplifying the relationship management.

One-to-Many Relationships

The 1-n table relationships are taken care of by the administration generator. As is depicted by Figure 14-1 earlier, the blog_comment table is related to the blog_article table through the article_id field. If you initiate the module of the Comment class with the administration generator, the comment/edit action will automatically display the article_id as a drop-down list showing the IDs of the available records of the blog_article table (check again Figure 14-9 for an illustration).

In addition, if you define a __toString() method in the Article object, the text of the drop-down options use it instead of the primary keys.

If you need to display the list of comments related to an article in the article module (n-1 relationship), you will need to customize the module a little by way of a partial field.

Many-to-Many Relationships

Symfony also takes care of n-n table relationships, but since you can't define them in the schema, you need to add a few parameters to the generator.yml file.

The implementation of many-to-many relationships requires an intermediate table. For instance, if there is an n-n relation between a blog_article and a blog_author table (an article can be written by more than one author and, obviously, an author can write more than one article), your database will always end up with a table called blog_article_author or similar, as in Figure 14-20.

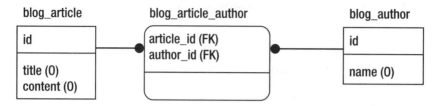

Figure 14-20. *Using a "through class" to implement many-to-many relationships*

The model then has a class called `ArticleAuthor`, and this is the only thing that the administration generator needs—but you have to pass it as a `through_class` parameter of the field.

For instance, in a generated module based on the `Article` class, you can add a field to create new n-n associations with the `Author` class if you write `generator.yml` as in Listing 14-30.

Listing 14-30. *Handling Many-to-Many Relationships with a `through_class` Parameter*

```
edit:
  fields:
    article_author: { type: admin_double_list,
                      params: through_class=ArticleAuthor }
```

Such a field handles links between existing objects, so a regular drop-down list is not enough. You must use a special type of input for that. Symfony offers three widgets to help relate members of two lists (illustrated in Figure 14-21):

- An `admin_double_list` is a set of two expanded select controls, together with buttons to switch elements from the first list (available elements) to the second (selected elements).

- An `admin_select_list` is an expanded select control in which you can select many elements.

- An `admin_check_list` is a list of check box tags.

Figure 14-21. *Available controls for many-to-many relationships*

Adding Interactions

Administration modules allow users to perform the usual CRUD operations, but you can also add your own interactions or restrict the possible interactions for a view. For instance, the interaction definition shown in Listing 14-31 gives access to all the default CRUD actions on the `article` module.

Listing 14-31. *Defining Interactions for Each View, in* `backend/modules/article/config/`
`generator.yml`

```
list:
  title:            List of Articles
  object_actions:
    _edit:          ~
    _delete:        ~
  actions:
    _create:        ~

edit:
  title:            Body of article %%title%%
  actions:
    _list:          ~
    _save:          ~
    _save_and_add:  ~
    _delete:        ~
```

In a `list` view, there are two action settings: the list of actions available for every object, and the list of actions available for the whole page. The `list` interactions defined in Listing 14-31 render like in Figure 14-22. Each line shows one button to edit the record and one to delete it. At the bottom of the list, a button allows the creation of a new record.

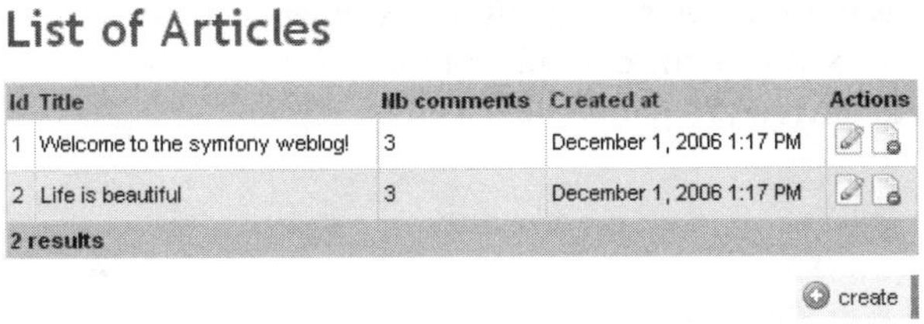

List of Articles

Figure 14-22. *Interactions in the* `list` *view*

In an `edit` view, as there is only one record edited at a time, there is only one set of actions to define. The `edit` interactions defined in Listing 14-31 render like in Figure 14-23. Both the save and the save_and_add actions save the current edits in the records, the difference being that the save action displays the edit view on the current record after saving, while the save_and_add action displays an empty edit view to add another record. The save_and_add action is a shortcut that you will find very useful when adding many records in rapid succession. As for the position of the delete action, it is separated from the other buttons so that users don't click it by mistake.

The interaction names starting with an underscore (_) tell symfony to use the default icon and action corresponding to these interactions. The administration generator understands _edit, _delete, _create, _list, _save, _save_and_add, and _create.

Body of article Life is beautiful

Content:

> The purpose of a weblog is usually to talk about one's mood. Mine is great today. How is yours?

▦ list │ ⊘ save │ ⊘ save and add │

⊖ delete │

Figure 14-23. *Interactions in the edit view*

But you can also add a custom interaction, in which case you must specify a name starting with no underscore, as in Listing 14-32.

Listing 14-32. *Defining a Custom Interaction*

```
list:
  title:          List of Articles
  object_actions:
    _edit:        -
    _delete:      -
    addcomment:   { name: Add a comment, action: addComment,
                    icon: backend/addcomment.png }
```

Each article in the list will now show the addcomment.png button, as shown in Figure 14-24. Clicking it triggers a call to the addComment action in the current module. The primary key of the current object is automatically added to the request parameters.

List of Articles

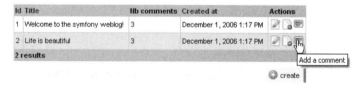

Id	Title	Nb comments	Created at	Actions
1	Welcome to the symfony weblog!	3	December 1, 2006 1:17 PM	🖉 🗋 ▤
2	Life is beautiful	3	December 1, 2006 1:17 PM	🖉 🗋 ▤
2 results				

Add a comment

⊕ create │

Figure 14-24. *Custom interaction in the list view*

The addComment action can be implemented as in Listing 14-33.

Listing 14-33. *Implementing the Custom Interaction Action, in actions/actions.class.php*

```
public function executeAddComment()
{
  $comment = new Comment();
  $comment->setArticleId($this->getRequestParameter('id'));
  $comment->save();
```

```
$this->redirect('comment/edit?id='.$comment->getId());
}
```

One last word about actions: If you want to suppress completely the actions for one category, use an empty list, as in Listing 14-34.

Listing 14-34. *Removing All Actions in the* list *View*

```
list:
  title:        List of Articles
  actions:      {}
```

Form Validation

If you take a look at the generated _edit_form.php template in your project cache/ directory, you will see that the form fields use a special naming convention. In a generated edit view, the input names result from the concatenation of the module name and the field name between angle brackets.

For instance, if the edit view for the article module has a title field, the template will look like Listing 14-35 and the field will be identified as article[title].

Listing 14-35. *Syntax of the Generated Input Names*

```
// generator.yml
generator:
  class:              sfPropelAdminGenerator
  param:
    model_class:      Article
    theme:            default
    edit:
      display: [title]

// Resulting _edit_form.php template
<?php echo object_input_tag($article, 'getTitle', array('control_name' =>
    'article[title]')) ?>

// Resulting HTML
<input type="text" name="article[title]" id="article[title]" value="My Title" />
```

This has plenty of advantages during the internal form-handling process. However, as explained in Chapter 10, it makes the form validation configuration a bit trickier, so you have to change square brackets, [ ], to curly braces, { }, in the fields definition. Also, when using a field name as a parameter for a validator, you should use the name as it appears in the generated HTML code (that is, with the square brackets, but between quotes). Refer to Listing 14-36 for a detail of the special validator syntax for generated forms.

Listing 14-36. *Validator File Syntax for Administration-Generated Forms*

```
## Replace square brackets by curly brackets in the fields list
fields:
  article{title}:
    required:
      msg: You must provide a title
    ## For validator parameters, use the original field name between quotes
    sfCompareValidator:
      check:        "user[newpassword]"
      compare_error: The password confirmation does not match the password.
```

Restricting User Actions Using Credentials

For a given administration module, the available fields and interactions can vary according to the credentials of the logged user (refer to Chapter 6 for a description of symfony's security features).

The fields in the generator can take a `credentials` parameter into account so as to appear only to users who have the proper credential. This works for the `list` view and the `edit` view. Additionally, the generator can also hide interactions according to credentials. Listing 14-37 demonstrates these features.

Listing 14-37. *Using Credentials in* `generator.yml`

```
## The id column is displayed only for users with the admin credential
    list:
      title:        List of Articles
      layout:       tabular
      display:      [id, =title, content, nb_comments]
      fields:
        id:         { credentials: [admin] }
```

```
## The addcomment interaction is restricted to the users with the admin credential
    list:
      title:        List of Articles
      object_actions:
        _edit:       -
        _delete:     -
        addcomment:  { credentials: [admin], name: Add a comment,
                       action: addComment, icon: backend/addcomment.png }
```

Modifying the Presentation of Generated Modules

You can modify the presentation of the generated modules so that it matches any existing graphical charter, not only by applying your own style sheet, but also by overriding the default templates.

Using a Custom Style Sheet

Since the generated HTML is structured content, you can do pretty much anything you like with the presentation.

You can define an alternative CSS to be used for an administration module instead of a default one by adding a `css` parameter to the generator configuration, as in Listing 14-38.

Listing 14-38. *Using a Custom Style Sheet Instead of the Default One*

```
generator:
  class:            sfPropelAdminGenerator
  param:
    model_class:    Comment
    theme:          default
    css:            mystylesheet
```

Alternatively, you can also use the mechanisms provided by the module `view.yml` to override the styles on a per-view basis.

Creating a Custom Header and Footer

The `list` and `edit` views systematically include a header and footer partial. There is no such partial by default in the `templates/` directory of an administration module, but you just need to add one with one of the following names to have it included automatically:

```
_list_header.php
_list_footer.php
_edit_header.php
_edit_footer.php
```

For instance, if you want to add a custom header to the `article/edit` view, create a file called `_edit_header.php` as in Listing 14-39. It will work with no further configuration.

Listing 14-39. *Example* edit *Header Partial, in* modules/articles/template/_edit_header.php

```php
<?php if ($article->getNbComments() > 0): ?>
  <h2>This article has <?php echo $article->getNbComments() ?> comments.</h2>
<?php endif; ?>
```

Notice that an `edit` partial always has access to the current object through a variable having the same name as the module, and that a `list` partial always has access to the current pager through the `$pager` variable.

CALLING THE ADMINISTRATION ACTIONS WITH CUSTOM PARAMETERS

The administration module actions can receive custom parameters using the `query_string` argument in a `link_to()` helper. For example, to extend the previous `_edit_header` partial with a link to the comments for the article, write this:

```
<?php if ($article->getNbComments() > 0): ?>
  <h2>This article has
  <?php echo link_to($article->getNbComments().' comments', 'comment/list',
      array('query_string' => 'filter=filter&filters%5Barticle_id%5D='.
      $article->getId())) ?></h2>
<?php endif; ?>
```

This query string parameter is an encoded version of the more legible

```
'filter=filter&filters[article_id]='.$article->getId()
```

It filters the comments to display only the ones related to `$article`. Using the `query_string` argument, you can specify a sorting order and/or a filter to display a custom `list` view. This can also be useful for custom interactions.

Customizing the Theme

There are other partials inherited from the framework that can be overridden in the module `templates/` folder to match your custom requirements.

The generator templates are cut into small parts that can be overridden independently, and the actions can also be changed one by one.

However, if you want to override those for several modules in the same way, you should probably create a reusable *theme*. A theme is a complete set of templates and actions that can be used by an administration module if specified in the theme value at the beginning of generator.yml. With the `default` theme, symfony uses the files defined in `$sf_symfony_data_dir/generator/sfPropelAdmin/default/`.

The theme files must be located in a project tree structure, in a `data/generator/sfPropelAdmin/[theme_name]/template/` directory, and you can bootstrap a new theme by copying the files from the `default` theme (located in `$sf_symfony_data_dir/generator/sfPropelAdmin/default/template/` directory). This way, you are sure that all the files required for a theme will be present in your custom theme:

```
// Partials, in [theme_name]/template/templates/
_edit_actions.php
_edit_footer.php
_edit_form.php
_edit_header.php
_edit_messages.php
_filters.php
```

```
_list.php
_list_actions.php
_list_footer.php
_list_header.php
_list_messages.php
_list_td_actions.php
_list_td_stacked.php
_list_td_tabular.php
_list_th_stacked.php
_list_th_tabular.php

// Actions, in [theme_name]/template/actions/actions.class.php
processFilters()     // Process the request filters
addFiltersCriteria() // Adds a filter to the Criteria object
processSort()
addSortCriteria()
```

Be aware that the template files are actually *templates of templates*, that is, PHP files that will be parsed by a special utility to generate templates based on generator settings (this is called the *compilation* phase). The generated templates must still contain PHP code to be executed during actual browsing, so the templates of templates use an alternative syntax to keep PHP code unexecuted for the first pass. Listing 14-40 shows an extract of a default template of template.

Listing 14-40. *Syntax of Templates of Templates*

```
<?php foreach ($this->getPrimaryKey() as $pk): ?>
[?php echo object_input_hidden_tag($<?php echo $this->getSingularName() ?>, ➥
 'get<?php echo $pk->getPhpName() ?>') ?]
<?php endforeach; ?>
```

In this listing, the PHP code introduced by <? is executed immediately (at compilation), the one introduced by [? is only executed at execution, but the templating engine finally transforms the [? tags into <? tags so that the resulting template looks like this:

```
<?php echo object_input_hidden_tag($article, 'getId') ?>
```

Dealing with templates of templates is tricky, so the best advice if you want to create your own theme is to start from the default theme, modify it step by step, and test it extensively.

■**Tip** You can also package a generator theme in a plug-in, which makes it even more reusable and easy to deploy across multiple applications. Refer to Chapter 17 for more information.

BUILDING YOUR OWN GENERATOR

The scaffolding and administration generators both use a set of symfony internal components that automate the creation of generated actions and templates in the cache, the use of themes, and the parsing of templates of templates.

This means that symfony provides all the tools to build your own generator, which can look like the existing ones or be completely different. The generation of a module is managed by the `generate()` method of the `sfGeneratorManager` class. For instance, to generate an administration, symfony calls the following internally:

```
$generator_manager = new sfGeneratorManager();
$data = $generator_manager->generate('sfPropelAdminGenerator', $parameters);
```

If you want to build your own generator, you should look at the API documentation of the `sfGeneratorManager` and the `sfGenerator` classes, and take as examples the `sfAdminGenerator` and `sfCRUDGenerator` classes.

Summary

To bootstrap your modules or automatically generate your back-end applications, the basis is a well-defined *schema and object model*. You can modify the PHP code of *scaffoldings*, but *administration-generated* modules are to be modified mostly through configuration.

The `generator.yml` file is the heart of the programming of generated back-ends. It allows for the complete customization of content, features, and the look and feel of the `list` and `edit` views. You can manage *field labels, tooltips, filters, sort order, page size, input type, foreign relationships, custom interactions*, and *credentials* directly in YAML, without a single line of PHP code.

If the administration generator doesn't natively support the feature you need, the *partial fields* and the *ability to override actions* provide complete extensibility. Plus, you can reuse your adaptations to the administration generator mechanisms thanks to the *theme* mechanisms.

CHAPTER 15

■■■

Unit and Functional Testing

Automated tests are one of the greatest advances in programming since object orientation. Particularly conducive to developing web applications, they can guarantee the quality of an application even if releases are numerous. Symfony provides a variety of tools for facilitating automated testing, and these are introduced in this chapter.

Automated Tests

Any developer with experience developing web applications is well aware of the time it takes to do testing well. Writing test cases, running them, and analyzing the results is a tedious job. In addition, the requirements of web applications tend to change constantly, which leads to an ongoing stream of releases and a continuing need for code refactoring. In this context, new errors are likely to regularly crop up.

That's why automated tests are a suggested, if not required, part of a successful development environment. A set of test cases can guarantee that an application actually does what it is supposed to do. Even if the internals are often reworked, the automated tests prevent accidental regressions. Additionally, they compel developers to write tests in a standardized, rigid format capable of being understood by a testing framework.

Automated tests can sometimes replace developer documentation since they can clearly illustrate what an application is supposed to do. A good test suite shows what output should be expected for a set of test inputs, and that is a good way to explain the purpose of a method.

The symfony framework applies this principle to itself. The internals of the framework are validated by automated tests. These unit and functional tests are not bundled with the standard symfony distribution, but you can check them out from the SVN repository or browse them online at `http://www.symfony-project.com/trac/browser/trunk/test`.

Unit and Functional Tests

Unit tests confirm that a unitary code component provides the correct output for a given input. They validate how functions and methods work in every particular case. Unit tests deal with one case at a time, so for instance a single method may need several unit tests if it works differently in certain situations.

Functional tests validate not a simple input-to-output conversion, but a complete feature. For instance, a cache system can only be validated by a functional test, because it involves more than one step: The first time a page is requested, it is rendered; the second time, it is taken from the cache. So functional tests validate a process and require a scenario. In symfony, you should write functional tests for all your actions.

For the most complex interactions, these two types may fall short. Ajax interactions, for instance, require a web browser to execute JavaScript, so automatically testing them requires a special third-party tool. Furthermore, visual effects can only be validated by a human.

If you have an extensive approach to automated testing, you will probably need to use a combination of all these methods. As a guideline, remember to keep tests simple and readable.

■**Note** Automated tests work by comparing a result with an expected output. In other words, they evaluate *assertions* (expressions like $a == 2). The value of an assertion is either `true` or `false`, and it determines whether a test passes or fails. The word "assertion" is commonly used when dealing with automated testing techniques.

Test-Driven Development

In the test-driven development (TDD) methodology, the tests are written before the code. Writing tests first helps you to focus on the tasks a function should accomplish before actually developing it. It's a good practice that other methodologies, like Extreme Programming (XP), recommend as well. Plus it takes into account the undeniable fact that if you don't write unit tests first, you never write them.

For instance, imagine that you must develop a text-stripping function. The function removes white spaces at the beginning and at the end of the string, replaces nonalphabetical characters by underscores, and transforms all uppercase characters to lowercase ones. In test-driven development, you would first think about all the possible cases and provide an example "nput and expected output for each, as shown in Table 15-1.

Table 15-1. *A List of Test Cases for a Text-Stripping Function*

Input	Expected Output
" foo "	"foo"
"foo bar"	"foo_bar"
"-)foo:..=bar?"	"_foo___bar_"
"FooBar"	"foobar"
"Don't foo-bar me!"	"don_t_foo_bar_me_"

You would write the unit tests, run them, and see that they fail. You would then add the necessary code to handle the first test case, run the tests again, see that the first one passes, and go on like that. Eventually, when all the test cases pass, the function is correct.

An application built with a test-driven methodology ends up with roughly as much test code as actual code. As you don't want to spend time debugging your tests cases, keep them simple.

■**Note** Refactoring a method can create new bugs that didn't use to appear before. That's why it is also a good practice to run all automated tests before deploying a new release of an application in production—this is called *regression testing*.

The Lime Testing Framework

There are many unit test frameworks in the PHP world, with the most well known being PhpUnit and SimpleTest. Symfony has its own, called *lime*. It is based on the `Test::More` Perl library, and is *TAP compliant*, which means that the result of tests is displayed as specified in the Test Anything Protocol, designed for better readability of test output.

Lime provides support for unit testing. It is more lightweight than other PHP testing frameworks and has several advantages:

- It launches test files in a sandbox to avoid strange side effects between each test run. Not all testing frameworks guarantee a clean environment for each test.

- Lime tests are very readable, and so is the test output. On compatible systems, lime uses color output in a smart way to distinguish important information.

- Symfony itself uses lime tests for regression testing, so many examples of unit and functional tests can be found in the symfony source code.

- The lime core is validated by unit tests.

- It is written in PHP, and it is fast and well coded. It is contained in a single file, `lime.php`, without any dependence.

The various tests described next use the lime syntax. They work out of the box with any symfony installation.

■**Note** Unit and functional tests are not supposed to be launched in production. They are developer tools, and as such, they should be run in the developer's computer, not in the host server.

Unit Tests

Symfony unit tests are simple PHP files ending in `Test.php` and located in the `test/unit/` directory of your application. They follow a simple and readable syntax.

What Do Unit Tests Look Like?

Listing 15-1 shows a typical set of unit tests for the strtolower() function. It starts by an instantiation of the lime_test object (you don't need to worry about the parameters for now). Each unit test is a call to a method of the lime_test instance. The last parameter of these methods is always an optional string that serves as the output.

Listing 15-1. *Example Unit Test File, in test/unit/strtolowerTest.php*

```php
<?php

include(dirname(__FILE__).'/../bootstrap/unit.php');
require_once(dirname(__FILE__).'/../../lib/strtolower.php');

$t = new lime_test(7, new lime_output_color());

// strtolower()
$t->diag('strtolower()');
$t->isa_ok(strtolower('Foo'), 'string',
    'strtolower() returns a string');
$t->is(strtolower('FOO'), 'foo',
    'strtolower() transforms the input to lowercase');
$t->is(strtolower('foo'), 'foo',
    'strtolower() leaves lowercase characters unchanged');
$t->is(strtolower('12#?@~'), '12#?@~',
    'strtolower() leaves non alphabetical characters unchanged');
$t->is(strtolower('FOO BAR'), 'foo bar',
    'strtolower() leaves blanks alone');
$t->is(strtolower('FoO bAr'), 'foo bar',
    'strtolower() deals with mixed case input');
$t->is(strtolower(''), 'foo',
    'strtolower() transforms empty strings into foo');
```

Launch the test set from the command line with the test-unit task. The command-line output is very explicit, and it helps you localize which tests failed and which passed. See the output of the example test in Listing 15-2.

Listing 15-2. *Launching a Single Unit Test from the Command Line*

```
> symfony test-unit strtolower
```

```
1..7
# strtolower()
ok 1 - strtolower() returns a string
ok 2 - strtolower() transforms the input to lowercase
ok 3 - strtolower() leaves lowercase characters unchanged
ok 4 - strtolower() leaves non alphabetical characters unchanged
ok 5 - strtolower() leaves blanks alone
```

```
ok 6 - strtolower() deals with mixed case input
not ok 7 - strtolower() transforms empty strings into foo
#     Failed test (.\batch\test.php at line 21)
#            got: ''
#       expected: 'foo'
# Looks like you failed 1 tests of 7.
```

■**Tip** The include statement at the beginning of Listing 15-1 is optional, but it makes the test file an independent PHP script that you can execute without the symfony command line, by calling php test/unit/ strtolowerTest.php.

Unit Testing Methods

The lime_test object comes with a large number of testing methods, as listed in Table 15-2.

Table 15-2. *Methods of the lime_test Object for Unit Testing*

Method	Description
diag($msg)	Outputs a comment but runs no test
ok($test, $msg)	Tests a condition and passes if it is true
is($value1, $value2, $msg)	Compares two values and passes if they are equal (==)
isnt($value1, $value2, $msg)	Compares two values and passes if they are not equal
like($string, $regexp, $msg)	Tests a string against a regular expression
unlike($string, $regexp, $msg)	Checks that a string doesn't match a regular expression
cmp_ok($value1, $operator, $value2, $msg)	Compares two arguments with an operator
isa_ok($variable, $type, $msg)	Checks the type of an argument
isa_ok($object, $class, $msg)	Checks the class of an object
can_ok($object, $method, $msg)	Checks the availability of a method for an object or a class
is_deeply($array1, $array2, $msg)	Checks that two arrays have the same values
include_ok($file, $msg)	Validates that a file exists and that it is properly included
fail()	Always fails—useful for testing exceptions
pass()	Always passes—useful for testing exceptions
skip($msg, $nb_tests)	Counts as $nb_tests tests—useful for conditional tests
todo()	Counts as a test—useful for tests yet to be written

The syntax is quite straightforward; notice that most methods take a message as their last parameter. This message is displayed in the output when the test passes. Actually, the best way to learn these methods is to test them, so have a look at Listing 15-3, which uses them all.

Listing 15-3. *Testing Methods of the* lime_test *Object, in* test/unit/exampleTest.php

```php
<?php

include(dirname(__FILE__).'/../bootstrap/unit.php');

// Stub objects and functions for test purposes
class myObject
{
  public function myMethod()
  {
  }
}

function throw_an_exception()
{
  throw new Exception('exception thrown');
}

// Initialize the test object
$t = new lime_test(16, new lime_output_color());

$t->diag('hello world');
$t->ok(1 == '1', 'the equal operator ignores type');
$t->is(1, '1', 'a string is converted to a number for comparison');
$t->isnt(0, 1, 'zero and one are not equal');
$t->like('test01', '/test\d+/', 'test01 follows the test numbering pattern');
$t->unlike('tests01', '/test\d+/', 'tests01 does not follow the pattern');
$t->cmp_ok(1, '<', 2, 'one is inferior to two');
$t->cmp_ok(1, '!==', true, 'one and true are not identical');
$t->isa_ok('foobar', 'string', '\'foobar\' is a string');
$t->isa_ok(new myObject(), 'myObject', 'new creates object of the right class');
$t->can_ok(new myObject(), 'myMethod', 'objects of class myObject do have a ➥
myMethod method');
$array1 = array(1, 2, array(1 => 'foo', 'a' => '4'));
$t->is_deeply($array1, array(1, 2, array(1 => 'foo', 'a' => '4')),
    'the first and the second array are the same');
$t->include_ok('./fooBar.php', 'the fooBar.php file was properly included');

try
{
  throw_an_exception();
  $t->fail('no code should be executed after throwing an exception');
}
```

```
catch (Exception $e)
{
  $t->pass('exception catched successfully');
}

if (!isset($foobar))
{
  $t->skip('skipping one test to keep the test count exact in the condition', 1);
}
else
{
  $t->ok($foobar, 'foobar');
}

$t->todo('one test left to do');
```

You will find a lot of other examples of the usage of these methods in the symfony unit tests.

■**Tip** You may wonder why you would use is() as opposed to ok() here. The error message output by is() is much more explicit; it shows both members of the test, while ok() just says that the condition failed.

Testing Parameters

The initialization of the lime_test object takes as its first parameter the number of tests that should be executed. If the number of tests finally executed differs from this number, the lime output warns you about it. For instance, the test set of Listing 15-3 outputs as Listing 15-4. The initialization stipulated that 16 tests were to run, but only 15 actually took place, so the output indicates this.

Listing 15-4. *The Count of Test Run Helps You to Plan Tests*

```
> symfony test-unit example
```

```
1..16
# hello world
ok 1 - the equal operator ignores type
ok 2 - a string is converted to a number for comparison
ok 3 - zero and one are not equal
ok 4 - test01 follows the test numbering pattern
ok 5 - tests01 does not follow the pattern
ok 6 - one is inferior to two
ok 7 - one and true are not identical
ok 8 - 'foobar' is a string
ok 9 - new creates object of the right class
```

```
ok 10 - objects of class myObject do have a myMethod method
ok 11 - the first and the second array are the same
not ok 12 - the fooBar.php file was properly included
#     Failed test (.\test\unit\testTest.php at line 27)
#        Tried to include './fooBar.php'
ok 13 - exception catched successfully
ok 14 # SKIP skipping one test to keep the test count exact in the condition
ok 15 # TODO one test left to do
# Looks like you planned 16 tests but only ran 15.
# Looks like you failed 1 tests of 16.
```

The diag() method doesn't count as a test. Use it to show comments, so that your test output stays organized and legible. On the other hand, the todo() and skip() methods count as actual tests. A pass()/fail() combination inside a try/catch block counts as a single test.

A well-planned test strategy must contain an expected number of tests. You will find it very useful to validate your own test files—especially in complex cases where tests are run inside conditions or exceptions. And if the test fails at some point, you will see it quickly because the final number of run tests won't match the number given during initialization.

The second parameter of the constructor is an output object extending the lime_output class. Most of the time, as tests are meant to be run through a CLI, the output is a lime_output_color object, taking advantage of bash coloring when available.

The test-unit Task

The test-unit task, which launches unit tests from the command line, expects either a list of test names or a file pattern. See Listing 15-5 for details.

Listing 15-5. *Launching Unit Tests*

```
// Test directory structure
test/
  unit/
    myFunctionTest.php
    mySecondFunctionTest.php
    foo/
      barTest.php


> symfony test-unit myFunction                        ## Run myFunctionTest.php
> symfony test-unit myFunction mySecondFunction  ## Run both tests
> symfony test-unit 'foo/*'                           ## Run barTest.php
> symfony test-unit '*'                               ## Run all tests (recursive)
```

Stubs, Fixtures, and Autoloading

In a unit test, the autoloading feature is not active by default. Each class that you use in a test must be either defined in the test file or required as an external dependency. That's why many test files start with a group of include lines, as Listing 15-6 demonstrates.

Listing 15-6. *Including Classes in Unit Tests*

```php
<?php

include(dirname(__FILE__).'/../bootstrap/unit.php');
include(dirname(__FILE__).'/../../config/config.php');
require_once($sf_symfony_lib_dir.'/util/sfToolkit.class.php');

$t = new lime_test(7, new lime_output_color());

// isPathAbsolute()
$t->diag('isPathAbsolute()');
$t->is(sfToolkit::isPathAbsolute('/test'), true,
    'isPathAbsolute() returns true if path is absolute');
$t->is(sfToolkit::isPathAbsolute('\\test'), true,
    'isPathAbsolute() returns true if path is absolute');
$t->is(sfToolkit::isPathAbsolute('C:\\test'), true,
    'isPathAbsolute() returns true if path is absolute');
$t->is(sfToolkit::isPathAbsolute('d:/test'), true,
    'isPathAbsolute() returns true if path is absolute');
$t->is(sfToolkit::isPathAbsolute('test'), false,
    'isPathAbsolute() returns false if path is relative');
$t->is(sfToolkit::isPathAbsolute('../test'), false,
    'isPathAbsolute() returns false if path is relative');
$t->is(sfToolkit::isPathAbsolute('..\\test'), false,
    'isPathAbsolute() returns false if path is relative');
```

In unit tests, you need to instantiate not only the object you're testing, but also the object it depends upon. Since unit tests must remain unitary, depending on other classes may make more than one test fail if one class is broken. In addition, setting up real objects can be expensive, both in terms of lines of code and execution time. Keep in mind that speed is crucial in unit testing because developers quickly tire of a slow process.

Whenever you start including many scripts for a unit test, you may need a simple autoloading system. For this purpose, the sfCore class (which must be manually included) provides an initSimpleAutoload() method, which expects an absolute path as parameter. All the classes located under this path will be autoloaded. For instance, if you want to have all the classes located under $sf_symfony_lib_dir/util/ autoloaded, start your unit test script as follows:

```php
require_once($sf_symfony_lib_dir.'/util/sfCore.class.php');
sfCore::initSimpleAutoload($sf_symfony_lib_dir.'/util');
```

■**Tip** The generated Propel objects rely on a long cascade of classes, so as soon as you want to test a Propel object, autoloading is necessary. Note that for Propel to work, you also need to include the files under the `vendor/propel/` directory (so the call to `sfCore` becomes `sfCore::initSimpleAutoload(array(SF_ROOT_DIR.'/lib/model', $sf_symfony_lib_dir.'/vendor/propel'));`) and to add the Propel core to the include path (by calling `set_include_path($sf_symfony_lib_dir.'/vendor'.PATH_SEPARATOR. SF_ROOT_DIR.PATH_SEPARATOR.get_include_path()`).

Another good workaround for the autoloading issues is the use of *stubs*. A stub is an alternative implementation of a class where the real methods are replaced with simple canned data. It mimics the behavior of the real class, but without its cost. A good example of stubs is a database connection or a web service interface. In Listing 15-7, the unit tests for a mapping API rely on a `WebService` class. Instead of calling the real `fetch()` method of the actual web service class, the test uses a stub that returns test data.

Listing 15-7. *Using Stubs in Unit Tests*

```
require_once(dirname(__FILE__).'/../../lib/WebService.class.php');
require_once(dirname(__FILE__).'/../../lib/MapAPI.class.php');

class testWebService extends WebService
{
  public static function fetch()
  {
    return file_get_contents(dirname(__FILE__).'/fixtures/data/ ➥
fake_web_service.xml');
  }
}

$myMap = new MapAPI();

$t = new lime_test(1, new lime_output_color());

$t->is($myMap->getMapSize(testWebService::fetch(), 100);
```

The test data can be more complex than a string or a call to a method. Complex test data is often referred to as *fixtures*. For coding clarity, it is often better to keep fixtures in separate files, especially if they are used by more than one unit test file. Also, don't forget that symfony can easily transform a YAML file into an array with the `sfYAML::load()` method. This means that instead of writing long PHP arrays, you can write your test data in a YAML file, as in Listing 15-8.

Listing 15-8. *Using Fixture Files in Unit Tests*

```
// In fixtures.yml:
-

  input:   '/test'
  output:  true
  comment: isPathAbsolute() returns true if path is absolute
-

  input:   '\\test'
  output:  true
  comment: isPathAbsolute() returns true if path is absolute
-

  input:   'C:\\test'
  output:  true
  comment: isPathAbsolute() returns true if path is absolute
-

  input:   'd:/test'
  output:  true
  comment: isPathAbsolute() returns true if path is absolute
-

  input:   'test'
  output:  false
  comment: isPathAbsolute() returns false if path is relative
-

  input:   '../test'
  output:  false
  comment: isPathAbsolute() returns false if path is relative
-

  input:   '..\\test'
  output:  false
  comment: isPathAbsolute() returns false if path is relative

// In testTest.php
<?php

include(dirname(__FILE__).'/../bootstrap/unit.php');
include(dirname(__FILE__).'/../../config/config.php');
require_once($sf_symfony_lib_dir.'/util/sfToolkit.class.php');
require_once($sf_symfony_lib_dir.'/util/sfYaml.class.php');

$testCases = sfYaml::load(dirname(__FILE__).'/fixtures.yml');

$t = new lime_test(count($testCases), new lime_output_color());
```

```
// isPathAbsolute()
$t->diag('isPathAbsolute()');
foreach ($testCases as $case)
{
  $t->is(sfToolkit::isPathAbsolute($case['input']), $case['output'], ➥
  $case['comment']);
}
```

Functional Tests

Functional tests validate parts of your applications. They simulate a browsing session, make requests, and check elements in the response, just like you would do manually to validate that an action does what it's supposed to do. In functional tests, you run a scenario corresponding to a use case.

What Do Functional Tests Look Like?

You could run your functional tests with a text browser and a lot of regular expression assertions, but that would be a great waste of time. Symfony provides a special object, called sfBrowser, which acts like a browser connected to a symfony application without actually needing a server—and without the slowdown of the HTTP transport. It gives access to the core objects of each request (the request, session, context, and response objects). Symfony also provides an extension of this class called sfTestBrowser, designed especially for functional tests, which has all the abilities of the sfBrowser object plus some smart assert methods.

A functional test traditionally starts with an initialization of a test browser object. This object makes a request to an action and verifies that some elements are present in the response.

For example, every time you generate a module skeleton with the init-module or the propel-init-crud tasks, symfony creates a simple functional test for this module. The test makes a request to the default action of the module and checks the response status code, the module and action calculated by the routing system, and the presence of a certain sentence in the response content. For a foobar module, the generated foobarActionsTest.php file looks like Listing 15-9.

Listing 15-9. *Default Functional Test for a New Module, in* tests/functional/frontend/ foobarActionsTest.php

```php
<?php

include(dirname(__FILE__).'/../../bootstrap/functional.php');

// Create a new test browser
$browser = new sfTestBrowser();
$browser->initialize();
```

```
$browser->
  get('/foobar/index')->
  isStatusCode(200)->
  isRequestParameter('module', 'foobar')->
  isRequestParameter('action', 'index')->
  checkResponseElement('body', '!/This is a temporary page/')
;
```

Tip The browser methods return an sfTestBrowser object, so you can chain the method calls for more readability of your test files. This is called a *fluid interface* to the object, because nothing stops the flow of method calls.

A functional test can contain several requests and more complex assertions; you will soon discover all the possibilities in the upcoming sections.

To launch a functional test, use the test-functional task with the symfony command line, as shown in Listing 15-10. This task expects an application name and a test name (omit the Test.php suffix).

Listing 15-10. *Launching a Single Functional Test from the Command Line*

```
> symfony test-functional frontend foobarActions
```

```
# get /comment/index
ok 1 - status code is 200
ok 2 - request parameter module is foobar
ok 3 - request parameter action is index
not ok 4 - response selector body does not match regex /This is a temporary page/
# Looks like you failed 1 tests of 4.
1..4
```

The generated functional tests for a new module don't pass by default. This is because in a newly created module, the index action forwards to a congratulations page (included in the symfony default module), which contains the sentence "This is a temporary page." As long as you don't modify the index action, the tests for this module will fail, and this guarantees that you cannot pass all tests with an unfinished module.

Note In functional tests, the autoloading is activated, so you don't have to include the files by hand.

Browsing with the sfTestBrowser Object

The test browser is capable of *making GET and POST requests*. In both cases, use a real URI as parameter. Listing 15-11 shows how to write calls to the sfTestBrowser object to simulate requests.

Listing 15-11. *Simulating Requests with the sfTestBrowser Object*

```
include(dirname(__FILE__).'/../../bootstrap/functional.php');

// Create a new test browser
$b = new sfTestBrowser();
$b->initialize();

$b->get('/foobar/show/id/1');                  // GET request
$b->post('/foobar/show', array('id' => 1));    // POST request

// The get() and post() methods are shortcuts to the call() method
$b->call('/foobar/show/id/1', 'get');
$b->call('/foobar/show', 'post', array('id' => 1));

// The call() method can simulate requests with any method
$b->call('/foobar/show/id/1', 'head');
$b->call('/foobar/add/id/1', 'put');
$b->call('/foobar/delete/id/1', 'delete');
```

A typical browsing session contains not only requests to specific actions, but also *clicks on links and on browser buttons*. As shown in Listing 15-12, the sfTestBrowser object is also capable of simulating those.

Listing 15-12. *Simulating Navigation with the sfTestBrowser Object*

```
$b->get('/');                  // Request to the home page
$b->get('/foobar/show/id/1');
$b->back();                    // Back to one page in history
$b->forward();                 // Forward one page in history
$b->reload();                  // Reload current page
$b->click('go');               // Look for a 'go' link or button and click it
```

The test browser handles a stack of calls, so the back() and forward() methods work as they do on a real browser.

■**Tip** The test browser has its own mechanisms to manage sessions (sfTestStorage) and cookies.

Among the interactions that most need to be tested, those associated with *forms* probably rank first. To simulate form input and submission, you have three choices. You can either make a POST request with the parameters you wish to send, call click() with the form parameters as an array, or fill in the fields one by one and click the submit button. They all result in the same POST request anyhow. Listing 15-13 shows an example.

Listing 15-13. *Simulating Form Input with the sfTestBrowser Object*

```
// Example template in modules/foobar/templates/editSuccess.php
<?php echo form_tag('foobar/update') ?>
  <?php echo input_hidden_tag('id', $sf_params->get('id')) ?>
  <?php echo input_tag('name', 'foo') ?>
  <?php echo submit_tag('go') ?>
  <?php echo textarea('text1', 'foo') ?>
  <?php echo textarea('text2', 'bar') ?>
</form>

// Example functional test for this form
$b = new sfTestBrowser();
$b->initialize();
$b->get('/foobar/edit/id/1');

// Option 1: POST request
$b->post('/foobar/update', array('id' => 1, 'name' => 'dummy', 'commit' => 'go'));

// Option 2: Click the submit button with parameters
$b->click('go', array('name' => 'dummy'));

// Option 3: Enter the form values field by field name then click the submit button
$b->setField('name', 'dummy')->
    click('go');
```

■**Note** With the second and third options, the default form values are automatically included in the form submission, and the form target doesn't need to be specified.

When an action finishes by a redirect(), the test browser doesn't automatically follow the redirection; you must follow it manually with followRedirect(), as demonstrated in Listing 15-14.

Listing 15-14. *The Test Browser Doesn't Automatically Follow Redirects*

```
// Example action in modules/foobar/actions/actions.class.php
public function executeUpdate()
{
  ...
  $this->redirect('foobar/show?id='.$this->getRequestParameter('id'));
}
```

```
// Example functional test for this action
$b = new sfTestBrowser();
$b->initialize();
$b->get('/foobar/edit?id=1')->
    click('go', array('name' => 'dummy'))->
    isRedirected()->    // Check that request is redirected
    followRedirect();    // Manually follow the redirection
```

There is one last method you should know about that is useful for browsing: restart() reinitializes the browsing history, session, and cookies—as if you restarted your browser.

Once it has made a first request, the sfTestBrowser object can *give access to the request, context, and response* objects. It means that you can check a lot of things, ranging from the text content to the response headers, the request parameters, and configuration:

```
$request  = $b->getRequest();
$context  = $b->getContext();
$response = $b->getResponse();
```

THE SFBROWSER OBJECT

All the browsing methods described in Listings 15-10 to 15-13 are also available out of the testing scope, throughout the sfBrowser object. You can call it as follows:

```
// Create a new browser
$b = new sfBrowser();
$b->initialize();
$b->get('/foobar/show/id/1')->
    setField('name', 'dummy')->
    click('go');
$content = $b()->getResponse()->getContent();
...
```

The sfBrowser object is a very useful tool for batch scripts, for instance, if you want to browse a list of pages to generate a cached version for each (refer to Chapter 18 for a detailed example).

Using Assertions

Due to the sfTestBrowser object having access to the response and other components of the request, you can do tests on these components. You could create a new lime_test object for that purpose, but fortunately sfTestBrowser proposes a test() method that returns a lime_test object where you can call the unit assertion methods described previously. Check Listing 15-15 to see how to do assertions via sfTestBrowser.

Listing 15-15. *The Test Browser Provides Testing Abilities with the* test() *Method*

```
$b = new sfTestBrowser();
$b->initialize();
$b->get('/foobar/edit/id/1');
$request  = $b->getRequest();
$context  = $b->getContext();
$response = $b->getResponse();

// Get access to the lime_test methods via the test() method
$b->test()->is($request->getParameter('id'), 1);
$b->test()->is($response->getStatuscode(), 200);
$b->test()->is($response->getHttpHeader('content-type'), 'text/html; ➡
charset=utf-8');
$b->test()->like($response->getContent(), '/edit/');
```

■**Note** The getResponse(), getContext(), getRequest(), and test() methods don't return an sfTestBrowser object, therefore you can't chain other sfTestBrowser method calls after them.

You can check incoming and outgoing cookies easily via the request and response objects, as shown in Listing 15-16.

Listing 15-16. *Testing Cookies with* sfTestBrowser

```
$b->test()->is($request->getCookie('foo'), 'bar');      // Incoming cookie
$cookies = $response->getCookies();
$b->test()->is($cookies['foo'], 'foo=bar');             // Outgoing cookie
```

Using the test() method to test the request elements ends up in long lines. Fortunately, sfTestbrowser contains a bunch of *proxy methods* that help you keep your functional tests readable and short—in addition to returning an sfTestBrowser object themselves. For instance, you can rewrite Listing 15-15 in a faster way, as shown in Listing 15-17.

Listing 15-17. *Testing Directly with* sfTestBrowser

```
$b = new sfTestBrowser();
$b->initialize();
$b->get('/foobar/edit/id/1')->
    isRequestParameter('id', 1)->
    isStatutsCode()->
    isResponseHeader('content-type', 'text/html; charset=utf-8')->
    responseContains('edit');
```

The status 200 is the default value of the parameter expected by isStatusCode(), so you can call it without any argument to test a successful response.

One more advantage of proxy methods is that you don't need to specify an output text as you would with a lime_test method. The messages are generated automatically by the proxy methods, and the test output is clear and readable.

```
# get /foobar/edit/id/1
ok 1 - request parameter "id" is "1"
ok 2 - status code is "200"
ok 3 - response header "content-type" is "text/html"
ok 4 - response contains "edit"
1..4
```

In practice, the proxy methods of Listing 15-17 cover most of the usual tests, so you will seldom use the test() method on an sfTestBrowser object.

Listing 15-14 showed that sfTestBrowser doesn't automatically follow redirections. This has one advantage: You can test a redirection. For instance, Listing 15-18 shows how to test the response of Listing 15-14.

Listing 15-18. *Testing Redirections with* sfTestBrowser

```
$b = new sfTestBrowser();
$b->initialize();
$b->
    get('/foobar/edit/id/1')->
    click('go', array('name' => 'dummy'))->
    isStatusCode(200)->
    isRequestParameter('module', 'foobar')->
    isRequestParameter('action', 'update')->

    isRedirected()->        // Check that the response is a redirect
    followRedirect()->      // Manually follow the redirection

    isStatusCode(200)->
    isRequestParameter('module', 'foobar')->
    isRequestParameter('action', 'show');
```

Using CSS Selectors

Many of the functional tests validate that a page is correct by checking for the presence of text in the content. With the help of regular expressions in the responseContains() method, you can check displayed text, a tag's attributes, or values. But as soon as you want to check something deeply buried in the response DOM, regular expressions are not ideal.

That's why the sfTestBrowser object supports a getResponseDom() method. It returns a libXML2 DOM object, much easier to parse and test than a flat text. Refer to Listing 15-19 for an example of using this method.

Listing 15-19. *The Test Browser Gives Access to the Response Content As a DOM Object*

```
$b = new sfTestBrowser();
$b->initialize();
$b->get('/foobar/edit/id/1');
$dom = $b->getResponseDom();
$b->test()->is($dom->getElementsByTagName('input')->item(1)->getAttribute('type'),➥
 'text');
```

But parsing an HTML document with the PHP DOM methods is still not fast and easy enough. If you are familiar with the CSS selectors, you know that they are an ever more powerful way to retrieve elements from an HTML document. Symfony provides a tool class called sfDomCssSelector that expects a DOM document as construction parameter. It has a getTexts() method that returns an array of strings according to a CSS selector, and a getElements() method that returns an array of DOM elements. See an example in Listing 15-20.

Listing 15-20. *The Test Browser Gives Access to the Response Content As an* sfDomCssSelector *Object*

```
$b = new sfTestBrowser();
$b->initialize();
$b->get('/foobar/edit/id/1');
$c = new sfDomCssSelector($b->getResponseDom())
$b->test()->is($c->getTexts('form input[type="hidden"][value="1"]'), array(''));
$b->test()->is($c->getTexts('form textarea[name="text1"]'), array('foo'));
$b->test()->is($c->getTexts('form input[type="submit"]'), array(''));
```

In its constant pursuit for brevity and clarity, symfony provides a shortcut for this: the checkResponseElement() proxy method. This method makes Listing 15-20 look like Listing 15-21.

Listing 15-21. *The Test Browser Gives Access to the Elements of the Response by CSS Selectors*

```
$b = new sfTestBrowser();
$b->initialize();
$b->get('/foobar/edit/id/1')->
    checkResponseElement('form input[type="hidden"][value="1"]', true->
    checkResponseElement('form textarea[name="text1"]', 'foo')->
    checkResponseElement('form input[type="submit"]', 1);
```

The behavior of the checkResponseElement() method depends on the type of the second argument that it receives:

- If it is a Boolean, it checks that an element matching the CSS selector exists.

- If it is an integer, it checks that the CSS selector returns this number of results.

- If it is a regular expression, it checks that the first element found by the CSS selector matches it.

- If it is a regular expression preceded by !, it checks that the first element doesn't match the pattern.

- For other cases, it compares the first element found by the CSS selector with the second argument as a string.

The method accepts a third optional parameter, in the shape of an associative array. It allows you to have the test performed not on the first element returned by the selector (if it returns several), but on another element at a certain position, as shown in Listing 15-22.

Listing 15-22. *Using the Position Option to Match an Element at a Certain Position*

```
$b = new sfTestBrowser();
$b->initialize();
$b->get('/foobar/edit?id=1')->
    checkResponseElement('form textarea', 'foo')->
    checkResponseElement('form textarea', 'bar', array('position' => 1));
```

The options array can also be used to perform two tests at the same time. You can test that there is an element matching a selector and how many there are, as demonstrated in Listing 15-23.

Listing 15-23. *Using the Count Option to Count the Number of Matches*

```
$b = new sfTestBrowser();
$b->initialize();
$b->get('/foobar/edit?id=1')->
    checkResponseElement('form input', true, array('count' => 3));
```

The selector tool is very powerful. It accepts most of the CSS 2.1 selectors, and you can use it for complex queries such as those of Listing 15-24.

Listing 15-24. *Example of Complex CSS Selectors Accepted by checkResponseElement()*

```
$b->checkResponseElement('ul#list li a[href]', 'click me');
$b->checkResponseElement('ul > li', 'click me');
$b->checkResponseElement('ul + li', 'click me');
$b->checkResponseElement('h1, h2', 'click me');
$b->checkResponseElement('a[class$="foo"][href*="bar.html"]', 'my link');
```

Working in the Test Environment

The sfTestBrowser object uses a special front controller, set to the test environment. The default configuration for this environment appears in Listing 15-25.

Listing 15-25. *Default Test Environment Configuration, in myapp/config/settings.php*

```
test:
  .settings:
    # E_ALL | E_STRICT & ~E_NOTICE = 2047
```

```
error_reporting:        2047
cache:                  off
web_debug:              off
no_script_name:         off
etag:                   off
```

The cache and the web debug toolbar are set to off in this environment. However, the code execution still leaves traces in a log file, distinct from the dev and prod log files, so that you can check it independently (myproject/log/myapp_test.log). In this environment, the exceptions don't stop the execution of the scripts—so that you can run an entire set of tests even if one fails. You can have specific database connection settings, for instance, to use another database with test data in it.

Before using the sfTestBrowser object, you have to initialize it. If you need to, you can specify a hostname for the application and an IP address for the client—that is, if your application makes controls over these two parameters. Listing 15-26 demonstrates how to do this.

Listing 15-26. *Setting Up the Test Browser with Hostname and IP*

```
$b = new sfTestBrowser();
$b->initialize('myapp.example.com', '123.456.789.123');
```

The test-functional Task

The test-functional task can run one or more functional tests, depending on the number of arguments received. The rules look much like the ones of the test-unit task, except that the functional test task always expects an application as first argument, as shown in Listing 15-27.

Listing 15-27. *Functional Test Task Syntax*

```
// Test directory structure
test/
  functional/
    frontend/
      myModuleActionsTest.php
      myScenarioTest.php
    backend/
      myOtherScenarioTest.php


## Run all functional tests for one application, recursively
> symfony test-functional frontend


## Run one given functional test
> symfony test-functional frontend myScenario


## Run several tests based on a pattern
> symfony test-functional frontend my*
```

Test Naming Practices

This section lists a few good practices to keep your tests organized and easy to maintain. The tips concern file organization, unit tests, and functional tests.

As for the *file structure*, you should name the unit test files using the class they are supposed to test, and name the functional test files using the module or the scenario they are supposed to test. See Listing 15-28 for an example. Your test/ directory will soon contain a lot of files, and finding a test might prove difficult in the long run if you don't follow these guidelines.

Listing 15-28. *Example File Naming Practice*

```
test/
  unit/
    myFunctionTest.php
    mySecondFunctionTest.php
    foo/
      barTest.php
  functional/
    frontend/
      myModuleActionsTest.php
      myScenarioTest.php
    backend/
      myOtherScenarioTest.php
```

For *unit tests*, a good practice is to group the tests by function or method, and start each test group with a diag() call. The messages of each unit test should contain the name of the function or method tested, followed by a verb and a property, so that the test output looks like a sentence describing a property of the object. Listing 15-29 shows an example.

Listing 15-29. *Example Unit Test Naming Practice*

```
// srttolower()
$t->diag('strtolower()');
$t->isa_ok(strtolower('Foo'), 'string', 'strtolower() returns a string');
$t->is(strtolower('FOO'), 'foo', 'strtolower() transforms the input to lowercase');
```

```
# strtolower()
ok 1 - strtolower() returns a string
ok 2 - strtolower() transforms the input to lowercase
```

Functional tests should be grouped by page and start by a request. Listing 15-30 illustrates this practice.

Listing 15-30. *Example Functional Test Naming Practice*

```
$browser->
  get('/foobar/index')->
  isStatusCode(200)->
  isRequestParameter('module', 'foobar')->
  isRequestParameter('action', 'index')->
  checkResponseElement('body', '/foobar/')
;
```

```
# get /comment/index
ok 1 - status code is 200
ok 2 - request parameter module is foobar
ok 3 - request parameter action is index
ok 4 - response selector body matches regex /foobar/
```

If you follow this convention, the output of your test will be clean enough to use as a developer documentation of your project—enough so in some cases to make actual documentation useless.

Special Testing Needs

The unit and functional test tools provided by symfony should suffice in most cases. A few additional techniques are listed here to resolve common problems in automated testing: launching tests in an isolated environment, accessing a database within tests, testing the cache, and testing interactions on the client side.

Executing Tests in a Test Harness

The `test-unit` and `test-functional` tasks can launch a single test or a set of tests. But if you call these tasks without any parameter, they launch all the unit and functional tests written in the `test/` directory. A particular mechanism is involved to isolate each test file in an independent sandbox, to avoid contamination risks between tests. Furthermore, as it wouldn't make sense to keep the same output as with single test files in that case (the output would be thousands of lines long), the tests results are compacted into a synthetic view. That's why the execution of a large number of test files uses a *test harness*, that is, an automated test framework with special abilities. A test harness relies on a component of the lime framework called `lime_harness`. It shows a test status file by file, and an overview at the end of the number of tests passed over the total, as you see in Listing 15-31.

Listing 15-31. *Launching All Tests in a Test Harness*

```
> symfony test-unit
```

```
unit/myFunctionTest.php...............ok
unit/mySecondFunctionTest.php..........ok
unit/foo/barTest.php.................not ok

Failed Test                   Stat  Total   Fail  List of Failed
----------------------------------------------------------------
unit/foo/barTest.php            0     2      2  62 63
Failed 1/3 test scripts, 66.66% okay. 2/53 subtests failed, 96.22% okay.
```

The tests are executed the same way as when you call them one by one, only the output is made shorter to be really useful. In particular, the final chart focuses on the failed tests and helps you locate them.

You can launch all the tests with one call using the `test-all` task, which also uses a test harness, as shown in Listing 15-32. This is something that you should do before every transfer to production, to ensure that no regression has appeared since the latest release.

Listing 15-32. *Launching All the Tests of a Project*

```
> symfony test-all
```

Accessing a Database

Unit tests often need to access a database. To initialize a database connection, use the `getConnection()` method of the `Propel` class, as in Listing 15-33.

Listing 15-33. *Initializing a Database in a Test*

```
$con = Propel::getConnection();
```

You should populate the database with fixtures before starting the tests. This can be done via the `sfPropelData` object. This object can load data from a file, just like the `propel-load-data` task, or from an array, as shown in Listing 15-34.

Listing 15-34. *Populating a Database from a Test File*

```
$data = new sfPropelData();

// Loading data from file
$data->loadData(sfConfig::get('sf_data_dir').'/fixtures/test_data.yml');
```

```
// Loading data from array
$fixtures = array(
  'Article' => array(
    'article_1' => array(
      'title'      => 'foo title',
      'body'       => 'bar body',
      'created_at' => time(),
    ),
    'article_2'   => array(
      'title'      => 'foo foo title',
      'body'       => 'bar bar body',
      'created_at' => time(),
    ),
  ),
);
$data->loadDataFromArray($fixtures);
```

Then, use the Propel objects as you would in a normal application, according to your testing needs. Remember to include their files in unit tests (you can use the sfCore:: sfSimpleAutoloading() method to automate it, as explained in a tip in the "Stubs, Fixtures, and Autoloading" section previously in this chapter). Propel objects are autoloaded in functional tests.

Testing the Cache

When you enable caching for an application, the functional tests should verify that the cached actions do work as expected.

The first thing to do is enable cache for the test environment (in the settings.yml file). Then, if you want to test whether a page comes from the cache or whether it is generated, you should use the isCached() test method provided by the sfTestBrowser object. Listing 15-35 demonstrates this method.

Listing 15-35. *Testing the Cache with the isCached() Method*

```php
<?php

include(dirname(__FILE__).'/../../bootstrap/functional.php');

// Create a new test browser
$b = new sfTestBrowser();
$b->initialize();

$b->get('/mymodule');
$b->isCached(true);        // Checks that the response comes from the cache
$b->isCached(true, true); // Checks that the cached response comes with layout
$b->isCached(false);       // Checks that the response doesn't come from the cache
```

■Note You don't need to clear the cache at the beginning of a functional test; the bootstrap script does it for you.

Testing Interactions on the Client

The main drawback of the techniques described previously is that they cannot simulate JavaScript. For very complex interactions, like with Ajax interactions for instance, you need to be able to reproduce exactly the mouse and keyboard input that a user would do and execute scripts on the client side. Usually, these tests are reproduced by hand, but they are very time consuming and prone to error.

The solution is called *Selenium* (http://www.openqa.org/selenium/), which is a test framework written entirely in JavaScript. It executes a set of actions on a page just like a regular user would, using the current browser window. The advantage over the sfBrowser object is that Selenium is capable of executing JavaScript in a page, so you can test even Ajax interactions with it.

Selenium is not bundled with symfony by default. To install it, you need to create a new selenium/ directory in your web/ directory, and in it unpack the content of the Selenium archive (http://www.openqa.org/selenium-core/download.action). This is because Selenium relies on JavaScript, and the security settings standard in most browsers wouldn't allow it to run unless it is available on the same host and port as your application.

■Caution Be careful not to transfer the selenium/ directory to your production server, since it would be accessible by anyone having access to your web document root via the browser.

Selenium tests are written in HTML and stored in the web/selenium/tests/ directory. For instance, Listing 15-36 shows a functional test where the home page is loaded, the link click me is clicked, and the text "Hello, World" is looked for in the response. Remember that in order to access the application in the test environment, you have to specify the myapp_test.php front controller.

Listing 15-36. *A Sample Selenium Test, in web/selenium/test/testIndex.html*

```
<!DOCTYPE html PUBLIC "-//W3C//DTD HTML 4.01 Transitional//EN">
<html>
<head>
  <meta content="text/html; charset=UTF-8" http-equiv="content-type">
  <title>Index tests</title>
</head>
<body>
<table cellspacing="0">
```

```
<tbody>
  <tr><td colspan="3">First step</td></tr>
  <tr><td>open</td>              <td>/myapp_test.php/</td> <td> </td></tr>
  <tr><td>clickAndWait</td>      <td>link=click me</td>    <td> </td></tr>
  <tr><td>assertTextPresent</td> <td>Hello, World!</td>    <td> </td></tr>
</tbody>
</table>
</body>
</html>
```

A test case is represented by an HTML document containing a table with three columns: command, target, and value. Not all commands take a value, however. In this case, either leave the column blank or use   to make the table look better. Refer to the Selenium website for a complete list of commands.

You also need to add this test to the global test suite by inserting a new line in the table of the TestSuite.html file, located in the same directory. Listing 15-37 shows how.

Listing 15-37. *Adding a Test File to the Test Suite, in* web/selenium/test/TestSuite.html

```
...
<tr><td><a href='./testIndex.html'>My First Test</a></td></tr>
...
```

To run the test, simply browse to

```
http://myapp.example.com/selenium/index.html
```

Select Main Test Suite, click the button to run all tests, and watch your browser as it reproduces the steps that you have told it to do.

■**Note** As Selenium tests run in a real browser, they also allow you to test browser inconsistencies. Build your test with one browser, and test them on all the others on which your site is supposed to work with a single request.

The fact that Selenium tests are written in HTML could make the writing of Selenium tests a hassle. But thanks to the Firefox Selenium extension (http://seleniumrecorder.mozdev.org/), all it takes to create a test is to execute the test once in a recorded session. While navigating in a recording session, you can add assert-type tests by right-clicking in the browser window and selecting the appropriate check under Append Selenium Command in the pop-up menu.

You can save the test to an HTML file to build a test suite for your application. The Firefox extension even allows you to run the Selenium tests that you have recorded with it.

■**Note** Don't forget to reinitialize the test data before launching the Selenium test.

Summary

Automated tests include *unit tests* to validate methods or functions and *functional tests* to validate features. Symfony relies on the *lime* testing framework for unit tests and provides an sfTestBrowser class especially for functional tests. They both provide many assertion methods, from basic to the most advanced, like *CSS selectors*. Use the *symfony command line* to launch tests, either one by one (with the test-unit and test-functional tasks) or in a *test harness* (with the test-all task). When dealing with data, automated tests use *fixtures* and *stubs*, and this is easily achieved within symfony unit tests.

If you make sure to write enough unit tests to cover a large part of your applications (maybe using the TDD methodology), you will feel safer when *refactoring* internals or adding new features, and you may even gain some time on the *documentation* task.

CHAPTER 16

■ ■ ■

Application Management Tools

During both the development and deployment phases, developers require a consistent stream of diagnostic information in order to determine whether the application is working as intended. This information is generally aggregated through logging and debugging utilities. Because of the central role frameworks, such as symfony, play in driving applications, it's crucial that such capabilities are tightly integrated to ensure efficient developmental and operational activities.

During the life of an application on the production server, the application administrator repeats a large number of tasks, from log rotation to upgrades. A framework must also provide tools to automate these tasks as much as possible.

This chapter explains how symfony application management tools can answer all these needs.

Logging

The only way to understand what went wrong during the execution of a request is to review a trace of the execution process. Fortunately, as you'll learn in this section, both PHP and symfony tend to log large amounts of this sort of data.

PHP Logs

PHP has an `error_reporting` parameter, defined in `php.ini`, that specifies which PHP events are logged. Symfony allows you to override this value, per application and environment, in the `settings.yml` file, as shown in Listing 16-1.

Listing 16-1. *Setting the Error Reporting Level, in* `myapp/config/settings.yml`

```
prod:
  .settings:
    error_reporting:  257

dev:
  .settings:
    error_reporting:  4095
```

The numbers are a short way of writing error levels (refer to the PHP documentation on error reporting for more details). Basically, 4095 is a shortcut for E_ALL | E_STRICT, and 257 stands for E_ERROR | E_USER_ERROR (the default value for every new environment).

In order to avoid performance issues in the production environment, the server logs only the critical PHP errors. However, in the development environment, all types of events are logged, so that the developer can have all the information necessary to trace errors.

The location of the PHP log files depends on your php.ini configuration. If you never bothered about defining this location, PHP probably uses the logging facilities provided by your web server (such as the Apache error logs). In this case, you will find the PHP logs under the web server log directory.

Symfony Logs

In addition to the standard PHP logs, symfony can log a lot of custom events. You can find all the symfony logs under the myproject/log/ directory. There is one file per application and per environment. For instance, the development environment log file of the myapp application is named myapp_dev.log, the production one is named myapp_prod.log, and so on.

If you have a symfony application running, take a look at its log files. The syntax is very simple. For every event, one line is added to the log file of the application. Each line includes the exact time of the event, the nature of the event, the object being processed, and any additional relevant details. Listing 16-2 shows an example of symfony log file content.

Listing 16-2. *Sample Symfony Log File Content, in* log/myapp_dev.php

```
Nov 15 16:30:25 symfony [info ] {sfAction} call "barActions->executemessages()"
Nov 15 16:30:25 symfony [debug] SELECT bd_message.ID, bd_message.SENDER_ID, bd_...
Nov 15 16:30:25 symfony [info ] {sfCreole} executeQuery(): SELECT bd_message.ID...
Nov 15 16:30:25 symfony [info ] {sfView} set slot "leftbar" (bar/index)
Nov 15 16:30:25 symfony [info ] {sfView} set slot "messageblock" (bar/mes...
Nov 15 16:30:25 symfony [info ] {sfView} execute view for template "messa...
Nov 15 16:30:25 symfony [info ] {sfView} render "/home/production/myproject/...
Nov 15 16:30:25 symfony [info ] {sfView} render to client
```

You can find many details in these files, including the actual SQL queries sent to the database, the templates called, the chain of calls between objects, and so on.

Symfony Log Level Configuration

There are eight levels of symfony log messages: emerg, alert, crit, err, warning, notice, info, and debug, which are the same as the PEAR::Log package (http://pear.php.net/package/Log/) levels. You can configure the maximum level to be logged in each environment in the logging.yml configuration file of each application, as demonstrated in Listing 16-3.

Listing 16-3. *Default Logging Configuration, in* `myapp/config/logging.yml`

```
prod:
  enabled: off
  level:   err
  rotate:  on
  purge:   off

dev:

test:

#all:
#  enabled:  on
#  level:    debug
#  rotate:   off
#  period:   7
#  history:  10
#  purge:    on
```

By default, in all environments except the production environment, all the messages are logged (up to the least important level, the debug level). In the production environment, logging is disabled by default; if you change `enabled` to `on`, only the most important messages (from `crit` to `emerg`) appear in the logs.

You can change the logging level in the `logging.yml` file for each environment to limit the type of logged messages. The `rotate`, `period`, `history`, and `purge` settings are described in the upcoming "Purging and Rotating Log Files" section.

■**Tip** The values of the logging parameters are accessible during execution through the `sfConfig` object with the `sf_logging_` prefix. For instance, to see if logging is enabled, call `sfConfig::get('sf_logging_enabled')`.

Adding a Log Message

You can manually add a message in the symfony log file from your code by using one of the techniques described in Listing 16-4.

Listing 16-4. *Adding a Custom Log Message*

```
// From an action
$this->logMessage($message, $level);

// From a template
<?php use_helper('Debug') ?>
<?php log_message($message, $level) ?>
```

$level can have the same values as in the log messages.

Alternatively, to write a message in the log from anywhere in your application, use the sfLogger methods directly, as shown in Listing 16-5. The available methods bear the same names as the log levels.

Listing 16-5. *Adding a Custom Log Message from Anywhere*

```
if (sfConfig::get('sf_logging_enabled'))
{
  sfContext::getInstance()->getLogger()->info($message);
}
```

CUSTOMIZING THE LOGGING

Symfony's logging system is very simple, yet it is also easy to customize. You can specify your own logging object by calling sfLogger::getInstance()->registerLogger(). For instance, if you want to use PEAR::Log, just add the following to your application's config.php:

```
require_once('Log.php');
$log = Log::singleton('error_log', PEAR_LOG_TYPE_SYSTEM, 'symfony');
sfLogger::getInstance()->registerLogger($log);
```

If you want to register your own logger class, the only prerequisite is that it must define a log() method. Symfony calls this method with two parameters: $message (the message to be logged) and $priority (the level).

Purging and Rotating Log Files

Don't forget to periodically purge the log/ directory of your applications, because these files have the strange habit of growing by several megabytes in a few days, depending, of course, on your traffic. Symfony provides a special log-purge task for this purpose, which you can launch regularly by hand or put in a cron table. For example, the following command erases the symfony log files in applications and environments where the logging.yml file specifies purge: on (which is the default value):

```
> symfony log-purge
```

For both better performance and security, you probably want to store symfony logs in several small files instead of one single large file. The ideal storage strategy for log files is to back up and empty the main log file regularly, but to keep only a limited number of backups. You can enable such a log rotation and specify the parameters in logging.yml. For instance, with a period of 7 days and a history (number of backups) of 10, as shown in Listing 16-6, you would work with one active log file plus ten backup files containing seven days' worth of history each. Whenever the next period of seven days ends, the current active log file goes into backup, and the oldest backup is erased.

Listing 16-6. *Configuring Log Rotation, in* `myapp/config/logging.yml`

```
prod:
  rotate:  on
  period:  7        ## Log files are rotated every 7 days by default
  history: 10       ## A maximum history of 10 log files is kept
```

To execute the log rotation, periodically execute the `log-rotate` task. This task only purges files for which `rotate` is on. You can specify a single application and environment when calling the task:

```
> symfony log-rotate myapp prod
```

The backup log files are stored in the `logs/history/` directory and suffixed with the date they were saved.

Debugging

No matter how proficient a coder you are, you will eventually make mistakes, even if you use symfony. Detecting and understanding errors is one of the keys of fast application development. Fortunately, symfony provides several debug tools for the developer.

Symfony Debug Mode

Symfony has a *debug mode* that facilitates application development and debugging. When it is on, the following happens:

- The configuration is checked at each request, so a change in any of the configuration files has an immediate effect, without any need to clear the configuration cache.

- The error messages display the full stack trace in a clear and useful way, so that you can more efficiently find the faulty element.

- More debug tools are available (such as the detail of database queries).

- The Propel debug mode is also activated, so any error in a call to a Propel object will display a detailed chain of calls through the Propel architecture.

On the other hand, when the debug mode is off, processing is handled as follows:

- The YAML configuration files are parsed only once, then transformed into PHP files stored in the `cache/config/` folder. Every request after the first one ignores the YAML files and uses the cached configuration instead. As a consequence, the processing of requests is much faster.

- To allow a reprocessing of the configuration, you must manually clear the configuration cache.

- An error during the processing of the request returns a response with code 500 (Internal Server Error), without any explanation of the internal cause of the problem.

The debug mode is activated per application in the front controller. It is controlled by the value of the SF_DEBUG constant, as shown in Listing 16-7.

Listing 16-7. *Sample Front Controller with Debug Mode On, in web/myapp_dev.php*

```php
<?php

define('SF_ROOT_DIR',    realpath(dirname(__FILE__).'/..'));
define('SF_APP',         'myapp');
define('SF_ENVIRONMENT', 'dev');
define('SF_DEBUG',       true);

require_once(SF_ROOT_DIR.DIRECTORY_SEPARATOR.'apps'.DIRECTORY_SEPARATOR ➥
.SF_APP.DIRECTORY_SEPARATOR.'config'.DIRECTORY_SEPARATOR.'config.php');

sfContext::getInstance()->getController()->dispatch();
```

■**Caution** In your production server, you should not activate the debug mode nor leave any front controller with debug mode on available. Not only will the debug mode slow down the page delivery, but it may also reveal the internals of your application. Even though the debug tools never reveal database connection information, the stack trace of exceptions is full of dangerous information for any ill-intentioned visitor.

Symfony Exceptions

When an exception occurs in the debug mode, symfony displays a useful exception notice that contains everything you need to find the cause of the problem.

The exception messages are clearly written and refer to the most probable cause of the problem. They often provide possible solutions to fix the problem, and for most common problems, the exception pages even contain a link to a symfony website page with more details about the exception. The exception page shows where the error occurred in the PHP code (with syntax highlighting), together with the full stack of method calls, as shown in Figure 16-1. You can follow the trace to the first call that caused the problem. The arguments that were passed to the methods are also shown.

■**Note** Symfony really relies on PHP exceptions for error reporting, which is much better than the way PHP 4 applications work. For instance, the 404 error can be triggered by an sfError404Exception.

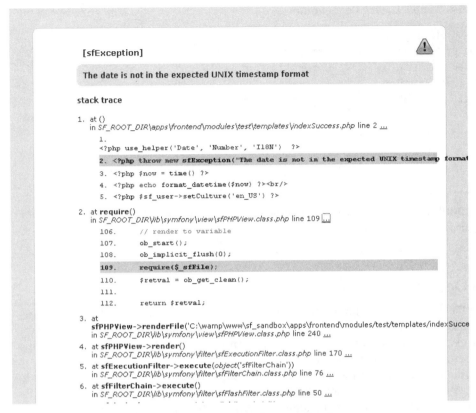

Figure 16-1. *Sample exception message for a symfony application*

During the development phase, the symfony exceptions will be of great use as you debug your application.

Xdebug Extension

The Xdebug PHP extension (http://xdebug.org/) allows you to extend the amount of information that is logged by the web server. Symfony integrates the Xdebug messages in its own debug feedback, so it is a good idea to activate this extension when you debug the application. The extension installation depends very much on your platform; refer to the Xdebug website for detailed installation guidelines. Once Xdebug is installed, you need to activate it manually in your php.ini file after installation. For *nix platforms, this is done by adding the following line:

```
zend_extension="/usr/local/lib/php/extensions/no-debug-non-zts-20041030/xdebug.so"
```

For Windows platforms, the Xdebug activation is triggered by this line:

```
extension=php_xdebug.dll
```

Listing 16-8 gives an example of Xdebug configuration, which must also be added to the php.ini file.

Listing 16-8. *Sample Xdebug Configuration*

```
;xdebug.profiler_enable=1
;xdebug.profiler_output_dir="/tmp/xdebug"
xdebug.auto_trace=1              ; enable tracing
xdebug.trace_format=0
;xdebug.show_mem_delta=0         ; memory difference
;xdebug.show_local_vars=1
;xdebug.max_nesting_level=100
```

You must restart your web server for the Xdebug mode to be activated.

■**Caution** Don't forget to deactivate Xdebug mode in your production platform. Not doing so will slow down the execution of every page a lot.

Web Debug Toolbar

The log files contain interesting information, but they are not very easy to read. The most basic task, which is to find the lines logged for a particular request, can be quite tricky if you have several users simultaneously using an application and a long history of events. That's when you start to need a *web debug toolbar*.

This toolbar appears as a semitransparent box superimposed over the normal content in the browser, in the top-right corner of the window, as shown in Figure 16-2. It gives access to the symfony log events, the current configuration, the properties of the request and response objects, the details of the database queries issued by the request, and a chart of processing times related to the request.

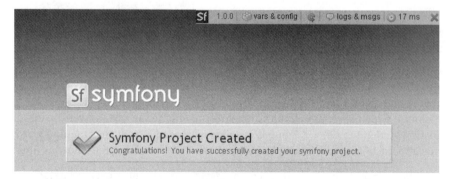

Figure 16-2. *The web debug toolbar appears in the top-right corner of the window.*

The color of the debug toolbar background depends on the highest level of log message issued during the request. If no message passes the debug level, the toolbar has a gray background. If a single message reaches the err level, the toolbar has a red background.

Note Don't confuse the *debug mode* with the *web debug toolbar*. The debug toolbar can be displayed even when the debug mode if off, although, in that case, it displays much less information.

To activate the web debug toolbar for an application, open the `settings.yml` file and look for the `web_debug` key. In the `prod` and `test` environments, the default value for `web_debug` is `off`, so you need to activate it manually if you want it. In the `dev` environment, the default configuration has it set to `on`, as shown in Listing 16-9.

Listing 16-9. *Web Debug Toolbar Activation, in* `myapp/config/settings.yml`

```
dev:
  .settings:
    web_debug:            on
```

When displayed, the web debug toolbar offers a lot of information/interaction:

- Click the *symfony logo* to toggle the visibility of the toolbar. When reduced, the toolbar doesn't hide the elements located at the top of the page.

- Click the *vars & config* section to show the details of the request, response, settings, globals, and PHP properties, as shown in Figure 16-3. The top line sums up the important configuration settings, such as the debug mode, the cache, and the presence of a PHP accelerator (they appear in red if they are deactivated and in green if they are activated).

Figure 16-3. *The vars & config section shows all the variables and constants of the request.*

- When the cache is enabled, a *green arrow* appears in the toolbar. Click this arrow to reprocess the page, regardless of what is stored in the cache (but the cache is not cleared).

- Click the *logs & msgs* section to reveal the log messages for the current request, as shown in Figure 16-4. According to the importance of the events, they are displayed in gray, yellow, or red lines. You can filter the events that are displayed by category using the links displayed at the top of the list.

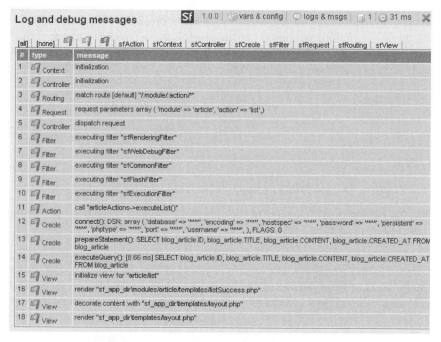

Figure 16-4. *The logs & msgs section shows the log messages for the current request.*

Note When the current action results from a redirect, only the logs of the latest request are present in the logs & msgs pane, so the log files are still indispensable for good debugging.

- For requests executing SQL queries, a *database icon* appears in the toolbar. Click it to see the detail of the queries, as shown in Figure 16-5.

- To the right of a *clock icon* is the total time necessary to process the request. Be aware that the web debug toolbar and the debug mode slow down the request execution, so try to refrain from considering the timings per se, and pay attention to only the differences between the execution time of two pages. Click the clock icon to see details of the processing time category by category, as shown in Figure 16-6. Symfony displays the time spent on specific parts of the request processing. Only the times related to the current request make sense for an optimization, so the time spent in the symfony core is not displayed. That's why these times don't sum up to the total time.

- Click the *red x* at the right end of the toolbar to hide the toolbar.

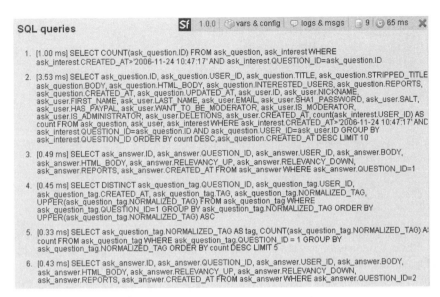

Figure 16-5. *The database queries section shows queries executed for the current request.*

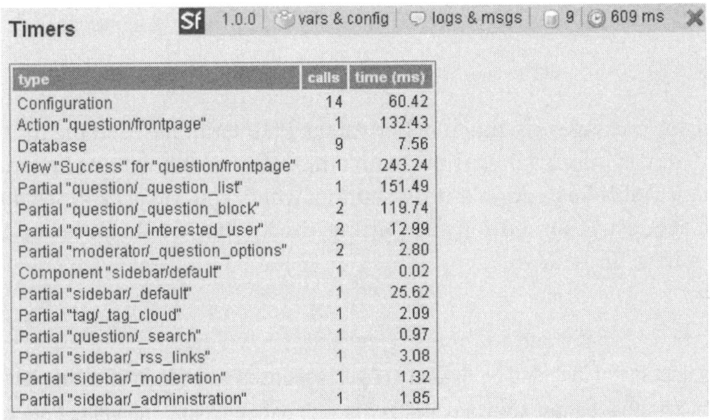

Figure 16-6. *The clock icon shows execution time by category.*

ADDING YOUR OWN TIMER

Symfony uses the `sfTimer` class to calculate the time spent on the configuration, the model, the action, and the view. Using the same object, you can time a custom process and display the result with the other timers in the web debug toolbar. This can be very useful when you work on performance optimizations.

To initialize timing on a specific fragment of code, call the `getTimer()` method. It will return an `sfTimer` object and start the timing. Call the `addTime()` method on this object to stop the timing. The elapsed time is available through the `getElapsedTime()` method, and displayed in the web debug toolbar with the others.

```
// Initialize the timer and start timing
$timer = sfTimerManager::getTimer('myTimer');

// Do things
...

// Stop the timer and add the elapsed time
$timer->addTime();

// Get the result (and stop the timer if not already stopped)
$elapsedTime = $timer->getElapsedTime();
```

The benefit of giving a name to each timer is that you can call it several times to accumulate timings. For instance, if the myTimer timer is used in a utility method that is called twice per request, the second call to the getTimer('myTimer') method will restart the timing from the point calculated when addTime() was last called, so the timing will add up to the previous one. Calling getCalls() on the timer object will give you the number of times the timer was launched, and this data is also displayed in the web debug toolbar.

```
// Get the number of calls to the timer
$nbCalls = $timer->getCalls();
```

In Xdebug mode, the log messages are much richer. All the PHP script files and the functions that are called are logged, and symfony knows how to link this information with its internal log. Each line of the log messages table has a double-arrow button, which you can click to see further details about the related request. If something goes wrong, the Xdebug mode gives you the maximum amount of detail to find out why.

Note The web debug toolbar is not included by default in Ajax responses and documents that have a non-HTML content-type. For the other pages, you can disable the web debug toolbar manually from within an action by simply calling sfConfig::set('sf_web_debug', false).

Manual Debugging

Getting access to the framework debug messages is nice, but being able to log your own messages is better. Symfony provides shortcuts, accessible from both actions and templates, to help you trace events and/or values during request execution.

Your custom log messages appear in the symfony log file as well as in the web debug toolbar, just like regular events. (Listing 16-4 gave an example of the custom log message syntax.) A custom message is a good way to check the value of a variable from a template, for instance. Listing 16-10 shows how to use the web debug toolbar for developer's feedback from a template (you can also use $this->logMessage() from an action).

Listing 16-10. *Inserting a Message in the Log for Debugging Purposes*

```
<?php use_helper('Debug') ?>
...
<?php if ($problem): ?>
  <?php log_message('{sfAction} been there', 'err') ?>
  ...
<?php endif ?>
```

The use of the err level guarantees that the event will be clearly visible in the list of messages, as shown in Figure 16-7.

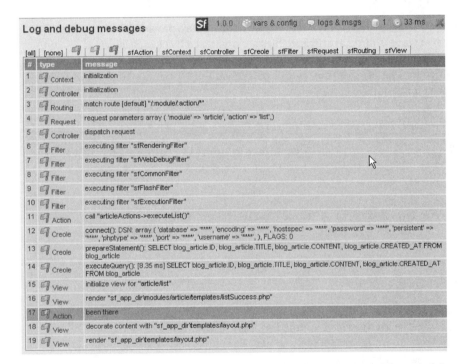

Figure 16-7. *A custom log message appears in the logs & msgs section of the web debug toolbar.*

If you don't want to add a line to the log, but just trace a short message or a value, you should use debug_message instead of log_message. This action method (a helper with the same name also exists) displays a message in the web debug toolbar, on top of the logs & msgs section. Check Listing 16-11 for an example of using the debug message writer.

Listing 16-11. *Inserting a Message in the Debug Toolbar*

```
// From an action
$this->debugMessage($message);

// From a template
<?php use_helper('Debug') ?>
<?php debug_message($message) ?>
```

Populating a Database

In the process of application development, developers are often faced with the problem of database population. A few specific solutions exist for some database systems, but none can be used on top of the object-relational mapping. Thanks to YAML and the sfPropelData object, symfony can automatically transfer data from a text source to a database. Although writing a text file source for data may seem like more work than entering the records by hand using a CRUD interface, it will save you time in the long run. You will find this feature very useful for automatically storing and populating the test data for your application.

Fixture File Syntax

Symfony can read data files that follow a very simple YAML syntax, provided that they are located under the data/fixtures/ directory. Fixture files are organized by class, each class section being introduced by the class name as a header. For each class, records labeled with a unique string are defined by a set of fieldname: value pairs. Listing 16-12 shows an example of a data file for database population.

Listing 16-12. *Sample Fixture File, in data/fixtures/import_data.yml*

```
Article:                              ## Insert records in the blog_article table
  first_post:                         ## First record label
    title:        My first memories
    content: |
      For a long time I used to go to bed early. Sometimes, when I had put
      out my candle, my eyes would close so quickly that I had not even time
      to say "I'm going to sleep."

  second_post:                        ## Second record label
    title:        Things got worse
    content: |
      Sometimes he hoped that she would die, painlessly, in some accident,
      she who was out of doors in the streets, crossing busy thoroughfares,
      from morning to night.
```

Symfony translates the column keys into setter methods by using a camelCase converter (setTitle(), setContent()). This means that you can define a password key even if the actual table doesn't have a password field—just define a setPassword() method in the User object, and you can populate other columns based on the password (for instance, a hashed version of the password).

The primary key column doesn't need to be defined. Since it is an auto-increment field, the database layer knows how to determine it.

The created_at columns don't need to be set either, because symfony knows that fields named that way must be set to the current system time when created.

Launching the Import

The `propel-load-data` task imports data from a YAML file to a database. The connection
settings come from the `databases.yml` file, and therefore need an application name to run.
Optionally, you can specify an environment name (dev by default).

```
> symfony propel-load-data frontend
```

This command reads all the YAML fixture files from the `data/fixtures/` directory and
inserts the records into the database. By default, it replaces the existing database content, but
if the last argument call is `append`, the command will not erase the current data.

```
> symfony propel-load-data frontend append
```

You can specify another fixture file or directory in the call. In this case, add a path relative
to the project `data/` directory.

```
> symfony propel-load-data frontend myfixtures/myfile.yml
```

Using Linked Tables

You now know how to add records to a single table, but how do you add records with foreign
keys to another table? Since the primary key is not included in the fixtures data, you need an
alternative way to relate records to one another.

Let's return to the example in Chapter 8, where a `blog_article` table is linked to a
`blog_comment` table, as shown in Figure 16-8.

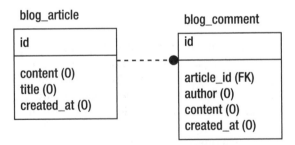

Figure 16-8. *A sample database relational model*

This is where the labels given to the records become really useful. To add a `Comment` field
to the `first_post` article, you simply need to append the lines shown in Listing 16-13 to the
`import_data.yml` data file.

Listing 16-13. *Adding a Record to a Related Table, in data/fixtures/import_data.yml*

```
Comment:
  first_comment:
    article_id:    first_post
    author:        Anonymous
    content:       Your prose is too verbose. Write shorter sentences.
```

The `propel-load-data` task will recognize the label that you gave to an article previously in `import_data.yml`, and grab the primary key of the corresponding `Article` record to set the `article_id` field. You don't even see the IDs of the records; you just link them by their labels—it couldn't be simpler.

The only constraint for linked records is that the objects called in a foreign key must be defined earlier in the file; that is, as you would do if you defined them one by one. The data files are parsed from the top to the bottom, and the order in which the records are written is important.

One data file can contain declarations of several classes. But if you need to insert a lot of data for many different tables, your fixture file might get too long to be easily manipulated.

The `propel-load-data` task parses all the files it finds in the `fixtures/` directory, so nothing prevents you from splitting a YAML fixture file into smaller pieces. The important thing to keep in mind is that foreign keys impose a processing order for the tables. To make sure that they are parsed in the correct order, prefix the files with an ordinal number.

```
100_article_import_data.yml
200_comment_import_data.yml
300_rating_import_data.yml
```

Deploying Applications

Symfony offers shorthand commands to synchronize two versions of a website. These commands are mostly used to deploy a website from a development server to a final host, connected to the Internet.

Freezing a Project for FTP Transfer

The most common way to deploy a project to production is to transfer all its files by FTP (or SFTP). However, symfony projects use the symfony libraries, and unless you develop in a sandbox (which is not recommended), or if the symfony `lib/` and `data/` directories are linked by `svn:externals`, these libraries are not in the project directory. Whether you use a PEAR installation or symbolic links, reproducing the same file structure in production can be time-consuming and tricky.

That's why symfony provides a utility to "freeze" a project—to copy all the necessary symfony libraries into the project `data/`, `lib/`, and `web/` directories. The project then becomes a kind of sandbox, an independent, stand-alone application.

```
> symfony freeze
```

Once a project is frozen, you can transfer the project directory into production, and it will work without any need for PEAR, symbolic links, or whatever else.

■**Tip** Various frozen projects can work on the same server with different versions of symfony without any problems.

To revert a project to its initial state, use the `unfreeze` task. It erases the `data/symfony/`, `lib/symfony/`, and `web/sf/` directories.

```
> symfony unfreeze
```

Note that if you had symbolic links to a symfony installation prior to the freeze, symfony will remember them and re-create the symbolic links in the original location.

Using rsync for Incremental File Transfer

Sending the root project directory by FTP is fine for the first transfer, but when you need to upload an update of your application, where only a few files have changed, FTP is not ideal. You need to either transfer the whole project again, which is a waste of time and bandwidth, or browse to the directories where you know that some files changed, and transfer only the ones with different modification dates. That's a time-consuming job, and it is prone to error. In addition, the website can be unavailable or buggy during the time of the transfer.

The solution that is supported by symfony is *rsync synchronization through an SSH layer*. Rsync (`http://samba.anu.edu.au/rsync/`) is a command-line utility that provides fast incremental file transfer, and it's open source. With *incremental* transfer, only the modified data will be sent. If a file didn't change, it won't be sent to the host. If a file changed only partially, just the differential will be sent. The major advantage is that rsync synchronizations transfer only a small amount of data and are very fast.

Symfony adds SSH on top of rsync to secure the data transfer. More and more commercial hosts support an SSH tunnel to secure file uploads on their servers, and that's a good practice to avoid security breaches.

The SSH client called by symfony uses connection settings from the `config/properties.ini` file. Listing 16-14 gives an example of connection settings for a production server. Write the settings of your own production server in this file before any synchronization. You can also define a single parameters setting to provide your own rsync command line parameters.

Listing 16-14. *Sample Connection Settings for a Server Synchronization, in* `myproject/config/properties.ini`

```
[symfony]
  name=myproject

[production]
  host=myapp.example.com
  port=22
  user=myuser
  dir=/home/myaccount/myproject/
```

■**Note** Don't confuse the *production server* (the host server, as defined in the `properties.ini` file of the project) with the *production environment* (the front controller and configuration used in production, as referred to in the configuration files of an application).

Doing an rsync over SSH requires several commands, and synchronization can occur a lot of times in the life of an application. Fortunately, symfony automates this process with just one command:

```
> symfony sync production
```

This command launches the rsync command in dry mode; that is, it shows which files must be synchronized but doesn't actually synchronize them. If you want the synchronization to be done, you need to request it explicitly by adding go.

```
> symfony sync production go
```

Don't forget to clear the cache in the production server after synchronization.

■**Tip** Sometimes bugs appear in production that didn't exist in development. In 90% of the cases, this is due to differences in versions (of PHP, web server, or database) or in configurations. To avoid unpleasant surprises, you should define the target PHP configuration in the php.yml file of your application, so that it checks that the development environment applies the same settings. Refer to Chapter 19 for more information about this configuration file.

IS YOUR APPLICATION FINISHED?

Before sending your application to production, you should make sure that it is ready for a public use. Check that the following items are done before actually deciding to deploy the application:

- The error pages should be customized to the look and feel of your application. Refer to Chapter 19 to see how to customize the error 500, error 404, and security pages, and to the "Managing a Production Application" section in this chapter to see how to customize the pages displayed when your site is not available.

- The session-handling mechanism uses a cookie on the client side, and this cookie is called symfony by default. Before deploying your application, you should probably rename it to avoid disclosing the fact that your application uses symfony. Refer to Chapter 6 to see how to customize the cookie name in the factories.yml file.

- The robots.txt file, located in the project's web/ directory, is empty by default. You should customize it to inform web spiders and other web robots about which parts of a website they can browse and which they should avoid. Most of the time, this file is used to exclude certain URL spaces from being indexed—for instance, resource-intensive pages, pages that don't need indexing (such as bug archives), or infinite URL spaces in which robots could get trapped.

- Modern browsers request a favicon.ico file when a user first browses to your application, to represent the application with an icon in the address bar and bookmarks folder. Providing such a file will not only make your application's look and feel complete, but it will also prevent a lot of 404 errors from appearing in your server logs.

Ignoring Irrelevant Files

If you synchronize your symfony project with a production host, a few files and directories should not be transferred:

- All the *version control directories* (.svn/, CVS/, and so on) and their content are necessary only for development and integration.

- The *front controller for the development environment* must not be available to the final users. The debugging and logging tools available when using the application through this front controller slow down the application and give information about the core variables of your actions. It is something to keep away from the public.

- The cache/ and log/ directories of a project must not be erased in the host server each time you do a synchronization. These directories must be ignored as well. If you have a stats/ directory, it should probably be treated the same way.

- The *files uploaded by users* should not be transferred. One of the good practices of symfony projects is to store the uploaded files in the web/uploads/ directory. This allows you to exclude all these files from the synchronization by pointing to only one directory.

To exclude files from rsync synchronizations, open and edit the rsync_exclude.txt file under the myproject/config/ directory. Each line can contain a file, a directory, or a pattern. The symfony file structure is organized logically, and designed to minimize the number of files or directories to exclude manually from the synchronization. See Listing 16-15 for an example.

Listing 16-15. *Sample rsync Exclusion Settings, in myproject/config/rsync_exclude.txt*

```
.svn
/cache/*
/log/*
/stats/*
/web/uploads/*
/web/myapp_dev.php
```

■Note The cache/ and log/ directories must not be synchronized with the development server, but they must at least exist in the production server. Create them by hand if the myproject/ project tree structure doesn't contain them.

Managing a Production Application

The command that is used most often in production servers is clear-cache. You must run it every time you upgrade symfony or your project (for instance, after calling the sync task), and every time you change the configuration in production.

```
> symfony clear-cache
```

■**Tip** If the command-line interface is not available in your production server, you can still clear the cache manually by erasing the contents of the cache/ folder.

You can temporarily disable your application—for instance, when you need to upgrade a library or a large amount of data.

```
> symfony disable APPLICATION_NAME ENVIRONMENT_NAME
```

By default, a disabled application displays the default/unavailable action (stored in the framework), but you can customize the module and action to be used in this case in the settings.yml file. Listing 16-16 shows an example.

Listing 16-16. *Setting the Action to Execute for an Unavailable Application, in* myapp/config/ settings.yml

```
all:
  .settings:
    unavailable_module:    mymodule
    unavailable_action:    maintenance
```

The enable task reenables the application and clears the cache.

```
> symfony enable APPLICATION_NAME ENVIRONMENT_NAME
```

DISPLAYING AN UNAVAILABLE PAGE WHEN CLEARING THE CACHE

If you set the check_lock parameter to on in the settings.yml file, symfony will lock the application when the cache is being cleared, and all the requests arriving before the cache is finally cleared are then redirected to a page saying that the application is temporarily available. If the cache is large, the delay to clear it may be longer than a few milliseconds, and if your site's traffic is high, this is a recommended setting.

This unavailable page is not the same as the one displayed when you call symfony disable (because while the cache is being cleared, symfony cannot work normally). It is located in the $sf_symfony_data_dir/ web/errors/ directory, but if you create your own unavailable.php file in your project's web/errors/ directory, symfony will use it instead. The check_lock parameter is deactivated by default because it has a very slight negative impact on performance.

The clear-controllers task clears the web/ directory of all controllers other than the ones running in a production environment. If you do not include the development front controllers in the rsync_exclude.txt file, this command guarantees that a backdoor will not reveal the internals of your application.

```
> symfony clear-controllers
```

The permissions of the project files and directories can be broken if you use a checkout from an SVN repository. The fix-perms task fixes directory permissions, to change the log/ and cache/ permissions to 0777, for example (these directories need to be writable for the framework to work correctly).

```
> symfony fix-perms
```

ACCESS TO THE SYMFONY COMMANDS IN PRODUCTION

If your production server has a PEAR installation of symfony, then the symfony command line is available from every directory and will work just as it does in development. For frozen projects, however, you need to add php before the symfony command to be able to launch tasks:

```
// With symfony installed via PEAR
> symfony [options] <TASK> [parameters]

// With symfony frozen in the project or symlinked
> php symfony [options] <TASK> [parameters]
```

Summary

By combining *PHP logs* and *symfony logs*, you can monitor and debug your application easily. During development, the *debug mode*, the *exceptions*, and the *web debug toolbar* help you locate problems. You can even *insert custom messages* in the log files or in the toolbar for easier debugging.

The *command-line interface* provides a large number of tools that facilitate the management of your applications, during development and production phases. Among others, the *data population, freeze,* and *synchronization* tasks are great time-savers.

CHAPTER 17

■ ■ ■

Extending Symfony

Eventually, you will need to alter symfony's behavior. Whether you need to modify the way a certain class behaves or add your own custom features, the moment will inevitably happen—all clients have specific requirements that no framework can forecast. As a matter of fact, this situation is so common that symfony provides a mechanism to extend existing classes, called a *mixin*. You can even replace the core symfony classes on your own, using the *factories* settings. Once you have built an extension, you can easily package it as a *plug-in*, so that it can be reused in other applications—or by other symfony users.

Mixins

Among the current limitations of PHP, one of the most annoying is you can't have a class extend more than one class. Another limitation is you can't add new methods to an existing class or override existing methods. To palliate these two limitations and to make the framework truly extendable, symfony introduces a class called sfMixer. It is in no way related to cooking devices, but to the concept of *mixins* found in object-oriented programming. A mixin is a group of methods or functions that can be mixed into a class to extend it.

Understanding Multiple Inheritance

Multiple inheritance is the ability for a class to extend more than one class and inherit these class properties and methods. Let's consider an example. Imagine a Story and a Book class, each with its own properties and methods—just like in Listing 17-1.

Listing 17-1. *Two Example Classes*

```
class Story
{
  protected $title = '';
  protected $topic = '';
  protected $characters = array();

  public function __construct($title = '', $topic = '', $characters = array())
  {
    $this->title = $title;
    $this->topic = $topic;
```

```
    $this->characters = $characters;
  }

  public function getSummary()
  {
    return $this->title.', a story about '.$this->topic;
  }
}

class Book
{
  protected $isbn = 0;

  function setISBN($isbn = 0)
  {
    $this->isbn = $isbn;
  }

  public function getISBN()
  {
    return $this->isbn;
  }
}
```

A ShortStory class extends Story, a ComputerBook class extends Book, and logically, a Novel should extend both Story and Book and take advantage of all their methods. Unfortunately, this is not possible in PHP. You *cannot* write the Novel declaration as in Listing 17-2.

Listing 17-2. *Multiple Inheritance Is Not Possible in PHP*

```
class Novel extends Story, Book
{
}

$myNovel = new Novel();
$myNovel->getISBN();
```

One possibility would be to have Novel *implements* two interfaces instead of having it *extend* two classes, but this would prevent you from having the methods actually written in the parent classes.

Mixing Classes

The sfMixer class takes another approach to the problem, taking an existing class and extending it *a posteriori*, provided that the class contains the proper hooks. The process involves two steps:

- Declaring a class as extendable

- Registering extensions (or mixins), after the class declaration

Listing 17-3 shows how you would implement the Novel class with sfMixer.

Listing 17-3. *Multiple Inheritance Is Possible via sfMixer*

```
class Novel extends Story
{
  public function __call($method, $arguments)
  {
    return sfMixer::callMixins();
  }
}

sfMixer::register('Novel', array('Book', 'getISBN'));
$myNovel = new Novel();
$myNovel->getISBN();
```

One of the classes (Story) is chosen as the main parent, in line with PHP's ability to only inherit from one class. The Novel class is declared as extendable by the code located in the __call() method. The method of the other class (Book) is added afterwards to the Novel class by a call to sfMixer::register(). The next sections will explicitly explain this process.

When the getISBN() method of the Novel class is called, everything happens as if the class had been defined as in Listing 17-2—except it's the magic of the __call() method and of the sfMixer static methods that simulate it. The getISBN() method is *mixed in* the Novel class.

WHEN TO USE MIXINS

The symfony mixin mechanism is useful in many cases. Simulating *multiple inheritance*, as described previously, is just one of them.

You can use mixins to *alter a method after its declaration*. For example, when building a graphic library, you will probably implement a Line object—representing a line. It will have four attributes (the coordinates for both ends) and a draw() method to render itself. A ColoredLine should have the same properties and methods, but with an additional attribute, color, to specify its color. Furthermore, the draw() method of a ColoredLine is a little different from the one of a simple Line, to use the object's color. You could package the abilities of a graphical element to deal with color into a ColoredElement class. This would allow you to reuse the color methods for other graphical elements (Dot, Polygon, and so on). In this case, the ideal implementation of the ColoredLine class would be an extension of the Line class, with methods from the ColoredElement class mixed in. The final draw() method would be a mix between the original one from Line and the one from ColoredElement.

Mixins can also be seen as a way to *add new methods to an existing class*. For instance, the symfony action class, called sfActions, is defined in the framework. One of the constraints of PHP is that you cannot change the sfActions definition after its initial declaration. You may want to add a custom method to sfActions in one of your applications only—for instance, to forward a request to a special web service. For that purpose, PHP alone falls short, but the mixin mechanism provides a perfect solution.

Declaring a Class As Extendable

To declare a class as extendable, you must insert one or several "hooks" into the code, which the sfMixer class can later identify. These hooks are calls to the sfMixer::callMixins() method. Many of the symfony classes already contain such hooks, including sfRequest, sfResponse, sfController, sfUser, sfAction, and others.

The hook can be placed in different parts of the class, according to the desired degree of extensibility:

- To be able to add new methods to a class, you must insert the hook *in the __call() method* and *return its result,* as demonstrated in Listing 17-4.

Listing 17-4. *Giving a Class the Ability to Get New Methods*

```
class SomeClass
{
  public function __call($method, $arguments)
  {
    return sfMixer::callMixins();
  }
}
```

- To be able to alter the way an existing method works, you must insert the hook *inside the method,* as demonstrated in Listing 17-5. The code added by the mixin class will be executed where the hook is placed.

Listing 17-5. *Giving a Method the Ability to Be Altered*

```
class SomeOtherClass
{
  public function doThings()
  {
    echo "I'm working...";
    sfMixer::callMixins();
  }
}
```

You may want to place more than one hook in a method. In this case, you must *name the hooks,* so that you can define which hook is to be extended afterwards, as demonstrated in Listing 17-6. A named hook is a call to callMixins() with a hook name as a parameter. This name will be used afterwards, when registering a mixin, to tell where in the method the mixin code must be executed.

Listing 17-6. *A Method Can Contain More Than One Hook, In Which Case They Must Be Named*

```
class AgainAnotherClass
{
  public function doMoreThings()
  {
    echo "I'm ready.";
    sfMixer::callMixins('beginning');
    echo "I'm working...";
    sfMixer::callMixins('end');
    echo "I'm done.";
  }
}
```

Of course, you can combine these techniques to create classes with the ability to be assigned new and extendable methods, as Listing 17-7 demonstrates.

Listing 17-7. *A Class Can Be Extendable in Various Ways*

```
class BicycleRider
{
  protected $name = 'John';

  public function getName()
  {
    return $this->name;
  }

  public function sprint($distance)
  {
    echo $this->name." sprints ".$distance." meters\n";
    sfMixer::callMixins(); // The sprint() method is extendable
  }

  public function climb()
  {
    echo $this->name.' climbs';
    sfMixer::callMixins('slope'); // The climb() method is extendable here
    echo $this->name.' gets to the top';
    sfMixer::callMixins('top'); // And also here
  }

  public function __call($method, $arguments)
  {
    return sfMixer::callMixins(); // The BicyleRider class is extendable
  }
}
```

■**Caution** Only the classes that are declared as extendable can be extended by sfMixer. This means that you cannot use this mechanism to extend a class that didn't "subscribe" to this service.

Registering Extensions

To register an extension to an existing hook, use the sfMixer::register() method. Its first argument is the element to extend, and the second argument is a PHP callable and represents the mixin.

The format of the first argument depends on what you try to extend:

- If you extend a class, use the class name.

- If you extend a method with an anonymous hook, use the class:method pattern.

- If you extend a method with a named hook, use the class:method:hook pattern.

Listing 17-8 illustrates this principle by extending the class defined in Listing 17-7. The extended object is automatically passed as first parameter to the mixin methods (except, of course, if the extended method is static). The mixin method also gets access to the parameters of the original method call.

Listing 17-8. *Registering Extensions*

```
class Steroids
{
  protected $brand = 'foobar';

  public function partyAllNight($bicycleRider)
  {
    echo $bicycleRider->getName()." spends the night dancing.\n";
    echo "Thanks ".$brand."!\n";
  }

  public function breakRecord($bicycleRider, $distance)
  {
    echo "Nobody ever made ".$distance." meters that fast before!\n";
  }

  static function pass()
  {
    echo " and passes half the peloton.\n";
  }
}
```

```
sfMixer::register('BicycleRider', array('Steroids', 'partyAllNight'));
sfMixer::register('BicycleRider:sprint', array('Steroids', 'breakRecord'));
sfMixer::register('BicycleRider:climb:slope', array('Steroids', 'pass'));
sfMixer::register('BicycleRider:climb:top', array('Steroids', 'pass'));

$superRider = new BicycleRider();
$superRider->climb();
=> John climbs and passes half the peloton
=> John gets to the top and passes half the peloton
$superRider->sprint(2000);
=> John sprints 2000 meters
=> Nobody ever made 2000 meters that fast before!
$superRider->partyAllNight();
=> John spends the night dancing.
=> Thanks foobar!
```

The extension mechanism is not only about adding methods. The `partyAllNight()` method uses an attribute of the `Steroids` class. This means that when you extend the `BicycleRider` class with a method of the `Steroids` class, you actually create a new `Steroids` instance inside the `BicycleRider` object.

■**Caution** You cannot add two methods with the same name to an existing class. This is because the `callMixins()` call in the `__call()` methods uses the mixin method name as a key. Also, you cannot add a method to a class that already has a method with the same name, because the mixin mechanism relies on the magic `__call()` method and, in that particular case, it would never be called.

The second argument of the `register()` call is a PHP callable, so it can be a `class::method` array, or an `object->method` array, or even a function name. See examples in Listing 17-9.

Listing 17-9. *Any Callable Can Be Registered As a Mixer Extension*

```
// Use a class method as a callable
sfMixer::register('BicycleRider', array('Steroids', 'partyAllNight'));

// Use an object method as a callable
$mySteroids = new Steroids();
sfMixer::register('BicycleRider', array($mySteroids, 'partyAllNight'));

// Use a function as a callable
sfMixer::register('BicycleRider', 'die');
```

The extension mechanism is dynamic, which means that even if you already instantiated an object, it can take advantage of further extensions in its class. See an example in Listing 17-10.

Listing 17-10. *The Extension Mechanism Is Dynamic and Can Occur Even After Instantiation*

```
$simpleRider = new BicycleRider();
$simpleRider->sprint(500);
=> John sprints 500 meters
sfMixer::register('BicycleRider:sprint', array('Steroids', 'breakRecord'));
$simpleRider->sprint(500);
=> John sprints 500 meters
=> Nobody ever made 500 meters that fast before!
```

Extending with More Precision

The sfMixer::callMixins() instruction is actually a shortcut to something a little bit more elaborate. It automatically loops over the list of registered mixins and calls them one by one, passing to it the current object and the current method parameters. In short, an sfMixer::callMixins() call behaves more or less like Listing 17-11.

Listing 17-11. *callMixin() Loops Over the Registered Mixins and Executes Them*

```
foreach (sfMixer::getCallables($class.':'.$method.':'.$hookName) as $callable)
{
  call_user_func_array($callable, $parameters);
}
```

If you want to pass other parameters or to do something special with the return value, you can write the foreach loop explicitly instead of using the shortcut method. Look at Listing 17-12 for an example of a mixin more integrated into a class.

Listing 17-12. *Replacing callMixin() by a Custom Loop*

```
class Income
{
  protected $amout = 0;

  public function calculateTaxes($rate = 0)
  {
    $taxes = $this->amount * $rate;
    foreach (sfMixer::getCallables('Income:calculateTaxes') as $callable)
    {
      $taxes += call_user_func($callable, $this->amount, $rate);
    }

    return $taxes;
  }
}
```

```
class FixedTax
{
  protected $minIncome = 10000;
  protected $taxAmount = 500;

  public function calculateTaxes($amount)
  {
    return ($amount > $this->minIncome) ? $this->taxAmount : 0;
  }
}

sfMixer::register('Income:calculateTaxes', array('FixedTax', 'calculateTaxes'));
```

PROPEL BEHAVIORS

Propel behaviors, discussed previously in Chapter 8, are a special kind of mixin: They extend Propel-generated objects. Let's look at an example.

The Propel objects corresponding to the tables of the database all have a `delete()` method, which deletes the related record from the database. But for an `Invoice` class, for which you can't delete a record, you may want to alter the `delete()` method to be able to keep the record in the database and change the value of an `is_deleted` attribute to `true` instead. Usual object retrieval methods (`doSelect()`, `retrieveByPk()`) would only consider the records for which `is_deleted` is false. You would also need to add another method called `forceDelete()`, which would allow you to really delete the record. In fact, all these modifications can be packaged into a new class, called `ParanoidBehavior`. The final `Invoice` class extends the Propel `BaseInvoice` class and has methods of the `ParanoidBehavior` mixed in.

So a behavior is a mixin on a Propel object. Actually, the term "behavior" in symfony covers one more thing: the fact that the mixin is packaged as a plug-in. The `ParanoidBehavior` class just mentioned corresponds to a real symfony plug-in called `sfPropelParanoidBehaviorPlugin`. Refer to the symfony wiki (`http://www.symfony-project.com/trac/wiki/sfPropelParanoidBehaviorPlugin`) for details on installation and use of this plug-in.

One last word about behaviors: To be able to support them, the generated Propel objects must contain quite a number of hooks. These may slow down execution a little and penalize performance if you don't use behaviors. That's why the hooks are not enabled by default. In order to add them and enable behavior support, you must first set the `propel.builder.addBehaviors` property to `true` in the `propel.ini` file and rebuild the model.

Factories

A *factory* is the definition of a class for a certain task. Symfony relies on factories for its core features such as the controller and session capabilities. For instance, when the framework needs to create a new request object, it searches in the factory definition for the name of the class to use for that purpose. The default factory definition for requests is `sfWebRequest`, so symfony creates an object of this class in order to deal with requests. The great advantage of using a factory definition is that it is very easy to alter the core features of the framework: Just change the factory definition, and symfony will use your custom request class instead of its own.

The factory definitions are stored in the `factories.yml` configuration file. Listing 17-13 shows the default factory definition file. Each definition is made of the name of an autoloaded class and (optionally) a set of parameters. For instance, the session storage factory (set under the `storage:` key) uses a `session_name` parameter to name the cookie created on the client computer to allow persistent sessions.

Listing 17-13. *Default Factories File, in* `myapp/config/factories.yml`

```
cli:
  controller:
    class: sfConsoleController
  request:
    class: sfConsoleRequest

test:
  storage:
    class: sfSessionTestStorage

#all:
#  controller:
#    class: sfFrontWebController
#
#  request:
#    class: sfWebRequest
#
#  response:
#    class: sfWebResponse
#
#  user:
#    class: myUser
#
#  storage:
#    class: sfSessionStorage
#    param:
#      session_name: symfony
#
#  view_cache:
#    class: sfFileCache
#    param:
#      automaticCleaningFactor: 0
#      cacheDir:                %SF_TEMPLATE_CACHE_DIR%
```

The best way to change a factory is to create a new class inheriting from the default factory and to add new methods to it. For instance, the user session factory is set to the `myUser` class (located in `myapp/lib/`) and inherits from `sfUser`. Use the same mechanism to take advantage of the existing factories. Listing 17-14 shows an example of a new factory for the request object.

Listing 17-14. *Overriding Factories*

```
// Create a myRequest.class.php in an autoloaded directory,
// For instance in myapp/lib/
<?php

class myRequest extends sfRequest
{
  // Your code here
}

// Declare this class as the request factory in factories.yml
all:
  request:
    class: myRequest
```

Bridges to Other Framework Components

If you need capabilities provided by a third-party class, and if you don't want to copy this class in one of the symfony lib/ dirs, you will probably install it outside of the usual places where symfony looks for files. In that case, using this class will imply a manual require in your code, unless you use the *symfony bridge* to take advantage of the autoloading.

Symfony doesn't (yet) provide tools for everything. If you need a PDF generator, an API to Google Maps, or a PHP implementation of the Lucene search engine, you will probably need a few libraries from the *Zend Framework*. If you want to manipulate images directly in PHP, connect to a POP3 account to read e-mails, or design a console interface, you might choose the libraries from *eZcomponents*. Fortunately, if you define the right settings, the components from both these libraries will work out of the box in symfony.

The first thing that you need to declare (unless you installed the third-party libraries via PEAR) is the path to the root directory of the libraries. This is to be done in the application settings.yml:

```
.settings:
  zend_lib_dir:   /usr/local/zend/library/
  ez_lib_dir:     /usr/local/ezcomponents/
```

Then, extend the autoload routine by specifying which library to consider when the autoloading fails with symfony:

```
.settings:
  autoloading_functions:
    - [sfZendFrameworkBridge, autoload]
    - [sfEzComponentsBridge,  autoload]
```

Note that this setting is distinct from the rules defined in autoload.yml (see Chapter 19 for more information about this file). The autoloading_functions setting specifies bridge classes, and autoload.yml specifies paths and rules for searching. The following describes what will happen when you create a new object of an unloaded class:

1. The symfony autoloading function (sfCore::splAutoload()) first looks for a class in the paths declared in the autoload.yml file.

2. If none is found, the callback methods declared in the sf_autoloading_functions setting will be called one after the other, until one of them returns true:

   • sfZendFrameworkBridge::autoload()

   • sfEzComponentsBridge::autoload()

3. If these also return false, if you use PHP 5.0.X, symfony will throw an exception saying that the class doesn't exist. Starting with PHP 5.1, the error will be generated by PHP itself.

This means that the other framework components benefit from the autoload mechanism, and you can use them even more easily than within their own environment. For instance, if you want to use the Zend_Search component in the Zend Framework to implement an equivalent of the Lucene search engine in PHP, you have to write this:

```
require_once 'Zend/Search/Lucene.php';
$doc = new Zend_Search_Lucene_Document();
$doc->addField(Zend_Search_Lucene_Field::Text('url', $docUrl));
...
```

With symfony and the Zend Framework bridge, it is simpler. Just write this:

```
$doc = new Zend_Search_Lucene_Document(); // The class is autoloaded
$doc->addField(Zend_Search_Lucene_Field::Text('url', $docUrl));
...
```

The available bridges are stored in the $sf_symfony_lib_dir/addon/bridge/ directory.

Plug-Ins

You will probably need to reuse a piece of code that you developed for one of your symfony applications. If you can package this piece of code into a single class, no problem: Drop the class in one of the lib/ folders of another application and the autoloader will take care of the rest. But if the code is spread across more than one file, such as a complete new theme for the administration generator or a combination of JavaScript files and helpers to automate your favorite visual effect, just copying the files is not the best solution.

Plug-ins offer a way to package code disseminated in several files and to reuse this code across several projects. Into a plug-in, you can package classes, filters, mixins, helpers, configuration, tasks, modules, schemas and model extensions, fixtures, web assets, etc. Plug-ins are easy to install, upgrade, and uninstall. They can be distributed as a .tgz archive, a PEAR package, or a simple checkout of a code repository. The PEAR packaged plug-ins have the advantage of managing dependencies, being easier to upgrade and automatically discovered. The symfony loading mechanisms take plug-ins into account, and the features offered by a plug-in are available in the project as if the plug-in code was part of the framework.

So, basically, a plug-in is *a packaged extension* for a symfony project. With plug-ins, not only can you reuse your own code across applications, but you can also reuse developments made by other contributors and add third-party extensions to the symfony core.

Finding Symfony Plug-Ins

The symfony project website contains a page dedicated to symfony plug-ins. It is in the symfony wiki and accessible with the following URL:

```
http://www.symfony-project.com/trac/wiki/SymfonyPlugins
```

Each plug-in listed there has its own page, with detailed installation instructions and documentation.

Some of these plug-ins are contributions from the community, and some come from the core symfony developers. Among the latter, you will find the following:

- sfFeedPlugin: Automates the manipulation of RSS and Atom feeds

- sfThumbnailPlugin: Creates thumbnails—for instance, for uploaded images

- sfMediaLibraryPlugin: Allows media upload and management, including an extension for rich text editors to allow authoring of images inside rich text

- sfShoppingCartPlugin: Allows shopping cart management

- sfPagerNavigationPlugin: Provides classical and Ajax pager controls, based on an sfPager object

- sfGuardPlugin: Provides authentication, authorization, and other user management features above the standard security feature of symfony

- sfPrototypePlugin: Provides prototype and script.aculo.us JavaScript files as a standalone library

- sfSuperCachePlugin: Writes pages in cache directory under the web root to allow the web server to serve them as fast as possible

- sfOptimizerPlugin: Optimizes your application's code to make it execute faster in the production environment (see the next chapter for details)

- sfErrorLoggerPlugin: Logs every 404 and 500 error in a database and provides an administration module to browse these errors

- sfSslRequirementPlugin: Provides SSL encryption support for actions

The wiki also proposes plug-ins designed to extend your Propel objects, also called behaviors. Among them, you will find the following:

- sfPropelParanoidBehaviorPlugin: Disables object deletion and replaces it with the updating of a deleted_at column

- sfPropelOptimisticLockBehaviorPlugin: Implements optimistic locking for Propel objects

You should regularly check out the symfony wiki, because new plug-ins are added all the time, and they bring very useful shortcuts to many aspects of web application programming.

Apart from the symfony wiki, the other ways to distribute plug-ins are to propose a plug-ins archive for download, to host them in a PEAR channel, or to store them in a public version control repository.

Installing a Plug-In

The plug-in installation process differs according to the way it's packaged. Always refer to the included README file and/or installation instructions on the plug-in download page. Also, always clear the symfony cache after installing a plug-in.

Plug-ins are installed applications on a per-project basis. All the methods described in the following sections result in putting all the files of a plug-in into a myproject/plugins/pluginName/ directory.

PEAR Plug-Ins

Plug-ins listed on the symfony wiki are bundled as PEAR packages attached to a wiki page. To install such a plug-in, use the plugin-install task with a full URL, as shown in Listing 17-15.

Listing 17-15. *Installing a Plug-In from the Symfony Wiki*

```
> cd myproject
> php symfony plugin-install http://plugins.symfony-project.com/pluginName
> php symfony cc
```

Alternatively, you can download the plug-in and install it from the disk. In this case, replace the channel name with the absolute path to the package archive, as shown in Listing 17-16.

Listing 17-16. *Installing a Plug-In from a Downloaded PEAR Package*

```
> cd myproject
> php symfony plugin-install /home/path/to/downloads/pluginName.tgz
> php symfony cc
```

Some plug-ins are hosted on PEAR channels. Install them with the plugin-install task, and don't forget to mention the channel name, as shown in Listing 17-17.

Listing 17-17. *Installing a Plug-In from a PEAR Channel*

```
> cd myproject
> php symfony plugin-install channelName/pluginName
> php symfony cc
```

These three types of installation all use a PEAR package, so the term "PEAR plug-in" will be used indiscriminately to talk about plug-ins installed from the symfony wiki, a PEAR channel, or a downloaded PEAR package.

Archive Plug-Ins

Some plug-ins come as a simple archive of files. To install those, just unpack the archive into your project's plugins/ directory. If the plug-in contains a web/ subdirectory, make a copy or a symlink of this directory into the project's web/ directory, as demonstrated in Listing 17-18. Finally, don't forget to clear the cache.

Listing 17-18. *Installing a Plug-In from an Archive*

```
> cd plugins
> tar -zxpf myPlugin.tgz
> cd ..
> ln -sf plugins/myPlugin/web web/myPlugin
> php symfony cc
```

Installing Plug-Ins from a Version Control Repository

Plug-ins sometimes have their own source code repository for version control. You can install them by doing a simple checkout in the plugins/ directory, but this can be problematic if your project itself is under version control.

Alternatively, you can declare the plug-in as an *external dependency* so that every update of your project source code also updates the plug-in source code. For instance, Subversion stores external dependencies in the svn:externals property. So you can add a plug-in by editing this property and updating your source code afterwards, as Listing 17-19 demonstrates.

Listing 17-19. *Installing a Plug-In from a Source Version Repository*

```
> cd myproject
> svn propedit svn:externals plugins
  pluginName   http://svn.example.com/pluginName/trunk
> svn up
> php symfony cc
```

■**Note** If the plug-in contains a web/ directory, you must create a symlink to it the same way as for an archive plug-in.

Activating a Plug-In Module

Some plug-ins contain whole modules. The only difference between module plug-ins and classical modules is that module plug-ins don't appear in the myproject/apps/myapp/modules/ directory (to keep them easily upgradeable). They also need to be activated in the settings.yml file, as shown in Listing 17-20.

Listing 17-20. *Activating a Plug-In Module, in myapp/config/settings.yml*

```
all:
  .settings:
    enabled_modules:  [default, sfMyPluginModule]
```

This is to avoid a situation where the plug-in module is mistakenly made available for an application that doesn't require it, which could open a security breach. Think about a plug-in that provides frontend and backend modules. You will need to enable the frontend modules only in your frontend application, and the backend ones only in the backend application. This is why plug-in modules are not activated by default.

■Tip The `default` module is the only enabled module by default. That's not really a plug-in module, because it resides in the framework, in `$sf_symfony_data_dir/modules/default/`. This is the module that provides the congratulations pages, and the default error pages for 404 and credentials required errors. If you don't want to use the symfony default pages, just remove this module from the `enabled_modules` setting.

Listing the Installed Plug-Ins

If a glance at your project's `plugins/` directory can tell you which plug-ins are installed, the `plugin-list` task tells you even more: the version number and the channel name of each installed plug-in (see Listing 17-21).

Listing 17-21. *Listing Installed Plug-Ins*

```
> cd myproject
> php symfony plugin-list
```

```
Installed plugins:
sfPrototypePlugin          1.0.0-stable # pear.symfony-project.com (symfony)
sfSuperCachePlugin         1.0.0-stable # pear.symfony-project.com (symfony)
sfThumbnail                1.1.0-stable # pear.symfony-project.com (symfony)
```

Upgrading and Uninstalling Plug-Ins

To uninstall a PEAR plug-in, call the `plugin-uninstall` task from the root project directory, as shown in Listing 17-22. You must prefix the plug-in name with its installation channel (use the `plugin-list` task to determine this channel).

Listing 17-22. *Uninstalling a Plug-In*

```
> cd myproject
> php symfony plugin-uninstall pear.symfony-project.com/sfPrototypePlugin
> php symfony cc
```

■Tip Some channels have an alias. For instance, the `pear.symfony-project.com` channel can also be seen as `symfony`, which means that you can uninstall the `sfPrototypePlugin` as in Listing 17-22 by calling simply `php symfony plugin-uninstall symfony/sfPrototypePlugin`.

To uninstall an archive plug-in or an SVN plug-in, remove manually the plug-in files from the project `plugins/` and `web/` directories, and clear the cache.

To upgrade a plug-in, either use the `plugin-upgrade` task (for a PEAR plug-in) or do an `svn update` (if you grabbed the plug-in from a version control repository). Archive plug-ins can't be upgraded easily.

Anatomy of a Plug-In

Plug-ins are written using the PHP language. If you can understand how an application is organized, you can understand the structure of the plug-ins.

Plug-In File Structure

A plug-in directory is organized more or less like a project directory. The plug-in files have to be in the right directories in order to be loaded automatically by symfony when needed. Have a look at the plug-in file structure description in Listing 17-23.

Listing 17-23. *File Structure of a Plug-In*

```
pluginName/
  config/
    *schema.yml        // Data schema
    *schema.xml
    config.php         // Specific plug-in configuration
  data/
    generator/
      sfPropelAdmin
        */             // Administration generator themes
          templates/
          skeleton/
    fixtures/
      *.yml            // Fixtures files
    tasks/
      *.php            // Pake tasks
  lib/
    *.php              // Classes
    helper/
      *.php            // Helpers
    model/
      *.php            // Model classes
  modules/
    */                 // Modules
      actions/
        actions.class.php
      config/
        module.yml
        view.yml
        security.yml
```

```
      templates/
        *.php
      validate/
        *.yml
  web/
    *                       // Assets
```

Plug-In Abilities

Plug-ins can contain a lot of things. Their content is automatically taken into account by your application at runtime and when calling tasks with the command line. But for plug-ins to work properly, you must respect a few conventions:

> *Database schemas* are detected by the `propel-` tasks. When you call `propel-build-model` in your project, you rebuild the project model and all the plug-in models with it. Note that a plug-in schema must always have a `package` attribute under the shape `plugins.pluginName.lib.model`, as shown in Listing 17-24.

Listing 17-24. *Example Schema Declaration in a Plug-In, in* `myPlugin/config/schema.yml`

```
propel:
  _attributes:     { package: plugins.myPlugin.lib.model }
  my_plugin_foobar:
    _attributes:     { phpName: myPluginFoobar }
      id:
      name:             { type: varchar, size: 255, index: unique }
      ...
```

> *The plug-in configuration* is to be included in the plug-in bootstrap script (`config.php`). This file is executed after the application and project configuration, so symfony is already bootstrapped at that time. You can use this file, for instance, to add directories to the PHP include path or to extend existing classes with mixins.

> *Fixtures files* located in the plug-in `data/fixtures/` directory are processed by the `propel-load-data` task.

> *Tasks* are immediately available to the symfony command line as soon as the plug-in is installed. It is a best practice to prefix the task by something meaningful—for instance, the plug-in name. Type `symfony` to see the list of available tasks, including the ones added by plug-ins.

> *Custom classes* are autoloaded just like the ones you put in your project `lib/` folders.

> *Helpers* are automatically found when you call `use_helper()` in templates. They must be in a `helper/` subdirectory of one of the plug-in's `lib/` directory.

> *Model classes* in `myplugin/lib/model/` specialize the model classes generated by the Propel builder (in `myplugin/lib/model/om/` and `myplugin/lib/model/map/`). They are, of course, autoloaded. Be aware that you cannot override the generated model classes of a plug-in in your own project directories.

Modules provide new actions accessible from the outside, provided that you declare them in the enabled_modules setting in your application.

Web assets (images, scripts, style sheets, etc.) are made available to the server. When you install a plug-in via the command line, symfony creates a symlink to the project web/ directory if the system allows it, or copies the content of the module web/ directory into the project one. If the plug-in is installed from an archive or a version control repository, you have to copy the plug-in web/ directory by hand (as the README bundled with the plug-in should mention).

Manual Plug-In Setup

There are some elements that the plugin-install task cannot handle on its own, and which require manual setup during installation:

Custom application configuration can be used in the plug-in code (for instance, by using sfConfig::get('app_myplugin_foo')), but you can't put the default values in an app.yml file located in the plug-in config/ directory. To handle default values, use the second argument of the sfConfig::get() method. The settings can still be overridden at the application level (see Listing 17-25 for an example).

Custom routing rules have to be added manually to the application routing.yml.

Custom filters have to be added manually to the application filters.yml.

Custom factories have to be added manually to the application factories.yml.

Generally speaking, all the configuration that should end up in one of the application configuration files has to be added manually. Plug-ins with such manual setup should embed a README file describing installation in detail.

Customizing a Plug-In for an Application

Whenever you want to customize a plug-in, *never alter the code found in the* plugins/ *directory*. If you do so, you will lose all your modifications when you upgrade the plug-in. For customization needs, plug-ins provide custom settings, and they support overriding.

Well-designed plug-ins use *settings* that can be changed in the application app.yml, as Listing 17-25 demonstrates.

Listing 17-25. *Customizing a Plug-In That Uses the Application Configuration*

```
// example plug-in code
$foo = sfConfig::get('app_my_plugin_foo', 'bar');

// Change the 'foo' default value ('bar') in the application app.yml
all:
  my_plugin:
    foo:       barbar
```

The module settings and their default values are often described in the plug-in's README file.

You can replace the default contents of a plug-in module by creating a module of the same name in your own application. It is not really overriding, since the elements in your application are used instead of the ones of the plug-in. It works fine if you create *templates* and *configuration files* of the same name as the ones of the plug-ins.

On the other hand, if a plug-in wants to offer a module with the ability to override its *actions*, the actions.class.php in the plug-in module must be empty and inherit from an auto-loading class, so that the method of this class can be inherited as well by the actions.class.php of the application module. See Listing 17-26 for an example.

Listing 17-26. *Customizing a Plug-In Action*

```
// In myPlugin/modules/mymodule/lib/myPluginmymoduleActions.class.php
class myPluginmymoduleActions extends sfActions
{
  public function executeIndex()
  {
    // Some code there
  }
}

// In myPlugin/modules/mymodule/actions/actions.class.php
class mymoduleActions extends myPluginmymoduleActions
{
  // Nothing
}

// In myapp/modules/mymodule/actions/actions.class.php
class mymoduleActions extends myPluginmymoduleActions
{
  public function executeIndex()
  {
    // Override the plug-in code there
  }
}
```

How to Write a Plug-In

Only plug-ins packaged as PEAR packages can be installed with the plugin-install task. Remember that such plug-ins can be distributed via the symfony wiki, a PEAR channel, or a simple file download. So if you want to author a plug-in, it is better to publish it as a PEAR package than as a simple archive. In addition, PEAR packaged plug-ins are easier to upgrade, can declare dependencies, and automatically deploy assets in the web/ directory.

File Organization

Suppose you have developed a new feature and want to package it as a plug-in. The first step is to organize the files logically so that the symfony loading mechanisms can find them when needed. For that purpose, you have to follow the structure given in Listing 17-23. Listing 17-27 shows an example of file structure for an sfSamplePlugin plug-in.

Listing 17-27. *Example List of Files to Package As a Plug-In*

```
sfSamplePlugin/
  README
  LICENSE
  config/
    schema.yml
  data/
    fixtures/
      fixtures.yml
    tasks/
      sfSampleTask.php
  lib/
    model/
      sfSampleFooBar.php
      sfSampleFooBarPeer.php
    validator/
      sfSampleValidator.class.php
  modules/
    sfSampleModule/
      actions/
        actions.class.php
      config/
        security.yml
      lib/
        BasesfSampleModuleActions.class.php
      templates/
        indexSuccess.php
  web/
    css/
      sfSampleStyle.css
    images/
      sfSampleImage.png
```

For authoring, the location of the plug-in directory (sfSamplePlugin/ in Listing 17-27) is not important. It can be anywhere on the disk.

■**Tip** Take examples of the existing plug-ins and, for your first attempts at creating a plug-in, try to reproduce their naming conventions and file structure.

Creating the package.xml File

The next step of plug-in authoring is to add a `package.xml` file at the root of the plug-in directory. The `package.xml` follows the PEAR syntax. Have a look at a typical symfony plug-in `package.xml` in Listing 17-28.

Listing 17-28. *Example `package.xml` for a Symfony Plug-In*

```
<?xml version="1.0" encoding="UTF-8"?>
<package packagerversion="1.4.6" version="2.0" xmlns="http://pear.php.net/dtd/ ➥
  package-2.0" xmlns:tasks="http://pear.php.net/dtd/tasks-1.0" xmlns:xsi="http ➥
  ://www.w3.org/2001/XMLSchema-instance" xsi:schemaLocation="http://pear.php.n ➥
  et/dtd/tasks-1.0 http://pear.php.net/dtd/tasks-1.0.xsd http://pear.php.net/d ➥
  td/package-2.0 http://pear.php.net/dtd/package-2.0.xsd">
 <name>sfSamplePlugin</name>
 <channel>pear.symfony-project.com</channel>
 <summary>symfony sample plugin</summary>
 <description>Just a sample plugin to illustrate PEAR packaging</description>
 <lead>
  <name>Fabien POTENCIER</name>
  <user>fabpot</user>
  <email>fabien.potencier@symfony-project.com</email>
  <active>yes</active>
 </lead>
 <date>2006-01-18</date>
 <time>15:54:35</time>
 <version>
  <release>1.0.0</release>
  <api>1.0.0</api>
 </version>
 <stability>
  <release>stable</release>
  <api>stable</api>
 </stability>
 <license uri="http://www.symfony-project.com/license">MIT license</license>
 <notes>-</notes>
 <contents>
  <dir name="/">
   <file role="data" name="README" />
   <file role="data" name="LICENSE" />
   <dir name="config">
    <!-- model -->
    <file role="data" name="schema.yml" />
   </dir>
   <dir name="data">
    <dir name="fixtures">
     <!-- fixtures -->
     <file role="data" name="fixtures.yml" />
```

```
  </dir>
  <dir name="tasks">
   <!-- tasks -->
   <file role="data" name="sfSampleTask.php" />
  </dir>
 </dir>
 <dir name="lib">
  <dir name="model">
   <!-- model classes -->
   <file role="data" name="sfSampleFooBar.php" />
   <file role="data" name="sfSampleFooBarPeer.php" />
  </dir>
  <dir name="validator">
   <!-- validators ->>
   <file role="data" name="sfSampleValidator.class.php" />
  </dir>
 </dir>
 <dir name="modules">
  <dir name="sfSampleModule">
   <file role="data" name="actions/actions.class.php" />
   <file role="data" name="config/security.yml" />
   <file role="data" name="lib/BasesfSampleModuleActions.class.php" />
   <file role="data" name="templates/indexSuccess.php" />
  </dir>
 </dir>
 <dir name="web">
  <dir name="css">
   <!-- stylesheets -->
   <file role="data" name="sfSampleStyle.css" />
  </dir>
  <dir name="images">
   <!-- images -->
   <file role="data" name="sfSampleImage.png" />
  </dir>
 </dir>
</dir>
</contents>
<dependencies>
 <required>
  <php>
   <min>5.0.0</min>
  </php>
  <pearinstaller>
   <min>1.4.1</min>
  </pearinstaller>
  <package>
   <name>symfony</name>
```

```
    <channel>pear.symfony-project.com</channel>
    <min>1.0.0</min>
    <max>1.1.0</max>
    <exclude>1.1.0</exclude>
   </package>
  </required>
 </dependencies>
 <phprelease />
 <changelog />
</package>
```

The interesting parts here are the `<contents>` and the `<dependencies>` tags, described next. For the rest of the tags, there is nothing specific to symfony, so you can refer to the PEAR online manual (`http://pear.php.net/manual/en/`) for more details about the `package.xml` format.

Contents

The `<contents>` tag is the place where you must describe the plug-in file structure. This will tell PEAR which files to copy and where. Describe the file structure with `<dir>` and `<file>` tags. All `<file>` tags must have a `role="data"` attribute. The `<contents>` part of Listing 17-28 describes the exact directory structure of Listing 17-27.

■**Note** The use of `<dir>` tags is not compulsory, since you can use relative paths as name values in the `<file>` tags. However, it is recommended so that the `package.xml` file remains readable.

Plug-In Dependencies

Plug-ins are designed to work with a given set of versions of PHP, PEAR, symfony, PEAR packages, or other plug-ins. Declaring these dependencies in the `<dependencies>` tag tells PEAR to check that the required packages are already installed, and to raise an exception if not.

You should always declare dependencies on PHP, PEAR, and symfony, at least the ones corresponding to your own installation, as a minimum requirement. If you don't know what to put, add a requirement for PHP 5.0, PEAR 1.4, and symfony 1.0.

It is also recommended to add a *maximum version number* of symfony for each plug-in. This will cause an error message when trying to use a plug-in with a more advanced version of the framework, and this will oblige the plug-in author to make sure that the plug-in works correctly with this version before releasing it again. It is better to have an alert and to download an upgrade rather than have a plug-in fail silently.

Building the Plug-In

The PEAR component has a command (`pear package`) that creates the `.tgz` archive of the package, provided you call the command shown in Listing 17-29 from a directory containing a `package.xml`.

Listing 17-29. *Packaging a Plug-In As a PEAR Package*

```
> cd sfSamplePlugin
> pear package
```

```
Package sfSamplePlugin-1.0.0.tgz done
```

Once your plug-in is built, check that it works by installing it yourself, as shown in Listing 17-30.

Listing 17-30. *Installing the Plug-In*

```
> cp sfSamplePlugin-1.0.0.tgz /home/production/myproject/
> cd /home/production/myproject/
> php symfony plugin-install sfSamplePlugin-1.0.0.tgz
```

According to their description in the `<contents>` tag, the packaged files will end up in different directories of your project. Listing 17-31 shows where the files of the sfSamplePlugin should end up after installation.

Listing 17-31. *The Plug-In Files Are Installed on the plugins/ and web/ Directories*

```
plugins/
  sfSamplePlugin/
    README
    LICENSE
    config/
      schema.yml
    data/
      fixtures/
        fixtures.yml
      tasks/
        sfSampleTask.php
    lib/
      model/
        sfSampleFooBar.php
        sfSampleFooBarPeer.php
      validator/
        sfSampleValidator.class.php
    modules/
      sfSampleModule/
        actions/
          actions.class.php
        config/
          security.yml
        lib/
```

```
          BasesfSampleModuleActions.class.php
      templates/
          indexSuccess.php
web/
  sfSamplePlugin/                    ## Copy or symlink, depending on system
    css/
      sfSampleStyle.css
    images/
      sfSampleImage.png
```

Test the way the plug-in behaves in your application. If it works well, you are ready to distribute it across projects—or to contribute it to the symfony community.

Hosting Your Plug-In in the Symfony Project Website

A symfony plug-in gets the broadest audience when distributed by the symfony-project.com website. Even your own plug-ins can be distributed this way, provided that you follow these steps:

1. Make sure the README file describes the way to install and use your plug-in, and that the LICENSE file gives the license details. Format your README with the Wiki Formatting syntax (http://www.symfony-project.com/trac/wiki/WikiFormatting).

2. Create a PEAR package for your plug-in by calling the pear package command, and test it. The PEAR package must be named sfSamplePlugin-1.0.0.tgz (1.0.0 is the plug-in version).

3. Create a new page on the symfony wiki named sfSamplePlugin (Plugin is a mandatory suffix). In this page, describe the plug-in usage, the license, the dependencies, and the installation procedure. You can reuse the contents of the plug-in README file. Check the existing plug-ins' wiki pages and use them as an example.

4. Attach your PEAR package to the wiki page (sfSamplePlugin-1.0.0.tgz).

5. Add the new plug-in wiki page ([wiki:sfSamplePlugin]) to the list of available plug-ins, which is also a wiki page (http://www.symfony-project.com/trac/wiki/SymfonyPlugins).

If you follow this procedure, users will be able to install your plug-in by simply typing the following command in a project directory:

```
> php symfony plugin-install http://plugins.symfony-project.com/sfSamplePlugin
```

Naming Conventions

To keep the plugins/ directory clean, ensure all the plug-in names are in camelCase and end with Plugin (for example, shoppingCartPlugin, feedPlugin, and so on). Before naming your plug-in, check that there is no existing plug-in with the same name.

■**Note** Plug-ins relying on Propel should contain `Propel` in the name. For instance, an authentication plug-in using the Propel data access objects should be called `sfPropelAuth`.

Plug-ins should always include a `LICENSE` file describing the conditions of use and the chosen license. You are also advised to add a `README` file to explain the version changes, purpose of the plug-in, its effect, installation and configuration instructions, etc.

Summary

The symfony classes contain `sfMixer` *hooks* that give them the ability to be modified at the application level. The *mixins* mechanism allows *multiple inheritance* and *class overriding at runtime* even if the PHP limitations forbid it. So you can easily extend the symfony features, even if you have to modify the core classes for that—the *factories configuration* is here for that.

Many such extensions already exist; they are packaged as *plug-ins*, to be easily installed, upgraded, and uninstalled through the symfony command line. *Creating a plug-in* is as easy as creating a *PEAR package*, and provides reusability across applications.

The *symfony wiki* contains many plug-ins, and you can even *add your own*. So now that you know how to do it, we hope that you will enhance the symfony core with a lot of useful extensions!

PART 5

■■■

Becoming a Symfony Expert

CHAPTER 18

■■■

Performance

If you expect your website will attract a crowd, performance and optimization issues should be a major factor during the development phase. Rest assured, performance has always been a chief concern among the core symfony developers.

While the advantages gained by accelerating the development process result in some overhead, the core symfony developers have always been cognizant of performance requirements. Accordingly, every class and every method have been closely inspected and optimized to be as fast as possible. The basic overhead, which you can measure by comparing the time to display a "hello, world" message with and without symfony, is minimal. As a result, the framework is scalable and reacts well to stress tests. And as the ultimate proof, some websites with extremely high traffic (that is, websites with millions of active subscribers and a lot of server-pressuring Ajax interactions) use symfony and are very satisfied with its performance. Check the list of websites developed with symfony in the wiki (http://www.symfony-project.com/trac/wiki/ApplicationsDevelopedWithSymfony) for names.

But, of course, high-traffic websites often have the means to expand the server farm and upgrade hardware as they see fit. If you don't have the resources to do this, or if you want to be sure the full power of the framework is always at your disposal, there are a few tweaks that you can use to further speed up your symfony application. This chapter lists some of the recommended performance optimizations at all levels of the framework and they are mostly for advanced users. Some of them were already mentioned throughout the previous chapters, but you will find it useful to have them all in one place.

Tweaking the Server

A well-optimized application should rely on a well-optimized server. You should know the basics of server performance to make sure there is no bottleneck outside symfony. Here are a few things to check to make sure that your server isn't unnecessarily slow.

Having `magic_quotes_gpc` turned on in the `php.ini` slows down an application, because it tells PHP to escape all quotes in request parameters, but symfony will systematically unescape them afterwards, and the only consequence will be a loss of time—and quotes-escaping problems on some platforms. Therefore, turn this setting off if you have access to the PHP configuration.

The more recent PHP release you use, the better. PHP 5.2 is faster than PHP 5.1, and PHP 5.1 is a lot faster than PHP 5.0. So make sure you upgrade your PHP version to benefit from the latest performance improvements.

The use of a PHP accelerator (such as APC, XCache, or eAccelerator) is almost compulsory for a production server, because it can make PHP run an average 50% faster, with no tradeoff. Make sure you install one of the accelerator extensions to feel the real speed of PHP.

On the other hand, make sure you deactivate any debug utility, such as the Xdebug or APD extension, in your production server.

■**Note** You might be wondering about the overhead caused by the `mod_rewrite` extension: it is negligible. Of course, loading an image with rewriting rules is slower than loading an image without, but the slowdown is orders of magnitude below the execution of any PHP statement.

Some symfony developers like to use `syck`, which is a YAML parser packaged as a PHP extension, as an alternative to the symfony internal parser. It is faster, but symfony's caching system already minimizes the overhead of YAML parsing, so the benefit is nonexistent in a production environment. You should also be aware that `syck` isn't completely mature yet, and that it may cause errors when you use it. However, if you are interested, install the extension (`http://whytheluckystiff.net/syck/`), and symfony will use it automatically.

■**Tip** When one server is not enough, you can still add another and use load balancing. As long as the `uploads/` directory is shared and you use database storage for sessions, a symfony project will react seamlessly in a load-balanced architecture.

Tweaking the Model

In symfony, the model layer has the reputation of being the slowest part. If benchmarks show that you have to optimize this layer, here are a few possible improvements.

Optimizing Propel Integration

Initializing the model layer (the core Propel classes) takes some time, because of the need to load a few classes and construct various objects. However, because of the way symfony integrates Propel, these initialization tasks occur only when an action actually needs the model—and as late as possible. The Propel classes will be initialized only when an object of your generated model is autoloaded. This means pages that don't use the model are not penalized by the model layer.

If your entire application doesn't require the use of the model layer, you can also save the initialization of the `sfDatabaseManager` by switching the whole layer off in your `settings.yml`:

```
all:
  .settings:
    use_database: off
```

The generated model classes (in lib/model/om/) are already optimized—they don't contain comments, and they benefit from the autoloading system. Relying on autoloading instead of manually including files means that classes are loaded only if it is really necessary. So in case one model class is not needed, having classes autoloaded will save execution time, while the alternative method of using include statements won't. As for the comments, they document the use of the generated methods but lengthen the model files—resulting in a minor overhead on slow disks. As the generated method names are pretty explicit, the comments are turned off by default.

These two enhancements are symfony-specific, but you can revert to the Propel defaults by changing two settings in your propel.ini file, as follows:

```
propel.builder.addIncludes = true    # Add include statements in generated classes
                                     # Instead of relying on the autoloading system
propel.builder.addComments = true    # Add comments to generated classes
```

Limiting the Number of Objects to Hydrate

When you use a method of a peer class to retrieve objects, your query goes through the *hydrating process* (creating and populating objects based on the rows of the result of the query). For instance, to retrieve all the rows of the article table with Propel, you usually do the following:

```
$articles = ArticlePeer::doSelect(new Criteria());
```

The resulting $articles variable is an array of objects of class Article. Each object has to be created and initialized, which takes time. This has one major consequence: Contrary to direct database queries, *the speed of a Propel query is directly proportional to the number of results it returns*. This means your model methods should be optimized to return only a given number of results. When you don't need all the results returned by a Criteria, you should limit it with the setLimit() and setOffset() methods. For instance, if you need only the rows 10 to 20 of a particular query, refine the Criteria as in Listing 18-1.

Listing 18-1. *Limiting the Number of Results Returned by a Criteria*

```
$c = new Criteria();
$c->setOffset(10);  // Offset of the first record returned
$c->setLimit(10);   // Number of records returned
$articles = ArticlePeer::doSelect($c);
```

This can be automated by the use of a pager. The sfPropelPager object automatically handles the offset and the limit of a Propel query to hydrate only the objects required for a given page. Refer to the API documentation for more information on this class.

Minimizing the Number of Queries with Joins

During application development, you should keep an eye on the number of database queries issued by each request. The web debug toolbar shows the number of queries for each page, and clicking the little database icon reveals the SQL code of these queries. If you see the number of queries rising abnormally, it is time to consider using a Join.

Before explaining the Join methods, let's review what happens when you loop over an array of objects and use a Propel getter to retrieve details about a related class, as in Listing 18-2. This example supposes that your schema describes an article table with a foreign key to an author table.

Listing 18-2. *Retrieving Details About a Related Class in a Loop*

```
// In the action
$this->articles = ArticlePeer::doSelect(new Criteria());

// Database query issued by doSelect()
SELECT article.id, article.title, article.author_id, ...
FROM   article

// In the template
<ul>
<?php foreach ($articles as $article): ?>
  <li><?php echo $article->getTitle() ?>,
    written by <?php echo $article->getAuthor()->getName() ?></li>
<?php endforeach; ?>
</ul>
```

If the $articles array contains ten objects, the getAuthor() method will be called ten times, which in turn executes one database query each time it is called to hydrate one object of class Author, as in Listing 18-3.

Listing 18-3. *Foreign Key Getters Issue One Database Query*

```
// In the template
$article->getAuthor()

// Database query issued by getAuthor()
SELECT author.id, author.name, ...
FROM   author
WHERE  author.id = ?                    // ? is article.author_id
```

So the page of Listing 18-2 will require a total of 11 queries: the one necessary to build the array of Article objects, plus the 10 queries to build one Author object at a time. This is a lot of queries to display only a list of articles and their author.

If you were using plain SQL, you would know how to reduce the number of queries to only one by retrieving the columns of the article table *and* those of the author table in the same query. That's exactly what the doSelectJoinAuthor() method of the ArticlePeer class does. It issues a slightly more complex query than a simple doSelect() call, but the additional columns in the result set allow Propel to hydrate both Article objects and the related Author objects. The code of Listing 18-4 displays exactly the same result as Listing 18-2, but it requires only one database query to do so rather than 11 and therefore is faster.

Listing 18-4. *Retrieving Details About Articles and Their Author in the Same Query*

```
// In the action
$this->articles = ArticlePeer::doSelectJoinAuthor(new Criteria());

// Database query issued by doSelectJoinAuthor()
SELECT article.id, article.title, article.author_id, ...
       author.id, author.name, ...
FROM   article, author
WHERE  article.author_id = author.id

// In the template (unchanged)
<ul>
<?php foreach ($articles as $article): ?>
  <li><?php echo $article->getTitle() ?>,
    written by <?php echo $article->getAuthor()->getName() ?></li>
<?php endforeach; ?>
</ul>
```

There is no difference in the result returned by a doSelect() call and a doSelectJoinXXX() method; they both return the same array of objects (of class Article in the example). The difference appears when a foreign key getter is used on these objects afterwards. In the case of doSelect(), it issues a query, and one object is hydrated with the result; in the case of doSelectJoinXXX(), the foreign object already exists and no query is required, and the process is much faster. So if you know that you will need related objects, call a doSelectJoinXXX() method to reduce the number of database queries—and improve the page performance.

The doSelectJoinAuthor() method is automatically generated when you call a propel-build-model because of the relationship between the article and author tables. If there were other foreign keys in the article table structure—for instance, to a category table—the generated BaseArticlePeer class would have other Join methods, as shown in Listing 18-5.

Listing 18-5. *Example of Available doSelect Methods for an ArticlePeer Class*

```
// Retrieve Article objects
doSelect()

// Retrieve Article objects and hydrate related Author objects
doSelectJoinAuthor()

// Retrieve Article objects and hydrate related Category objects
doSelectJoinCategory()

// Retrieve Article objects and hydrate related Author and Category objects
doSelectJoinAuthorAndCategory()

// Synonym of
doSelectJoinAll()
```

The peer classes also contain Join methods for doCount(). The classes with an i18n counterpart (see Chapter 13) provide a doSelectWithI18n() method, which behaves the same as Join methods but for i18n objects. To discover the available Join methods in your model classes, you should inspect the generated peer classes in lib/model/om/. If you don't find the Join method needed for your query (for instance, there is no automatically generated Join method for many-to-many relationships), you can build it yourself and extend your model.

■Tip Of course, a doSelectJoinXXX() call is a bit slower than a call to doSelect(), so it only improves the overall performance if you use the hydrated objects afterwards.

Avoid Using Temporary Arrays

When using Propel, objects are already hydrated, so there is no need to prepare a *temporary array* for the template. Developers not used to ORMs usually fall into this trap. They want to prepare an array of strings or integers, whereas the template can rely directly on an existing array of objects. For instance, imagine that a template displays the list of all the titles of the articles present in the database. A developer who doesn't use OOP would probably write code similar to what is shown in Listing 18-6.

Listing 18-6. *Preparing an Array in the Action Is Useless If You Already Have One*

```
// In the action
$articles = ArticlePeer::doSelect(new Criteria());
$titles = array();
foreach ($articles as $article)
{
  $titles[] = $article->getTitle();
}
$this->titles = $titles;

// In the template
<ul>
<?php foreach ($titles as $title): ?>
  <li><?php echo $title ?></li>
<?php endforeach; ?>
</ul>
```

The problem with this code is that the hydrating is already done by the doSelect() call (which takes time), making the $titles array superfluous, since you can write the same code as in Listing 18-7. So the time spent to build the $titles array could be gained to improve the application performance.

Listing 18-7. *Using an Array of Objects Exempts You from Creating a Temporary Array*

```
// In the action
$this->articles = ArticlePeer::doSelect(new Criteria());

// In the template
<ul>
<?php foreach ($articles as $article): ?>
  <li><?php echo $article->getTitle() ?></li>
<?php endforeach; ?>
</ul>
```

If you feel that you really need to prepare a temporary array because some processing is necessary on objects, the right way to do so is to create a new method in your model class that directly returns this array. For instance, if you need an array of article titles and the number of comments for each article, the action and the template should look like Listing 18-8.

Listing 18-8. *Using a Custom Method to Prepare a Temporary Array*

```
// In the action
$this->articles = ArticlePeer::getArticleTitlesWithNbComments();

// In the template
<ul>
<?php foreach ($articles as $article): ?>
  <li><?php echo $article[0] ?> (<?php echo $article[1] ?> comments)</li>
<?php endforeach; ?>
</ul>
```

It's up to you to build a fast-processing getArticleTitlesWithNbComments() method in the model—for instance, by bypassing the whole object-relational mapping and database abstraction layers.

Bypassing the ORM

When you don't really need objects but only a few columns from various tables, as in the previous example, you can create specific methods in your model that bypass completely the ORM layer. You can directly call the database with Creole, for instance, and return a custom-built array. Listing 18-9 illustrates this idea.

Listing 18-9. *Using Direct Creole Access for Optimized Model Methods, in* lib/model/ ArticlePeer.php

```
class ArticlePeer extends BaseArticlePeer
{
  public static function getArticleTitlesWithNbComments()
  {
    $connection = Propel::getConnection();
    $query = 'SELECT %s as title, COUNT(%s) AS nb FROM %s LEFT JOIN %s ON %s = %s ➥
```

```
  GROUP BY %s';
  $query = sprintf($query,
    ArticlePeer::TITLE, CommentPeer::ID,
    ArticlePeer::TABLE_NAME, CommentPeer::TABLE_NAME,
    ArticlePeer::ID, CommentPeer::ARTICLE_ID,
    ArticlePeer::ID
  );
  $statement = $connnection->prepareStatement($query);
  $resultset = $statement->executeQuery();
  $results = array();
  while ($resultset->next())
  {
    $results[] = array($resultset->getString('title'), $resultset->getInt('nb'));
  }

  return $results;
 }
}
```

When you start building these sorts of methods, you may end up writing one custom method for each action, and lose the benefit of the layer separation—not to mention the fact that you lose database-independence.

Tip If Propel doesn't suit you as a model layer, consider using other ORMs before writing your queries by hand. For instance, check the sfDoctrine plug-in for an interface with the *PhpDoctrine* ORM. In addition, you can use another database abstraction layer than Creole to access your database directly. As of PHP 5.1, PDO is bundled with PHP and provides a faster alternative to Creole.

Speeding Up the Database

There are many database-specific optimization techniques that can be applied regardless of whether you're using symfony. This section briefly outlines the most common database optimization strategies, but a good knowledge of database engines and administration is required to get the most out of your model layer.

Tip Remember that the web debug toolbar displays the time taken by each query in a page, and that every tweak should be monitored to determine whether it really improves performance.

Table queries are often based on non–primary key columns. To improve the speed of such queries, you should define *indexes* in your database schema. To add a single column index, add the `index: true` property to the column definition, as in Listing 18-10.

Listing 18-10. *Adding a Single Column Index, in* `config/schema.yml`

```
propel:
  article:
    id:
    author_id:
    title: { type: varchar(100), index: true }
```

You can use the alternative `index: unique` syntax to define a unique index instead of a classic one. You can also define multiple column indices in `schema.yml` (refer to Chapter 8 for more details about the indexing syntax). You should strongly consider doing this, because it is often a good way to speed up a complex query.

After adding an index to a schema, you should do the same in the database itself, either by issuing an `ADD INDEX` query directly in the database or by calling the `propel-build-all` command (which will not only rebuild the table structure, but also erase all the existing data).

■**Tip** Indexing tends to make `SELECT` queries faster, but `INSERT`, `UPDATE`, and `DELETE` queries are slower. Also, database engines use only one index per query, and they infer the index to be used for each query based on internal heuristics. Adding an index can sometimes be disappointing in terms of performance boost, so make sure you measure the improvements.

Unless specified otherwise, each request uses a single database connection in symfony, and the connection is closed at the end of the request. You can enable *persistent database connections* to use a pool of database connections that remain open between queries, by setting `persistent: true` in the `databases.yml` file, as shown in Listing 18-11.

Listing 18-11. *Enabling Persistent Database Connection Support, in* `config/databases.yml`

```
prod:
  propel:
    class:        sfPropelDatabase
    param:
      persistent:  true
      dsn:         mysql://login:passwd@localhost/blog
```

This may or may not improve the overall database performance, depending on numerous factors. The documentation on the subject is abundant on the Internet. Make sure you benchmark your application performance before and after changing this setting to validate its interest.

MYSQL-SPECIFIC TIPS

Many settings of the MySQL configuration, found in the `my.cnf` file, may alter database performance. Make sure you read the online documentation (`http://dev.mysql.com/doc/refman/5.0/en/option-files.html`) on this subject.

One of the tools provided by MySQL is the *slow queries log*. All SQL statements that take more than `long_query_time` seconds to execute (this is a setting that can be changed in the `my.cnf`) are logged in a file that is quite difficult to construe by hand, but that the `mysqldumpslow` command summarizes usefully. This is a great tool to detect the queries that require optimizations.

Tweaking the View

According to how you design and implement the view layer, you may notice small slowdowns or speedups. This section describes the alternatives and their tradeoffs.

Using the Fastest Code Fragment

If you don't use the caching system, you have to be aware that an `include_component()` is slightly slower than an `include_partial()`, which itself is slightly slower than a simple PHP `include`. This is because symfony instantiates a view to include a partial and an object of class `sfComponent` to include a component, which collectively add some minor overhead beyond what's required to include the file.

However, this overhead is insignificant, unless you include a lot of partials or components in a template. This may happen in lists or tables, and every time you call an `include_partial()` helper inside a `foreach` statement. When you notice that a large number of partial or component inclusions have a significant impact on your performance, you may consider caching (see Chapter 12), and if caching is not an option, then switch to simple `include` statements.

As for slots and component slots, the difference in performance is perceptible. The process time necessary to set and include a slot is negligible—it is equivalent to a variable instantiation. But component slots rely on a view configuration, and they require a few objects to be initiated to work. However, component slots can be cached independently from the calling templates, while slots are always cached within the template that includes them.

Speeding Up the Routing Process

As explained in Chapter 9, every call to a link helper in a template asks the routing system to process an internal URI into an external URL. This is done by finding a match between the URI and the patterns of the `routing.yml` file. Symfony does it quite simply: It tries to match the first rule with the given URI, and if it doesn't work, it tries with the following, and so on. As every test involves regular expressions, this is quite time consuming.

There is a simple workaround: Use the rule name instead of the module/action couple. This will tell symfony which rule to use, and the routing system won't lose time trying to match all previous rules.

In concrete terms, consider the following routing rule, defined in your `routing.yml` file:

```
article_by_id:
  url:          /article/:id
  param:        { module: article, action: read }
```

Then instead of outputting a hyperlink this way:

```
<?php echo link_to('my article', 'article/read?id='.$article->getId()) ?>
```

you should use the fastest version:

```
<?php echo link_to('my article', '@article_by_id?id='.$article->getId()) ?>
```

The difference starts being noticeable when a page includes a few dozen routed hyperlinks.

Skipping the Template

Usually, a response is composed of a set of headers and content. But some responses don't need content. For instance, some Ajax interactions need only a few pieces of data from the server in order to feed a JavaScript program that will update different parts of the page. For this kind of short response, a set of headers alone is faster to transmit. As discussed in Chapter 11, an action can return only a JSON header. Listing 18-12 reproduces an example from Chapter 11.

Listing 18-12. *Example Action Returning a JSON Header*

```
public function executeRefresh()
{
  $output = '[["title", "My basic letter"], ["name", "Mr Brown"]]';
  $this->getResponse()->setHttpHeader("X-JSON", '('.$output.')');

  return sfView::HEADER_ONLY;
}
```

This skips the template and the layout, and the response can be sent at once. As it contains only headers, it is more lightweight and will take less time to transmit to the user.

Chapter 6 explained another way to skip the template by returning content text directly from the action. This breaks the MVC separation, but it can increase the responsiveness of an action greatly. Check Listing 18-13 for an example.

Listing 18-13. *Example Action Returning Content Text Directly*

```
public function executeFastAction()
{
  return $this->renderText("<html><body>Hello, World!</body></html>");
}
```

Restricting the Default Helpers

The standard helper groups (Partial, Cache, and Form) are loaded for every request. If you are sure that you won't use some of them, removing a helper group from the list of standard ones will save you the parsing of the helper file. In particular, the `Form` helper group, although included by default, is quite heavy and slows down pages with no forms just because of its size. So it might be a good idea to edit the `standard_helpers` setting in the `settings.yml` file to remove it:

```
all:
  .settings:
    standard_helpers: [Partial, Cache]    # Form is removed
```

The tradeoff is that you must declare the `Form` helper group on each template using it with `use_helper('Form')`.

Compressing the Response

Symfony compresses the response before sending it to the user. This feature is based on the PHP zlib module. You can save a little CPU time for each request by deactivating it in the `settings.yml` file:

```
all:
  .settings:
    compressed: off
```

Be aware that the CPU gain will be balanced by the bandwidth loss, so the performance won't increase in all configurations with this change.

■**Tip** If you deactivate zip compression in PHP, you can enable it at the server level. Apache has a compression extension of its own.

Tweaking the Cache

Chapter 12 already described how to cache parts of a response or all of it. The response cache results in a major performance improvement, and it should be one of your first optimization considerations. If you want to make the most out of the cache system, read further, for this section unveils a few tricks you might not have thought of.

Clearing Selective Parts of the Cache

During application development, you have to clear the cache in various situations:

- *When you create a new class:* Adding a class to an autoloading directory (one of the project's `lib/` folders) is not enough to have symfony find it automatically. You must clear the autoloading configuration cache so that symfony browses again all the directories of the `autoload.yml` file and references the location of autoloadable classes—including the new ones.

- *When you change the configuration in production:* The configuration is parsed only during the first request in production. Further requests use the cached version instead. So a change in the configuration in the production environment (or any environment where `SF_DEBUG` is turned off) doesn't take effect until you clear the cached version of the file.

- *When you modify a template in an environment where the template cache is enabled:* The valid cached templates are always used instead of existing templates in production, so a template change is ignored until the template cache is cleared or outdated.

- *When you update an application with the* sync *command:* This case usually covers the three previous modifications.

The problem with clearing the whole cache is that the next request will take quite long to process, because the configuration cache needs to be regenerated. Besides, the templates that were not modified will be cleared from the cache as well, losing the benefit of previous requests.

That means it's a good idea to clear only the cache files that really need to be regenerated. Use the options of the clear-cache task to define a subset of cache files to clear, as demonstrated in Listing 18-14.

Listing 18-14. *Clearing Only Selective Parts of the Cache*

```
// Clear only the cache of the myapp application
> symfony clear-cache myapp

// Clear only the HTML cache of the myapp application
> symfony clear-cache myapp template

// Clear only the configuration cache of the myapp application
> symfony clear-cache myapp config
```

You can also remove files by hand in the cache/ directory, or clear template cache files selectively from the action with the $cacheManager->remove() method, as described in Chapter 12.

All these techniques will minimize the negative performance impact of any of the changes listed previously.

■**Tip** When you upgrade symfony, the cache is automatically cleared, without manual intervention (if you set the check_symfony_version parameter to true in settings.yml).

Generating Cached Pages

When you deploy a new application to production, the template cache is empty. You must wait for users to visit a page once for this page to be put in the cache. In critical deployments, the overhead of page processing is not acceptable, and the benefits of caching must be available as soon as the first request is issued.

The solution is to automatically browse the pages of your application in the staging environment (where the configuration is similar to the one in production) to have the template cache generated, then to transfer the application *with the cache* to production.

To browse the pages automatically, one option is to create a shell script that looks through a list of external URLs with a browser (curl for instance). But there is a better and faster solution:

a symfony batch using the sfBrowser object, already discussed in Chapter 15. That's an internal browser written in PHP (and used by sfTestBrowser for functional tests). It takes an external URL and returns a response, but the interesting thing is that it triggers the template cache just like a regular browser. As it only initializes symfony once and doesn't pass by the HTTP transport layer, this method is a lot faster.

Listing 18-15 shows an example batch script used to generate template cache files in a staging environment. Launch it by calling php batch/generate_cache.php.

Listing 18-15. *Generating the Template Cache, in batch/generate_cache.php*

```php
<?php

define('SF_ROOT_DIR',    realpath(dirname(__FILE__).'/..'));
define('SF_APP',         'myapp');
define('SF_ENVIRONMENT', 'staging');
define('SF_DEBUG',       false);

require_once(SF_ROOT_DIR.DIRECTORY_SEPARATOR.'apps'.DIRECTORY_SEPARATOR.SF_APP ➡
.DIRECTORY_SEPARATOR.'config'.DIRECTORY_SEPARATOR.'config.php');

// Array of URLs to browse
$uris = array(
  '/foo/index',
  '/foo/bar/id/1',
  '/foo/bar/id/2',
  ...
);

$b = new sfBrowser();
foreach ($uris as $uri)
{
  $b->get($uri);
}
```

Using a Database Storage System for Caching

The default storage system for the template cache in symfony is the file system: Fragments of HTML or serialized response objects are stored under the cache/ directory of a project. Symfony proposes an alternative way to store cache: a SQLite database. Such a database is a simple file that PHP natively knows how to query very efficiently.

To tell symfony to use SQLite storage instead of file system storage for the template cache, open the factories.yml file and edit the view_cache entry as follows:

```
view_cache:
  class: sfSQLiteCache
  param:
    database: %SF_TEMPLATE_CACHE_DIR%/cache.db
```

The benefits of using SQLite storage for the template cache are faster read and write operations when the number of cache elements is important. If your application makes heavy use of caching, the template cache files end up scattered in a deep file structure; in this case, switching to SQLite storage will increase performance. In addition, clearing the cache on file system storage may require a lot of files to be removed from the disk; this operation may last a few seconds, during which your application is unavailable. With a SQLite storage system, the cache clearing process results in a single file operation: the deletion of the SQLite database file. Whatever the number of cache elements currently stored, the operation is instantaneous.

Bypassing Symfony

Perhaps the best way to speed symfony up is to bypass it completely . . . this is said only partly in jest. Some pages don't change and don't need to be reprocessed by the framework at each request. The template cache is already here to speed up the delivery of such pages, but it still relies on symfony.

A couple of tricks described in Chapter 12 allow you to bypass symfony completely for some pages. The first one involves the use of HTTP 1.1 headers for asking the proxies and client browsers to cache the page themselves, so that they don't request it again the next time the page is needed. The second one is the *super fast cache* (automated by the sfSuperCachePlugin plug-in), which consists of storing a copy of the response in the web/ directory and modifying the rewriting rules so that Apache first looks for a cached version before handing a request to symfony.

Both these methods are very effective, and even if they only apply to static pages, they will take the burden of handling these pages off from symfony, and the server will then be fully available to deal with complex requests.

Caching the Result of a Function Call

If a function doesn't rely on context-sensitive values nor on randomness, calling it twice with the same parameters should return the same result. That means the second call could very well be avoided if the result had been stored the first time. That's exactly what the sfFunctionCache class does. This class has a call() method, which expects a callable and a set of parameters. When called, this method creates an md5 hash with all its arguments and looks in the cache directory for a file named by this hash. If such a file is found, the function returns the result stored in the file. If not, the sfFunctionCache executes the function, stores the result in the cache, and returns it. So the second execution of Listing 18-16 will be faster than the first one.

Listing 18-16. *Caching the Result of a Function*

```
$function_cache_dir = sfConfig::get('sf_cache_dir').'/function';
$fc = new sfFunctionCache($function_cache_dir);
$result1 = $fc->call('cos', M_PI);
$result2 = $fc->call('preg_replace', '/\s\s+/', ' ', $input);
```

The sfFunctionCache constructor expects an absolute directory path as argument (the directory must exist prior to the object instantiation). The first argument of the call() method must be a callable, so it can be a function name, an array of a class name and static method name, or an array of an object name and public method name. As for the other arguments of the call() method, you can include as many as you need—they are all handed to the callable.

This object is especially useful for CPU-intensive functions, because the file I/O overhead exceeds the time required to process a simple function. It relies on the sfFileCache class, which is the component also used by the symfony template cache engine. Refer to the API documentation for more details.

Caution The clear-cache task erases only the contents of the cache/ file. If you store the function cache somewhere else, it will not be cleared automatically when you clear the cache through the command line.

Caching Data in the Server

PHP accelerators provide special functions to store data in memory so that you can reuse it across requests. The problem is that they all have a different syntax, and each has its own specific way of performing this task. Symfony provides a class called sfProcessCache, which abstracts all these differences and works with whatever accelerator you are using. See its syntax in Listing 18-17.

Listing 18-17. *Syntax of the sfProcessCache Methods*

```
// Storing data in the process cache
sfProcessCache::set($name, $value, $lifetime);

// Retrieving data
$value = sfProcessCache::get($name);

// Checking if a piece of data exists in the process cache
$value_exists = sfProcessCache::has($name);

// Clear the process cache
sfProcessCache::clear();
```

The set() method returns false if the caching didn't work. The cached value can be anything (a string, an array, an object); the sfProcessCache class will deal with the serialization. The get() method returns null if the required variable doesn't exist in the cache.

The methods of the sfProcessCache class work even if no accelerator is installed. Therefore, there is no risk in trying to retrieve data from the process cache, as long as you provide a fallback value. For instance, Listing 18-18 shows how to retrieve a configuration setting in the process cache.

Listing 18-18. *Using the Process Cache Safely*

```
if (sfProcessCache::has('myapp_parameters'))
{
  $params = sfProcessCache::get('myapp_parameters');
}
else
{
  $params = retrieve_parameters();
}
```

■**Tip** If you want to go further into memory caching, make sure you take a look at the *memcache* extension for PHP. It can help decrease the database load on load-balanced applications, and PHP 5 provides an OO interface to it (`http://www.php.net/memcache/`).

Deactivating the Unused Features

The default symfony configuration activates the most common features of a web application. However, if you happen to not need all of them, you should deactivate them to save the time their initialization takes on each request.

For instance, if your application doesn't use the session mechanism, or if you want to start the session handling by hand, you should turn the `auto_start` setting to `false` in the `storage` key of the `factories.yml` file, as in Listing 18-19.

Listing 18-19. *Turning Sessions Off, in* `myapp/config/factories.yml`

```
all:
  storage:
    class: sfSessionStorage
    param:
      auto_start: false
```

The same applies for the database (as explained in the "Tweaking the Model" section earlier in this chapter) and output escaping feature (see Chapter 7). If your application makes no use of them, deactivate them for a small performance gain, this time in the `settings.yml` file (see Listing 18-20).

Listing 18-20. *Turning Features Off, in* `myapp/config/settings.yml`

```
all:
  .settings:
    use_database:      off    # Database and model features
    escaping_strategy: off    # Output escaping feature
```

As for the security and the flash attribute features (see Chapter 6), you can deactivate them in the `filters.yml` file, as shown in Listing 18-21.

Listing 18-21. *Turning Features Off, in* `myapp/config/filters.yml`

```
rendering: ~
web_debug: ~
security:
  enabled: off

# generally, you will want to insert your own filters here

cache:     ~
common:    ~
flash:
  enabled: off

execution: ~
```

Some features are useful only in development, so you should not activate them in production. This is already the case by default, since the production environment in symfony is really optimized for performance. Among the performance-impacting development features, the `SF_DEBUG` mode is the most severe. As for the symfony logs, the feature is also turned off in production by default.

You may wonder how to get information about failed requests in production if logging is disabled, and argue that problems arise not only in development. Fortunately, symfony can use the `sfErrorLoggerPlugin` plug-in, which runs in the background in production and logs the details of 404 and 500 errors in a database. It is much faster than the file logging feature, because the plug-in methods are called only when a request fails, while the logging mechanism, once turned on, adds a nonnegligible overhead whatever the level. Check the installation instructions and manual at `http://www.symfony-project.com/trac/wiki/sfErrorLoggerPlugin`.

Tip Make sure you regularly check the server error logs—they also contain very valuable information about 404 and 500 errors.

Optimizing Your Code

It's also possible to speed up your application by optimizing the code itself. This section offers some insight regarding how to do that.

Core Compilation

Loading ten files requires more I/O operations than loading one long file, especially on slow disks. Loading a very long file requires more resources than loading a smaller file—especially if a large share of the file content is of no use for the PHP parser, which is the case for comments.

So merging a large number of files and stripping out the comments they contain is an operation that improves performance. Symfony already does that optimization; it's called the *core compilation*. At the beginning of the first request (or after the cache is cleared), a symfony application concatenates all the core framework classes (sfActions, sfRequest, sfView, and so on) into one file, optimizes the file size by removing comments and double blanks, and saves it in the cache, in a file called config_core_compile.yml.php. Each subsequent request only loads this single optimized file instead of the 30 files that compose it.

If your application has classes that must always be loaded, and especially if they are big classes with lots of comments, it may be beneficial to add them to the core compile file. To do so, just add a core_compile.yml file in your application config/ directory, and list in it the classes that you want to add, as in Listing 18-22.

Listing 18-22. *Adding Your Classes to the Core Compile File, in myapp/config/core_compile.yml*

```
- %SF_ROOT_DIR%/lib/myClass.class.php
- %SF_ROOT_DIR%/apps/myapp/lib/myToolkit.class.php
- %SF_ROOT_DIR%/plugins/myPlugin/lib/myPluginCore.class.php
...
```

The sfOptimizer Plug-In

Symfony also offers another optimization tool, called sfOptimizer. It applies various optimization strategies to the symfony and application code, which may further speed up the execution.

The symfony code counts many tests that rely on configuration parameters—and your application may also do so. For instance, if you take a look at the symfony classes, you will often see a test on the value of the sf_logging_enabled parameter before a call to the sfLogger object:

```
if (sfConfig::get('sf_logging_enabled'))
{
    $this->getContext()->getLogger()->info('Been there');
}
```

Even if the sfConfig registry is very well optimized, the number of calls to its get() method during the processing of each request is important—and it counts in the final performance. One of the sfOptimizer optimization strategies is to replace configuration constants by their value—as long as these constants are not subject to change at runtime. That's the case, for instance, with the sf_logging_enabled parameter; when it is defined as false, the sfOptimizer transforms the previous code into the following:

```
if (0)
{
    $this->getContext()->getLogger()->info('Been there');
}
```

And that's not all, because an evident test like the preceding one also gets optimized to an empty string.

To apply the optimizations, you must first install the plug-in from http://www.symfony-project.com/trac/wiki/sfOptimizerPlugin and then call the optimize task, specifying an application and an environment:

```
> symfony optimize myapp prod
```

If you want to apply other optimization strategies to your code, the `sfOptimizer` plug-in might be a good starting place.

Summary

Symfony is already a very optimized framework and is able to handle high-traffic websites without a problem. But if you really need to optimize your application's performance, *tweaking the configuration* (whether the server configuration, the PHP configuration, or the application settings) will gain you a small boost. You should also follow good practices to write *efficient model methods*; and since the database is often a bottleneck in web applications, this point should require all your attention. *Templates* can also benefit from a few tricks, but the best boost will always come from *caching*. Finally, don't hesitate to look at existing *plug-ins*, since some of them provide innovative techniques to further speed up the delivery of web pages (`sfSuperCache`, `sfOptimizer`).

CHAPTER 19

■■■

Mastering Symfony's Configuration Files

Now that you know symfony very well, you are already able to dig into its code to understand its core design and discover new hidden abilities. But before extending the symfony classes to match your own requirements, you should take a closer look at some of the configuration files. Many features are already built into symfony and can be activated by just changing configuration settings. This means that you can tweak the symfony core behavior without overriding its classes. This chapter takes you deep into the configuration files and their powerful capabilities.

Symfony Settings

The `myapp/config/settings.yml` file contains the main symfony configuration for the `myapp` application. You have already seen the function of many settings from this file in the previous chapters, but let's revisit them.

As explained in Chapter 5, this file is environment-dependent, which means that each setting can take a different value for each environment. Remember that each parameter defined in this file is accessible from inside the PHP code via the `sfConfig` class. The parameter name is the setting name prefixed with `sf_`. For instance, if you want to get the value of the `cache` parameter, you just need to call `sfConfig::get('sf_cache')`.

Default Modules and Actions

When a routing rule doesn't define the `module` or the `action` parameter, values from the `settings.yml` file are used instead:

> `default_module`: Default `module` request parameter. Defaults to the `default` module.

> `default_action`: Default `action` request parameter. Defaults to the `index` action.

Symfony provides default pages for special situations. In the case of a routing error, symfony executes an action of the `default` module, which is stored in the `$sf_symfony_data_dir/modules/default/` directory. The `settings.yml` file defines which action is executed depending on the error:

`error_404_module` and `error_404_action`: Action called when the URL entered by the user doesn't match any route or when an `sfError404Exception` occurs. The default value is `default/error404`.

`login_module` and `login_action`: Action called when a nonauthenticated user tries to access a page defined as secure in `security.yml` (see Chapter 6 for details). The default value is `default/login`.

`secure_module` and `secure_action`: Action called when a user doesn't have the credentials required for an action. The default value is `default/secure`.

`module_disabled_module` and `module_disabled_action`: Action called when a user requests a module declared as disabled in `module.yml`. The default value is `default/disabled`.

`unavailable_module` and `unavailable_action`: Action called when a user requests a page from a disabled application. The default value is `default/unavailable`. To disable an application, set the `available` parameter to `off` in `settings.yml`.

Before deploying an application to production, you should customize these actions, because the `default` module templates include the symfony logo on the page. See Figure 19-1 for a screenshot of one of these pages, the error 404 page.

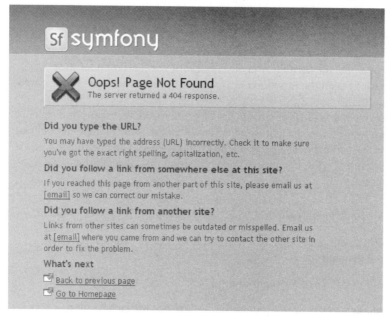

Figure 19-1. *Default 404 error page*

You can override the default pages in two ways:

- You can create your own `default` module in the application's `modules/` directory, override all the actions defined in the `settings.yml` file (`index`, `error404`, `login`, `secure`, `disabled`, and `unavailable`) and all the related templates (`indexSuccess.php`, `error404Success.php`, `loginSuccess.php`, `secureSuccess.php`, `disabledSuccess.php`, and `unavailableSuccess.php`).

- You can change the default module and action settings of the `settings.yml` file to use pages of your application.

Two other pages bear a symfony look and feel, and they also need to be customized before deployment to production. These pages are not in the `default` module, because they are called when symfony cannot run properly. Instead, you will find these default pages in the `$sf_symfony_data_dir/web/errors/` directory:

`error500.php`: Page called when an internal server error occurs in the production environment. In other environments (where `SF_DEBUG` is set to `true`), when an error occurs, symfony displays the full execution stack and an explicit error message (see Chapter 16 for details).

`unavailable.php`: Page called when a user requests a page while the cache is being cleared (that is, between a call to the `symfony clear-cache` task and the end of this task execution). On systems with a very large cache, the cache-clearing process can take several seconds. Symfony cannot execute a request with a partially cleared cache, so requests received before the end of the process are redirected to this page. The `unavailable.php` page is also used when an application is disabled via the `symfony disable` command (see Chapter 16 for details).

To customize these pages, simply create `error500.php` and `unavailable.php` pages in your application's `web/errors/` directory. Symfony will use these instead of its own.

■Note To have requests redirected to the `unavailable.php` page when needed, you need to set the `check_lock` setting to on in the application `settings.yml`. The check is deactivated by default, because it adds a very slight overhead for every request.

Optional Feature Activation

Some parameters of the `settings.yml` file control optional framework features that can be enabled or disabled. Deactivating unused features boosts performances a bit, so make sure to review the settings listed in Table 19-1 before deploying your application.

Table 19-1. *Optional Features Set Through* `settings.yml`

Parameter	Description	Default Value
use_database	Enables the database manager. Set it to off if you don't use a database.	on
use_security	Enables security features (secure actions and credentials; see Chapter 6). The default security filter (sfBasicSecurityFilter) is enabled only if it is on.	on
use_flash	Enables the flash parameter feature (see Chapter 6). Set it to off if you never use the set_flash() method in your actions. The flash filter (sfFlashFilter) is enabled only if it is on.	on
i18n	Enables interface translation (see Chapter 13). Set it to on for multilingual applications.	off
logging_enabled	Enables logging of symfony events. Set it to off when you want to ignore the logging.yml settings and turn symfony logging off completely.	on
escaping_strategy	Enables and defines the policy of the output escaping feature (see Chapter 7). Set it to off if you don't use the $sf_data container in your templates.	bc
cache	Enables template caching (see Chapter 12). Set it to on if one of your modules includes cache.yml file. The cache filter (sfCacheFilter) is enabled only if it is on.	off in development, on in production
web_debug	Enables the web debug toolbar for easy debugging (see Chapter 16). Set it to on to display the toolbar on every page. The web debug filter (sfWebDebugFilter) is enabled ony if it is on.	on in development, off in production
check_symfony_version	Enables the check of the symfony version for every request. Set it to on for automatic cache clearing after a framework upgrade. Leave it set to off if you always clear the cache after an upgrade.	off
check_lock	Enables the application lock system, triggered by the clear-cache and disable tasks (see the previous section). Set it to on to have all requests to disabled applications redirected to the $sf_symfony_data_dir/web/errors/unavailable.php page.	off
compressed	Enables PHP response compression. Set it to on to compress the outgoing HTML via the PHP compression handler.	off

Table 19-1. *Optional Features Set Through* `settings.yml`

Parameter	Description	Default Value
`use_process_cache`	Enables symfony optimizations based on PHP accelerators. When such an accelerator (for instance, APC, XCache, or eAccelerator) is installed, symfony takes advantage of its features to keep objects and configuration in memory between requests. Set the parameter to `off` in development or when you don't want PHP accelerator optimizations. Note that even if you don't have any accelerator installed, leaving it set to `on` will not harm performance.	on

Feature Configuration

Symfony uses some parameters of `settings.yml` to alter the behavior of built-in features such as form validation, cache, and third-party modules.

Output Escaping Settings

Output escaping settings control the way the variables are accessible in the template (see Chapter 7). The `settings.yml` file includes two settings for this feature:

- The `escaping_strategy` setting can take the value `bc`, `both`, `on`, or `off`.

- The `escaping_method` setting can be set to `ESC_RAW`, `ESC_ENTITIES`, `ESC_JS`, or `ESC_JS_NO_ENTITIES`.

Routing Settings

Two routing settings (see Chapter 9) are stored in `settings.yml`:

- The `suffix` parameter sets the default suffix for generated URLs. The default value is a period (`.`), and it corresponds to no suffix. Set it to `.html`, for instance, to have all generated URLs look like static pages.

- The `no_script_name` parameter enables the front controller name in generated URLs. The `no_script_name` setting can be `on` only for a single application in a project, unless you store the front controllers in various directories and alter the default URL rewriting rules. It is usually on for the production environment of your main application and `off` for the others.

Form Validation Settings

Form validation settings control the way error messages output by the `Validation` helpers look (see Chapter 10). These errors are included in `<div>` tags, and they use the `validation_error_class` setting as a `class` attribute and the `validation_error_id_prefix` setting to build up the `id` attribute. The default values are `form_error` and `error_for_`, so the attributes output by a call to the `form_error()` helper for an input named `foobar` will be `class="form_error"` `id="error_for_foobar"`.

Two settings determine which characters precede and follow each error message: `validation_error_prefix` and `validation_error_suffix`. You can change them to customize all error messages at once.

Cache Settings

Cache settings are defined in `cache.yml` for the most part, except for two in `settings.yml`: `cache` enables the template cache mechanism, and `etag` enables ETag handling on the server side (see Chapter 15).

Logging Settings

Two logging settings (see Chapter 16) are stored in `settings.yml`:

- `error_reporting` specifies which events are logged in the PHP logs. By default, it is set to 341 for the production environment (so the logged events are E_PARSE, E_COMPILE_ERROR, E_ERROR, E_CORE_ERROR, and E_USER_ERROR) and to 4095 for the development environment (E_ALL and E_STRICT).

- The `web_debug` setting activates the web debug toolbar. Set it to on only in the development and test environments.

Paths to Assets

The `settings.yml` file also stores paths to assets. If you want to use another version of the asset than the one bundled with symfony, you can change these path settings:

- Rich text editor JavaScript files stored in `rich_text_js_dir` (by default, `js/tiny_mce`)

- Prototype libraries stored in `prototype_web_dir` (by default, `/sf/prototype`)

- Files needed by the administration generator stored in `admin_web_dir`

- Files needed by the web debug toolbar stored in `web_debug_web_dir`

- Files needed by the javascript calendar stored in `calendar_web_dir`

Default Helpers

Default helpers, loaded for every template, are declared in the `standard_helpers` setting (see Chapter 7). By default, these are the `Partial`, `Cache`, and `Form` helper groups. If you use a helper group in all templates of an application, adding its name to the `standard_helpers` setting saves you the hassle of declaring it with `use_helper()` on each template.

Activated Modules

Activated modules from plug-ins or from the symfony core are declared in the `enabled_modules` parameter. Even if a plug-in bundles a module, users can't request this module unless it is declared in `enabled_modules`. The `default` module, which provides the default symfony pages (congratulations, page not found, and so on), is the only enabled module by default.

Character Set

The character set of the responses is a general setting of the application, because it is used by many components of the framework (templates, output escaper, helpers, and so on). Defined in the charset setting, its default (and advised) value is utf-8.

Miscellaneous Configuration

The settings.yml file contains a few more parameters, used internally by symfony for core behaviors. Listing 19-1 lists them as they appear in the configuration file.

Listing 19-1. *Miscellaneous Configuration Settings, in myapp/config/settings.yml*

```
# Remove comments in core framework classes as defined in the core_compile.yml
strip_comments:        on
# Functions called when a class is requested and not already loaded
# Expects an array of callables. Used by the framework bridges.
autoloading_functions:  ~
# Session timeout, in seconds
timeout:               1800
# Maximum number of forwards followed by the action before raising an exception
max_forwards:          5
# Global constants
path_info_array:       SERVER
path_info_key:         PATH_INFO
url_format:            PATH
```

ADDING YOUR APPLICATION SETTINGS

The settings.yml file defines symfony settings for an application. As discussed in Chapter 5, when you want to add new parameters, the best place to do so is in the myapp/config/app.yml file. This file is also environment-dependent, and the settings it defines are available through the sfConfig class with the app_ prefix.

```
all:
  creditcards:
    fake:             off    # app_creditcards_fake
    visa:             on     # app_creditcards_visa
    americanexpress:  on     # app_creditcards_americanexpress
```

You can also write an app.yml file in the *project* configuration directory, and this provides a way to define custom project settings. The configuration cascade also applies to this file, so the settings defined in the application app.yml file override the ones defined at the project level.

Extending the Autoloading Feature

The autoloading feature, briefly explained in Chapter 2, exempts you from requiring classes in your code if they are located in specific directories. This means that you can just let the framework do the job for you, allowing it to load only the necessary classes at the appropriate time, and only when needed.

The `autoload.yml` file lists the paths in which autoloaded classes are stored. The first time this configuration file is processed, symfony parses all the directories referenced in the file. Each time a file ending with `.php` is found in one of these directories, the file path and the class names found in this file are added to an internal list of autoloading classes. This list is saved in the cache, in a file called `config/config_autoload.yml.php`. Then, at runtime, when a class is used, symfony looks in this list for the class path and includes the `.php` file automatically.

Autoloading works for all `.php` files containing classes and/or interfaces.

By default, classes stored in the following directories in your projects benefit from the autoloading automatically:

- `myproject/lib/`

- `myproject/lib/model`

- `myproject/apps/myapp/lib/`

- `myproject/apps/myapp/modules/mymodule/lib`

There is no `autoload.yml` file in the default application configuration directory. If you want to modify the framework settings—for instance, to autoload classes stored somewhere else in your file structure—create an empty `autoload.yml` file and override the settings of `$sf_symfony_data_dir/config/autoload.yml` or add your own.

The `autoload.yml` file must start with an `autoload:` key and list the locations where symfony should look for classes. Each location requires a label; this gives you the ability to override symfony's entries. For each location, provide a `name` (it will appear as a comment in `config_autoload.yml.php`) and an absolute `path`. Then define if the search must be `recursive`, which directs symfony to look in all the subdirectories for `.php` files, and `exclude` the subdirectories you want. Listing 19-2 shows the locations used by default and the file syntax.

Listing 19-2. *Default Autoloading Configuration, in $sf_symfony_data_dir/config/autoload.yml*

```
autoload:

  # symfony core
  symfony:
    name:         symfony
    path:         %SF_SYMFONY_LIB_DIR%
    recursive:    on
    exclude:      [vendor]
```

```
propel:
  name:          propel
  path:          %SF_SYMFONY_LIB_DIR%/vendor/propel
  recursive:     on

creole:
  name:          creole
  path:          %SF_SYMFONY_LIB_DIR%/vendor/creole
  recursive:     on

propel_addon:
  name:          propel addon
  files:
    Propel:      %SF_SYMFONY_LIB_DIR%/addon/propel/sfPropelAutoload.php

# plugins
plugins_lib:
  name:          plugins lib
  path:          %SF_PLUGINS_DIR%/*/lib
  recursive:     on

plugins_module_lib:
  name:          plugins module lib
  path:          %SF_PLUGINS_DIR%/*/modules/*/lib
  prefix:        2
  recursive:     on

# project
project:
  name:          project
  path:          %SF_LIB_DIR%
  recursive:     on
  exclude:       [model, symfony]

project_model:
  name:          project model
  path:          %SF_MODEL_LIB_DIR%
  recursive:     on

# application
application:
  name:          application
  path:          %SF_APP_LIB_DIR%
  recursive:     on
```

```
modules:
  name:         module
  path:         %SF_APP_DIR%/modules/*/lib
  prefix:       1
  recursive:    on
```

A rule path can contain wildcards and use the file path parameters from the `constants.php` file (see the next section). If you use these parameters in the configuration file, they must appear in uppercase and begin and end with %.

Editing your own `autoload.yml` will add new locations to symfony's autoloading, but you may want to extend this mechanism and add your own autoloading handler to symfony's handler. This is possible through the `autoloading_functions` parameter in the `settings.yml` file. It expects an array of callables as a value, as follows:

```
.settings:
  autoloading_functions:
    - [myToolkit, autoload]
```

When symfony encounters a new class, it will first try its own autoloading system (and use the locations defined in `autoload.yml`). If it doesn't find a class definition, it will then try the other autoloading functions from `settings.yml`, until the class is found. So you can add as many autoloading mechanisms as you want—for instance, to provide a bridge to other framework components (see Chapter 17).

Custom File Structure

Each time the framework uses a path to look for something (from core classes to templates, plug-ins, configurations, and so on), it uses a path variable instead of an actual path. By changing these variables, you can completely alter the directory structure of a symfony project, and adapt to the file organization requirements of any client.

■**Caution** Customizing the directory structure of a symfony project is possible but not necessarily a good idea. One of the strengths of a framework like symfony is that any web developer can look at a project built with it and feel at home, because of the respect for conventions. Make sure you consider this issue before deciding to use your own directory structure.

The Basic File Structure

The path variables are defined in the `$sf_symfony_data_dir/config/constants.php` file, included when the application bootstraps. These variables are stored in the `sfConfig` object, and so they are easy to override. Listing 19-3 shows a listing of the path variables and the directory they reference.

Listing 19-3. *Default File Structure Variables, from $sf_symfony_data_dir/config/ constants.php*

```
sf_root_dir              # myproject/
                         #   apps/
sf_app_dir               #     myapp/
sf_app_config_dir        #       config/
sf_app_i18n_dir          #       i18n/
sf_app_lib_dir           #       lib/
sf_app_module_dir        #       modules/
sf_app_template_dir      #       templates/
sf_bin_dir               #   batch/
                         #   cache/
sf_base_cache_dir        #     myapp/
sf_cache_dir             #       prod/
sf_template_cache_dir    #         templates/
sf_i18n_cache_dir        #         i18n/
sf_config_cache_dir      #         config/
sf_test_cache_dir        #         test/
sf_module_cache_dir      #         modules/
sf_config_dir            #   config/
sf_data_dir              #   data/
sf_doc_dir               #   doc/
sf_lib_dir               #   lib/
sf_model_lib_dir         #     model/
sf_log_dir               #   log/
sf_test_dir              #   test/
sf_plugins_dir           #   plugins/
sf_web_dir               #   web/
sf_upload_dir            #     uploads/
```

Every path to a key directory is determined by a parameter ending with _dir. Always use the path variables instead of real (relative or absolute) file paths, so that you will be able to change them later, if necessary. For instance, when you want to move a file to the uploads/ directory in an application, you should use sfConfig::get('sf_upload_dir') for the path instead of SF_ROOT_DIR.'/web/uploads/'.

The module directory structure is defined at runtime, when the routing system determines the module name ($module_name). It is automatically built according to the path names defined in the constants.php file, as shown in Listing 19-4.

Listing 19-4. *Default Module File Structure Variables*

```
sf_app_module_dir                # modules/
module_name                      #   mymodule/
sf_app_module_action_dir_name    #     actions/
sf_app_module_template_dir_name  #     templates/
sf_app_module_lib_dir_name       #     lib/
sf_app_module_view_dir_name      #     views/
```

```
sf_app_module_validate_dir_name    #    validate/
sf_app_module_config_dir_name      #    config/
sf_app_module_i18n_dir_name        #    i18n/
```

So, for instance, the path to the validate/ directory of the current module is built dynamically at runtime:

```
sfConfig::get('sf_app_module_dir').'/'.$module_name.'/'.sfConfig::get('sf_app_ ➥
module_validate_dir_name')
```

Customizing the File Structure

You will probably need to modify the default project file structure if you develop an application for a client who already has a defined directory structure and who is not willing to change it to comply with the symfony logic. By overriding the sf_*XXX*_dir and sf_*XXX*_dir_name variables with sfConfig, you can make symfony work for a totally different directory structure than the default structure. The best place to do this is in the application config.php file.

■**Caution** Use the *application* config.php and not the *project* one to override the sf_*XXX*_dir and sf_*XXX*_dir_name variables with sfConfig. The project config/config.php file is loaded very early in the life of a request, at a time when the sfConfig class doesn't exist yet, and when the constants.php file is not yet loaded.

For instance, if you want all applications to share a common directory for the template layouts, add this line to the myapp/config/config.php file to override the sf_app_template_dir settings:

```
sfConfig::set('sf_app_template_dir', sfConfig::get('sf_root_dir'). ➥
DIRECTORY_SEPARATOR.'templates');
```

Note that the application config.php file is not empty, so if you need to include file structure definitions there, do it at the end of the file.

Modifying the Project Web Root

All the paths built in constants.php rely on the project root directory, which is a constant defined in the front controller (SF_ROOT_DIR). Usually, the root directory is one level above the web/ directory, but you can use a different structure. Suppose that your main directory structure is made of two directories, one public and one private, as shown in Listing 19-5. This typically happens when hosting a project on a shared host.

Listing 19-5. *Example of Custom Directory Structure for a Shared Host*

```
symfony/    # Private area
  apps/
  batch/
  cache/
  ...
www/        # Public area
  images/
  css/
  js/
  index.php
```

In this case, the root directory is the symfony/ directory. So the index.php front controller simply needs to define the SF_ROOT_DIR as follows for the application to work:

```
define('SF_ROOT_DIR', dirname(__FILE__).'/../symfony');
```

In addition, since the public area is www/ instead of the usual web/, you must override two file paths in the application config.php file, as follows:

```
sfConfig::add(array(
  'sf_web_dir'    => SF_ROOT_DIR.DIRECTORY_SEPARATOR.'www',
  'sf_upload_dir' => SF_ROOT_DIR.DIRECTORY_SEPARATOR.'www'.DIRECTORY_SEPARATOR ➥
                     .sfConfig::get('sf_upload_dir_name'),
));
```

Linking to Symfony Libraries

The paths to the framework files are defined in the project config.php file, as you can see in Listing 19-6.

Listing 19-6. *The Paths to the Framework Files, in myproject/config/config.php*

```php
<?php

// symfony directories
$sf_symfony_lib_dir  = '/path/to/symfony/lib';
$sf_symfony_data_dir = '/path/to/symfony/data';
```

These paths are initialized when you call a symfony init-project from the command line, and refer to the symfony installation used to build the project. They are used both by the command line and by the MVC architecture.

This means that you can switch to another installation of symfony by changing the paths to the framework files.

These paths should be absolute, but by using dirname(__FILE__), you can refer to files inside the project structure and preserve independence of the chosen directory for the project installation. For instance, many projects choose to have the symfony lib/ directory appear as a symbolic link in the project lib/symfony/ directory, and do the same for the symfony data/ directory, as follows:

```
myproject/
  lib/
    symfony/ => /path/to/symfony/lib
  data/
    symfony/ => /path/to/symfony/data
```

In this case, the project config.php file just needs to define the symfony directories as follows:

```
$sf_symfony_lib_dir  = dirname(__FILE__).'/../lib/symfony';
$sf_symfony_data_dir = dirname(__FILE__).'/../data/symfony';
```

The same principle also applies if you choose to include the symfony files as a svn:externals in the project lib/vendor/ directory:

```
myproject/
  lib/
    vendor/
      svn:externals symfony http://svn.symfony-project.com/trunk/
```

In this case, the config.php file should look like this:

```
$sf_symfony_lib_dir  = dirname(__FILE__).'/../lib/vendor/symfony/lib';
$sf_symfony_data_dir = dirname(__FILE__).'/../lib/vendor/symfony/data';
```

■**Tip** Sometimes, the different servers running an application don't have the same path to the symfony libraries. One way to enable that is to exclude the project config.php file from the synchronization (by adding it to rsync_exclude.txt). Another method is to keep the same paths in the development and production versions of config.php, but to have these paths point to symbolic links that can vary according to the server.

Understanding Configuration Handlers

Each configuration file has a handler. The job of configuration handlers is to manage the configuration cascade, and to do the translation between the configuration files and the optimized PHP code executable at runtime.

Default Configuration Handlers

The default handler configuration is stored in $sf_symfony_data_dir/config/config_handlers.yml. This file links the handlers to the configuration files according to a file path. Listing 19-7 shows an extract of this file.

Listing 19-7. *Extract of $sf_symfony_data_dir/config/config_handlers.yml*

```
config/settings.yml:
  class:    sfDefineEnvironmentConfigHandler
  param:
    prefix: sf_

config/app.yml:
  class:    sfDefineEnvironmentConfigHandler
  param:
    prefix: app_

config/filters.yml:
  class:    sfFilterConfigHandler

modules/*/config/module.yml:
  class:    sfDefineEnvironmentConfigHandler
  param:
    prefix: mod_
    module: yes
```

For each configuration file (config_handlers.yml identifies each file by a file path with wildcards), the handler class is specified under the class key.

The settings of configuration files handled by sfDefineEnvironmentConfigHandler can be made available directly in the code via the sfConfig class, and the param key contains a prefix value.

You can add or modify the handlers used to process each configuration file—for instance, to use INI or XML files instead of YAML files.

■**Note** The configuration handler for the config_handlers.yml file is sfRootConfigHandler and, obviously, it cannot be changed.

If you ever need to modify the way the configuration is parsed, create an empty config_handlers.yml file in your application's config/ folder and override the class lines with the classes you wrote.

Adding Your Own Handler

Using a handler to deal with a configuration file provides two important benefits:

- The configuration file is transformed into executable PHP code, and this code is stored in the cache. This means that the configuration is parsed only once in production, and the performance is optimal.

- The configuration file can be defined at different levels (project and application) and the final parameter values will result from a cascade. So you can define parameters at a project level and override them on a per-application basis.

If you feel like writing your own configuration handler, follow the example of the structure used by the framework in the $sf_symfony_lib_dir/config/ directory.

Let's suppose that your application contains a myMapAPI class, which provides an interface to a third-party web service delivering maps. This class needs to be initialized with a URL and a user name, as shown in Listing 19-8.

Listing 19-8. *Example of Initialization of the myMapAPI Class*

```
$mapApi = new myMapAPI();
$mapApi->setUrl($url);
$mapApi->setUser($user);
```

You may want to store these two parameters in a custom configuration file called map.yml, located in the application config/ directory. This configuration file might contain the following:

```
api:
  url:  map.api.example.com
  user: foobar
```

In order to transform these settings into code equivalent to Listing 19-8, you must build a configuration handler. Each configuration handler must extend sfConfigHandler and provide an execute() method, which expects an array of file paths to configuration files as a parameter, and must return data to be written in a cache file. Handlers for YAML files should extend the sfYamlConfigHandler class, which provides additional facilities for YAML parsing. For the map.yml file, a typical configuration handler could be written as shown in Listing 19-9.

Listing 19-9. *A Custom Configuration Handler, in myapp/lib/myMapConfigHandler.class.php*

```php
<?php

class myMapConfigHandler extends sfYamlConfigHandler
{
  public function execute($configFiles)
  {
    $this->initialize();

    // Parse the yaml
    $config = $this->parseYamls($configFiles);

    $data  = "<?php\n";
    $data. = "\$mapApi = new myMapAPI();\n";

    if (isset($config['api']['url'])
    {
      $data. = sprintf("\$mapApi->setUrl('%s');\n", $config['api']['url']);
    }
```

```
  if (isset($config['api']['user']))
  {
    $data. = sprintf("\$mapApi->setUser('%s');\n", $config['api']['user']);
  }

  return $data;
 }
}
```

The `$configFiles` array that symfony passes to the `execute()` method will contain a path to all the `map.yml` files found in the `config/` folders. The `parseYamls()` method will handle the configuration cascade.

In order to associate this new handler with the `map.yml` file, you must create a `config_handlers.yml` configuration file with the following content:

```
config/map.yml:
  class: myMapConfigHandler
```

■**Note** The `class` must either be autoloaded (that's the case here) or defined in the file whose path is written in a `file` parameter under the `param` key.

When you need the code based on the `map.yml` file and generated by the `myMapConfigHandler` handler in your application, call the following line:

```
include(sfConfigCache::getInstance()->checkConfig(sfConfig::get( ➥
'sf_app_config_dir_name').'/map.yml'));
```

When calling the `checkConfig()` method, symfony looks for existing `map.yml` files in the configuration directories and processes them with the handler specified in the `config_handlers.yml` file, if a `map.yml.php` does not already exist in the cache or if the `map.yml` file is more recent than the cache.

■**Tip** If you want to handle *environments* in a YAML configuration file, the handler can extend the `sfDefineEnvironmentConfigHandler` class instead of `sfYamlConfigHandler`. After calling the `parseYaml()` method to retrieve configuration, you should call the `mergeEnvironment()` method. You can do it all in one line by calling `$config = $this->mergeEnvironment($this->parseYamls($configFiles));`.

USING EXISTING CONFIGURATION HANDLERS

If you just need to allow users to retrieve values from the code via sfConfig, you can use the sfDefineEnvironmentConfigHandler configuration handler class. For instance, to have the url and user parameters available as sfConfig::get('map_url') and sfConfig::get('map_user'), define your handler as follows:

config/map.yml:
```
  class: sfDefineEnvironmentConfigHandler
  param:
    prefix: map_
```

Be careful not to choose a prefix already used by another handler. Existing prefixes are sf_, app_, and mod_.

Controlling PHP Settings

In order to have a PHP environment compatible with the rules and best practices of agile development, symfony checks and overrides a few settings of the php.ini configuration. This is the purpose of the php.yml file. Listing 19-10 shows the default php.yml file.

Listing 19-10. *Default PHP Settings for Symfony, in $sf_symfony_data_dir/config/php.yml*

```
set:
  magic_quotes_runtime:      off
  log_errors:                on
  arg_separator.output:      |
    &amp;

check:
  zend.ze1_compatibility_mode: off

warn:
  magic_quotes_gpc:          off
  register_globals:          off
  session.auto_start:        off
```

The main purpose of this file is to check that the PHP configuration is compatible with your application. It is also very useful to check that your development server configuration is as similar as possible to the production server. That's why you should inspect the production server configuration at the beginning of a project, and report its PHP settings in a php.yml file in your project. You can then develop and test with confidence that you will not encounter any compatibility errors once you deploy your project to the production platform.

The variables defined under the set header are modified (despite how they were defined in the server php.ini file). The variables defined under the warn category cannot be modified on the fly, but symfony can run even if they are not properly set. It is just considered bad practice to have these settings set to on, and symfony will log a warning in this case. The variables defined under the check category cannot be modified on the fly either, but they must have a certain value for symfony to run. So, in this case, an exception is raised if the php.ini file is not correct.

The default php.yml file sets log_errors to on so that you can trace errors in symfony projects. It also recommends that the register_globals be set to off to prevent security breaches.

If you don't want symfony to apply these settings, or if you want to run a project with magic_quotes_gpc and register_globals set to on without warning, then create a php.yml file in your application config/ directory, and override the settings you want to change.

Additionally, if your project requires an extension, you can specify it under the extensions category. It expects an array of extension names, as follows:

```
extensions: [gd, mysql, mbstring]
```

Summary

The configuration files can heavily modify the way the framework works. Because symfony relies on configuration even for its core features and file loading, it can adapt to many more environments than just the standard dedicated host. This great configurability is one of the main strengths of symfony. Even if it sometimes frightens newcomers, who see in configuration files a lot of conventions to learn, it allows symfony applications to be compatible with a very large number of platforms and environments. Once you become a master of symfony's configuration, no server will ever refuse to run your applications!

GNU Free Documentation License

Version 1.2, November 2002

0. PREAMBLE

The purpose of this License is to make a manual, textbook, or other functional and useful document "free" in the sense of freedom: to assure everyone the effective freedom to copy and redistribute it, with or without modifying it, either commercially or noncommercially. Secondarily, this License preserves for the author and publisher a way to get credit for their work, while not being considered responsible for modifications made by others.

This License is a kind of "copyleft", which means that derivative works of the document must themselves be free in the same sense. It complements the GNU General Public License, which is a copyleft license designed for free software.

We have designed this License in order to use it for manuals for free software, because free software needs free documentation: a free program should come with manuals providing the same freedoms that the software does. But this License is not limited to software manuals; it can be used for any textual work, regardless of subject matter or whether it is published as a printed book. We recommend this License principally for works whose purpose is instruction or reference.

1. APPLICABILITY AND DEFINITIONS

This License applies to any manual or other work, in any medium, that contains a notice placed by the copyright holder saying it can be distributed under the terms of this License. Such a notice grants a worldwide, royalty-free license, unlimited in duration, to use that work under the conditions stated herein. The "Document", below, refers to any such manual or work.

Any member of the public is a licensee, and is addressed as "you". You accept the license if you copy, modify or distribute the work in a way requiring permission under copyright law.

A "Modified Version" of the Document means any work containing the Document or a portion of it, either copied verbatim, or with modifications and/or translated into another language.

A "Secondary Section" is a named appendix or a front-matter section of the Document that deals exclusively with the relationship of the publishers or authors of the Document to the Document's overall subject (or to related matters) and contains nothing that could fall directly within that overall subject. (Thus, if the Document is in part a textbook of mathematics, a Secondary Section may not explain any mathematics.) The relationship could be a matter of historical connection with the subject or with related matters, or of legal, commercial, philosophical, ethical or political position regarding them.

The "Invariant Sections" are certain Secondary Sections whose titles are designated, as being those of Invariant Sections, in the notice that says that the Document is released under this License. If a section does not fit the above definition of Secondary then it is not allowed to be designated as Invariant. The Document may contain zero Invariant Sections. If the Document does not identify any Invariant Sections then there are none.

The "Cover Texts" are certain short passages of text that are listed, as Front-Cover Texts or Back-Cover Texts, in the notice that says that the Document is released under this License. A Front-Cover Text may be at most 5 words, and a Back-Cover Text may be at most 25 words.

A "Transparent" copy of the Document means a machine-readable copy, represented in a format whose specification is available to the general public, that is suitable for revising the document straightforwardly with generic text editors or (for images composed of pixels) generic paint programs or (for drawings) some widely available drawing editor, and that is suitable for input to text formatters or for automatic translation to a variety of formats suitable for input to text formatters. A copy made in an otherwise Transparent file format whose markup, or absence of markup, has been arranged to thwart or discourage subsequent modification by readers is not Transparent. An image format is not Transparent if used for any substantial amount of text. A copy that is not "Transparent" is called "Opaque".

Examples of suitable formats for Transparent copies include plain ASCII without markup, Texinfo input format, LaTeX input format, SGML or XML using a publicly available DTD, and standard-conforming simple HTML, PostScript or PDF designed for human modification. Examples of transparent image formats include PNG, XCF and JPG. Opaque formats include proprietary formats that can be read and edited only by proprietary word processors, SGML or XML for which the DTD and/or processing tools are not generally available, and the machine-generated HTML, PostScript or PDF produced by some word processors for output purposes only.

The "Title Page" means, for a printed book, the title page itself, plus such following pages as are needed to hold, legibly, the material this License requires to appear in the title page. For works in formats which do not have any title page as such, "Title Page" means the text near the most prominent appearance of the work's title, preceding the beginning of the body of the text.

A section "Entitled XYZ" means a named subunit of the Document whose title either is precisely XYZ or contains XYZ in parentheses following text that translates XYZ in another language. (Here XYZ stands for a specific section name mentioned below, such as "Acknowledgements", "Dedications", "Endorsements", or "History".) To "Preserve the Title" of such a section when you modify the Document means that it remains a section "Entitled XYZ" according to this definition.

The Document may include Warranty Disclaimers next to the notice which states that this License applies to the Document. These Warranty Disclaimers are considered to be included by reference in this License, but only as regards disclaiming warranties: any other implication that these Warranty Disclaimers may have is void and has no effect on the meaning of this License.

2. VERBATIM COPYING

You may copy and distribute the Document in any medium, either commercially or noncommercially, provided that this License, the copyright notices, and the license notice saying this License applies to the Document are reproduced in all copies, and that you add no other conditions whatsoever to those of this License. You may not use technical measures to obstruct or control the reading or further copying of the copies you make or distribute. However, you may accept compensation in exchange for copies. If you distribute a large enough number of copies you must also follow the conditions in section 3.

You may also lend copies, under the same conditions stated above, and you may publicly display copies.

3. COPYING IN QUANTITY

If you publish printed copies (or copies in media that commonly have printed covers) of the Document, numbering more than 100, and the Document's license notice requires Cover Texts, you must enclose the copies in covers that carry, clearly and legibly, all these Cover Texts: Front-Cover Texts on the front cover, and Back-Cover Texts on the back cover. Both covers must also clearly and legibly identify you as the publisher of these copies. The front cover must present the full title with all words of the title equally prominent and visible. You may add other material on the covers in addition.

Copying with changes limited to the covers, as long as they preserve the title of the Document and satisfy these conditions, can be treated as verbatim copying in other respects.

If the required texts for either cover are too voluminous to fit legibly, you should put the first ones listed (as many as fit reasonably) on the actual cover, and continue the rest onto adjacent pages.

If you publish or distribute Opaque copies of the Document numbering more than 100, you must either include a machine-readable Transparent copy along with each Opaque copy, or state in or with each Opaque copy a computer-network location from which the general network-using public has access to download using public-standard network protocols a complete Transparent copy of the Document, free of added material. If you use the latter option, you must take reasonably prudent steps, when you begin distribution of Opaque copies in quantity, to ensure that this Transparent copy will remain thus accessible at the stated location until at least one year after the last time you distribute an Opaque copy (directly or through your agents or retailers) of that edition to the public.

It is requested, but not required, that you contact the authors of the Document well before redistributing any large number of copies, to give them a chance to provide you with an updated version of the Document.

4. MODIFICATIONS

You may copy and distribute a Modified Version of the Document under the conditions of sections 2 and 3 above, provided that you release the Modified Version under precisely this License, with the Modified Version filling the role of the Document, thus licensing distribution and modification of the Modified Version to whoever possesses a copy of it. In addition, you must do these things in the Modified Version:

A. Use in the Title Page (and on the covers, if any) a title distinct from that of the Document, and from those of previous versions (which should, if there were any, be listed in the History section of the Document). You may use the same title as a previous version if the original publisher of that version gives permission.

B. List on the Title Page, as authors, one or more persons or entities responsible for authorship of the modifications in the Modified Version, together with at least five of the principal authors of the Document (all of its principal authors, if it has fewer than five), unless they release you from this requirement.

C. State on the Title page the name of the publisher of the Modified Version, as the publisher.

D. Preserve all the copyright notices of the Document.

E. Add an appropriate copyright notice for your modifications adjacent to the other copyright notices.

F. Include, immediately after the copyright notices, a license notice giving the public permission to use the Modified Version under the terms of this License, in the form shown in the Addendum below.

G. Preserve in that license notice the full lists of Invariant Sections and required Cover Texts given in the Document's license notice.

H. Include an unaltered copy of this License.

I. Preserve the section Entitled "History", Preserve its Title, and add to it an item stating at least the title, year, new authors, and publisher of the Modified Version as given on the Title Page. If there is no section Entitled "History" in the Document, create one stating the title, year, authors, and publisher of the Document as given on its Title Page, then add an item describing the Modified Version as stated in the previous sentence.

J. Preserve the network location, if any, given in the Document for public access to a Transparent copy of the Document, and likewise the network locations given in the Document for previous versions it was based on. These may be placed in the "History" section. You may omit a network location for a work that was published at least four years before the Document itself, or if the original publisher of the version it refers to gives permission.

K. For any section Entitled "Acknowledgements" or "Dedications", Preserve the Title of the section, and preserve in the section all the substance and tone of each of the contributor acknowledgements and/or dedications given therein.

L. Preserve all the Invariant Sections of the Document, unaltered in their text and in their titles. Section numbers or the equivalent are not considered part of the section titles.

M. Delete any section Entitled "Endorsements". Such a section may not be included in the Modified Version.

N. Do not retitle any existing section to be Entitled "Endorsements" or to conflict in title with any Invariant Section.

O. Preserve any Warranty Disclaimers.

If the Modified Version includes new front-matter sections or appendices that qualify as Secondary Sections and contain no material copied from the Document, you may at your option designate some or all of these sections as invariant. To do this, add their titles to the list of Invariant Sections in the Modified Version's license notice. These titles must be distinct from any other section titles.

You may add a section Entitled "Endorsements", provided it contains nothing but endorsements of your Modified Version by various parties—for example, statements of peer review or that the text has been approved by an organization as the authoritative definition of a standard.

You may add a passage of up to five words as a Front-Cover Text, and a passage of up to 25 words as a Back-Cover Text, to the end of the list of Cover Texts in the Modified Version. Only one passage of Front-Cover Text and one of Back-Cover Text may be added by (or through arrangements made by) any one entity. If the Document already includes a cover text for the same cover, previously added by you or by arrangement made by the same entity you are acting on behalf of, you may not add another; but you may replace the old one, on explicit permission from the previous publisher that added the old one.

The author(s) and publisher(s) of the Document do not by this License give permission to use their names for publicity for or to assert or imply endorsement of any Modified Version.

5. COMBINING DOCUMENTS

You may combine the Document with other documents released under this License, under the terms defined in section 4 above for modified versions, provided that you include in the combination all of the Invariant Sections of all of the original documents, unmodified, and list them all as Invariant Sections of your combined work in its license notice, and that you preserve all their Warranty Disclaimers.

The combined work need only contain one copy of this License, and multiple identical Invariant Sections may be replaced with a single copy. If there are multiple Invariant Sections with the same name but different contents, make the title of each such section unique by adding at the end of it, in parentheses, the name of the original author or publisher of that section if known, or else a unique number. Make the same adjustment to the section titles in the list of Invariant Sections in the license notice of the combined work.

In the combination, you must combine any sections Entitled "History" in the various original documents, forming one section Entitled "History"; likewise combine any sections Entitled "Acknowledgements", and any sections Entitled "Dedications". You must delete all sections Entitled "Endorsements".

6. COLLECTIONS OF DOCUMENTS

You may make a collection consisting of the Document and other documents released under this License, and replace the individual copies of this License in the various documents with a single copy that is included in the collection, provided that you follow the rules of this License for verbatim copying of each of the documents in all other respects.

You may extract a single document from such a collection, and distribute it individually under this License, provided you insert a copy of this License into the extracted document, and follow this License in all other respects regarding verbatim copying of that document.

7. AGGREGATION WITH INDEPENDENT WORKS

A compilation of the Document or its derivatives with other separate and independent documents or works, in or on a volume of a storage or distribution medium, is called an "aggregate" if the copyright resulting from the compilation is not used to limit the legal rights of the compilation's users beyond what the individual works permit. When the Document is included in an aggregate, this License does not apply to the other works in the aggregate which are not themselves derivative works of the Document.

If the Cover Text requirement of section 3 is applicable to these copies of the Document, then if the Document is less than one half of the entire aggregate, the Document's Cover Texts may be placed on covers that bracket the Document within the aggregate, or the electronic equivalent of covers if the Document is in electronic form. Otherwise they must appear on printed covers that bracket the whole aggregate.

8. TRANSLATION

Translation is considered a kind of modification, so you may distribute translations of the Document under the terms of section 4. Replacing Invariant Sections with translations requires special permission from their copyright holders, but you may include translations of some or all Invariant Sections in addition to the original versions of these Invariant Sections. You may include a translation of this License, and all the license notices in the Document, and any Warranty Disclaimers, provided that you also include the original English version of this License and the original versions of those notices and disclaimers. In case of a disagreement between the translation and the original version of this License or a notice or disclaimer, the original version will prevail.

If a section in the Document is Entitled "Acknowledgements", "Dedications", or "History", the requirement (section 4) to Preserve its Title (section 1) will typically require changing the actual title.

9. TERMINATION

You may not copy, modify, sublicense, or distribute the Document except as expressly provided for under this License. Any other attempt to copy, modify, sublicense or distribute the Document is void, and will automatically terminate your rights under this License. However, parties who have received copies, or rights, from you under this License will not have their licenses terminated so long as such parties remain in full compliance.

10. FUTURE REVISIONS OF THIS LICENSE

The Free Software Foundation may publish new, revised versions of the GNU Free Documentation License from time to time. Such new versions will be similar in spirit to the present version, but may differ in detail to address new problems or concerns. See `http://www.gnu.org/copyleft/`.

Each version of the License is given a distinguishing version number. If the Document specifies that a particular numbered version of this License "or any later version" applies to it, you have the option of following the terms and conditions either of that specified version or of any later version that has been published (not as a draft) by the Free Software Foundation. If the Document does not specify a version number of this License, you may choose any version ever published (not as a draft) by the Free Software Foundation.

Index

Find it faster at http://superindex.apress.com

You Need the Companion eBook

Your purchase of this book entitles you to buy the companion PDF-version eBook for only $10. Take the weightless companion with you anywhere.

We believe this Apress title will prove so indispensable that you'll want to carry it with you everywhere, which is why we are offering the companion eBook (in PDF format) for $10 to customers who purchase this book now. Convenient and fully searchable, the PDF version of any content-rich, page-heavy Apress book makes a valuable addition to your programming library. You can easily find and copy code—or perform examples by quickly toggling between instructions and the application. Even simultaneously tackling a donut, diet soda, and complex code becomes simplified with hands-free eBooks!

Once you purchase your book, getting the $10 companion eBook is simple:

❶ Visit **www.apress.com/promo/tendollars/**.

❷ Complete a basic registration form to receive a randomly generated question about this title.

❸ Answer the question correctly in 60 seconds, and you will receive a promotional code to redeem for the $10.00 eBook.

2560 Ninth Street • Suite 219 • Berkeley, CA 94710

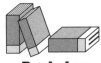
eBookshop

THE EXPERT'S VOICE™

Offer valid through 7/29/07.